Stuarts' Field Guide to

MAMMALS

of Southern Africa
INCLUDING ANGOLA, ZAMBIA & MALAWI

Chris & Mathilde Stuart

Published by Struik Nature (an imprint of Penguin Random House (Pty) Ltd)
Reg. No. 1953/000441/07
The Estuaries No 4, Century Avenue (Oxbow Crescent), Century City, 7441
PO Box 1144, Cape Town, 8000 South Africa

Visit **www.penguinrandomhouse.co.za** and join the Struik Nature Club for updates, news,
events and special offers
Visit Chris and Mathilde Stuart at **www.stuartonnature.com**

First published 1988
Second edition 1993
Third edition 2001
Fourth edition 2007
Fifth edition 2015

10 9 8 7 6 5 4 3

Publisher: Pippa Parker
Managing editor: Helen de Villiers
Editor: Colette Alves
Design manager: Janice Evans
Designer: Gillian Black
Cartography: Mathilde Stuart
Illustrator (marine mammals): David Thorpe
Proofreader: Emsie du Plessis

Reproduction by Hirt & Carter Cape (Pty) Ltd
Printing and binding: 1010 Printing International Ltd, China

ISBN 978 1 77584 111 1
E-pub (Eng) 978 1 77584 266 8
E-PDF (Eng) 978 1 77584 267 5

Also available in Afrikaans:
Stuarts se Veldgids tot Soogdiere van Suider-Afrika 978 1 77584 112 8

Front cover: Leopard
Back cover: Aardvark, Plains Zebra

ACKNOWLEDGEMENTS

We gratefully acknowledge the help we have received over the years from friends and colleagues. No doubt many more names should appear below, and we ask pardon of those who assisted us in different ways but whose names have unintentionally escaped mention. Pierre Swanepoel and the late Lloyd Wingate of the Amathole Museum in King William's Town, Naas Rautenbach previously of the Ditsong National Museum of Natural History, and the staff of the Iziko South African Museum are thanked for allowing us access to the mammal collections in their care. More recently, we have photographed specimens at the Smithsonian Institution Natural History Museum, Washington DC, and would like to express special thanks to Darrin P. Lunde for facilitating our work there. A special word of thanks to Jay Villemarette, Museum of Osteology, Oklahoma City, for allowing us to photograph his fine collection of skulls and skeletons.

Our sincere thanks for information, photographs and other assistance go to the following: Paul K. Anderson (University of Calgary); Laila Bahaa-el-din; Ric Bernard (Rhodes University); Hu Berry; John Carlyon; Alan Channing (University of the Western Cape); Nico Dippenaar; Anthony Duckworth and Laura Fielden (University of KwaZulu-Natal); Patrick J. Frere (Langata Bird Sanctuary); Mike Griffin; Malan Lindeque; Ian Manning; Daan Marais; Penny Meakin; Gus Mills; David R. Mills; Peter le S. Milstein; Pam Newby; Harald Nicolay; Guy Palmer; Debbie Peake (for elephant skull measurements); Mike Perrin (University of KwaZulu-Natal); Graham Ross; Judith A. Rudnai; the late Reay Smithers; the late H. van Rompaey; Alan Weaving; the late Viv Wilson (Chipangali Wildlife Trust).

Our special thanks go to Merlin Tuttle, founder of Bat Conservation International, for his encouragement and photographs. A special word of thanks to Ara Monadjem and Ernest Seamark for allowing us to use many of their fine images of bats in this edition. Miki Sugimoto (Curator of Toba Aquarium, Tokyo, Japan) is thanked for providing images of the West African Manatee. Mark Williams (Ashanti African Tours, Ghana, **www.ashantiafricantours.com**) is thanked for allowing us to use some of his fine images. Bill Stanley and Rebecca Banasiak of the Field Museum of Natural History, Chicago, are sincerely thanked for providing images of living mammals and study skins.

Finally, we should also like to express our appreciation to the former and present staff of Struik Nature: in particular Peter Borchert and Eve Gracie for their support and advice at the start, John Comrie-Greig for editing the original manuscript, and Pippa Parker and her team for successfully steering it through three subsequent editions.

Chris and Mathilde Stuart (**www.stuartonnature.com**)
Clearwater/Caloosahatchee River, 2013

CONTENTS

MAJOR BIOTIC ZONES OF SOUTHERN AFRICA

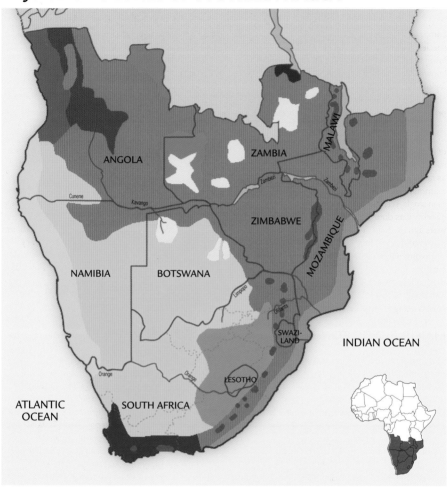

▨ Desert	▨ Mixed wood- / grassland
▨ Arid zone	▨ Savanna grassland
▨ Lowland forest & woodland	▨ Dry forest & western Zambezi grasslands
▨ Broadleaf evergreen forest	▨ Seasonally flooded grasslands
▨ Tropical savanna	▨ Montane & tropical forest
▨ Savanna woodland including miombo & mopane	▨ Cape heathland / fynbos
▨ Itigi-Sumbu thicket	

INTRODUCTION

The worldwide mammal group is a small one when compared with birds (9,500 species) or fish (30,000 species). It comprises between 4,700 and 5,500 living species, of which almost 400 are currently known to occur in the greater southern African region. Why this disparity in the number of species? New species are constantly being described, principally as a result of genetic investigation and species splits; very few are newly discovered species. In 2011 one group of taxonomists raised the number of ungulates (hoofed mammals) from 257 species to 450 worldwide by recognizing many subspecies as full species in their own right. Some of the smaller mammals, however, are known from very few, or even single, records. The richest period of mammal diversity was during the late Tertiary (5–2 million years ago), when an estimated three times as many mammal species roamed the earth than do so today.

Taxonomists are constantly revising and reassessing the scientific status of many mammals, particularly the smaller species such as bats, shrews and small rodents. This often results in scientific names being changed and, on occasion, new species being described; Juliana's Golden Mole, for example, was described from the former Transvaal in 1972 and the Long-tailed Forest Shrew from the southern coastal belt of South Africa as recently as 1978. Recent genetic research has resulted in the Hottentot Golden Mole (*Amblysomus hottentotus*) being split into five new species. The bats are especially mobile, and it is very likely that additional species from this group will be discovered and added to the faunal complement of southern Africa in due course. Recently, taxonomists have been reassessing the status of many of the hoofed mammals and, according to some authorities, many more species should be recognized. Where we feel that this is relevant we have made note of such potential changes.

Mammals have a number of common characters that set them apart from other vertebrates: they breathe with lungs; they possess a four-chambered heart; they have three delicate bones in the middle ear; the females have mammary glands that produce milk for suckling the young; and nearly all species have a covering of body hair.

MAJOR BIOTIC ZONES OF SOUTHERN AFRICA

The greater southern African region – defined as that part of the African continent and its coastal waters that includes and extends southwards from Angola, Zambia, Malawi and Mozambique – can be divided into 11 major biotic zones, each differing in climate and vegetation. This does, however, present an oversimplified picture, and each of these zones can be further subdivided into many different habitat and vegetation types. Many mammal species are restricted to one particular vegetation type or habitat, whereas others range over several.

Desert

Desert is characterized by very low rainfall (usually less than 100mm per year) and sparse plant growth. Extensive areas may be devoid of any vegetation, being covered by sand-dunes or consisting of flat gravel plains and rugged hill country. Several species of mammal have evolved mechanisms that help them to survive in this harsh environment. In the southern African region, this biotic zone is represented by the Namib, which stretches along the coast of Namibia, marginally in the north-west of South Africa and into south-western Angola.

Arid (semi-desert) zone

Areas classed as 'arid' receive higher rainfall than true desert, but this rarely exceeds 500mm per year. In southern Africa, rainfall is at its lowest in the west, gradually increasing towards the east. The Kalahari, Karoo, Bushmanland, Namaqualand and Damaraland fall within the arid zone. The southern section, namely Bushmanland, Namaqualand and the Karoo, consists mainly of extensive rocky plains and isolated hills and hill ranges, with a vegetation comprising low, woody shrubs and succulents. Much of the area is veined with river courses,

Desert

Arid (semi-desert) zone

Savanna woodland

which are vegetated along their banks with bushes and low trees. In the northern parts, for example, the Kalahari 'desert' of the Northern Cape and Botswana, sandy soils are more prevalent with low (often acacia) trees and bushes, and relatively good grass cover. This zone once supported vast numbers of ungulates, but the free-roaming herds of Springbok, Red Hartebeest, Blue Wildebeest, Eland and Plains Zebra have diminished greatly and are now restricted to the more sparsely populated parts of Botswana.

Savanna woodland (including the miombo across much of Angola and Zambia) and savanna grassland

The savanna biome can be divided into two principal zones, namely savanna woodland mostly in the north, and savanna grassland in the south. Savanna woodland includes mopane woodland, thorn scrub (thicket) and dense woodland habitats in the east. These woodlands extend in a broad swathe across large areas of Angola, most of Zambia and Malawi, as well as the inland areas of Mozambique, and in South Africa from Limpopo down the coastal belt of KwaZulu-Natal to the Eastern Cape. In the north of the region these extensive woodlands are referred to as

miombo. Grass cover ranges from sparse to good. It is within this zone that many of the region's major game reserves are situated.

Within the savanna woodland there are a number of distinctive divisions. Lowland forest and woodland is restricted to the coastal plain from Port Elizabeth in the south to the Mozambique/Tanzania border. Much of this vegetation in South Africa has been lost or modified for development. In north-central Angola extensive areas of tropical savanna intrude into the miombo woodlands and differ in having additional tree species not found further to the east. The Itigi-Sumbu thicket in extreme north-east Zambia is a particularly dense deciduous thicket with woody shrubs ranging in height from 3–5m and is surrounded by miombo woodland. Much of this unique thicket has been lost due to the actions of humans. Dry forest and Zambezi grassland, as well as mixed wood-grassland also fall within the extensive miombo belt and share many species, but also have some unique to them. Many other vegetation types are recognized within the vast miombo zone, but these are beyond the scope of this field guide.

Savanna grassland consists largely of mixed grassland, with tree and shrub growth more or less restricted to the edges of watercourses and to hills

Savanna grassland

Miombo woodland

Miombo woodland

Cape fynbos

and more rugged terrain. Much of the formerly extensive savanna grassland of east-central South Africa has been destroyed by cultivation or modified by overgrazing.

Although falling within the larger savanna zone, the wetlands and **seasonally flooded grasslands** of the Okavango and Linyanti swamps deserve separate mention. The Okavango Swamp of north-western Botswana is the largest inland river delta in the world and one of southern Africa's most important wetlands. The Linyanti Swamp is situated in eastern Caprivi, Namibia. These two areas are home to many species of water-adapted mammal, including Sitatunga, Lechwe and Hippopotamus. All southern African swamps and seasonally flooded grasslands are under increasing human pressure and there is an urgent need for careful resource management and conservation planning. Zambia also has critically important swamps and seasonally flooded wetlands, such as the Bangweulu, Kafue and Barotse plains. Many smaller areas of seasonally flooded grasslands, known as dambos, are scattered through the miombo woodlands.

Cape fynbos or heathland

This small but significant zone is largely restricted to the Western and Eastern Cape provinces of South Africa, and its vegetation can be broadly divided into mountain and lowland fynbos. Elements of the Cape heathland vegetation can be found in several other locations in South Africa, as well as in Zimbabwe, Malawi and Zambia. This very limited area is so rich in plant species that it is classed as one of the world's six 'floristic kingdoms', although it covers only 0.04 per cent of the world's land surface area. The vegetation is dominated largely by evergreen shrubs and bushes. The fynbos zone has suffered more than any other in the region from agriculture and other human influences. It is not a mammal-rich region.

Indigenous forest

Indigenous forest can be divided into **lowland forest** and **montane forest**. Poorly represented in southern Africa, it is restricted, in fragmented and widely scattered pockets, to the southern and eastern areas of South Africa, the eastern highlands of Zimbabwe and the adjacent areas of Mozambique, and extreme north-eastern Zambia. There are areas of tropical **broadleaf evergreen forest** in northern Angola. Several mammal species, such as the Giant Golden Mole and Sykes's Monkey, are found only in this habitat.

Indigenous forest

Broadleaf evergreen forest

Geographically, this book covers the area stretching south of the Congo River in the west, Lake Tanganyika in the east and the Ruvuma River that forms much of the border between Tanzania and Mozambique. The Atlantic Ocean laps the western seaboard, and the southern and eastern shores are bounded by the Indian Ocean. The southern African region is usually defined as the area south of the Cunene and Zambezi rivers. In a break from this definition, we have elected to include Angola, Zambia, Malawi and northern Mozambique in what we shall call greater southern Africa. We have chosen to expand the area covered by this field guide for several reasons: the ranges of many species that occur south of the Cunene/Zambezi rivers also extend northwards beyond this point; and there is a lack of popular literature dealing with the full spectrum of mammal species in Zambia, Malawi and Mozambique, despite the increase in eco-tourism to these countries thanks to their conservation areas and great wildlife diversity. Angola still has some way to go in this regard, but over time its network of national parks is likely to be developed and become more accessible to visitors interested in wildlife. We have also included, for the sake of completeness, those species that do not occur south of the Cunene/Zambezi line.

The main purpose of a field guide is to enable the observer to identify mammals in the wild. While there should be little difficulty in identifying the larger, medium-sized and some small mammals to species level, this is not always the case with many smaller species. Many of these are secretive and therefore only rarely seen or difficult to find. Furthermore, many small species can be identified only by specialists with access to comparative study material of skins and skulls, usually through a museum. For some small species, identification is possible normally only to family and generic level; this applies particularly to golden moles, shrews, bats and many small rodents, where positive identification may require expert examination of the skull, teeth and sometimes even their genetic material. Where this is the case, it is pointed out in the text.

As the marine environment simply does not lend itself to easy observation, illustrations instead of photographs are used to depict most whales and dolphins.

Each species account is divided into sections under subheadings to enable the reader to look up any aspect that is of particular interest. Take care when identifying juvenile animals, as they may differ considerably from the adults. This applies particularly to the antelopes, where the sub-adults of one species may be easily confused with the adults of another species. Another thing to bear in mind is that a number of species possess one or more subspecies, or races, that differ from each other in colour, pattern or size. Where this is applicable, it is mentioned in the species account.

The tools of the mammal-watcher are simple: a good pair of binoculars, a notebook and pencil, and a suitable mammal reference book.

The mysteries of changing taxonomy

In recent years, the use of modern techniques in mammal taxonomy has resulted in a number of changes in mammal classification. Some changes make good sense to us, a few do not, but there is no doubt that taxonomy is in a state of ongoing evolution. Cytogenetics, molecular technologies and protein electrophoresis are among the principal forces driving the taxonomic convulsions that are giving us a better understanding of the origins and roots of our mammalian fauna.

Where possible, this edition has incorporated these changes. In some cases we question these changes, or proposed changes, but make mention of them for the sake of completeness. However, the reader should be aware that, as research techniques continue to be refined, more changes will come into play. Taxonomy is a very fluid field of study that promises to produce much discussion and debate in the future.

Identification pointers

The main aids to identifying a species are summarized in each species account, and prominent features are highlighted under the heading 'Identification pointers'. Where one species is similar to, or could be confused with, another species, their distinguishing features are also mentioned (for example, the Side-striped and Black-backed Jackals).

Distribution

A glance at the distribution maps will give a quick indication of species' distribution within greater southern Africa. Remember that the scale of the maps is such that only general distribution patterns can be given. For example, although the Rock Hyrax (Dassie) is shown to have a continuous distribution, it can clearly only occur where suitable habitat is available. Always consult

Six steps to identify a mammal

Descriptions in this field guide concentrate on external features that will help with species identification. Follow the six steps below when identifying a mammal:

1. **Decide to which group the mammal belongs.** Is it an antelope, or does it belong to the dog family, for instance?
2. **Estimate the shoulder height, total length and tail length if possible.** Is the tail shorter than the head and body? Are the ears long or short?
3. **Look for outstanding features.** Does it have white or black stripes, spots or a bushy tail?
4. **Check the distribution map to ascertain whether the animal occurs in the area.**
5. **Check the habitat preference of the mammal.** You will not see a Klipspringer bounding across open plains, or a Black-backed Jackal in dense forest.
6. **Make a note of specific behavioural traits that may aid in identification.** Did you see a large group together or just a few animals; was an individual digging a burrow?

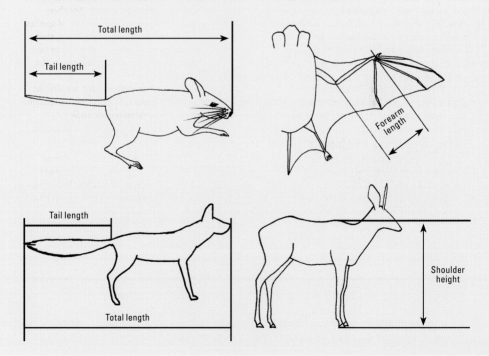

the notes on a species' habitat preference in conjunction with the distribution map. You will notice that on some maps, principally of the larger species, we have included historic range. In recent years many species, especially larger ungulates and carnivores, have been widely reintroduced to areas where they were hunted to local or regional extinction in the past.

Habitat

An indication is given in the text of the habitats favoured by each species. However, you should bear in mind that a species may be encountered within other habitats.

Behaviour

Behavioural characters that may aid in identification are given preference, but other aspects of interest are also mentioned.

Food and Reproduction

The notes under these headings may assist in identifying a mammal, but are usually given for general interest.

Spoor drawings

As a further aid to identification, spoor drawings have been provided for many species. These show the tracks of species most likely to be encountered, or tracks that are particularly distinctive. 'Reading' tracks and signs adds a fascinating dimension to mammal-watching; a great deal of information may be gleaned without the animal itself being observed. The measurements given are usually the average for each species but in some cases ranges are given.

Measurements

The most useful measurement in the field identification of larger and medium-sized mammals is shoulder height. Other measurements are given as an aid to determining whether a mammal is 'small', 'medium-sized' or 'large', often when compared with an average human body, or a part of it, such as a hand or forearm. A useful method of learning to judge measurements is to cut pieces of wood into known lengths and place these at different distances. With practice, you should be able to apply these estimates to mammals in the field.

All measurements given are metric, and it is important to note that average figures are given for each species. These measurements can vary considerably within a species and the figures given in this book should be taken only as a guide. In the case of antelope, two horn measurements are provided: the average length, and the record length as given in Rowland Ward's *African Records of Big Game*, the 'bible' of international hunting statistics.

CONSERVATION AND WILDLIFE MANAGEMENT

During the past 2,000 years, approximately 200 species of mammal and bird are believed to have become extinct, an average of one species every 10 years. This rate has accelerated, with many of these species having disappeared during the last 100 years. In southern Africa, one mammal species (Blue Antelope or Bluebuck, *Hippotragus leucophaeus*) and one subspecies (Quagga, *Equus quagga quagga*) have become extinct in recent times.

The Quagga once occurred in large herds on the southern and central plains of southern Africa, but was driven to extinction by hunting and by competition with domestic stock; the last Quagga died in Amsterdam Zoo in 1883. Present thinking is leaning towards the belief that the Quagga was simply the southernmost subspecies of the Plains (Burchell's) Zebra but, even if current research should prove this to be the case, the extinction of this distinctive subspecies is still inexcusable.

The Blue Antelope, on the other hand, was almost certainly a full species. When the first European settlers arrived at the Cape of Good Hope in the mid-17th century, it would appear that this close relative of the Roan and Sable Antelopes was already declining in numbers and range. At that time it was restricted to the area now known as the Overberg in the Western Cape, although the fossil and sub-fossil record shows that it was once spread more widely along the coastal plain to the east and west. It is theorized that the decline of the Blue Antelope, like the Quagga, was a result of its having to compete for grazing with the sheep, goats and cattle of the indigenous people of the Cape, and was accelerated by the arrival of the colonists and their firearms. It finally disappeared around 1799–1800, gaining the dubious distinction of being the first mammal on the African continent recorded as becoming extinct in historical times.

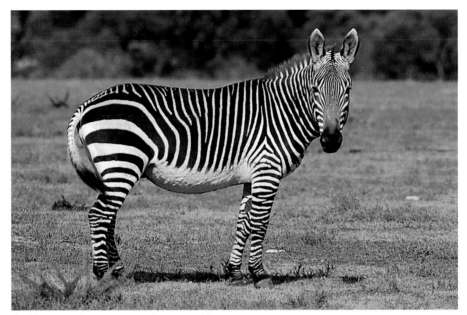

Sound conservation management has secured the futures of the Cape Mountain Zebra (**above**) and Black Wildebeest (**right**).

The Cape Mountain Zebra, Bontebok, Black Wildebeest and Square-lipped Rhinoceros have all come perilously close to the brink of extinction. Fortunately, however, these once-numerous species were protected in good time, and their futures now seem secure. Regrettably, many species have been eradicated from their original ranges, and we will never again see elephant herds making their way across the sandy flats within sight of Cape Town. The Hook-lipped Rhinoceros was once found throughout southern Africa; today, it occurs in only a handful of sanctuaries in the north and east. Other species, such as Oribi, Roan and Sable Antelopes, African Wild Dog and Riverine Rabbit are all currently a cause for concern to conservationists. In earlier editions of this field guide we stated that Lion, once abundant in the area, would never be heard again calling on the Nuweveld escarpment above the town of Beaufort West! We were wrong, as towards the end of 2010 a pride of eight were released in the Karoo National Park, and by all accounts they are doing well. This, after the last wild lions in the district had been shot some 170 years previously. Lions have also been reintroduced into Addo Elephant National Park and Mountain Zebra National Park, as well as most recently in Malawi, where the last wild lions were killed 20 years ago.

Modern technology has frequently encouraged the wasteful and exploitative use of the natural environment. Apart from the deliberate hunting of wild mammals, probably the single greatest factor that has influenced wildlife in the region is the uncontrolled manner in which agriculture has modified or completely changed the character of many habitats and vegetation types.

Food cultivation, overgrazing, soil erosion, destruction of woodland and forest, and competition with domestic stock are all factors that have contributed to the decline of wild mammal populations.

Another issue is the trapping or poisoning of predators that include domestic animals in their diet. Because it is impossible to restrict control to just the species that has caused the damage, many thousands of non-target animals, including the Bat-eared Fox, Small Grey Mongoose and a variety of harmless rodents, are killed each year. Problem animal management (or 'vermin control' as it used to be called) is a field that deserves far greater attention in order to reduce the death toll among harmless species and to increase selectivity for the real problem animals.

The pivotal problem, of course, is human overpopulation and the resulting demands it places on the environment. Man creates or exacerbates pressure on the environment and, as a result, the mammal fauna is adversely affected. It is our responsibility to achieve a compromise between development and destruction that will allow man and nature to co-exist in harmony.

Although it is often difficult to balance economics and conservation, there is a growing awareness that wildlife can increasingly help to pay its way. Each year, southern Africa's vast, but diminishing mammal resources draw tens of thousands of tourists to its reserves, wildlife sanctuaries and game farms, creating a wide range of employment opportunities that boost local, regional and national coffers.

In the case of privately owned game farms, some landowners have found that combining conservation initiatives with hunting concessions results in a profitable form of land use. Many such farms are situated on marginal agricultural land, with low livestock-carrying capacities. Game species, long adapted to these areas, are able to thrive without the costly dipping and dosing programmes associated with sheep, goat and cattle husbandry. In parts of northern South Africa and Namibia, this may be the only economically viable form of land use. However, many conservation-orientated people find the commercial aspects of wildlife utilization objectionable, and believe that man has a moral duty to protect, rather than to exploit, the environment and its biota. Although this is a morally correct standpoint, it is one that is becoming increasingly unrealistic. It would be difficult to convince a farmer to conserve large numbers of Springbok and Blesbok merely for the sake of conservation; if he cannot be assured of a cash return for his large game herds, he would go back to sheep- and goat-farming. By the same token, the suburban gardener cannot be expected to accept with equanimity the regular destruction of his or her potato or flower patch by mole-rats. In recent years there has been an unfortunate trend to introduce game species into areas where they never occurred previously. For example, one can drive past a game farm in South Africa's Eastern Cape province and see Lechwe, Sable Antelope and Giraffe, all great distances from their natural range! During a drive through the Karoo plateau you may glimpse Common Waterbuck and Impala far away from their natural habitats. Surprisingly, many of these reintroductions thrive. This has now reached such a level, especially in South Africa and Namibia, that it would be virtually impossible to reverse the trend. In fact, if it was decided to undertake such a massive removal, it would result in a slaughter that would be unacceptable to the public at large. In South Africa, especially, many game farmers now maintain and breed colour variants that bring high trophy prices, such as white, black and copper Springbok, golden Blue Wildebeest and black Impala. Even more disturbing, in our eyes, is the running of Blue Wildebeest and Black Wildebeest, Bontebok and Blesbok, not only on the same game farms but not infrequently in the same camps, even though this is against the law. Both crosses may produce fertile hybrids, resulting in the loss of genetic purity.

Programmes to conserve the mammals of southern Africa are closely tied to habitat conservation. It is no good conserving a species, or group of species, if the habitat to which they are adapted is not also protected. But, in the last resort, mankind must also be convinced of the necessity of managing its own population and keeping it in check. A seemingly forlorn hope!

MAJOR PARKS AND RESERVES OF SOUTHERN AFRICA

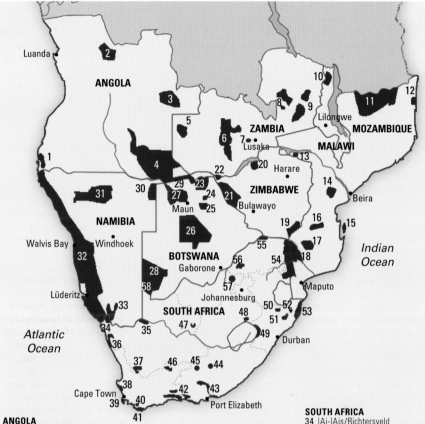

ANGOLA
1 Iona National Park
2 Cangandala National Park
3 Cameia National Park
4 Luiana & Longa-Mavinga
   National Parks

ZAMBIA
5 Liuwa Plains
6 Kafue National Park
7 Blue Lagoon National Park
8 Kasanka / Bengweulu/Lavushi-Manda
   Park Complex
9 South & North Luangwa National Parks

MALAWI
10 Nyika National Park

MOZAMBIQUE
11 Niassa Reserve
12 Quirimbas National Park
13 Magoe National Park
14 Gorongoza National Park
15 Bazaruto National Park
16 Zinave National Park
17 Banhine National Park
18 Limpopo National Park

ZIMBABWE
19 Gonarezhou National Park
20 Mana Pools National Park
21 Hwange National Park
22 Zambezi National Park

BOTSWANA
23 Chobe National Park
24 Nxai Pan National Park
25 Makgadikgadi Game Reserve
26 Central Kalahari Game Reserve
27 Moremi Game Reserve
28 Kgalagadi Transfrontier Park

NAMIBIA
29 Bwabwata/Nkasa Rupara/
    Mudumu National Parks
30 Khaudom National Park
31 Etosha National Park
32 Skeleton Coast/Namib-Naukluft/
    Dorob National Park Complex
33 |Ai-|Ais/Richtersveld
    Transfrontier Park

SOUTH AFRICA
34 |Ai-|Ais/Richtersveld
    Transfrontier Park
35 Augrabies Falls National Park
36 Namaqua National Park
37 Tankwa Karoo National Park
38 West Coast National Park
39 Table Mountain National Park
40 Bontebok National Park
41 Agulhas National Park
42 Garden Route National Park
43 Addo Elephant National Park
44 Mountain Zebra National Park
45 Camdeboo National Park
46 Karoo National Park
47 Mokala National Park
48 Golden Gate Highlands
    National Park
49 Ukhahlamba Drakensberg Park
50 Ithala Game Reserve
51 Hluhluwe-iMfolozi Game Reserve
52 uMkhuzi Game Reserve
53 iSimangaliso Wetland Park
54 Kruger National Park
55 Mapungubwe National Park
56 Marakele National Park
57 Pilanesberg Game Reserve
58 Kgalagadi Transfrontier Park

FAMILY INTRODUCTIONS

The following are general accounts of the mammal families and subfamilies occurring in southern Africa.

GOLDEN MOLES & OTTER SHREWS   Order Afrosoricida

GOLDEN MOLES   Family Chrysochloridae   (p.36)

Twenty species occur in greater southern Africa. Most are inadequately known as they are difficult
to trap and are rarely seen because of their subterranean life-style; some are known only from very
restricted geographical areas. They leave characteristic domed tunnels just below the soil surface, not the
mounds or heaps normally pushed up by mole-rats. All golden moles are small (the largest has a total
length of 23cm), and have no external tail. The head is wedge-shaped, with a horny pad at the tip of the
muzzle, which is used for burrowing. They are blind and their ears are merely small openings through the
fur without pinnae. The hind legs (with five digits each) are less developed than the forelegs (with four
digits); the third digit of each forefoot carries a long, heavy claw to facilitate digging.

Eighteen species have smooth, dense, glossy fur but the two larger species have longer, coarse hair. As
a group, the golden moles have been aptly described as 'animated powder-puffs'. They show a marked
preference for looser, sandy soils. They are not related to rodent moles (family Bathyergidae, p.162).
Key features: Tail, eyes and ears not visible; glossy fur; surface tunnels; do not have pair of large incisors
in upper and lower jaw.

GIANT OTTER SHREW   Family Tenrecidae   (p.42)

One species of otter shrew occurs within the region, and only in northern Angola. It may reach a total
length of 65cm, of which roughly half is tail, and a weight averaging 1kg. The tail is muscular and
latterly flattened to aid in swimming and the short, dense fur is dark brown above and cream to white
below. They occupy a variety of aquatic habitats, from swiftly flowing streams to swamps. Closely
resemble a small otter.
Key features: Long, flattened tail; otter-like appearance and habitat.

SENGIS   Order Macroscelidea

SENGIS (ELEPHANT-SHREWS)   Family Macroscelididae   (p.42)

Twelve species occur in the region. All are small (the largest has a head-and-body length of 30cm) and
characterized by the elongated, constantly twitching, trunk-like snout. The ears are rounded and prominent,
and the eyes are large. Hind legs and feet are much longer than forelegs and -feet. The tail is about the same
length as the head and body and is only sparsely haired. If disturbed, sengis can move very rapidly.
Key features: All but two of the species in the region are small and mouse-like, with a long, mobile
trunk-like snout.

HEDGEHOGS & SHREWS   Order Eulipotyphla

The Shrews are sometimes placed in their own Order Soricomorpha.

HEDGEHOGS   Family Erinaceidae   (p.48)

Two species of hedgehog occur in the region, one restricted to limited areas of Malawi and Zambia.
Characterized by their small size (total length 22cm), and the short, stiff spines on the back and sides. The
snout is pointed, and the muzzle is black with a white forehead band. The tail is not visible. Nocturnal.
Key features: Spine-covered back and sides; usually brownish; curls up if threatened.

At least 27 species have been recorded from the region. All are small to very small (largest has head-and-body length of 12cm) with a long, narrow and wedge-shaped muzzle (not as elongated and mobile as in sengis). The tail is usually shorter than the head-and-body length and the legs are short. The fur is short, soft and, in most species, dark in colour. Most species are associated with damp habitats. Some species are extremely difficult to identify in the field and careful examination of the teeth, skull and even chromosome structure is often required.

Key features: Small and mouse-like; long, wedge-shaped head; tiny eyes.

BATS Order Chiroptera

All bats belong to the order Chiroptera. Until recently, this was divided into the suborder Megachiroptera containing the fruit-eating bats and the suborder Microchiroptera containing the insect-eating bats. Based on recent genetic and other research, such as species-specific echolocation calls, this division has been changed and new suborders have been suggested: Yinpterochiroptera and Yangochiroptera or Pteropodiformes and Vespertilioniformes. Some of the insect-eating bat families will be included with the fruit-eating bats in the new suborders, but the final verdict is still outstanding.. At the present time, 20 species of fruit-bat and 88 species of insectivorous bat have been recorded as occurring in greater southern Africa, but it is highly probable that several more bat species will be added to the region's faunal list in the near future, after more intensive biological surveying and genetic investigations. We have made mention of newly described species in the body of the text.

Bats are the only mammals capable of true flight. The forelimbs, with their greatly elongated fingers, have evolved into wings, over which the skin of the upper and lower surfaces has fused to form a very thin wing-membrane. This membrane extends along the side of the body to the ankles. When at rest, bats usually hang head-downwards, suspended by the claws of the hind feet and with the wings either folded against the body, or enveloping it. The fruit-eating and insect-eating bats differ in several ways (see box below):

Character	Fruit-bat	Insectivorous bat
Size	Usually large	Usually small
Wing-claws	2 (in southern Africa)	1
Tail	Absent or short	Medium to long
Interfemoral (tail) membrane	Poorly developed	Usually well-developed
Ear tragus	Absent	Usually well-developed but absent in horseshoe bats
Eyes	Large	Usually small
Echolocation	Absent, except in *Rousettus* species	Present

Fruit-bat: two wing-claws

Insectivorous bat: one wing-claw

Bats rely to a great extent on their hearing and this is particularly so in the case of the microchiropterans or insect-eating bats, which have perfected the art of echolocation. Their ears are extremely well developed and most microchiropteran species, with the exception of the horseshoe bats, have a small lobe, the tragus, in front of the ear opening. While in flight, insectivorous bats emit high-frequency sound waves through the mouth (e.g. the family Vespertilionidae) or nostrils (e.g. the family Hipposideridae). These clicks and bleeps are reflected by objects in the immediate vicinity of the bat and are picked up on the rebound by the bats' ears, thus providing information on obstacles, potential predators and prey to the bat. The different calls emitted during echolocation can help identify the bat species.

Anyone who has observed bats in flight will appreciate the rapidity with which they analyse and react to these 'messages'. The time between the emission of the call, the reception of the bounced echo and the bat's physical reaction to the stimulus may in fact be as little as one hundredth of a second. Among the fruit-bats, only the two *Rousettus* fruit-bats in the region possess the ability to echolocate; the clicks are made with the tongue, emitted through the mouth, and are of a lower frequency than those of insect-eating bats.

FRUIT-BATS (p.58)
Family Pteropodidae (p.58)

Twenty species occur in the region but only three are regularly encountered. Dobson's Fruit-bat is known mainly from the miombo belt. Local bats that were previously assigned to the Gambian Epauletted Fruit-bat *(Epomophorus gambianus)* have been reassigned to Peters's Epauletted Fruit-bat *(E. crypturus)*. Two species, the Little Epauletted Fruit-bat *(E. labiatus)* and Bergman's Collared Fruit-bat *(Myonycteris relicta)*, have been added to the local fauna and a further one has been reassigned. The latter is Harrison's Soft-furred Fruit-bat *(Lissonycteris goliath)*, which replaces Bocage's Fruit-bat *(L. angolensis)*. Ten species are known from one to just a few records in the north of greater southern Africa, most notably in Angola.

Most fruit-bats recorded from the region are large in size with pointed, dog-like heads. Their ears are fairly prominent but lack ear extensions or tragi. The tail is very short and the tail (interfemoral) membrane is indistinct (fig 1.1, below). Unlike the insectivorous bats, the fruit-bats in the region have two claws on each wing. Two of the more common species have white tufts at the base of the ears and roost in trees; the Egyptian Fruit-bat lacks such white tufts, roosts in caves and is one of only two fruit-bats in the region that can echolocate.

Key features: Large size; dog-like faces.

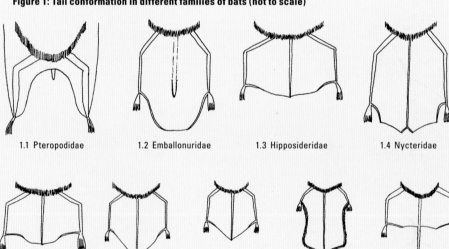

Figure 1: Tail conformation in different families of bats (not to scale)

1.1 Pteropodidae

1.2 Emballonuridae

1.3 Hipposideridae

1.4 Nycteridae

1.5 Rhinolophidae

1.6 Vespertilionidae (subfamily Miniopterinae)

1.7 Vespertilionidae (subfamily Vespertilioninae)

1.8 Vespertilionidae (subfamily Kerivoulinae)

1.9 Molossidae

Figure 2: Face and ear conformation of different bat groups (not to scale)

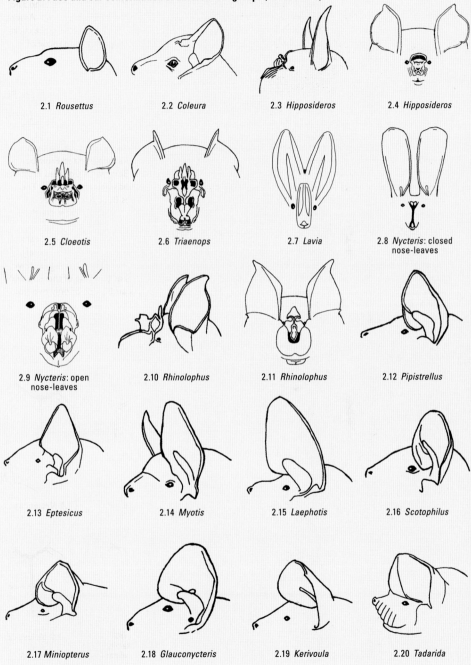

2.1 *Rousettus*

2.2 *Coleura*

2.3 *Hipposideros*

2.4 *Hipposideros*

2.5 *Cloeotis*

2.6 *Triaenops*

2.7 *Lavia*

2.8 *Nycteris*: closed nose-leaves

2.9 *Nycteris*: open nose-leaves

2.10 *Rhinolophus*

2.11 *Rhinolophus*

2.12 *Pipistrellus*

2.13 *Eptesicus*

2.14 *Myotis*

2.15 *Laephotis*

2.16 *Scotophilus*

2.17 *Miniopterus*

2.18 *Glauconycteris*

2.19 *Kerivoula*

2.20 *Tadarida*

INSECTIVOROUS BATS (p.70)

There are eight families and at least 88 species of insectivorous bats in the region. Many species are difficult to separate without detailed examination. Unlike the fruit-bats, insectivorous bats have only one claw on each wing and they are generally, but not always, much smaller in size. The conformation of the tail and the interfemoral membrane, which it helps to support, are useful diagnostic features at family level (see fig. 1, p.18).

SHEATH-TAILED & TOMB BATS Family Emballonuridae (p.70)

Four species occur in southern Africa, of which one is known from only a single locality in the region. They are easily separated from other bats by the distinctive tail conformation: somewhat more than half of the tail is enclosed by the interfemoral membrane, the remainder being free. The tail-tip, however, does not reach the outer edge of the membrane as it does in the free-tailed bats (figs. 1.2 and 1.9, p.18). The eyes are larger than those of most insectivorous bats. They roost against a surface and never hang free.
Key features: Tail distinctive – partly free but not projecting beyond outer edge of membrane; simple face with no nose-leaves.

TRIDENT & LEAF-NOSED BATS Family Hipposideridae (p.72)

Five species occur in the region, four leaf-nosed bats and two trident bats (but note that the Trident Bat *Triaenops persicus* is usually called the Persian Leaf-nosed Bat outside the region). They are all similar in general appearance to horseshoe bats but can be separated from the latter by their more simple nose-leaves. Their tail conformation resembles that of horseshoe bats (figs. 1.3 and 1.5, p.18). Trident bats have a three-pronged process on the top edge of the nose-leaves. The leaf-nosed bats have large ears and tiny tragi. The Giant and Striped Leaf-nosed Bats are the largest insect-eating bats in southern Africa. All species usually roost in caves.
Key features: Similar to horseshoe bats but nose-leaf structure simpler and less 'horseshoe'-like.

SLIT-FACED BATS Family Nycteridae (p.76)

Nine species occur in the region, but only one has a wide distribution range. Several are known from one, or very few, records. Bats of this family have disproportionately long ears (nearly 4cm in the case of Egyptian Slit-faced Bat), which are parallel-sided and are held more or less vertically, unlike, for example, the ears of the long-eared bats (fig. 2.15, p.19), which are held at an angle of 45° to the head. There is a slit in the skin down the middle of the face which, when unfolded, reveals small nose-leaves. The terminal vertebra of the tail is bifurcated, giving a Y-tipped appearance, a feature diagnostic of this family (fig. 1.4, p.18). Slit-faced bats tend to roost singly or in small numbers, hanging free rather than pressed against a vertical surface. All species in the region belong to the genus *Nycteris*.
Key features: Very long, vertically held ears; Y-shaped tail-tip; groove down middle of face.

HORSESHOE BATS Family Rhinolophidae (p.80)

The 17 species of horseshoe bat in the region are difficult to separate to species level but in most cases can be separated by their echolocation calls. All have complex nose-leaves, which play an important role in echolocation. The plate-like or horseshoe-shaped main nose-leaf above the upper lip varies little in shape between the different species. Above the horseshoe, however, there is a protruding saddle-shaped outgrowth known as the sella, and in the region of the forehead is an erect, triangular fold of skin called the lancet (fig. 2.11, p.19). It is these outgrowths, together with the tooth structure, which allow taxonomists to distinguish the different species. The ears are prominent and widely separated, but have no tragi; the horseshoe bats are the only family of insectivorous bats in the region to lack the tragus. The interfemoral membrane is more or less

squared off between feet and tail-tip, as in the leaf-nosed and trident bats (figs. 1.5 and 1.3, p.18). Most species roost in caves and crevices and they hang free, not pressed against the walls of the roost. The wings are short and rounded and, when the bat is at rest, they envelop the body.
Key features: Horseshoe-shaped nose-leaf with projections; no tragus.

FALSE VAMPIRE BATS Family Megadermatidae (p.84)

Just one species, the Yellow-winged Bat, occurs in the region and is restricted to north-eastern Zambia and Malawi. It has large, rounded ears and a large, spearhead-shaped nose-leaf that runs the full length of the face.
Key features: Large ears; spear-head shaped nose-leaf.

LONG-FINGERED BATS Family Miniopteridae (p.84)

Three species occur in southern Africa. The members of this family are characterized by the second phalanx of the third digit being about three times as long as the first phalanx; in the other vesper bats it is not especially elongated. At present, the three species can only be conclusively identified and separated by examination of various skull features or DNA analysis, which is beyond the scope of this book. As with most insectivorous bats, the echolocation calls can be diagnostic.
Key feature: Second phalanx of third digit greatly elongated.

VESPER BATS Family Vespertilionidae (p.88)

By far the largest bat family in the southern African region, with at least 34 species recorded to date, although more than one third of these species are known only from very few records. All vesper bats have simple mouse-like muzzles and lack any out-of-the-ordinary facial structures. Their ears are well developed and carry tragi, which vary in shape according to the species. The tail is completely enclosed by the interfemoral membrane, which tapers towards the tail-tip and projects backwards in a V-shape (figs. 1.6, 1.7, 1.8, p.18). The bats of this group are difficult to identify to species level in most cases.
Key features: Mouse-like faces; membrane extends to tail-tip in V-shape.

VARIOUS VESPER BATS Subfamily Vespertilioninae (p.88)

This subfamily contains 11 genera and about 32 species. Members of two genera are relatively simple to place but the remainder are generally confusing and variable in appearance even within a single species. Many species occur only marginally in the region and are rarely encountered. The Variegated Butterfly Bat (p.98) has distinctive reticulated venation on the wings. The long-eared bats (*Laephotis*) are represented in the region by four species with very large ears which are held at an angle of 45° to the head (unlike, for example, the long ears of the slit-faced bats, which are held vertically). The wing-gland bats (hairy bats) of the genera *Myotis* and *Cistugo* (p.88) can be separated from other vesper bats by their longer, more pointed muzzles and their soft, erect fur. Note, however, that the individual hairs are straight, not curled at the tip like those of the woolly bats.
Key feature: Mouse-like faces.

WOOLLY BATS Subfamily Kerivoulinae (p.106)

Two species occur. They are small and are characterized by a long, woolly coat, the individual hairs of which are curled at the tip, unlike that of the wing-gland bats (p.88). The interfemoral membrane is fringed with short hairs – a feature peculiar to this subfamily (see fig. 1.8, p.18).
Key features: Long, woolly hair; fringe of hair around tail membrane.

FREE-TAILED BATS Family Molossidae (p.108)

Of the 15 species recorded from the region, only four are regularly encountered. Members of the family are characterized by having the first third to half of the tail encased in the interfemoral membrane to its end, with the remainder of the tail projecting beyond the outer edge of the membrane (fig. 1.9, p.18). In the family Emballonuridae (p.70) the end of the tail is also free, but it is shorter than the membrane and projects from the central area of the membrane at an angle (fig. 1.2, p.18). All but one species, the Large-eared Giant Mastiff Bat, have shortened faces and this is emphasized by the relatively large ears. A tragus is present but is small. Many species have distinctively wrinkled upper lips (and are often called bulldog bats; see fig. 2.20, p.19). Males of two species in the region have a prominent crest on top of the head. The feet have a fringe of prominent hairs. The fur is short and flattened and usually dark brown or reddish-brown. Unlike most bats, free-tailed bats can scuttle around rapidly on walls and on the ground. Several species commonly roost in houses.

Key features: Partly free tail projecting beyond edge of interfemoral membrane; wrinkled lips in many species.

BABOONS, MONKEYS & GALAGOS Order Primates

BABOONS & MONKEYS Family Cercopithecidae (p.112)

Eleven species occur in greater southern Africa. Nine are long-tailed 'typical' monkeys – including two Vervet Monkeys, which are pale in colour and open woodland dwellers, and the Sykes's and Blue Monkeys, darker in colour and forest-dwellers. The two baboons are large, with dog-like muzzles, and have a marked kink in the tail about one-third of the way along its length. They are largely terrestrial but will readily climb trees. All are diurnal.

Key features: Unmistakable monkey-like appearance; diurnal.

POTTOS Family Lorisidae (p.126)

A single species in the region that is restricted to northern Angola. The Potto weighs between 600 and 1,600g and has a woolly grey-brown coat and a very short tail. Almost entirely arboreal.

Key features: Very short tail; arboreal and nocturnal.

GALAGOS (BUSHBABIES) Family Galagidae (p.126)

Eight species, one of which is apparently restricted to Mozambique, occur in the region. All are small, slender animals, the largest being the Thick-tailed Galagos (Bushbabies), with a total length of 70–80cm, a long bushy tail, dense, soft fur and very large eyes. The ears are large, membranous and mobile. Its harsh, screaming call is often the only indication of its presence. The smaller species have long but less-bushy tails and each has a distinctive call. All species are nocturnal and largely arboreal, although the Thick-tailed Galagos commonly come to the ground. It is likely that more species could be described over time.

Key features: Large eyes and ears; long furry tails; mainly arboreal; nocturnal.

PANGOLINS Order Pholidota

PANGOLINS Family Manidae (p.132)

Only two species occur in the region. They are quite unmistakable with the upperparts and sides covered entirely in large, hard, plate-like brown scales. One is a ground-dweller, the other arboreal.

Key feature: Body covered with large, overlapping brown scales.

HARES & RABBITS Order Lagomorpha

HARES & RABBITS Family Leporidae (p.134)

At least eight species occur naturally in the region and a ninth, the European Rabbit, has been introduced on a few offshore islands. All have short, fluffy tails but the three true hares have black-and-white tails while the rabbits have uniformly brown or reddish-brown tails. The true hares have long, well-developed hind legs whereas those of the red rock rabbits, the Central African Rabbit, which may occur in northern Angola, and the Riverine Rabbit are less developed. The Riverine Rabbit is very rare and localized. All species are primarily nocturnal.

Key features: Unmistakable rabbit appearance; short, fluffy tails; long ears.

RODENTS Order Rodentia

Only the rodents have the characteristic large pair of chisel-like incisor teeth at the front of both the upper and lower jaw (hyraxes have one pair of incisors above and two pairs below, see p.29). Rodents are very varied in size and appearance, from the +20kg Porcupine to the 6g Pygmy Mouse. At least 133 species occur in the region; four more have been introduced (three accidentally, one deliberately) from other countries.

Key features: Two prominent pairs of large incisor teeth, one pair in upper jaw, one pair in lower jaw.

SCALY-TAILED SQUIRRELS Family Anomaluridae (p.142)

Just two species occur in the north of the region; characterized by pointed, raised scales on underside of tail towards its base and ability to glide.

Key features: Gliding membranes along sides; mainly nocturnal.

SQUIRRELS Family Sciuridae (p.144)

Twelve species of arboreal (tree-dwelling) and two species of partly fossorial (burrowing) squirrels occur in the region. They are characterized by having long, bushy tails. The arboreal species have soft hair and the burrowing species have coarse hair. Sometimes confused with much smaller (similarly bushy-tailed) dormice (p.158). All are diurnal (dormice are nocturnal).

Key features: Bushy tails; tail often held erect or curved forward over back.

DORMICE Family Myoxidae (p.158)

At least 10 species have been recorded in the region. They are small, grey, mouse-like creatures with bushy, squirrel-like tails. They do not, however, sit erect or with tail raised like squirrels and they are all nocturnal in habit.

Key features: Greyish and mouse-like but with bushy tails; nocturnal.

SPRINGHARES Family Pedetidae (p.160)

This family contains two species, one in southern Africa and the other in East Africa. With its well-developed hind legs, small forelegs and long bushy tail, it resembles a small kangaroo. Its eyes are large and its ears long. It lives in burrows in sandy soils and is nocturnal in habit.

Key features: Like miniature kangaroo; reddish-fawn colour; nocturnal.

RODENT MOLES (MOLE-RATS) Family Bathyergidae   (p.162)

At least 13 species of these burrowing rodents occur in the region. The largest is the Cape Dune Mole-rat, which has a mass of up to, and exceeding, 750g. The name 'mole-rat' is misleading, as these animals are neither moles nor rats. The eyes and ear openings are tiny but visible; the tail is very short and flattened. All species have short legs with long digging claws on the forefeet. They have a round, pig-like snout-tip. The fur is soft but not glossy as in golden moles (p.36). All species push up mounds or heaps of soil, unlike golden moles, which tend to raise long meandering ridges just under the soil surface.
Key features: Tiny eyes and ears; very short tail; pig-like snout-tip; obvious two pairs of incisor teeth; push 'mole-hills' in runs.

PORCUPINE Family Hystricidae   (p.166)

Only one species occurs in southern Africa and it is unmistakable. It is the largest rodent in the region with a mass of up to 24kg. The upperparts of its body are covered with long black-and-white banded flexible spines and rigid quills. It is nocturnal in habit.
Key features: Long black-and-white quills and spines; large size.

CANE-RATS Family Thryonomyidae   (p.168)

Two species found in the region. They are similar in general appearance with large, stocky bodies and short tails. The brown bristly body hair looks a little like short, soft quills. The Greater Cane-rat is widespread in the east where it inhabits reed beds and other moist, well-vegetated areas; the Lesser Cane-rat will also use drier habitats. Both species are mainly nocturnal.
Key features: Large size; brown bristly, quill-like hair; moist habitats.

DASSIE RAT (NOKI) Family Petromuridae   (p.170)

This family contains only one species, which is restricted to rocky habitats in the arid west of the region, to south-west Angola. It is somewhat squirrel-like in appearance but its tail is hairy rather than bushy. It is diurnal in habit.
Key features: Brown and squirrel-like, but tail not bushy; rocky habitat.

RATS & MICE Family Muridae   (p.170)

Larger species are usually called rats and the smaller mice but there is no clear-cut distinction between the two terms. At least 99 species occur in the region. The majority of species are nocturnal. Three species, the House Rat, Brown Rat and the House Mouse, are alien to the region; they are cosmopolitan invaders associated with human settlements.
Key feature: Varied but typically mouse- and rat-like.

Rats & mice – orientation table

This table is intended to help you more easily identify rats and mice that have distinguishing features to either genus or species level. Not all species are included here. Sometimes the type of habitat can help narrow down your choice of species.

Identifying feature 1	Identifying feature 2	Description	Principal habitat	Genus	Species	Page
Tail light or white	Tail shorter than head and body	Tail short and all white	Arid areas	*Zelotomys*	*woosnami*	170
			Grassland and heath	*Mystromys*	*albicaudatus*	172
		Tail short and grey-white	Wide tolerance	*Saccostomys*	*campestris*	174
		Short and lighter (not white) tail	Forest and savanna	*Zelotomys*	*hildegardeae*	172
		Tail pale to white below	Wide tolerance	*Steatomys*		178
		Wholly white tail in some areas	Wide tolerance	*Steatomys*	*parvus*	178
	Tail longer than head and body	Last third of tail white, very large size	Forest and woodland	*Cricetomys*	*gambianus*	174
		White tail tip	Forest and woodland	*Beamys*	*hindei*	176
Distinctive markings on back	Single dark stripe on back	Very small, long tail	Grasslands and reed beds	*Dendromus*		180
		Medium size	Grasslands and woodland	*Lemniscomys*	*rosalia*	194
		Dark coat with dark stripe	Wetlands and fringes	*Hybomys*		196
		Moderate size, rat-like	Wetland	*Pelomys*		206
	Multiple stripes on back	Multiple stripes (> 4) and lines of dots	Grasslands and woodland	*Lemniscomys*	*striatus griselda roseveari*	196
		Four distinct longitudinal stripes	Wide tolerance	*Rhabdomys*		194
	Other distinctive markings	Dark middle line on back and patches on side, very short tail, very large, rounded ears, small size	Arid areas	*Malacothrix*		180

Identifying feature 1	Identifying feature 2	Description	Principal habitat	Genus	Species	Page
Distinctive markings on back	Other distinctive markings	Broad, dark rump patch; long, slender tail	Forest and wetland	Colomys		198
Other coat features	Reddish-yellow on sides		Forests	Malacomys		198
	Erectile, spiny hairs on back and sides	Small size	Rocky habitats and woodland	Acomys		186
	Bristle-like rump hairs		Floodplains	Uranomys		208
	Coarse hair, brush-like to touch	On back and sides	Wooded grasslands	Lophuromys		212
	Obviously glossy coat		High-altitude grasslands	Mylomys		206
Facial features	White patch at ear bases and narrow, tall ears	Tail shorter than head and body	Arid areas	Desmodillus		182
		Tail longer than head and body (some animals may not have the white ear patches)	Mostly arid areas	Gerbillurus		182
	Narrow, tall ears, no white patch at base		Grasslands and woodland	Gerbilliscus		184
	Variable dark ring around eye	Tail longer than head and body; arboreal	Savanna woodland	Thallomys		202
		Tail longer than head and body; not arboreal	Cape heathland	Myomyscus	verreauxii	208
	Reddish snout and sides of face		Forest	Oenomys		212
			Wide tolerance	Rhabdomys		194
			Grasslands and woodland	Lemniscomys		194
Soles of feet	Hairy hind feet undersides	See also facial features	Arid areas	Desmodillus		182
			Mostly arid areas	Gerbillurus		182

Identifying feature 1	Identifying feature 2	Description	Principal habitat	Genus	Species	Page
Guinea-pig like	Stocky build; short legs; tails one third to half of total length; blunt snout; relatively large	1 species highly social; sharp whistling call diagnostic for both	Arid areas	*Parotomys*		214
			Mainly wetlands	*Otomys*		216
		Build large lodges	Arid areas	*Myotomys*		216
			Seasonal floodplains	*Arvicanthis*		190
			Wet habitats	*Dasymys*		192
No distinguishing features	Mouse-like	Soft fur; smaller; tail shorter or equal to head and body length	Wide tolerance	*Mastomys*		208
				Praomys		208
				Hylomyscus		210
	Rat-like	Larger; tail obviously longer than head and body	Rocky habitats and woodland	*Aethomys*		188
				Micaelamys		188
	Typical rat	Large; associated with human settlements	Human settlements	*Rattus*		214
	Very tiny size	Usually less than 10g; tail usually shorter than head and body; most species have white bellies	Wide tolerance	*Nannomys*		200
		Between 10 and 20g; tail slightly longer than head and body; grey belly	Human settlements	*Mus*	*musculus*	202
		Less than 20g; occurs only in rocky areas	Arid rocky habitats	*Petromyscus*		220
	Very long slender tail	Tail almost two-thirds of total length; arboreal	Forest and woodland	*Grammomys*		204

CARNIVORES Order Carnivora

FOXES, JACKALS & AFRICAN WILD DOG Family Canidae (p.222)

Five canids occur in the region, ranging in size from the Cape Fox to the African Wild Dog. All have dog-like features – elongated muzzle, fairly long legs, prominent ears and variably bushy tails. They may have short hair (as in the African Wild Dog) or long hair (as in the Bat-eared Fox) and all have non-retractile claws. They are mainly nocturnal in habit, except for the African Wild Dog.
Key feature: Dog-like features.

OTTERS, BADGER, WEASEL & POLECAT Family Mustelidae (p.230)

Five species of mustelid are found in southern Africa. They are small to medium-sized carnivores. The two otter species are associated mainly with aquatic habitats, and have heavy, broad-based, rudder-like tails. Both the Striped Weasel, with its short legs and sinuous body, and the Striped Polecat, have distinctive black-and-white striping along the back, while the Honey Badger has silvery-coloured upperparts and black underparts. All species are mainly nocturnal.
Key features: Varied but distinctive group of carnivores: see species accounts.

MONGOOSES, GENETS & CIVETS Families Herpestidae, Viverridae
& Nandiniidae (pp.236, 256, 260)

These families are varied and have 20 southern African representatives: one civet, one palm civet, possibly five genets and 13 mongooses. They are small to medium-sized carnivores (260g to 15kg) with relatively long bodies and muzzles. Most species have medium to long, well-haired tails. The civets and genets are spotted. The mongooses and the African Civet are terrestrial (the Palm Civet is mainly arboreal) and the genets are at least partly arboreal. Most members of these families have nocturnal habits, but several mongooses are diurnal.
Key features: Varied but distinctive group of carnivores; long bodies, long muzzles and disproportionately short legs in some species.

HYAENAS & AARDWOLF Family Hyaenidae (pp.262, 266)

(Family Protelidae often applied to Aardwolf)
Two species of Hyaena and the Aardwolf occur in the region. The hyaenas are moderately large carnivores but the Aardwolf is considerably smaller (and sometimes placed in its own family, the Protelidae). The Spotted Hyaena has a distinctive short, spotted coat and rounded ears, and its hindquarters are lower than its shoulders. The Aardwolf and Brown Hyaena have long hair, the former with vertical black body stripes. Predominantly nocturnal.
Key feature: Appear higher at the shoulder than at the rump.

CATS Family Felidae (p.268)

Eight species occur naturally in the region and a ninth, the domestic cat, takes readily to the wild. All are highly specialized carnivores with short muzzles and, except in the case of Cheetah, have fully retractile claws. They range in size from the 1.5kg Small Spotted Cat to the 225kg Lion. Most smaller species are mainly nocturnal, as is the Leopard, but the Lion is partly diurnal and the Cheetah predominantly so.
Key features: All have short muzzles and typically cat-like faces.

AARDVARK Order Tubulidentata

AARDVARK Family Orycteropodidae (p.282)

There is only one species in this order. It cannot be confused with any other mammal, with its large size (up to 65kg), arched back, long, pig-like snout and very heavy tail and legs. The ears are long and mule-like.

Key features: Large; pig-like; arched back; elongated snout.

ELEPHANT Order Proboscidea

ELEPHANT Family Elephantidae (p.284)

A single species in the region and the largest land mammal. Unmistakable.

DASSIES (HYRAXES) Order Hyracoidea

DASSIES (HYRAXES) Family Procaviidae (p.286)

At least two rock-dwelling and one tree-living species occur in the region. Small (up to 4.6kg), stoutly built animals, with short legs, small rounded ears and no tail. The muzzle is pointed and they have well-developed incisors, one pair above and two pairs below, as opposed to rodents, which have chisel-shaped incisors, one pair above, one pair below. Dassies are often called 'rock rabbits', although they are not related to rabbits.

Key features: Stocky build; tailless; small patch of different-coloured hair in centre of back.

ODD-TOED UNGULATES Order Perissodactyla

ZEBRAS Family Equidae (p.294)

Two species occur in the region. Both are boldly striped in black and white but where Plains Zebra has a 'shadow' stripe in the white stripes, particularly on its hindquarters, this feature is absent in the Mountain Zebra. In the north of the region this 'shadow' stripe is absent. A dewlap on the throat and grid-iron pattern on the rump also distinguish the Mountain Zebra from the Plains Zebra.

Key features: Horse-like; striped in black and white.

RHINOCEROSES Family Rhinocerotidae (p.296)

The two species of the region are easy to separate on size and the structure of the lips. The Hook-lipped (Black) Rhinoceros is a browser with a hooked, prehensile upper lip; the Square-lipped (White) Rhinoceros is a grazer with broad, squared-off upper and lower lips. Both species carry two horns on the front of the head and are almost hairless.

Key features: Large size; two horns, one above the other on front of head.

HIPPOPOTAMUS   Order Whippomorpha Suborder Ancodonta

HIPPOPOTAMUSES Family Hippopotamidae   (p.302)

Only one of the two hippopotamus species occurs in the region. It is distinctively large with a massive head and a barrel-shaped body. It usually spends the day in water, emerging after dark to feed. It is now believed to be closely related to the whales and dolphins and is placed in the same Order Whippomorpha by many taxonomists.
Key features: Large, barrel-shaped body; aquatic habitat.

PIGS & HOGS Order Suiformes

Family Suidae   (p.304)

Two species, Warthog and Bushpig, occur in greater southern Africa. Both are clearly recognizable as pigs. It is possible that a third species, Red Forest Hog, may occur in the extreme north of Angola. The head has a typically elongated, mobile snout, and the Warthog carries large, curved tusk-like canines. Separated largely by habitat – Warthog preferring open woodland savanna and Bushpig favouring denser cover. The Warthog is diurnal in habit and the Bushpig is nocturnal. Some authorities now place the pigs within the order Cetartiodactyla.
Key feature: Pig-like.

EVEN-TOED UNGULATES Order Cetartiodactyla

(previously Order Ruminantia)
We would like to stress again that modern taxonomic thinking is in a state of flux and some scientists now favour replacing the Order Ruminantia with the Order Cetartiodactyla to cover all even-toed ungulates, including pigs, hippopotamus, deer, cattle and antelopes, among others. In addition, many subspecies have been raised to full species status by some taxonomists but some of these are being contested in certain quarters. In the authors' opinion, some changes are valid but others require further research to determine whether they should be accepted! Where these changes might occur we have mentioned them in the species accounts and, wherever possible, have included images of the different taxonomic forms.

GIRAFFE Family Giraffidae   (p.308)

A single species, with greatly elongated neck and legs.
Key features: Unmistakable; large size and very long neck.

BUFFALO & ANTELOPES Family Bovidae   (p.310)

This large family is represented in greater southern Africa by 36 indigenous species. Recent taxonomic changes have greatly increased the number of antelope species, with most recognized subspecies having been elevated to full species level. This has been noted in the species accounts. All have cloven or centrally split hooves. The males of all species carry horns, as do the females of slightly less than half of the species. Most live in herds of varying size but a number of the smaller species lead more solitary lives. There are 10 subfamilies and tribes, as described below.
Key features: Cloven hooves; all males carry horns, some females also.

BUFFALO, ELAND, KUDU, NYALA, SITATUNGA, BUSHBUCK
Subfamily Bovinae (Tribes Bovini and Tragelaphini)   (p.310)

Six species (eight if one follows the new taxonomy) of this subfamily occur in the region. The Buffalo is unmistakable, uniformly coloured and cow-like and includes the savanna and red forest subspecies. The other five species, known as tragelaphine, or spiral-horned, antelopes, range from medium to very large in size. There is a crest of long hair, least noticeable in the Eland, along the neck and back. Only males of tragelaphine antelopes have horns – except for Eland where the females are also horned; horns are always spirally twisted and ridged at front and back; they are never ringed. Body colour varies from grey through to chestnut-brown but all tragelaphines have white stripes or spots to a greater or lesser extent, and thus differ from other antelopes.

Key features: Buffalo uniformly coloured and cow-like; colour generally variable but white spots or stripes usually present on body, unlike other antelope. Males of tragelaphine antelopes have spirally twisted horns (female Eland is the exception).

ROAN, SABLE & GEMSBOK (ORYX)
Subfamily Antilopinae (Tribe Hippotragini)   (p.320)

Three species of this subfamily occur in the region. They are large antelope with well-developed horns in both sexes. Horns are straight and rapier-like in the Gemsbok (Oryx); sabre-like and backwardly curving in the other two species, and are distinctly ringed. All three species have a long, tufted tail and distinctive black-and-white facial markings.

Key features: Large size; distinctive horns; black-and-white facial markings.

WATERBUCK, LECHWE, PUKU, REEDBUCK, GREY RHEBOK
Subfamily Reduncinae (Tribe Reduncini)   (p.326)

Six species (10 species under the new taxonomy) of this subfamily occur in the region. They range from medium to large in size. They are generally heavily built and only the males carry horns. These curve back, up and then forward, and are strongly ringed. The Grey Rhebok is restricted to South Africa, Swaziland and Lesotho. It is of medium size and only the male has short erect horns, ringed for about half their length.

Key features: Horn form of males; association with watery or damp habitats (except in case of Mountain Reedbuck and Grey Rhebok). Rhebok has grey body; white underparts; straight, erect, short horns.

WILDEBEEST, HARTEBEEST, BONTEBOK/BLESBOK &
TSESSEBE Subfamily Alcelaphinae (Tribe Alcelaphini)   (p.334)

Six species (seven under the new taxonomic order) of this subfamily occur in the region: two wildebeest, two hartebeest, the Tsessebe and the Bontebok/Blesbok. They are medium to large antelope, with shoulders higher than the rump and with a long, narrow face. Each species has a distinctive horn structure and both sexes have horns. They are usually found in herds on the open plains or ecotone (zone) of woodland and grassland.

Key features: Back slopes down towards rump; long faces.

IMPALA Subfamily Aepycerotinae (Tribe Aepycerotini)   (p.346)

This subfamily has only one member (two under the new taxonomic order), the Impala. It is of medium size and slender build. Only the males carry the slender, well-ringed, lyre-shaped horns. It is the only antelope with a tuft of black hair just above the ankle-joint of each hind leg.

Key features: Medium size; males with lyrate horns; characteristic tuft of black hair on each hind leg above ankle-joint.

GAZELLES & DWARF ANTELOPES (Tribe Antilopini; Tribe Oreotragini: Klipspringer; Tribe Neotragini: Suni) (p.348)

Eight species (up to 13 species under the new order) of this subfamily (Springbok, Dik-dik, Steenbok, Oribi, Klipspringer, Suni, Cape Grysbok and Sharpe's Grysbok) occur in the region. The Springbok, whose male and female both carry horns, is placed in a separate tribe from the other species, only the males of which possess horns. Springbok congregate in herds but the other species live singly or in small family parties. The Steenbok, Oribi and Springbok prefer open habitat; the Klipspringer is found only in rocky areas; and the other four species show a preference for well-wooded or bushy habitats.
Key features: Small species, except for medium-sized Springbok. Diverse in habit and habitat. See species accounts.

DUIKERS Subfamily Cephalophinae (Tribe Cephalophini) (p.360)

Six species of this subfamily occur in the region, of which five are forest or dense-bush dwellers while the sixth prefers more open bush country. Of the forest species, four are small, one much larger, and all have arched backs and short, back-pointing horns in both sexes. There is a distinct tuft of hair present between the horns of all species. The Common Duiker has a straight back and is longer in the leg; only the male carries horns. All species have short tails. All usually occur solitarily or in pairs.
Key features: Small size except Yellow-backed Duiker; skulking habits; tuft of hair between ears.

DEER Family Cervidae (p.368)

Although several species of deer have been introduced to South Africa, only the Fallow Deer is numerous enough to warrant mention here. It has been widely distributed to game farms and private estates throughout the country. Escapes have resulted in free-ranging populations, especially on South Africa's central Karoo plateau. Only the males carry the bony antlers, which are shed and regrown annually. While growing, the antlers are covered by skin richly supplied with blood-vessels and are said to be 'in velvet'.
Key features: Males carry branched and palmate antlers for much of the year; females lack antlers; summer coat deep fawn with white spots.

MARINE MAMMALS

SEALS Order Carnivora

(Although seals are classified in Order Carnivora, in this book they have been placed before Suborder Cetacea under a heading of convenience: 'Marine Mammals'.)

FUR SEALS Family Otariidae (p.370)

Three species of this family occur in the region, one as a resident, the others as rare vagrants. Their hind flippers can be turned forward under the body when moving on land. They possess small but clearly visible ears.
Key features: Hind flippers can be turned forward on land; small ears present.

TRUE SEALS Family Phocidae (p.374)

Four species of 'true' seal occur as very rare vagrants off the southern African coastline. They lack external ears and their hind flippers cannot bend forward under the body. Southern Elephant Seal male has a prominent, bulbous proboscis.
Key features: Hind flippers cannot be turned forward; no external ears.

WHALES & DOLPHINS Order Whippomorpha

Suborder Cetacea

All the region's 45 whales and dolphins – known collectively as cetaceans – fall into one of two infraorders: the Odontoceti, which includes the toothed whales and dolphins, and the Mysticeti, or baleen whales. Ongoing genetic research is revealing an ever greater array of species, even among the great whales.

The toothed whales have a single nostril or blowhole, and the baleen whales have two. Whales and dolphins differ a great deal in shape, size, coloration and markings. In addition, as they are mammals, they must surface periodically to breathe and, in the case of the great whales, the 'blow' or spout can be used to aid identification (see pp.34, 35). The blow is not composed of water, but is a cloud of vapour produced by condensation when the whale's warm breath – forcibly expelled on surfacing – comes into contact with the cooler air. Although baleen whales have two blowholes, not all produce a V-shaped spout; the rorquals, for example, tend to produce a single spout. All species can remain under water for long periods but the Sperm Whale is the master of this art and is able to dive to great depths for up to at least 120 minutes.

The baleen whales are so named from the great plates of baleen that hang from the roof of the mouth. Baleen is composed of keratin – the horny material of which human hair and fingernails are composed – and grows in long, thin, closely layered plates. The outer edges of the plates are smooth and the inner edges are frayed into interlocking strands. Baleen whales feed on plankton and can be separated into two groups, the 'gulpers' and the 'skimmers', each with different feeding behaviour. The gulpers take huge 'bites' of sea-water, then strain the plankton through the baleen plates by expelling the water through the sides of the mouth; the plankton residue is then licked off by the large tongue. The skimmers swim with their mouths open, filtering the water until enough plankton has accumulated on the baleen to be scraped off and swallowed. The Sei Whale uses a combination of both methods.

The toothed whales take a wide variety of food, which includes squid, fish and crustaceans. The only true flesh-eater is the Killer Whale.

Social behaviour in this interesting group is poorly known. Some species are thought to be solitary, others move in small groups or 'pods', while several species may congregate in schools of several hundreds or even thousands.

The toothed whales and dolphins, in particular, have highly developed communication faculties, based on the emission of clicks and whistles, some ranging beyond the limits of audible human perception. The Humpback Whale (not toothed), which has been intensively studied, has an amazingly complex repertoire of sounds. The toothed whales also use their calls for echolocation, to pinpoint their fish and squid prey, but this ability has not yet been shown to exist in the baleen whales. There is no doubt that, as a group, the cetaceans are highly intelligent, but the level of their intelligence is still the subject of considerable debate and argument among scientists.

Unlike in other mammals, the young of the whales and dolphins obtain milk not by sucking but by having the mother 'pump' the milk into its mouth from a mammary slit on either side of the genital opening. This may take place underwater but the female commonly lies on her side on the surface, which allows the young to breathe while suckling. Cetacean milk is much thicker than that of other mammals and may have the consistency of toothpaste, cream or cottage cheese.

Whales and dolphins usually give birth to a single, well-developed young that can immediately follow its mother. Gestation periods vary from 9-16 months, relatively short considering the size of the adults.

As whales and dolphins are usually only fleetingly seen, it is important to take note of the following points to assist in identification:

1. Overall size (length) – small, medium or large
2. Dorsal fin – present or absent; size, shape and position
3. Blow (air exhalation) – single or double spout; estimated height
4. Tail-flukes – shape; markings
5. Body patterns or markings
6. Body shape and general colour
7. Jumping or breaching – the form it takes
8. Presence of other whales and size of group or pod

Whale spout shape and height

Southern Right Whale (from side)

Southern Right Whale (from front)

Humpback Whale (from side)

BALEEN OR WHALEBONE WHALES Infraorder Mysticeti

Ten species of baleen whales have been recorded off the coasts of southern Africa, ranging in size from the 6m-long Pygmy Right Whale to the 33m Blue Whale – the largest mammal that has ever existed. In 2013 a Gray Whale was repeatedly sighted close to Walvis Bay, a first record for southern Africa and in fact the south Atlantic Ocean.

RORQUALS (PLEATED WHALES) Family Balaenopteridae   (p.380)

Seven of the nine baleen whales in southern African waters belong to this family. They are long, slender and streamlined and have flattened heads, pointed flippers and a small, back-curved dorsal fin set far back along the body. They are characterized by a large number of grooves or pleats running longitudinally from the throat and chest to the upper abdomen; these grooves allow for the massive expansions and contractions of the whale's mouth as it first engulfs its prey, then expels the water while sieving out the food organisms through the baleen plates. The other baleen whales (see below) have smooth, ungrooved throats.
Key features: Large size; back-curved dorsal fin; diagnostic longitudinal throat grooves.

RIGHT WHALES Family Balaenidae & Cetotheriidae   (p.388)

The right whales, of which two species, the Southern Right and the Pygmy Right, occur in southern African waters, were so called because they are slow-moving and hence were easily caught by the early whalers; when killed they floated, allowing the whalers to tow the carcasses to land. They were the 'right' whales to hunt. They are characterized by their large heads with arched jaw-line and smooth, ungrooved throat. The larger of the two species, the Southern Right Whale, has a smooth back lacking any fin or hump. The Pygmy Right is no longer believed to be related to the true Right Whales.
Key features: Large size; smooth, ungrooved throat; dorsal fin only in the smaller of the two species.

TOOTHED WHALES & DOLPHINS Infraorder Odontoceti

Thirty-five species of toothed whales and dolphins have been recorded off the coasts of greater southern Africa. The smallest of these appears to be Haviside's Dolphin with a total length of about 1.3m. The largest is the Sperm Whale, with a total length of over 15m. The two nasal cavities of the toothed whales fuse to form a single blowhole, unlike those of baleen whales, which open separately (although situated together). All toothed whales have teeth, but the number is variable, from two in some beaked whales to over 120 in the Long-snouted Dolphin. In the beaked whales, the female's teeth do not normally erupt through the gums.

BEAKED WHALES Family Ziphiidae   (p.390)

Eleven species of beaked whales have been recorded from southern African waters but most are known from very few specimens and sightings. All members of this family are distinguished by having two grooves on the throat, which converge (but do not meet) to form a V-shape, and the males have either one or two pairs of prominent teeth on the lower jaw and none in the upper jaw. The form, position and number of the teeth are important characters in identifying the different species. In all 11 species, with the exception of Arnoux's Beaked Whale, the females are apparently toothless in that the teeth do not erupt from the gums. The flippers are small and the dorsal fin is usually prominent and set well back on the body. The tail-flukes do not have a central notch. All species are also characterized by a more or less developed bulbous swelling on the forehead

Sperm Whale (from side)   Blue Whale (from side)

and head, known as a 'melon'. Most are extremely difficult to identify to species level when seen at sea.
Key features: Between 4 and 9m long; prominent 'beak' and bulbous forehead; prominent dorsal fin; one or two pairs of teeth in males only.

SPERM WHALES Family Physeteridae   (p.398)

There is only one species in this family, and it is regularly recorded from region waters. It has a distinctly blunt and squared head. Functional teeth occur on the lower jaw but very rarely on the upper jaw. The head contains the spermaceti organ, whose white waxy product is believed to assist in regulating buoyancy when diving deep and perhaps also to focus sound used by the whales in echolocation.
Key features: Blunt, square head; dorsal fin present in two smaller species (Family Kogiidae).

PYGMY & DWARF SPERM WHALES Family Kogiidae   (p.398)

These small whales have well-developed spermaceti organs, as is found in their larger cousin, and distinct dorsal fins. Teeth are present only on the lower jaw.
Key features: Blunt, square head; dorsal fin present; small size.

WHALE DOLPHINS, PILOT WHALES, KILLER & FALSE KILLER WHALES Family Delphinidae   (p.400)

Of the 23 species of this family recorded from the coastal waters of the region, only a handful are regularly seen close inshore. Lengths vary from about 1.3m to >8m. All have long, more or less centrally situated dorsal fins, with the exception of the Southern Right Whale Dolphin, which lacks the fin. Members of the family are typically slender and sleek; 12 species have a well-developed beak (mostly the smaller species), four have a short beak and seven have no beak and somewhat globose heads. All have numerous teeth in both jaws except for Risso's Dolphin, which lacks teeth in the upper jaw.
Key features: Numerous teeth in both jaws (except Risso's Dolphin); dorsal fin present (except Southern Right Whale Dolphin).

DUGONG & WEST AFRICAN MANATEE Order Sirenia

DUGONG Family Dugongidae   (p.422)

One species occurs in the region. It is a marine but strictly coastal mammal with a long cigar-shaped body. Its forelimbs are paddle-like flippers and its boneless tail is broad and horizontally flattened. The snout is broad, rounded and well bristled. It could be confused with seals but the head shape is different. Less agile than seals.
Key features: Large (>3m) body; large blunt head; bristles around mouth.

MANATEES Family Trichechidae   (p.424)

One species, West African Manatee, occurs in north-western Angola. Occurs in sheltered inshore coastal waters and far up river systems. Similar to Dugong but ranges do not overlap.
Key features: Aquatic along coast and into river systems; large with blunt head; naked except for bristles around mouth.

GOLDEN MOLES Family Chrysochloridae

■ *Chrysospalax trevelyani*
■ *Chrysospalax villosus*
□ *Cryptochloris wintoni*
■ *Cryptochloris zyli*

The golden moles are endemic to Africa south of the Sahara, with 19 species occurring in southern Africa, and the possibility that an additional species, **Stuhlmann's Golden Mole** *(Chrysochloris stuhlmanni)*, may occur in northern Malawi. Material records for several species are scant, however, with **Van Zyl's Golden Mole** and **Visagie's Golden Mole** each being known from only a single specimen. The biology of all the golden moles is poorly known. They are all basically similar in appearance, with no visible eyes, no external ear pinnae and no external tails. The golden moles are not related to the rodent moles (mole-rats, p.162). The latter are rodents, and have small but visible eyes, short tails, massively developed incisor teeth on both the upper and lower jaw, and five claws on each forefoot.

Giant Golden Mole *Chrysospalax trevelyani*
Total length 23cm; mass 410–538g.

Rough-haired Golden Mole *Chrysospalax villosus*
Total length 15cm; mass to 125g.

De Winton's Golden Mole *Cryptochloris wintoni*
Total length 9cm.

■ *Chrysochloris asiatica*
■ *Chrysochloris visagiei*

Van Zyl's Golden Mole *Cryptochloris zyli*
Total length 8cm.

Cape Golden Mole *Chrysochloris asiatica*
Total length 11cm.

Visagie's Golden Mole *Chrysochloris visagiei* (cf. *C. asiatica*)
Total length 10.5cm.

Grant's Golden Mole *Eremitalpa granti*
Total length 7cm; mass 16–30g.

Arends's Golden Mole *Carpitalpa arendsi*
Total length 12cm; mass 40–76g.

□ *Eremitalpa granti*
■ *Carpitalpa arendsi*
■ *Chlorotalpa duthieae*
■ *Chlorotalpa sclateri*

Duthie's Golden Mole *Chlorotalpa duthieae*
Total length 10cm; 30g.

Sclater's Golden Mole *Chlorotalpa sclateri*
Total length 10cm; 22–54g.

Yellow Golden Mole *Calcochloris obtusirostris*
Total length 10cm; mass 20–30g.

Congo Golden Mole *(Calcochloris) leucorhinus*
Total length 6–12cm.

Gunning's Golden Mole *Neamblysomus gunningi*
Total length 12cm; 40–70g.

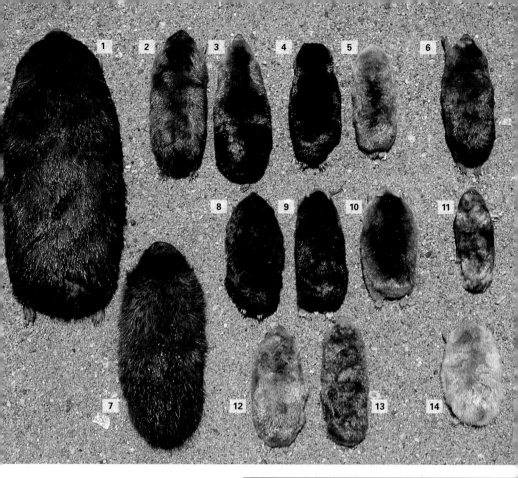

1. Giant Golden Mole
2. Cape Golden Mole
3. Hottentot (Fynbos) Golden Mole
4. Gunning's Golden Mole
5. Zulu Golden Mole
6. Juliana's Golden Mole
7. Rough-haired Golden Mole
8. Arends's Golden Mole
9. Duthie's Golden Mole
10. Sclater's Golden Mole
11. Yellow Golden Mole
12. De Winton's Golden Mole
13. Van Zyl's Golden Mole
14. Grant's Golden Mole
15. Dark form of Congo Golden Mole

Giant Golden Mole

Grant's Golden Mole

■ *Calcochloris obtusirostris*
■ *Calcochloris leucorhinus*

■ *Neamblysomus gunningi*
■ *Neamblysomus julianae*

■ *Amblysomus corriae*
■ *Amblysomus septentrionalis*
■ *Amblysomus hottentotus*
□ *Amblysomus marleyi*

Amblysomus robustus

Juliana's Golden Mole *Neamblysomus julianae*
Total length 10cm; mass 21–23g.

Hottentot Golden Mole *Amblysomus hottentotus*
Total length 13cm; mass 75g.

The genus *Amblysomus* has five recognized species, falling within the range of what used to be taken as just *A. hottentotus*. All are very similar in external appearance and their exact distribution limits have still to be defined. Use distribution map to aid identification.

Fynbos Golden Mole *Amblysomus corriae*
Range: Humansdorp to Cape Town.
Total length 12cm; mass 56g.

Highveld Golden Mole *Amblysomus septentrionalis*
Range: north-east Free State to south-east Mpumalanga.
Total length 13cm.

Hottentot Golden Mole *Amblysomus hottentotus*
Range: Eastern Cape into KwaZulu-Natal.
Total length 13cm; mass 37–85g.

Marley's Golden Mole *Amblysomus marleyi*
Range: Lebombo Mountains, northern KwaZulu-Natal.
Total length 10cm; mass 32g.

Robust Golden Mole *Amblysomus robustus*
Range: Steenkamps Range, eastern Mpumalanga.
Total length 9–14cm, mass 61-98g.

Identification pointers: All golden moles lack external tails, and have no visible eyes or external ears. Only two, the **Giant** and the **Rough-haired Golden Moles**, have long, coarse hair; the others have soft, silky hair. The forefeet carry four claws, of which the third is particularly well developed. The teeth are small and pointed, unlike the heavy chisel-like teeth of the mole-rats. The snouts are tipped with a leathery pad and are unlike the pig-like snout of the mole-rats. With the exception of a few species, the golden moles do not push up heaps or mounds like the mole-rats, but long, meandering ridges just under the surface.

Description: Only descriptions of the more widespread or distinctive species are given below:
  Giant Golden Mole has long, coarse hair; upperparts dark glossy-brown with paler underparts; small, light-coloured patches at sites of eyes and ears. **Rough-haired Golden Mole** has long, coarse hair; similar to **Giant Golden Mole** but has greyer underparts, and the sides of the face and top of the muzzle are pale grey. **De Winton's** and **Grant's Golden Moles** are similar to one another, their upperparts being pale yellowish to yellow-grey, with paler underparts. **Cape Golden Mole** has dark brown upperparts with changing sheen of purple, green and bronze; paler, duller underparts. Pale eye-spots, with pale brown line running from each spot to pale brown chin. **Sclater's Golden Mole** has rich glossy red-brown to dark brown upperparts, with dull grey underparts with a reddish tinge; chin paler than rest of body. **Duthie's Golden Mole** is very dark, almost black, with distinct green sheen; pale, triangular cheek-patches. **Hottentot Golden Mole** has usually rich reddish-brown upperparts with bronze sheen; underparts lighter with grey tinge; cheeks

Grant's Golden Mole has a silvery coat and has a total length of just 7cm.

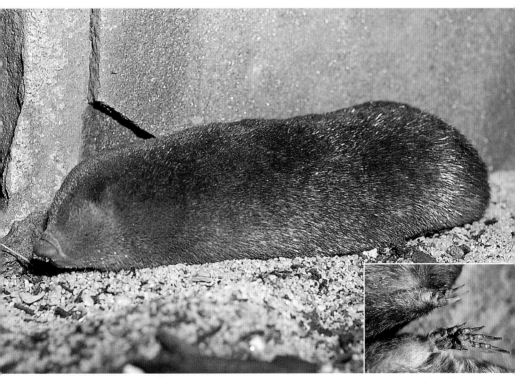

The Cape Golden Mole has pale eye-spots, with pale brown lines running from the eye-spots to the chin.
Inset: Front foot of Golden Mole (**above**) and Mole-rat (**below**), showing difference in toes and claws.

very pale; top of muzzle greyish-brown. Wherever possible, a specimen should be submitted to a natural history museum for confirmation of an identification. These small mammals are rarely seen, except when caught by domestic cats, which seldom eat them. However, the use of the distribution maps will assist in narrowing down the number of species involved in any particular area.

Distribution: Consult the distribution maps as most species have very restricted distributions. For example, **De Winton's Golden Mole** is only known from Port Nolloth on the west coast of South Africa; **Van Zyl's Golden Mole** has also only been collected at one site on the west coast; **Visagie's Golden Mole** is known from a solitary specimen taken in the western Karoo. There is some doubt as to the validity of several of these species but recent research has shown that the **Hottentot Golden Mole** is, in fact, a complex of at least five genetically separated species. **Grant's Golden Mole** is restricted to a narrow belt of sand-dunes in the Namib Desert. Both **Gunning's Golden Mole** and **Juliana's Golden Mole** also have extremely restricted distribution ranges. **Congo Golden Mole** only occurs in far northern Angola adjacent to the border with DR Congo.

Habitat: **Giant Golden Mole** has a patchy and limited distribution as it occurs only in the relict areas of indigenous high forest in the Eastern Cape. **Gunning's Golden Mole** is also associated with forested areas. **Congo Golden Mole** occurs in various forest and woodland types but also in more open areas. The vast majority of species are associated with sandy soils, although **Hottentot Golden Mole** and its related species, as well as a few other species, may also utilize clay or loamy soils. **Duthie's Golden Mole** has a broad habitat range, extending into montane areas. None of the species are able to cope with heavy clay or water-logged soils.

Behaviour: All golden moles are subterranean dwellers, although foraging on the surface may be commoner than is generally believed. Certainly **Grant's Golden Mole** spends much of its nocturnal foraging time moving about above ground. Because of this habit, many fall prey to owls and other predators. As far as is known, all species have deeper-running, permanent tunnels, with the surface tunnels being purely for foraging. **Giant Golden Mole** pushes mounds with soil removed from newly excavated burrows, in much the same way as the mole-rats. **Rough-haired Golden Mole** creates both surface tunnels and loose mounds, the latter always having an opening. Both of the larger species also forage frequently on the surface. In areas where more than one species occurs they are usually separated by differences in soil preference. Most, if not all, species are believed to be territorial and have to be kept separate in captivity to prevent fighting. Poorly known, but **Giant Golden Mole** more social.

Although some species may be nocturnal, at least several actively forage during the day. Where they occur in gardens they are usually considered a nuisance because of the soil disturbance but they are valuable allies as they eat large quantities of potentially harmful insects and other invertebrates. Virtually nothing is known about their social structure or general behaviour.

Food: All species feed on insects and other invertebrates. **Giant Golden Mole** apparently feeds mainly on giant earthworms (*Microchaetus* spp.). Several (if not all) species also eat small reptiles, particularly legless lizards and worm-snakes that share their underground habitat.

Reproduction: From the meagre records it seems that, depending on species, 1–3 young are born, naked and helpless. Those of **Hottentot Golden Mole** average 4.5g in weight. Young are probably born during the rainy season when food is most abundant. At least some species have been recorded breeding in the cooler, drier months. Some species line the birth nest with grass. Mammae: Probably 2 pairs (1 inguinal; 1 thoracic) in all species but definitely known for four species.

Longevity: No records.

The Hottentot Golden Mole, like most smaller golden moles, has a distinctive fur sheen.

Most golden moles push foraging runways such as those shown **above**. Deeper tunnels lead to resting and breeding chambers.

Potamogale velox

Giant Otter Shrew *Potamogale velox*

Total length 53–65cm; tail 29–35cm; mass 300–950g.
Identification pointers: Resembles very small otter; flattened face and stiff whiskers; swims like monitor lizard.

Description: Not a true shrew but a tenrec (Tenrecidae). Superficially similar to otters but lacks foot webbing and swims only with laterally flattened tail. Coat dense and double-layered, especially silky on tail. Dark brown on back and flanks, white to yellowish underparts. Eyes and ears are small, legs short.
Distribution: Main forest block of Central Africa, extending into northern Angola and marginally into Zambia.
Habitat: Wetlands, streams and slow-moving rivers within tropical forest zone. Occurs from sea level to 1,800m.
Behaviour: A solitary species that is principally nocturnally active. It excavates burrows in banks with entrances usually located below the waterline, and is said to add lining to the burrow ending. Does not remain in one burrow but may have several within its home range. Each adult has a linear territory of 500–1,000m in length. Forages at night, covering as much as 800m but usually less. Otter shrews make use of dung middens, which probably mark territories. May travel on land, where they are clumsy, but most, if not all, hunting takes place in water.
Food: Crabs and other crustaceans, amphibians and fish make up much of the diet but some aquatic insects and molluscs are also taken.
Reproduction: Breeding takes place during the rains, with 1 or 2 litters per year, each with 1 or 2 pups; birth weights not known. Mammae: 2 abdominal.
Longevity: Survives only a few days in captivity; in the wild, unknown.

SENGIS (ELEPHANT-SHREWS) Order Macroscelidea
SENGIS (ELEPHANT-SHREWS) Family Macroscelididae

Petrodromus tetradactylus

Rhynchocyon cirnei

Elephant-shrews originally derived their name from their elongated, trunk-like snout, but the name is unfortunate and they should more correctly be called sengis, as they are not related to either elephants or shrews. The hind legs and feet are considerably longer than the forelegs and -feet and rapid locomotion is achieved by a series of hops, or bounds, on all four feet. Within the region, they fall into four genera, *Petrodromus* (one species), *Rhynchocyon* (one species), *Macroscelides* (to three species but only two covered here), with the remainder designated as *Elephantulus* (seven species).

Four-toed Sengi *Petrodromus tetradactylus*
Total length 35cm; tail 16cm; mass 160–280g.

Chequered Giant Sengi *Rhynchocyon cirnei*
Total length 40–56cm; tail 18–25cm; mass 410–550g.

Round-eared Sengi *Macroscelides proboscideus*
Recent research indicates that this sengi may in fact be a complex of three species. A very pale form now recognized from northern Namibia, *Macroscelides flavicaudatus*, and *M. micus* in a very limited area of the same country.
Total length 23cm; tail 12cm; mass 31–47g.

Giant Otter Shrew

Some populations of Four-toed Sengi have knob-tipped bristles on the lower edge of the tail; believed to act as scent dispersers.

The Four-toed Sengi is the second largest sengi in the region.

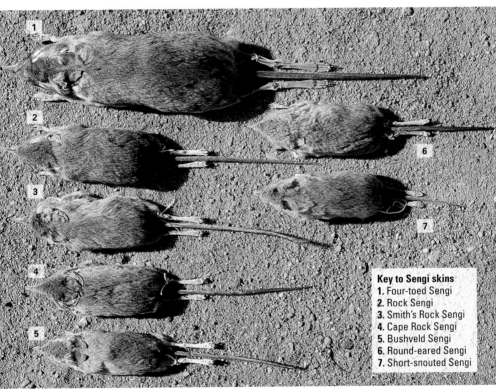

Key to Sengi skins
1. Four-toed Sengi
2. Rock Sengi
3. Smith's Rock Sengi
4. Cape Rock Sengi
5. Bushveld Sengi
6. Round-eared Sengi
7. Short-snouted Sengi

Sengis range in size from the 35cm-long Four-toed Sengi to the 21cm-long Short-snouted Sengi, as these skins show.

Giant Otter Shrew

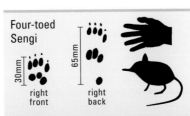
Four-toed Sengi

30mm
65mm
right front
right back

Chequered Giant Sengi

43

Peters's Short-snouted Sengi _Elephantulus fuscus_
Total length 21cm; mass approximately 40g; tail 8.6-11.6 cm.

Short-snouted Sengi _Elephantulus brachyrhynchus_
Total length 21cm; tail 10cm; mass 44g.

Western Rock Sengi _Elephantulus rupestris_
Total length 28cm; tail 15cm; mass 65g.

■ _Macroscelides proboscideus_
■ _Macroscelides flavicaudatus_

Karoo Rock Sengi _Elephantulus pilicaudus_
Measurements are similar to those of the Western Rock Sengi (above).

Bushveld Sengi _Elephantulus intufi_
Total length 24cm; tail 12cm; mass 50g.

Eastern Rock Sengi _Elephantulus myurus_
Total length 26cm; tail 14cm; mass 60g.

Cape Rock Sengi _Elephantulus edwardii_
Total length 25cm; tail 13cm; mass 50g.

■ _Elephantulus fuscus_
■ _Elephantulus pilicaudus_
▫ _Elephantulus intufi_

Identification pointers: Elongated, highly mobile snout – nostrils at tip; large thin ears; tail fairly long and sparsely haired; large eyes. Apart from **Four-toed Sengi** and **Round-eared Sengi**, the other species are generally difficult to tell apart in the field. Use distribution maps; note habitat preferences.

Description: Four-toed Sengi easily distinguished by its larger size. From head to base of tail the back is reddish-brown; sides are grey to grey-brown; white ring around eye; white patch at each ear base; underparts are white. Largest of all, **Chequered Giant Sengi**, is distinguished by its size and by its dark and pale markings on the back. Within the region these markings are often weakly defined. Cannot be confused with any other sengi species in the region. **Round-eared Sengi** is one of the smallest; variable in colour, but most commonly brownish-grey above, paler below; sometimes whitish-grey (northern Namibia); no white eye-ring. All other species have white or greyish-white rings around the eyes. The four rock sengis, two short-snouted sengis and **Bushveld Sengi** have reddish-brown to brown patches at the base of the ears. Colour of upperparts varies considerably in all species. Underparts are always paler than upperparts.

■ _Elephantulus brachyrhynchus_
■ _Elephantulus rupestris_

Distribution: See maps. The recently described **Karoo Rock Sengi** is endemic to the southern edge of Northern Cape province and adjacent parts of Western Cape province (Nama Karoo), South Africa (see map).

Habitat: Habitat preferences taken together with geographical locality considerably help in the identification of members of this group. The **Four-toed Sengi** is a forest and dense dry woodland species, associated with fairly thick undergrowth, usually in fairly high-rainfall areas. Four species, the **Eastern Rock Sengi**, **Cape Rock Sengi**, **Karoo Rock Sengi** and **Western Rock Sengi**, are restricted to rocky environments. It is possible that the ranges of the **Cape**, **Karoo** and **Western Rock Sengis** may overlap in part but they are impossible to tell apart in the field. The **Short-snouted Sengi**, Peters's Short-snouted Sengi and the **Bushveld Sengi** occur in areas with sandy soils. Although the **Eastern Rock Sengi** and the **Short-snouted Sengi** occur in the same geographical areas, they are clearly separated by their habitat requirements.

■ _Elephantulus myurus_
■ _Elephantulus edwardii_

Behaviour: All of the sengis are almost entirely diurnal, although the **Round-eared Sengi** may be partly nocturnal. They are all terrestrial and usually solitary, but in areas of high density, several animals may be observed in close proximity to one another. The rock-dwelling species keep to the shade of overhanging rocks and boulders

Three species of Round-eared Sengi are currently recognized: *M. flavicaudatus* (**above**), *M. proboscideus* (**left inset**) and *M. micus* (**right inset**).

Chequered Giant Sengi

Short-snouted Sengi

Above left, inset and above right: two colour variations of the Western Rock Sengi

Bushveld Sengi

Western Rock Sengi

7mm
right front

18mm
right back

during the hot midday hours, making occasional dashes to seize an insect. Those species relying more on bush or grass cover generally have regularly used pathways between shelters. The pathways tend to consist of evenly spaced, well-worn patches, a result of their rapid, hopping or bounding gait. In the case of **Four-toed Sengi**, these pathways are kept clear of debris such as leaves and are marked by distinctive heaps of droppings spaced along the edges of the runways. This is the only sengi in the region known to make use of dung middens. Those species associated with sandy soil usually live in burrows. Although sengis are not particularly vocal, they do communicate regularly by rapid tapping of the hind feet on the ground. This serves to warn of the presence of a predator or other threat, as well as in conflict situations between individuals. Although it has been claimed that the foot drumming tempo differs from species to species, there is, in fact, much overlap and it is not a useful or reliable identification character. May mate for life, and in the case of the **Chequered Giant Sengi** at least, pairs occupy the same territory, with the male driving out intruding males and the female other females. This species clears a saucer-like depression on the forest floor and covers it with leaves, under which it takes shelter.

Food: All sengis eat insects and other invertebrates, with a marked preference for ants and termites. At least two of the rock-dwelling sengis will, on occasion, forage for insects attracted to the dung middens of Hyrax (Dassies) and Red Rock Rabbits *(Pronolagus)*. In captivity, several species readily eat seed and other vegetable matter and it is possible that these items are included in their natural diet. **Round-eared Sengis** are known to eat a great deal of vegetation, including leaves, flowers and seeds. At certain times of the year this may make up between 50 and 90 per cent of their diet. Up to half the food intake of the **Short-snouted Sengi** is made up of plant parts, especially green leaves. Some sengis are important pollinators of certain ground-hugging plants. At least the two larger sengi species will kill and eat small mammals and other vertebrates.

Reproduction: The young of all species are born fully haired with their eyes open and are able to move around shortly after birth. Litter of 1 or 2 young born usually in association with the rainy season, but some throughout the year. At least some species form monogamous pairs within greatly overlapping home ranges. **Cape Rock Sengi** gives birth from November–January on the western escarpment of South Africa. By far the majority of females in this species drop twins. Gestation period in the **Round-eared Sengi** is about 64 days, with twins usual, each weighing 6–8g and births probably year-round. The **Short-snouted Sengi** female may have several litters in a year. **Bushveld Sengis** differ in birthing seasons in different parts of their range, probably throughout the year in Namibia but only during the summer in the east, with 1–3 young per litter, each averaging 8g, dropped after a 56-day gestation. **Four-toed Sengi** usually has a single young, weighing about 32g, after a 60-day gestation, with most births August–October. **Western Rock Sengi** has 1 or 2 young, weighing 9–10g, after a 56-day gestation, approximately. Mammae: Most species have 1 pair pectoral, 2 pairs abdominal but **Bushveld Sengi** has 2 pairs abdominal, 1 pair inguinal. Members of the genus *Rhynchocyon* have 2 pairs abdominal/inguinal; the **Four-Toed Sengi** has 2 pairs abdominal/inguinal.

Longevity: One captive **Round-eared Sengi** lived just over 6 years; **Four-toed Sengi** captive lived 6 years 7 months.

Note: A new species of sengi, Etendeka Round-eared Sengi *(Macroscelides micus)*, the third in this genus, is now recognized. Only known from the rust-coloured gravel plains at the foot of the Etendeka Plateau, north of the Huob River and Brandberg, Namibia. Dorsal pelage rusty brown, underparts off-white, ears shorter than in other two members of genus, and with a unique, elongated, naked gland on undersurface of tail. Also smallest in the genus (total length 18.6cm; tail 9cm; mass 27g).

Karoo Rock Sengi

Cape Rock Sengi

Bushveld Sengi

Eastern Rock Sengi, Soutpansberg, Limpopo

Eastern Rock Sengi, KwaZulu-Natal

HEDGEHOGS & SHREWS Order Eulipotyphla

The Shrews are sometimes placed in their own Order Soricomorpha.

HEDGEHOGS Family Erinaceidae

Atelerix frontalis

Atelerix albiventris

■ known
  distribution

▨ presumed
  distribution

Southern African Hedgehog *Atelerix frontalis*

Total length 20cm; tail 2cm; mass 400g.

Identification pointers: Small size; covered in short spines; pointed face; white stripe from ear to ear across forehead.

Description: The hedgehog's upperparts are covered with short but strong sharp spines. These spines extend from the forehead and the area just in front of the ears over the back to the rump. Although there is some variation, the spines are usually white at the base and tip with a dark brown or black band in between. The face, legs and tail are covered in dark to grey-brown hair. The underparts vary widely in colour from off-white to black. A prominent white band of hair extends across the forehead down beyond each ear. Contrary to popular belief, hedgehogs have quite long legs, but this is only revealed when they move rapidly.
Distribution: Two populations, possibly linked, occur in southern Africa; one in Namibia and the other extending from the eastern part of the Eastern Cape north into Zimbabwe and eastern Botswana. However, recent records show that the Southern African Hedgehog occurs further west into the Northern Cape than previously thought, including the dry pan country from Van Wyksvlei to Brandvlei, between Bo-Karoo and the Kaiingveld. This shows that this hedgehog can tolerate drier conditions than was previously thought. It occurs in south-western Angola in a continuation of the Namibian population.
Habitat: Occurs in a wide variety of habitats, excluding desert and high-rainfall areas. To date it has not been recorded from regions receiving >800mm of rain per year, as its habitat must provide suitable dry cover for lying up during the day.
Behaviour: Mainly nocturnal, although they are known to emerge during the day at the start of the rainy season. During the day they rest among dry vegetation or in the burrows of other species. Fixed resting-places are only used by females with young and by hibernating animals. At other times they use different sites. Hedgehogs hibernate chiefly between the winter months of May and July with peak activity occurring during the warmer, wetter months. They are nearly always solitary, only coming together to mate, or when a female is accompanied by young. The hedgehog has an excellent sense of smell, as well as good hearing but its eyesight is poor. When disturbed or threatened it curls itself into a tight ball with the spines protecting the vulnerable head and underparts.
Food: The hedgehog eats a wide variety of foods, including insects, millipedes, earthworms, mice, lizards, fungi and certain fruits. It eats approximately 30 per cent of its body weight in one night of feeding.
Reproduction: The young, weighing 9–11g, are born during the summer months after a gestation period of about 35 days. Newborn hedgehogs are blind and only the tips of the infant spines are visible. At about 6 weeks they have replaced the infant spines with a full covering of adult spines and it is at this time that they start to go foraging with the mother. Litters may contain 1–9 young, with an average of 4. Mammae: 2 pairs pectoral, 1 pair abdominal, some may have more.
Longevity: 3–7 years, captive and wild.
General: Although the spiny coat is adequate protection against many predators, including Lion, hedgehogs are a favourite prey of Verreaux's (Giant) Eagle-Owl (*Bubo lacteus*). Predation by humans for food or the alleged medicinal properties

Note: The White-bellied Hedgehog *Atelerix albiventris* is similar in size to the Southern African Hedgehog but differs in having pale to white underparts. In the region, known to occur only in Malawi and a limited area of south-eastern Zambia. Not studied in our area but in most aspects similar to the Southern African Hedgehog.

The Southern African Hedgehog is mainly nocturnal, but is known to emerge during the day at the start of the rainy season.

When disturbed, the hedgehog curls up into a tight ball.

Some hedgehogs have a pale patch below the eye.

The White-bellied Hedgehog *Atelerix albiventris*

Southern African Hedgehog

26mm

right
front

26mm

right
back

of the skin and spines occurs in some districts. Some areas have recorded a decline in hedgehog numbers in recent years, due to a number of factors, including road mortality, predation by humans, capture for pets, detrimental agricultural practices and, possibly, climatic factors such as extended droughts.

SHREWS Family Soricidae

Small, short-legged, mouse-like mammals, with long, wedge-shaped snouts and very small eyes. Three genera – *Myosorex*, *Crocidura* and *Suncus* – with at least 27 species, are currently recognized as occurring in the region.

FOREST SHREWS Genus *Myosorex*

Four species of forest shrew (sometimes called mouse shrews) occur in the region:

■ *Myosorex longicaudatus*
▨ *Myosorex sclateri*
■ *Myosorex tenuis*

Long-tailed Forest Shrew *Myosorex longicaudatus*
Total length 15cm; tail 6cm.

Dark-footed Forest Shrew *Myosorex cafer*
Total length 12cm; tail 4cm; mass 9–16g.

Sclater's Forest Shrew *Myosorex sclateri*
Total length 14cm; tail 5cm.

Forest Shrew *Myosorex varius*
Total length 12cm; tail 4cm; mass 12–16g.
A fifth species, the Thin (Tiny) Mouse Shrew *M. tenuis*, is sometimes recognized but it is closely related to the Dark-footed Forest Shrew.

Myosorex cafer

Identification pointers: Long-tailed Forest Shrew restricted to small area of southern South Africa; overlaps with **Forest Shrew** but has marginally longer tail. Area of overlap of the two shorter-tailed species is limited to the eastern coastal belt and the eastern escarpment of the north-east.

Description: Long-tailed Forest Shrew is dark brown to black, with slightly paler underparts. The main distinguishing character is the proportionally longer tail, which is black-brown above and slightly paler below. **Forest Shrew** and **Dark-footed Forest Shrew** are similar but it is possible to distinguish them where their ranges overlap in the Eastern Cape: there, **Forest Shrew** has more greyish underparts and the under-surface of its tail is paler than the upper-surface, while **Dark-footed Forest Shrew** has browner underparts and a uniformly coloured tail. Although hairy, the short tail of the forest shrews lacks the long hairs or vibrissae found in the musk shrews and dwarf shrews.

Myosorex varius

Distribution: See 'Identification pointers' and maps.
Habitat: All species are associated with well-vegetated and moist areas, with the Long-tailed Forest Shrew found mainly in the transition zone between forest and fynbos. Although named 'forest shrews', they occur in a wide range of habitats, and are sometimes referred to as mouse shrews.

Forest Shrew tail (left) lacks the long hairs, or vibrissae, found on the tail of Musk and Dwarf shrews (right; see also pp.52 and 56).

Behaviour: Virtually nothing is known about **Long-tailed Forest Shrew**'s behaviour. Like all other shrew species in the region, however, *Myosorex* species may be active at any time of night or day. **Forest Shrew** is an active digger, excavating shallow burrows, but it will also use holes dug by other species. In one study of **Forest Shrew**, it was found that individuals caught at high altitude (to 1,900m) were less aggressive than those caught at low altitudes (600m). The reason is not clear.

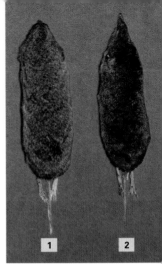

Above: Long-tailed Forest Shrew occurs in the transition zone between forest and fynbos.
Right: 1. Forest Shrew; 2. Dark-footed Forest Shrew. The two species overlap in the east.

1   2

The Forest Shrew feeds on a wide range of invertebrates, including earthworms, as pictured here.

Long-tailed Forest Shrew

Forest Shrew

7mm   15mm

right front   right back

Food: All four species are insectivorous but will take other invertebrates such as earthworms and small vertebrates, e.g. lizards and frogs.

Reproduction: Forest Shrew and Dark-footed Forest Shrew mainly give birth in the summer months (but in some areas in cooler months) to 2–4 naked young, weighing 1g. Young of at least Forest Shrew nipple-cling up to the fifth day, then follow the mother in 'caravan' to just past the third week.

Longevity: Forest Shrew rarely more than 1 year in the wild.

Note: Forest shrews, also called mouse shrews, are believed to be among the most primitive of all African shrews. Evidence for this lies with their teeth and certain other anatomical features. Although at present only four (perhaps five) *Myosorex* species are recognized for southern Africa, it seems highly likely that more will be described in the future based on genetic studies.

Crocidura olivieri

■ *Crocidura maquassiensis*
■ *Crocidura erica*

MUSK (WHITE-TOOTHED) SHREWS Genus *Crocidura*

Seventeen species of musk shrew occur in southern Africa. Apart from the two largest species, the only way to distinguish one from another is by detailed examination of skull structure, dentition and chromosome composition, although some can be identified based on distribution. Eight species are poorly known – Heather Shrew *(C. erica)*; Blackish White-toothed Shrew *(C. nigricans)*; African Black Shrew *(C. nigrofusca)*; Small-footed Shrew *(C. parvipes)*; Roosevelt's Shrew *(C. roosevelti)*; Turbo Shrew *(C. turba)*; Ansell's Shrew *(C. ansellorum)*; and Pitman's Shrew *(C. pitmani)*. These species all occur to the north of the Cunene/Zambezi line. Some are known from very few specimens, others are widespread but least known from the southern African region. Habitat varies greatly, with some occupying the forest-savanna ecotone, and others montane areas and riparian woodland. Most species occur at low to very low densities, where they have been trapped, but the Turbo Shrew, for example, is considered to be common. Several of these musk shrew species are believed to be species complexes – the Small-footed Shrew may in fact be five species and the African Black Shrew at least four species. Consulting the distribution maps will facilitate identification.

Olivier's Musk Shrew *Crocidura olivieri*
Total length 20cm; tail 8cm; mass 31–37g.

Swamp Musk Shrew *Crocidura mariquensis*
Total length 13cm; tail 5cm; mass 10g.

Tiny Musk Shrew *Crocidura fuscomurina*
Total length 10cm; tail 4cm; mass 6g.

Crocidura fuscomurina

Maquassie Musk Shrew *Crocidura maquassiensis*
Total length 10cm; tail 4cm; mass 6g.

Reddish-grey Musk Shrew *Crocidura cyanea*
Total length 13cm; tail 5cm; mass 9g.

Lesser Grey-brown Musk Shrew *Crocidura silacea*
Total length 12cm; tail 5cm; mass 6–8g.

Crocidura mariquensis

Swamp Musk Shrew

Tiny Musk Shrew

The Tiny Musk Shrew measures just 10cm from nose to tail-tip.

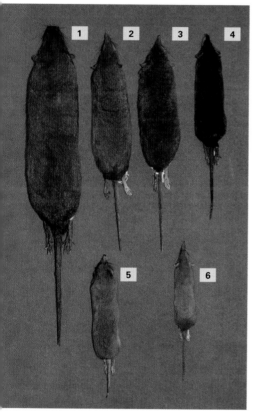

1. Greater Red Musk Shrew
2. Lesser Red Musk Shrew
3. Greater Grey-brown Musk Shrew
4. Swamp Musk Shrew
5. Reddish-grey Musk Shrew
6. Tiny Musk Shrew

Maquassie Musk Shrew

Olivier's Musk Shrew

Tiny Musk Shrew

53

Crocidura cyanea

■ Crocidura silacea
■ Crocidura ansellorum
▢ Crocidura pitmani

■ Crocidura flavescens
■ Crocidura nigricans
▢ Crocidura nigrofusca

Crocidura luna

Crocidura hirta

Greater Red Musk Shrew *Crocidura flavescens*
Total length 16cm; tail 6cm; mass 39g.

Greater Grey-brown Musk Shrew *Crocidura luna*
Total length 14.5cm; tail 5.5cm.

Lesser Red Musk Shrew *Crocidura hirta*
Total length 13cm; tail 4.5cm; mass 15g.

Identification pointers: Typical shrew appearance; prominent vibrissae on tail. Occupy wide range of habitats, so identification is aided by consulting distribution maps. Positive identification requires expert examination.

Description: Vary considerably in pelage colour, ranging from blackish-brown to greyish-fawn above, dark brown to pale grey below. **Reddish-grey Musk Shrew,** the most widespread, is greyish-red to reddish-brown on the upperparts depending on whether the specimen comes from western or eastern southern Africa; upper-surfaces of the feet are paler than the rest of the body. **Swamp Musk Shrew** is very dark brown to blackish-brown all over, including tail and upper-surface of feet. **Olivier's** and **Greater Red Musk Shrews** are distinguishable by their comparatively large size and pale fawn to reddish-brown upperparts, with fawn-grey to off-white underparts. **Lesser Red Musk Shrew** is similar in appearance but smaller. Musk shrew tails are sparsely covered with fairly long vibrissae, a feature shared with dwarf shrews, but not with the Climbing Dwarf Shrew or forest shrews.

Distribution: **Greater Grey-brown Musk Shrew** is restricted to Eastern Highlands of Zimbabwe and adjacent areas of Mozambique, Malawi and Zambia. **Maquassie Musk Shrew** is known only from a few scattered localities in eastern South Africa and Zimbabwe but extends further northwards. Most widespread species is **Reddish-grey Musk Shrew.**

Habitat: Mostly found in association with moist habitats, although **Reddish-grey Musk Shrew** is also found in very dry areas. **Lesser Red Musk Shrew** also extends into drier areas. All species show a preference for dense, matted vegetation.

Behaviour: Musk shrews have alternating periods of activity and rest throughout the 24-hour cycle. Foraging is probably solitary in all species. They actively defend territories within fixed home ranges. In the Karoo the **Reddish-grey Musk Shrew** is commonly associated with the stick lodges of the Bush Karoo Rat.

Food: Insects, other invertebrates and possibly small vertebrates.

Reproduction: Litters of 2–6 naked, helpless young born in warm, wet summer months. Gestation period of **Lesser Red** is 18 days. Nothing known about reproduction of **Maquassie, Lesser Grey-brown** or **Greater Grey-brown Musk Shrews.** Mammae: All species 3 pairs inguinal.

Longevity: As little as 16–18 months in the wild, often less.

Reddish-grey Musk Shrew

Reddish-grey Musk Shrew

Greater Red Musk Shrew

Greater Grey-brown Musk Shrew

The Lesser Red Musk Shrew occurs in drier areas.

Suncus lixus

Suncus varilla

■ confirmed range

▨ presumed overall range

Suncus infinitesimus

DWARF SHREWS Genus *Suncus*

Four species of dwarf shrew occur in southern Africa:

Greater Dwarf Shrew *Suncus lixus*
Total length 11cm; tail 4.5cm; mass 8g.

Lesser Dwarf Shrew *Suncus varilla*
Total length 9cm; tail 3.3cm; mass 6.5g.

Least Dwarf Shrew *Suncus infinitesimus*
Total length 8cm; tail 3cm; mass 3.5g.

Identification pointers: Very small size; could be confused with Tiny Musk Shrew where ranges overlap.

Description: Dwarf shrews are very small; only Tiny Musk Shrew (total length 10cm) and Maquassie Musk Shrew (10cm) are as small as **Least** and **Lesser** Dwarf Shrews. All three dwarf shrews are greyish-brown above with paler silver-fawn underparts; **Lesser Dwarf Shrew** has a clear demarcation between the colours of upper- and underparts but in the others the colours merge gradually. Upper-surfaces of feet are very pale or white in **Greater** and **Lesser** but somewhat darker in **Least Dwarf Shrew**. Body colouring of all species can vary considerably. Like musk shrews, but unlike forest shrews and the Climbing Dwarf Shrew, dwarf shrews have long hairs (vibrissae) interspersed between shorter hairs on the tail.

Distribution: Although dwarf shrews have patchy distributions, this may be apparent rather than real as they are difficult to catch, and may be more common and widespread than present records indicate. **Lesser Dwarf Shrew** is widespread in South Africa, whereas the other two species appear to have more limited distribution ranges and are absent from Namibia. All three extend into East Africa, with **Least Dwarf Shrew** widely distributed through sub-Saharan Africa.

Habitat: The dwarf shrews, particularly **Greater Dwarf Shrew**, occur in a broad range of habitats. **Least** and **Lesser Dwarf Shrews** are commonly found in association with termitaria, which provide shelter and probably also food.

Behaviour: Largely unknown, but at least two species build domed nests of grass and other debris within termite mounds (usually those without resident termites, although the authors have found them resident in active mounds).

Food: These shrews eat insects and probably other small invertebrates. In captivity the **Greater Dwarf Shrew** will readily attack grasshoppers equalling its own size.

Reproduction: Probably seasonal breeders and mainly during the rainy season. Young 2–4 per litter in at least two species; up to 7 young recorded in **Lesser Dwarf Shrew**. Mammae: Not recorded.

Longevity: Maximum of 24–30 months in **Lesser Dwarf Shrew** but usually less; probably little more than 12 months in all species.

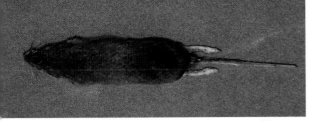

Although dwarf shrews are usually light in colour, some individuals have darker coats, such as this Lesser Dwarf Shrew.

The Greater Dwarf Shrew is greyish brown above with silvery underparts.

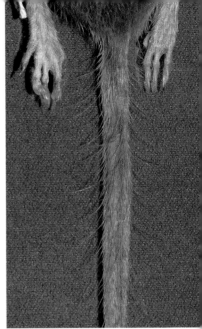

Long vibrissae are characteristic of the dwarf and musk shrews.

The Lesser Dwarf Shrew, one of the smallest shrews, measures just 9cm in length.

Greater Dwarf Shrew

Least Dwarf Shrew

Climbing Dwarf Shrew *Suncus megalura*
Total length 16cm; tail 8.5cm; mass 5–7g.
Identification pointers: Thin tail longer than head and body; typical shrew with long, wedge-shaped snout.

Suncus megalura

Description: The only southern African shrew with a tail longer than the length of the head and body. Upperparts are grey with a brownish tinge and underparts may be pale brown to off-white. The tail is long and thin, dark above and pale below. Previously classified in the genus *Sylvisorex*.
Distribution: Recorded from eastern Zimbabwe and adjacent Mozambique and more extensively in Malawi, Zambia and Angola; occurs widely south of the Sahara.
Habitat: High-rainfall areas with dense scrub and grass cover. Mainly in, or in association with, lowland and montane forests.
Behaviour: Unknown.
Food: Unknown but probably small invertebrates.
Reproduction: May breed throughout the year and mean litter size is 2.
Mammae: Not recorded.
Longevity: Not known.

BATS Order Chiroptera
FRUIT-BATS Family Pteropodidae

Twenty species of fruit-bat have been recorded from southern Africa. They may be divided into two groups based on the presence or absence of tufts of white hair at the base of the ears and pouched epaulettes on the shoulders of males. All fruit-bat and nearly all insectivorous bat females have one pair of pectoral mammae.

Straw-coloured Fruit-bat *Eidolon helvum*
Total length 19cm; tail 1.5cm; forearm 10–13cm; wingspan 75cm; mass to 300g (mean 170g).
Identification pointers: Large size; dog-like face; no white tufts of hair at base of ears or other obvious markings; black wings. Considerably larger than Egyptian Fruit-bat and with yellowish body fur, particularly on the shoulders and back.

Eidolon helvum
• vagrants
x largest known seasonal roost
? probably seasonally present

Description: Straw-coloured Fruit-bat is the largest bat in the region but see Hammer-headed Fruit-bat. Like other fruit-bats, it has a dog-like face. Wings long and tapered, and dark brown to black. General body colour is variable and may be dull yellow-brown to rich yellowish-brown, and often with distinct orange-coloured collar around the neck. The underparts are always paler. The hindquarters and limbs are usually darker than the rest of the body. The tail is very short.
Distribution: This large bat occurs widely within southern Africa, although it is least likely to be encountered in drier areas. A migrant from the tropics, it is found from Guinea in West Africa through the DR Congo to Uganda, Kenya and Tanzania in East Africa. A colony of at least five million bats is present in north-eastern Zambia seasonally, and recent records indicate that at least one breeding colony may be present in central Mozambique. Most records in the region are from the higher-lying plateaus but it has been recorded from a few coastal locations.
Habitat: Typically a species of tropical forest and some types of woodland, but in southern Africa it even penetrates into the Namib Desert along wooded watercourses in search of ripe fruit.

The Climbing Dwarf Shrew has the longest tail in relation to total length of any shrew species in southern Africa.

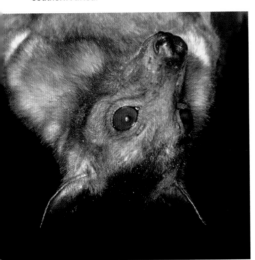

Fruit-bats have two claws on each wing.

As is typical of fruit-bats, the Straw-coloured has large eyes.

The foot claws of the Straw-coloured Fruit-bat are very well developed.

Straw-coloured Fruit-bats roost in tight clusters in trees.

Straw-coloured Fruit-bats have elongated, fox-like faces.

Climbing Dwarf Shrew

Straw-coloured Fruit-bat

Behaviour: In southern Africa it is usually encountered singly or in small groups, although in the tropics colonies may number well in excess of 100,000 individuals. Normally they hang in clusters of 10–50 animals in trees. Radio-tracking of several of these bats in the Zambian colony showed that they would forage for fruit up to 59km away from the day-roost. The Kasanka colony attracts animals from over 2,500km from known and unknown breeding colonies, and a single individual covered 370km in a single night. At large colonies, such as that at Kasanka, the bats are hunted by a wide range of predators, such as Nile crocodiles, several raptors (including African Fish Eagle) and White-backed Vultures, as well as pythons, Leopard and African Civet. Ground-hunters, such as crocodiles, take the bats when branches break and either kill or injure these aerial mammals.

Food: It eats a wide range of both wild and cultivated fruit. Seasonal movements are probably triggered by the presence or absence of fruiting trees.

Reproduction: Known to breed at the Kasanka colony (matings and births), and the Marromeu location in Mozambique is believed to be a breeding colony. In East Africa, births have been recorded from December–February, with similar timing in the Kasanka colony. A single young, weighing about 40–50g, dropped after a 120-day gestation, is the norm. When small, the young is carried by the mother, but as it grows it is 'parked.' Mammae: 1 pair pectoral.

Longevity: One captive lived over 21 years.

PLAIN FRUIT-BATS

Rousettus aegyptiacus

Egyptian Fruit-bat *Rousettus aegyptiacus*
Total length 15cm; forearm 9–10.5cm; wingspan 60cm; mass 130g.

Long-haired Rousette *Rousettus lanosus*
Total length 12–19cm; forearm 9.2cm; wingspan 61cm; mass 145g.

Harrison's Soft-furred Fruit-bat *Lissonycteris goliath*
Total length 12cm; forearm 8.1–8.8cm; wingspan 40cm; mass 70–100g.

Angolan Soft-furred Fruit-bat *Lissonycteris angolensis*
Total length 15cm; forearm 7.2–8.3cm; wingspan >20cm; mass 75g.

Bergman's Collared Fruit-bat *Myonycteris relicta*
Total length 10cm; forearm 7cm; tail 9mm; mass 54g.

Little Collared Fruit-bat *Myonycteris torquata*
Total length 10.2cm; forearm 6.3cm; wingspan 28–30cm; mass 46g.

Rousettus lanosus

Identification pointers: These species do not have white tufts at the base of the ears. Two species are large but **Bergman's Collared Fruit-bat** is obviously smaller. Uniformly coloured upper- and underparts, but underparts always lighter. Male of **Harrison's Soft-furred Fruit-bat** has collar of stiff, orange hair on throat and side of neck; female's throat and neck are sparsely haired.

Lissonycteris goliath

Description: Egyptian Fruit-bat plain without distinctive markings. Upperparts dark brown to greyish-brown, and underparts are grey. Neck has a paler, usually yellowish collar and throat may have a brownish tinge. Round-tipped wings are dark brown or nearly black and tail is short. **Harrison's Soft-furred Fruit-bat** is similar but is smaller with richer brown upperparts. Male has distinctive brown-orange collar of stiff hairs on throat and sides of neck, not found in male Egyptian Fruit-bat. Male **Bergman's Collared Fruit-bat** has reddish-brown ruff on neck, throat and upper chest.

Egyptian Fruit-bat

Egyptian Fruit-bats have a dog-like face and short tail.

Egyptian Fruit-bats serve as plant pollinators.

Harrison's Soft-furred Fruit-bat

Egyptian Fruit-bat

Long-haired Rousette

Lissonycteris
angolensis

■ known range

▦ probable range

■ *Myonycteris*
relicta
■ *Myonycteris*
torquata

Distribution: Egyptian Fruit-bat occurs from Cape Town eastwards through KwaZulu-Natal into Mozambique and inland to north-eastern South Africa and Zimbabwe. Also occurs widely through sub-Saharan Africa and north-eastwards to Egypt and the southern Arabian Peninsula. Harrison's Soft-furred Fruit-bat is known only from eastern Zimbabwe and the adjacent parts of Mozambique, where it is apparently endemic. Bergman's Collared Fruit-bat is known from the Haroni Forest at the southern tip of Chimanimani Mountains on the Zimbabwe/Mozambique border, as well as Chinizuia Forest in central Mozambique. Bergman's Collared Fruit-bat is considered to be very rare, with only a few records from southern and East Africa.

Habitat: Forested areas or savanna and riverine woodland with plentiful supply of ripe fruit. A second essential prerequisite is the presence of caves or old mine-shafts to provide roosts for Egyptian Fruit-bat and it is suspected that Harrison's Soft-furred Fruit-bat may roost in cave entrances but that Bergman's Collared Fruit-bat is possibly a tree rooster. The Angolan soft-furred Fruit-bat has been recorded roosting in cave entrances and hollow trees.

Behaviour: Both rousette *(Rousettus)* species roost in caves during the day but the Egyptian Fruit-bat, being one of only two fruit-bats known to echolocate in the region, utilizes the darkest areas; it does, however, have good eyesight. Harrison's Soft-furred Fruit-bat is reliant on sight for orientation and will roost in the lighter areas of a cave; it also roosts in hollow trees. Bergman's Collared Fruit-bat is believed to roost in trees. Egyptian Fruit-bat may form colonies several thousands strong; Harrison's and Bergman's probably live in small colonies. Suitable roosting-caves may be several kilometres from feeding-grounds and caves may be vacated at certain times of the year when the bats need to travel too far in search of food. Egyptian Fruit-bat may roost in dozens, hundreds or even several thousand. Nothing is known about the roosting habits of Harrison's or Bergman's but it is likely they roost in much smaller numbers.

Food: A wide range of soft fruit is eaten, especially figs. Egyptian Fruit-bat is sometimes blamed for damaging commercial fruit crops.

Reproduction: The single young (rarely 2) of the Egyptian Fruit-bat is born, weighing 18–25g, after a gestation of about 105 days, in wet summer months (October–February) in the north with some births in June in the south. Young first begin to fly at about 10 weeks. Nothing is known about the reproduction of Harrison's Soft-furred or Bergman's Collared Fruit-bats in southern Africa, or the other species for that matter. Mammae: As far as is known, females of all species have 1 pair pectoral.

Longevity: One captive Egyptian Fruit-bat lived for 22 years and 9 months but it is likely to be less in the wild.

Megaloglossus
woermanni

Woermann's Long-tongued Bat *Megaloglossus*
woermanni
Total length 6–8.2cm; wingspan 23–25cm; forearm 4cm; mass 14g (8–20g).
Identification pointers: Africa's smallest fruit-eating bat; no distinguishing markings; no tail.

Description: The smallest fruit-bat in Africa, with a uniformly brown coat with marginally paler underparts; adult males have a patch of longish, lighter-coloured hairs on the throat. The snout is notably narrow and rather elongated.

Distribution: Widespread through the tropical forest belt but from the region only known from a few records in northern Angola.

Habitat: Closed-canopy forest but may enter cleared fringe areas.

Angolan Soft-furred Fruit-bat

Little Collared Fruit-bat

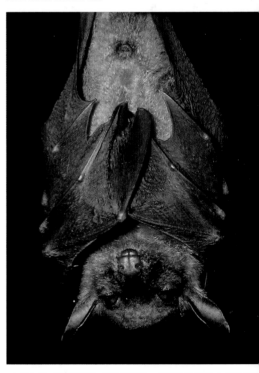

Above: Bergman's Collared Fruit-bat
Right: Woermann's Long-tongued Bat

Angolan Soft-furred
Fruit-bat

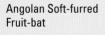

Woermann's Long-
tongued Bat

Behaviour: In parts of its range, said to roost among dense shrubbery but little known.

Food: A specialist nectar and pollen feeder; among others, visits blossoms of *Kigelia* and *Musa*. Said to visit flowers of coffee bushes.

Reproduction: Possibly breeds throughout the year; single young. Mammae: 1 pair pectoral.

Longevity: Not known.

FRUIT-BATS WITH WHITE MARKINGS

Epomophorus wahlbergi

Wahlberg's Epauletted Fruit-bat *Epomophorus wahlbergi*
Male: total length 14cm; forearm 8.4cm; wingspan 50cm; mass 70-160g.

Peters's Epauletted Fruit-bat *Epomophorus crypturus*
Male: total length 15cm; forearm 8.3cm; wingspan 56cm; mass 65-140g.

Angolan Epauletted Fruit-bat *Epomophorus angolensis*
Male: total length 15cm; forearm 8.3cm; wingspan 50cm; mass 86g.

Little Epauletted Fruit-bat *Epomophorus labiatus*
Male: total length 11cm; forearm 6.3cm; tail 2cm; wingspan <50cm; mass 32-65g.

■ *Epomophorus crypturus*
■ *Epomophorus angolensis*

Ansell's Epauletted Fruit-bat *Epomophorus anselli*
Forearm 6.4-7.7cm; mass 70g.

Dobson's Epauletted Fruit-bat *Epomops dobsonii*
Male: total length 16cm; forearm 8.5cm; mass 125g.

Franquet's Epauletted Fruit-bat *Epomops franqueti*
Total length 11-15cm; forearm 9.3cm; wingspan 60cm; mass 72-180g. (Females of all species smaller than males.)

Sanborn's Epauletted Fruit-bat *(Epomophorus grandis)* is known from just two specimens in the region, collected in extreme north-east Angola.

Epomophorus labiatus

Identification pointers: Large size; white hair tufts at ear bases; white or yellowish 'pouched' epaulettes on shoulders of males; uniform fur in various shades of brown, but lighter underparts. Dog-like faces. See distribution maps.

Description: Distinguished by tufts of white hair at the base of the brown ears in both sexes, and by males having a glandular pouch on each shoulder covered in long white hair (or yellowish in the case of **Dobson's Epauletted Fruit-bat**); when the pouch is spread, the light hair forms a prominent 'epaulette' – hence the group name. Length of the epaulette hairs varies between species but the longest are carried by **Dobson's Epauletted Fruit-bat** at about 18mm. Tails either absent or extremely short. Overall body colour of all seven species is buff to brown with paler underparts, but colour can vary; **Peters's Epauletted Fruit-bat**, for example, can be yellowish-cream above and off-white below, while **Wahlberg's** tends to be darker brown on average. **Wahlberg's** and Peters's Epauletted Fruit-bats are quite common in our region (see maps) and often associate. They are, however, difficult to separate in the field. The only certain way of distinguishing between the species of epauletted fruit-bats is by examining the number and situation of the transverse ridges on the palate (not possible in the living animal).

■ *Epomophorus anselli*
■ *Epomophorus grandis*

Distribution: Wahlberg's Epauletted Fruit-bat largely restricted to the eastern coastal belt. It extends inland along watercourses in the north above the miombo

Like all fruit-bats, Wahlberg's Epauletted Fruit-bat folds the wings around the body when at rest.

A female Wahlberg's Epauletted Fruit-bat with her large young

Wahlberg's Epauletted Fruit-bat in flight. **Inset:** A Little Epauletted Fruit-bat being held.

Wahlberg's Epauletted Fruit-bat

Franquet's Epauletted Fruit-bat

Epomops dobsonii

Epomops franqueti

belt. **Peters's Epauletted Fruit-bat** is largely restricted to the north-eastern part of the region, with isolated records from the south-eastern coastal area. The **Angolan Epauletted Fruit-bat** is restricted to south-western Angola and north-western Namibia. The **Little Epauletted Fruit-bat** occurs through Malawi and adjacent areas of Zambia and Mozambique, thus just marginally within the region, but it is likely that its local range is greater than records indicate. Refer to maps for all species.

Habitat: Forest and riverine woodland. May occasionally forage and roost away from the preferred woodland habitat, particularly in the case of the two more common species; **Wahlberg's**, for example, commonly roosts in trees in parks and along busy streets in Mozambique's coastal cities. **Peters's** occurs further west into more arid woodland types than does **Wahlberg's**, although with all epauletted fruit-bats riverine forest is a feature of their distribution, in large part because these are often associated with abundant fruiting trees.

Behaviour: Tree-roosters, with the two more common species coming together in noisy colonies of a few to several hundred individuals. **Peters's** usually roosts singly or in small groups; **Wahlberg's** is similar but may also gather in the hundreds at suitable sites. One of the best-known colonies is in the restaurant complex in Skukuza, Kruger National Park. Recent research in that park has shown that **Wahlberg's** may fly more than 13km between roost and suitable fruiting trees. The distinctive 'singing' calls are common to all epauletted fruit-bats.

Food: Most soft fruits, but possibly all species also feed from flowers. Most epauletted fruit-bats show a strong preference for a range of fig species but eat many other tree fruits. It is known that **Wahlberg's** also feeds from baobab flowers and in the process acts as a pollinator. These bats may feed at a fruiting tree, or pluck fruit with the mouth and carry it to a feeding perch. The authors have observed **Wahlberg's** removing fruit pulp from large pawpaws with the folded wing and then licking it clean.

Reproduction: Most young probably born in the early summer months, although **Peters's** in the north of the region may drop young at any time of year but with a distinct birthing peak at the onset of the rains; this also seems to apply to **Little Epauletted Fruit-bat**, which produces a single 11g pup. **Wahlberg's** also is an aseasonal breeder but with birthing peaks in July and during the summer rains. Females usually carry a single young (twins are rare) weighing about 20g. Full gestation of **Wahlberg's** is believed to be 150–180 days. As in most bat species, delayed implantation is known in most epauletted fruit-bats.

Mammae: As far as is known, all species have 1 pair pectoral.

Longevity: The Gambian Epauletted Fruit-bat *(Epomophorus gambianus)* of West Africa has an average lifespan of 21 years but may reach 28 years.

■ *Micropteropus intermedius*
■ *Micropterus pusillus*

Hayman's Lesser Epauletted Fruit-bat *Micropteropus intermedius*
Forearm 5.7–6.4cm; mass 35–40g.

Peters's Lesser Epauletted Fruit-bat *Micropterus pusillus*
Forearm 4.9–6cm; mass 30g.

Identification pointers: Small size; white patches of hair at ear bases; males with distinctive epaulettes.

Description: The two species very similar, with characteristic white ear patches and males with white shoulder epaulettes. Overall fur colour is medium brown with slightly paler underparts and brown wings.

Epauletted Fruit-bats roost in trees.

Franquet's Epauletted Fruit-bat

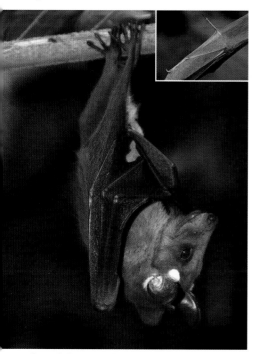
Peters's Epauletted Fruit-bat. **Inset:** All epauletted fruit-bats have two claws on each wing.

Angolan Epauletted Fruit-bat

67

Distribution: Peters's very widespread in the tropics but **Hayman's** known from just a few specimens collected in extreme northern Angola and adjacent DR Congo.
Habitat: Both species occur in areas of open woodland and forest savanna mix.
Behaviour: Peters's is mainly a solitary rooster in low bushes. Otherwise little is known, although it can be abundant in suitable habitat.
Food: Wide range of wild and cultivated fruits, as well as flowers.
Reproduction: A single pup is born after a gestation of 150–180 days (including period of delayed implantation). Mammae: 1 pair pectoral.
Longevity: Not known.

Anchieta's Broad-faced Fruit-bat *Plerotes anchietae*
Total length 7–9.6cm (8.2cm); forearm 5cm; mass 30g.
Identification pointers: Small size; white patch at ear bases; no epaulettes.

Plerotes anchietae

Description: A small fruit-bat with a yellowish-brown coat and slightly paler underparts. Both sexes have white hair tufts at the ear bases but male does not have shoulder epaulettes. They have a yellowish-white moustache and beard – no other fruit-bat has this. Very narrow tail, interfemoral membrane.
Distribution: Known from a few records in central Angola, north-eastern Zambia and northern Malawi.
Habitat: Miombo woodlands.
Behaviour: Nothing known.
Food: Apparently a specialized nectar and pollen feeder but its relatively short tongue indicates that it probably also feeds on fruits.
Reproduction: Nothing known.
Longevity: Not known.

Hammer-headed Fruit-bat *Hypsignathus monstrosus*
Total length 19–27cm; forearm 11–13cm; wingspan 90cm; mass 230–450g (male larger than female).
Identification pointers: Large size; distinctive muzzle shape; white hair tufts at ear bases; distinctive male call.

Hypsignathus monstrosus

Description: Very large bat with an overall light to reddish-brown coat and some white spotting on the belly. Light coloured collar usually present across shoulders. Head and shoulders with greyish tinge and white patches at ear bases. Wings overall brown. Main distinguishing feature the large snout with flattened tip; almost pig-like snout, most developed in male.
Distribution: Wide range across the tropical forest belt but only in northern Angola within the region.
Habitat: Forests with closed canopies, riparian forests; reported along forest edges.
Behaviour: Common throughout much of its range and apparently roosts singly, or in small numbers in trees.
Food: Feeds on a wide range of fruits, which it plucks while hovering and then carries to a perch, where juices are squeezed out and the rest is discarded.
Reproduction: Several males call from the same tree; call a distinctive honking noise, to attract females. At least in parts of range a seasonal breeder. and usually a single young, rarely twins, weighing on average 40g, is dropped. Mammae: 1 pair pectoral.
Longevity: May live up to 30 years.

Anchieta's Broad-faced Fruit-bat

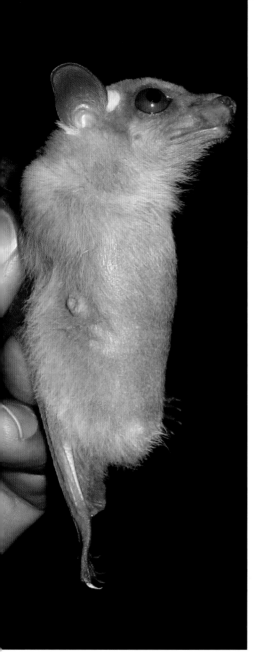

Peters's Lesser Epauletted Fruit-bat

Hammer-headed Fruit-bat female

Hammer-headed Fruit-bat

INSECTIVOROUS BATS

SHEATH-TAILED & TOMB BATS Family Emballonuridae

Bats of this family can be distinguished by the form of the tail, about one half of which is enclosed by the interfemoral membrane, the remainder not being attached to the membrane but not extending beyond it (fig. 1.2, p.18). They have simple faces without any projections or nose-leaves. The ears are triangular with rounded tips and each species has a differently shaped tragus. All have large eyes, and the wings are narrow and pointed at the tips for rapid flight.

African Sheath-tailed Bat *Coleura afra*
Total length 7cm; tail 1.5cm; forearm 4.4–5.3cm; wingspan 24cm; mass 11g.

Mauritian Tomb Bat *Taphozous mauritianus*
Total length 10cm; tail 2cm; forearm 6cm; wingspan 34cm; mass 28g.

Egyptian Tomb Bat *Taphozous perforatus*
Total length 10cm; tail 2.6cm; forearm 6cm; wingspan 34cm; mass 30g.

■ *Coleura afra*
■ *Taphozous perforatus*
■ *Saccolaimus peli*

A fourth species, Pel's Pouched Bat *(Saccolaimus peli)*, is only known from one locality in the region, in east-central Angola. Has typical large eyes, smooth muzzle and tail structure, but is very large (wingspan >60cm; mass 90g) with overall colouring dark brown to almost black, including the wings.

Taphozous mauritianus

Identification pointers: Tail partly enclosed by membrane, with remainder free but not projecting beyond membrane (see fig. 1.2, p.18; compare with free-tailed bats, fig. 1.9). Much smaller size of **Sheath-tailed Bat**; **Mauritian Tomb Bat** with white underparts and wings; **Egyptian Tomb Bat** only outer two-thirds of wings white, remainder very dark; underparts light brown to grey with some white hairs on lower belly, but not all white as in **Mauritian Tomb Bat**.

Description: Tail as described above. **African Sheath-tailed Bat** uniform deep brown body but slightly paler below and on wings. **Mauritian Tomb Bat** has grizzled grey upperparts, pure white underparts and greyish-white wing-membranes. Males have a deep glandular sac in the throat; females have only a shallow fold. **Egyptian Tomb Bat** has dark brown upperparts and slightly paler underparts, although belly is usually off-white; only outer two-thirds of the wing-membranes white, inner third almost black. No throat gland. Main features are the naked, to near-naked, muzzle and very large eyes for microbats.
Distribution: **African Sheath-tailed Bat** occurs only in extreme north-east of region and is known from a single record in central Mozambique, and north-central coast of Angola. **Mauritian Tomb Bat** restricted to northern and eastern areas of the region but extends in the south-west along the coastal plain to the Eastern Cape. **Egyptian Tomb Bat** only known from scattered localities in northern Botswana and Zimbabwe, and just 28 records from the region.
Habitat: Open woodland. **Mauritian Tomb Bat** frequently roosts in more exposed positions, such as outer walls of buildings and on tree trunks; **Egyptian Tomb Bat** hides in dark cracks and crevices in caves or buildings.
Behaviour: **Mauritian Tomb Bat** usually roosts singly or in pairs and **Egyptian Tomb Bat** roosts in clusters of 6–10. **African Sheath-tailed Bat** in East Africa forms colonies of 50,000 individuals or more. Roosts with belly flat against surface and, if disturbed, scuttles around a corner. Can detect movement from some distance away indicating that they have good eyesight in contrast to most other insect-eating bats. Sometimes hunt by day.

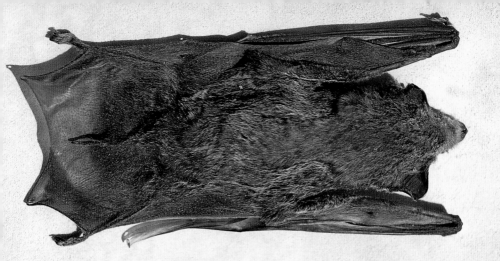

Tomb Bat skin showing part of the tail enclosed by the interfemoral membrane, with the remainder not extending beyond it.

Above and left inset: The Mauritian Tomb Bat frequently roosts on tree trunks, or on the outer walls of buildings. **Inset right:** The naked muzzle of this bat is diagnostic.

African Sheath-tailed Bat	Mauritian Tomb Bat Egyptian Tomb Bat

Food: Insects. The Mauritian Tomb Bat's diet consists mainly of moths, termite alates and small beetles.

Reproduction: Tomb bats give birth to a single young (rarely 2 in **Mauritian Tomb Bat**) during summer with some evidence of 2 birth peaks, in early summer and in late summer. Sheath-tailed bats probably similar but little information from region, although full gestation is about 114–122 days. Gestation in the **Mauritian Tomb Bat** given as from 60–90 days but needs confirmation. Mammae: 1 pair pectoral. **Longevity:** No records.

TRIDENT & LEAF-NOSED BATS Family Hipposideridae

This distinctive group of bats consists of three genera and five species in southern Africa, of which three have a single nose-leaf and two have three spear-shaped leaves mounted at the back of the main nose-leaf. These bats are sometimes also known as roundleaf bats.

Giant Leaf-nosed Bat *Hipposideros gigas*
Total length 13–15cm; forearm 10–12cm; wingspan up to 60cm; mass 52–175g (female much smaller than male; adult male in breeding to 200g).

Striped Leaf-nosed Bat *Hipposideros vittatus*
Similar measurements to Giant Leaf-nosed Bat but slightly smaller.

Hipposideros gigas & Hipposideros vittatus

Sundevall's Leaf-nosed Bat *Hipposideros caffer*
Total length 8cm; forearm 5cm; wingspan 20cm; mass 8g.

Noack's Leaf-nosed Bat *Hipposideros ruber*
Total length 9cm; forearm 5cm; wingspan 31cm; mass 10g.

Identification pointers: Giant and Striped very large; distinctive but simple nose-leaf, which lacks the triangular pointed process pointing backwards over the head typical of the horseshoe bats; short hair with overall pale fawn appearance; **Striped** males and females with white shoulder tufts; black feet. **Sundevall's** small; similar nose-leaf; colour variable; long woolly hair. Should not be confused with other bats (see horseshoe bats, p.80 and tail diagrams, p.18).

Hipposideros caffer

Description: The Giant and Striped Leaf-nosed Bats are much bigger than Sundevall's. Southern African Giant Leaf-nosed Bats were previously believed to be subspecies of Commerson's Leaf-nosed Bat *(H. commersoni)*, which has a wide range to the north of the region. Have well-developed nose-leaves and are related to horseshoe bats; unlike the latter, however, they do not have the prominent triangular posterior nose-leaf processes. Ears are large, pointed and leaf-like. Giant and Striped have short hair but this varies between the sexes, sandy-brown upperparts, but paler neck and head. Underparts also paler, with white, sparsely haired flanks; males and females of **Striped** have white tufts on sides of shoulders. **Sundevall's** is much smaller and its dorsal hair is long and woolly. Variable in colour, with some individuals being almost white (especially from Namibia) and others deep yellow-brown or dark grey-brown. **Noack's** impossible to separate in the field from **Sundevall's**. Tail structure like horseshoe bats (fig. 1.3, p.18).

Hipposideros ruber

Distribution: Giant and Striped occur only in the north of the region, but colonies numbering in the thousands have been recorded in Namibia and Zimbabwe, with one cave in Zimbabwe said to harbour as many as 100,000 individuals. At this stage it is not possible to separate the ranges of these two species accurately and

Leaf-nosed bat skin showing tail conformation.

Striped Leaf-nosed Bats roost in caves, sometimes in very large colonies.

Striped Leaf-nosed Bat

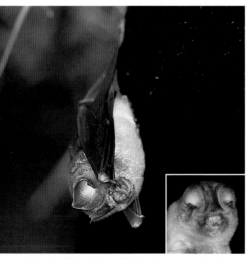
Sundevall's Leaf-nosed Bat is also a cave-dweller. **Inset:** Facial structure and ears can be seen here.

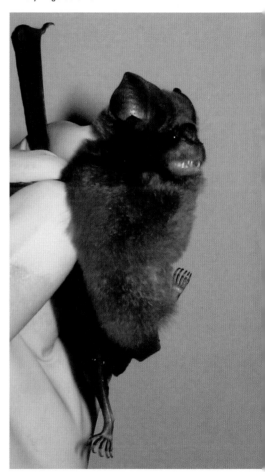
Noack's Leaf-nosed Bat

Giant Leaf-nosed Bat

Sundevall's Leaf-nosed Bat

they are dealt with on the one map. **Sundevall's** has a similar range, but it extends further south, over much of north-eastern South Africa (see map). **Noack's** in scattered locations across the north (Angola, Zambia, Malawi and Mozambique). **Habitat:** Savanna woodland; roost in caves, mine-shafts, buildings. **Noack's** apparently mainly from forested areas.

Behaviour: These species roost in colonies of hundreds, to hundreds of thousands, of individuals; **Sundevall's** sometimes in small groups of 2 or 3 but usually larger numbers. Hang free at the roosts in clusters but not in contact with neighbours. Slow but agile fliers.

Food: **Giant** and **Striped** believed to feed mainly on beetles but also termite alates and will often hunt from a perch, whereas **Sundevall's** takes mainly moths.

Reproduction: For **Sundevall's**, births have been recorded in early December in south-east of region. In **Striped**, mating and fertilization June–July in Zimbabwe with births in late October; pregnant females leave the breeding roost for about 2 months to feed, returning to the birthing cave in October. In all species a single young is the norm. Mammae: 1 pair pectoral.

Longevity: No records.

Cloeotis percivali

Percival's (Short-eared) Trident Bat *Cloeotis percivali*

Total length 7cm; forearm 3.5cm; wingspan 19-23cm; mass 4–5g.

Identification pointers: Three-pointed process at top of nose-leaf – a feature shared only with the African Trident Bat. Similar to the African Trident Bat but total length only 7cm to the latter's 8.2–10cm.

Description: Distinctive 3-pronged trident-like process at back of nose-leaf between eyes. Upperparts usually pale grey; underparts are grey-white to greyish-yellow; wings are dark. Face normally whitish-yellow. Ears are small and may be almost hidden by long fur.

Distribution: Patchy distribution in east of region but extends northwards into East Africa.

Habitat: Unknown but probably associated mainly with woodland types. Roosts in caves and mine-shafts, apparently favouring narrow cracks and fissures.

Behaviour: Colonies of several hundreds but also small groups. Roosts in darkest areas of caves or mines. Only known to occur in about 20 caves in the region, with a total population of probably in the very low thousands.

Food: Insects, apparently mainly moths.

Reproduction: A single young is born in early summer. Mammae: 1 pair pectoral.

Longevity: No records.

Triaenops afer

African Trident Bat *Triaenops afer*

Recent taxonomic thinking places this as *T. afer* through its African range, with *T. persicus* being extralimital.

Total length 8.2–10cm; tail 2.5–3.8cm; forearm 5–6cm; wingspan 35cm; mass 12g.

Identification pointers: Much larger than Percival's Trident Bat. Three spear-shaped leaves at top of nose-leaf. Only known from north-eastern part of southern African region.

Above: The tiny Percival's Trident Bat has a wingspan of 15cm and weighs just 5g on average.
Left: Head of Percival's Trident Bat clearly showing the three-pointed process at the top of the nose-leaf and the short, rounded ears.

Percival's Trident Bat

African Trident Bat

Description: Nose-leaf pitted with small cavities and folds; three large spear-shaped leaves mounted at back of nose-leaf. Ears are small, pointed and sharply notched on outer edge. Upperparts from light brown to reddish-brown; underparts paler and sides of face yellowish. Wings dark brown.

Distribution: Eastern Highlands of Zimbabwe and neighbouring Mozambique, marginally into Zambia.

Habitat: Little known but most records from Mozambique were in riparian and other woodland. Roosts in caves or old mines but possibly also hollow tree trunks.

Behaviour: Usually forms large colonies, in hundreds of thousands, in other parts of its range, particularly coastal regions. In roosting-caves hang from ceiling in clusters, but not touching one another. Have a slow, flapping flight.

Food: Insects; in Mozambique, apparently mainly moths.

Reproduction: Unknown in the region. Single young. Mammae: 1 pair pectoral.

Longevity: Not known.

Note: The Trident and Leaf-nosed Bats (Family Hipposideridae) are an Old World group of insect-eating bats. It is a large group with at least 69 species and nine genera. They occupy tropical and subtropical regions of Africa, South Asia and Australia. The greatest diversity of species is in South Asia, but Africa is home to at least 17 different species.

SLIT-FACED BATS Family Nycteridae

Immediately recognizable by the long, lobed slit that runs down the centre of the face; when this slit is opened nose-leaves can be seen. Slit-faced bats possess ear tragi and have large, more or less straight- and parallel-sided ears. The wings are broad and rounded at the tips. Also known as 'whispering bats' because of the low-intensity calls they use in echolocation.

Nycteris hispida

■ confirmed range

■ presumed range

Nycteris woodi

Hairy Slit-faced Bat *Nycteris hispida*
Total length 9cm; forearm 4cm; wingspan 28cm; ear length 2.2cm; mass 9g.

Large Slit-faced Bat *Nycteris grandis*
Total length 16cm; tail 7.5cm; forearm 6.1–6.5cm; wingspan 35cm; ear length 3.1cm; mass 40g.

Wood's Slit-faced Bat *Nycteris woodi*
Total length 9–10cm; tail 5cm; forearm 4cm; wingspan 28cm; ear length 3.2cm; mass 6g.

Large-eared (Greater) Slit-faced Bat *Nycteris macrotis*
Total length 11–13cm; tail 4.5–6.5cm; forearm 4.7cm; wingspan 33–35cm; ear length 2.9cm; mass 17g.

Egyptian Slit-faced Bat *Nycteris thebaica*
Total length 10cm (8–13cm); tail 5cm; forearm 4.7cm (3.4–5.2cm); wingspan 24–30cm; ear length 3.4cm; mass 11g.

Bates's Slit-faced Bat *Nycteris arge*
Total length 9–13cm; tail 5.4cm; forearm 4.2cm; winspan 27.5cm; mass 11g.

Intermediate Slit-faced Bat *Nycteris intermedia*
Total length 9.6cm; tail 5cm; forearm 3.6–3.8cm; wingspan 24.5cm; mass 7g.

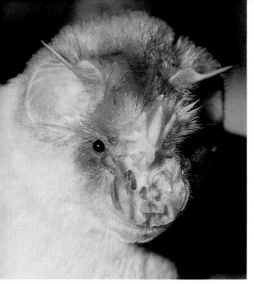

An African Trident Bat, showing the distinctive three-pronged trident-like process at the back of the nose-leaf between the eyes.

African Trident Bat

Slit-faced bat skin showing bifurcated tail-tip.

The Large Slit-faced Bat is by far the largest member of the genus in the region.

Hairy Slit-faced Bat

Large Slit-faced Bat

- ■ Nycteris grandis
- ░ Nycteris arge
- ■ Nycteris intermedia
- ■ Nycteris major
- ■ Nycteris nana

Nycteris macrotis

Nycteris thebaica

Dja Slit-faced Bat *Nycteris major*

Total length 10.6–13.7cm; tail 6cm; forearm 4.7cm; wingspan 31cm; mass 12g (8–16g).

Dwarf Slit-faced Bat *Nycteris nana*

Total length 7.4–9.2cm; tail 4.3cm; forearm 3.4cm; wingspan 22cm; mass 6g. Bates's, Intermediate, Dja and Dwarf Slit-Faced Bats are known from few records in the region but may be more widespread than records indicate. See maps.

Identification pointers: Very long, erect ears; facial slit; bifurcated tail-tip. Most likely to encounter Egyptian Slit-faced Bat. Should not be confused with other bats, but see long-eared bats of the genus *Laephotis* (p.98).

Description: All slit-faced bats have long, rounded ears, a split running down the length of the face, a long tail bifurcated at the tip and wings rounded at the tips. Large Slit-faced Bat can be separated by its much larger size. Colour in all species is variable but upperparts are always darker than underparts. Large and Large-eared (Greater) Slit-faced Bats usually have reddish-brown upperparts and greyer underparts. Egyptian Slit-faced Bat usually has light brown upperparts (occasionally reddish-orange) and underparts that range from pale brown to dirty white with palest animals in west of region. Wood's Slit-faced Bats in Zimbabwe usually have white underparts.

Distribution: Large-eared (Greater) Slit-faced Bat is widespread in equatorial Africa. Hairy Slit-faced Bat has a limited distribution in northern Zimbabwe, adjacent Botswana, into Mozambique and South Africa's KwaZulu-Natal province, but occurs widely south of the Sahara outside the region. Large Slit-faced Bat is known only from eastern Zimbabwe and Mozambique within the region, but has a wide sub-Saharan African range. Wood's Slit-faced Bat is known from several localities in Zimbabwe, adjacent South Africa along the Limpopo River and from scattered records in Mozambique, Zambia and Malawi. Egyptian Slit-faced Bat has a wide distribution in the region, extending northwards through Africa to Europe. This species probably occurs through much of Angola and northern Mozambique, but records lacking.

Habitat: Egyptian Slit-faced Bat has wide habitat tolerance, as has Hairy Slit-faced Bat, although the latter avoids more arid areas. Large and Large-eared Slit-faced Bats show a preference for riverine woodland. Some species are also found in tropical forests and their fringes. Roosts include caves, buildings, hollow trees and among leaves in trees and bushes. Some species have been recorded using man-made structures as both day and night roosts.

Behaviour: Although most species of slit-faced bat roost in small numbers and are often found roosting alone or in pairs, the Egyptian Slit-faced Bat sometimes forms roosts consisting of several hundred individuals. All are slow but highly efficient fliers. Insect and other prey is taken on the wing and even from the ground and vegetation and then carried to a regularly used perch to feed. Such perches may be recognized by the accumulation of non-edible parts such as moth wings and beetle elytra (horny front wings) on the ground below.

Food: Insects and other invertebrates are the usual prey but the Large Slit-faced Bat will also take vertebrate prey, including fish and frogs.

Reproduction: Egyptian Slit-faced Bat: a single young is born during the early summer months (October–November) and is carried by the mother during feeding forays; more than 1 young may be dropped in a season. This species is known to copulate in flight. Young of Wood's are dropped November–January, and those of Large are born September–December. Mammae: 1 pair pectoral.

Longevity: No records.

Slit-faced bats sometimes roost in caves, but have a wide habitat tolerance.

Above: Hairy Slit-faced Bat
Right: Head of Egyptian Slit-faced Bat

Egyptian Slit-faced Bat

Dja Slit-faced Bat

HORSESHOE BATS Family Rhinolophidae

Horseshoe bats are characterized by elaborate nose-leaves over the face between the mouth and forehead. Thirteen species have been recorded in southern Africa. Although only 13 species are recognized from the region at present, ongoing genetic research is showing that at least three, if not more, species are actually complexes and will be divided into several new species in the near future. Needless to say, it will not be possible to separate these species in the field, except for those with knowledge of their calls. Within a 'single species' such as Hildebrandt's, several different echolocation calls from various locations have been identified, indicating that several new species are involved *(R. smithersi; R. mossambicus; R. cohenae; R. mabuensis)*. Most microbats have species-specific echolocation calls. Specimens of *R. darlingi* in the west of South Africa and Namibia now believed to be Damara Horseshoe Bat *(R. damarensis)*. Ongoing research indicates that more species may be described.

■ *Rhinolophus hildebrandtii*
■ *Rhinolophus denti*

Hildebrandt's Horseshoe Bat *Rhinolophus hildebrandtii*
May in fact not occur in southern Africa and has been shown to be a species complex – see above.
Total length 11cm; tail 4cm; forearm 6.5cm; wingspan 39cm; mass 27g.

Rüppell's Horseshoe Bat *Rhinolophus fumigatus*
Total length 9.6cm; tail 3.2cm; forearm 5cm; wingspan 33cm; mass 14g.

Geoffroy's Horseshoe Bat *Rhinolophus clivosus*
Total length 9.7cm; tail 2.2–4cm; forearm 5.4cm; wingspan 32cm; mass 17g.

Rhinolophus fumigatus

Darling's Horseshoe Bat *Rhinolophus darlingi*
Total length 8.5cm; tail 3cm; forearm 4.7cm; wingspan 29cm; mass 9-12g.

Lander's Horseshoe Bat *Rhinolophus landeri*
Total length 8cm; tail 2.2cm; forearm 4.4cm; wingspan 29cm; mass 8g.

Peak-saddle (Blasius's) Horseshoe Bat *Rhinolophus blasii*
Total length 7.6cm; tail 2.7cm; forearm 4.5cm; wingspan 29cm; mass 4-12g.

Cape Horseshoe Bat *Rhinolophus capensis*
Total length 8.5cm; tail 2.8cm; forearm 4.8-5.2cm; wingspan 32cm; mass 11g.

Rhinolophus clivosus

Bushveld Horseshoe Bat *Rhinolophus simulator*
Total length 7cm; tail 2.4g; forearm 4.3cm; wingspan 29.5cm; mass 8-10g.

Dent's Horseshoe Bat *Rhinolophus denti*
Total length 7cm; tail 2.1cm; forearm 4.2cm; wingspan 20cm; mass 6-9g.

Swinny's Horseshoe Bat *Rhinolophus swinnyi*
Total length 7cm; tail 2.1cm; forearm 4.3cm; wingspan 26cm; mass 7.5g.

Decken's Horseshoe Bat *Rhinolophus deckenii*
Total length 9cm; tail 2.6cm; forearm 5.3cm; wingspan 34cm; mass 15g.

Rhinolophus darlingi

Maendeleo Horseshoe Bat *Rhinolophus maendeleo*
Total length 7.2cm; tail 2.5cm; forearm 4.9cm; mass 15g.

Horseshoe bat skin, showing squared-off tail.

Darling's Horseshoe Bat

Horseshoe bats roost with their wings wrapped around the body.

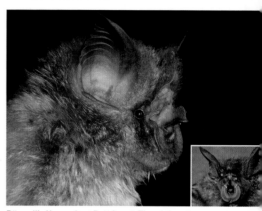

Rüppell's Horseshoe Bat. **Inset:** The elaborate nose-leaves are clearly evident.

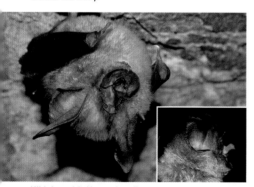

Hildebrandt's Horseshoe Bat

Geoffroy's Horseshoe Bats

Hildebrandt's
Horseshoe Bat

Dent's Horseshoe Bat

Sakeji Horseshoe Bat *Rhinolophus sakejiensis*

Total length 8.8cm; tail 3cm; forearm 5.4cm; mass 20g.

Identification pointers: Facial structure characteristic, with main nose-leaf base in the form of a horseshoe; large ears lacking tragi but with pronounced skin fold at ear base. When at rest, wings wrap around the body.

Rhinolophus landeri

■ *Rhinolophus blasii*
■ *Rhinolophus capensis*
■ *Rhinolophus deckenii*
■ *Rhinolophus maendeleo*
■ *Rhinolophus sakejiensis*

Rhinolophus simulator

Rhinolophus swinnyi

Description: For the non-expert this is a very difficult group to identify to species level. Hildebrandt's Horseshoe Bat can be separated by its much larger size, pale grey-brown upperparts and light grey to cream underparts. Most species are variable in colour but Dent's Horseshoe Bat is usually pale brown or even cream above with off-white underparts and pale translucent brown wing-membranes edged with white. Swinny's Horseshoe Bat is similar in colour to Dent's Horseshoe Bat but lacks the white edging of the membranes. Another pale species is Darling's Horseshoe Bat, which has dull-grey upper- and pale grey underparts and pale grey-brown wing-membranes. The Peak-saddle (Blasius's) Horseshoe Bat is characterized by long, woolly hair, which is very pale to white, with the palest area at the back of the neck and underparts. The Bushveld Horseshoe Bat is dark brown above with contrasting greyish-white underparts. The other species have brown upperparts and usually lighter underparts. In all cases, however, careful examination of calls, teeth, facial structures and forearm length is necessary for positive identification. Tail form is shown in fig. 1.5, p.18.

Distribution: Consult the distribution maps. Decken's is known from the region from only a single specimen collected in the Chinizuia Forest in central Mozambique. However, it may be found to be more widespread in that country, as the bat fauna is poorly known. Maendeleo Horseshoe Bat has only been collected at Mount Namuli, northern Mozambique, in the region, although some believe it may prove to be a new species and not the Maendeleo. Sakeji Horseshoe Bat is currently only known from extreme north-western Zambia.

Habitat: Most species are associated with savanna habitats, ranging from moist to arid types. Much of the range of Cape Horseshoe Bat lies within the Cape Heathland (fynbos) vegetation zone but does spill over marginally into other habitats. In the region, Swinny's seems to be mainly associated with temperate Afromontane forest. All are principally cave and mine adit roosters but some use dark buildings or road culverts; Hildebrandt's Horseshoe Bat utilizes tree hollows.

Behaviour: Rüppell's, Lander's, Peak-saddle and Swinny's Horseshoe Bats all roost in small numbers, whereas the other species may also roost in much larger colonies. Geoffroy's and Cape Horseshoe Bats sometimes roost in their thousands, hanging free by the feet, singly or in well-spaced groups. All horseshoe bats wrap their wings around their bodies in the manner of fruit-bats. Within at least one species, Rüppell's, there are regional differences in roost size, with those in the east roosting mainly solitarily and those in the west roosting in several hundreds. This has led scientists to suspect that they are possibly two separate species. A few species are known to go into torpor during cold and wet weather, but never for long periods. Although most species hunt and feed on the wing, a few species, such as Geoffroy's, carry larger prey back to a feeding roost. The ground below these roosts becomes littered with inedible insect parts, such as moth wings.

Food: Insects. Moths are particularly important in the diet of all species but some also take variable numbers of beetles.

Reproduction: In all species in the region, a single young is born in summer,

Geoffroy's Horseshoe Bat; orange phase

Cape Horseshoe Bat

Peak-saddle (Blasius's) Horseshoe Bat

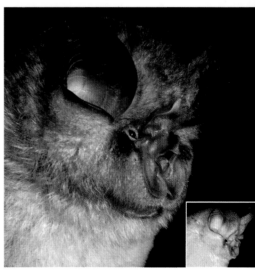

Bushveld Horseshoe Bat

mainly October–December, coinciding with the first rains, when insects are particularly abundant. However, in the northern parts of southern Africa seasonality may not be important. In **Cape Horseshoe Bat**, full gestation is around 110 days, and in **Bushveld Horseshoe Bat**, young are weaned at about 50 days. Mammae: All species have 1 pair pectoral.

Longevity: Not known for any African species but the **European Horseshoe Bat** *(Rhinolophus ferrumequinum)* has exceeded 24 years. Records for several non-African horseshoe bat species range from 18–30 years.

FALSE VAMPIRE BATS Family Megadermatidae

Five species across Africa but only one in the region, in the extreme north-east.

Lavia frons

Yellow-winged (False Vampire) Bat *Lavia frons*
Total length 6–8cm; forearm 6.2cm; wingspan 36cm; mass 28–36g.
Identification pointers: Should not be mistaken for any other species in the region; large size, bright yellow wings, large ears and spearhead-like nose-leaf.

Description: A relatively large bat with body fur ranging from pearly grey to slate-grey with contrasting reddish-yellow wings, tail membrane, ears and nose-leaf. The ears are long (about 4cm) and the spearhead-shaped nose-leaf (1.9–2.6cm long) is pointed at the tip and runs the length of the face. There is no visible external tail.
Distribution: In the region, only in north-eastern Zambia and northern Malawi.
Habitat: Mainly relatively open country with clumps of bush and a scattering of small trees and bushes. May roost in exposed positions.
Behaviour: Frequently forages during the day and probably at night. It is a wait-and-pounce hunter, hawking passing prey from a perch. During the breeding season pairs form monogamous bonds and defend a feeding territory. They are very alert and wary of close approach.
Food: Wide range, including moths and beetles.
Reproduction: After a gestation of around 90 days, a single young is born; births take place at the end of the dry season in Zambia. Mammae: 1 pair pectoral.
Longevity: Not known.

LONG-FINGERED BATS Family Miniopteridae

Miniopterus inflatus

Three species, which can only be distinguished on skull size and genetic makeup, occur in southern Africa. The **Greater Long-fingered Bat** is only known from a few localities in the region, the **Lesser** is considered to be rare, and only **Natal Long-fingered Bat** is common and widespread. All three species have a greatly elongated second phalanx on the third digit, or finger; 3–4 times as long as first phalanx. This allows the wing to 'bend' back on itself, hence the alternative name of 'bent-wing' bats.

Greater Long-fingered Bat *Miniopterus inflatus*
Total length 11cm; tail 5.5cm; forearm 4.7cm; wingspan 32–38cm; mass 15g.

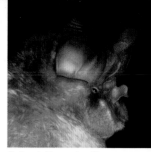

Dent's Horseshoe Bat   Decken's Horseshoe Bat   Swinny's Horseshoe Bat

Yellow-winged (False Vampire) Bat. **Inset left:** Note the long ears and distinctive nose-leaf.
Inset right: The long hind limbs are obvious in this image.

Yellow-winged Bat

Greater Long-fingered Bat

Miniopterus fraterculus

Miniopterus natalensis

Note: A fourth species of *Miniopterus* bat, the Mozambique Long-fingered Bat (*M. mossambicus*), known only from the northern province of Nampula, was recently described.

Lesser Long-fingered Bat *Miniopterus fraterculus*
Total length 10cm; tail 5cm; forearm 4.2cm; wingspan 30cm; mass 8g.

Natal (Schreibers's) Long-fingered Bat *Miniopterus natalensis*
Total length 11cm; tail 5.3cm; forearm 4.5cm; wingspan 28cm; mass 10g.

Identification pointers: All three very similar, with greatly elongated second phalanx of the third finger, which distinguishes them from bats of the family Vespertilionidae. Distinctive head profile with high, domed forehead and short muzzle.

Description: All three species are variable in measurements and in colour; Natal Long-fingered Bat, however, is usually dark brown above and slightly paler below, with almost black wings and interfemoral membrane. This bat has recently been recognized as comprising several different species, and the population in southern Africa is now referred to as *M. natalensis*. The upperparts of Lesser Long-fingered Bat are usually more reddish-brown to almost black, with black wing-membranes and dark brown interfemoral membrane. Greater Long-fingered Bat is similar but chocolate-brown above. In all species the wings are long and pointed and the ears are small and rounded.

Distribution: Greater Long-fingered Bat is only known from a few localities in eastern South Africa, Zimbabwe, Mozambique and northern Namibia, with scattered records from East Africa and the west coast of equatorial Africa. The Lesser Long-fingered Bat is restricted to the south and east of the region, with a few scattered localities from southern Central Africa and Madagascar, but is rather uncommon throughout. Natal Long-fingered Bat is widespread in the southern, eastern and northern parts of southern Africa. The population in Namibia may be a distinct species, *M. smitianus* has been proposed. Outside of the region in Africa, Asia and Europe, genetic work has shown that other species are involved and accurate range limits are unknown.

Habitat: All three species roost in caves or mine-shafts although they will also roost in crevices and holes in trees. The type of surrounding vegetation seems to play no significant role in habitat selection, although the Lesser Long-fingered Bat is said to favour areas of montane grasslands.

Behaviour: Natal Long-fingered Bat usually roosts in very large numbers, with up to 260,000 individuals known to occur in a single roost. The other two long-fingered species are frequently found in close association with Natal Long-fingered Bat, but always in much smaller numbers. In the roosts they form very dense clusters. Natal Long-fingered Bat females are subject to seasonal migrations to and from 'maternity' caves split between summer and winter. This movement between caves also applies to at least the Lesser Long-fingered Bat. Hibernation has been recorded in winter. They are rapid fliers.

Food: These bats take a wide range of flying insects, including moths, beetles, bugs, flies and termite alates.

Reproduction: A single young is born during the summer, particularly October–December; the gestation period is about 240 days, including a period of delayed implantation. The newborn young remains clinging to the mother for only a few hours and then it is left to hang independently from the rock among other juveniles. Mammae: 1 pair pectoral.

Longevity: A wild-living Natal Long-fingered Bat lived to 14 years.

Long-fingered bat skin, showing triangular tail conformation typical of long-fingered and vesper bats.

Natal Long-fingered Bat roosts in caves or disused mine shafts, often in dense clusters.

Greater Long-fingered Bat

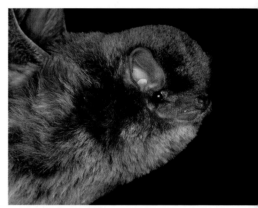

Natal Long-fingered Bat

Natal Long-fingered Bat is dark brown above.

Lesser Long-fingered Bat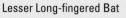

Natal Long-fingered Bat

'Vesper bats' is a group name for bats of the family Vespertilionidae, and includes the serotine, wing-gland, pipistrelle, butterfly, long-eared, house and woolly bats. It is by far the largest bat family occurring in the region, with two subfamilies, and about 34 species. Many can only be identified by examination of their dental and cranial characters, DNA and calls. All have somewhat mouse-like faces without nose-leaves; the ears are widely separated and usually prominent. Ear tragi are present and are useful in identification when the bat is 'in hand'. The tails are long and entirely enclosed in the interfemoral membrane (figs. 1.6, 1.7 and 1.8, p.18). With the exception of the woolly and hairy bats, all have short hair, which lies close to the body.

WING-GLAND AND MYOTIS (HAIRY) BATS Genera *Myotis*, *Cistugo* (Subfamily Vespertilioninae)

The five species of the *Myotis/Cistugo* group in the southern African region can be separated from other vesper bats by their longer, more pointed muzzles, and their soft, erect fur. The yellow-reddish fur and long, narrow tragus separate the *Cistugo* species from other members of the Vespertilionidae family.

Angolan Wing-gland (Hairy) Bat *Cistugo seabrae*
Total length 8–9cm; tail 3.5–4cm; forearm 3.2cm; mass 3–4.5g.

Lesueur's Wing-gland (Hairy) Bat *Cistugo lesueuri*
Total length 9.5cm; tail 4.3cm; forearm 3.6cm; mass 4–9g.

Welwitsch's Myotis (Hairy Bat) *Myotis welwitschii*

■ *Cistugo seabrae*
■ *Cistugo lesueuri*

Total length 12cm; tail 6cm; forearm 5.5cm; wingspan 38cm; mass 14g.

Temminck's Myotis (Hairy Bat) *Myotis tricolor*
Total length 12cm; tail 5cm; forearm 5cm; wingspan 28cm; mass 12.5g.

Rufous Myotis (Hairy Bat) *Myotis bocagii*
Total length 10cm; tail 4cm; forearm 4cm; wingspan 27cm; mass 6–10g.

Identification pointers: Fairly large ears; elongated muzzle; rich reddish-brown fur on upperparts of all except **Lesueur's Wing-gland Bat**; fur stands erect.

Myotis welwitschii

Description: Most *Myotis* and wing-gland bats have similarly coloured upperparts of rich reddish brown, although this can be variable; the **Angolan Wing-gland Bat's** upperparts may have a yellow tinge while **Lesueur's Wing-gland Bat** is honey-yellow. The underparts are usually off-white with a reddish-brown tinge except again for **Lesueur's Wing-gland Bat** where they are a light yellow-white. **Welwitsch's Myotis** has bold red-and-black patterning on the wings and the interfemoral membrane is reddish-brown and speckled with numerous small black spots; its ears are the same colour as the fur on the upperparts but are black around the edges. The wing-membranes of **Temminck's Myotis** are dark brown and the interfemoral membrane has a covering of reddish-brown hair; its ears are brown; upperparts are usually rich orange with slightly paler underparts. The rare **Rufous Myotis** has virtually grey-black ears, wing-membranes and interfemoral membrane, with coppery orange upperparts and off-white underparts. The wing- and interfemoral membranes of the **Angola** and **Lesueur's Wing-gland Bats** are dark brown.

Myotis tricolor

Hairy bat skin, showing tail
conformation

Lesueur's Wing-gland Bat

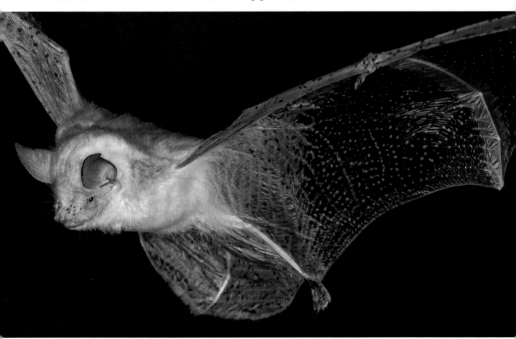

Welwitsch's Myotis has bold red-and-black patterning on the wings.

Welwitsch's Myotis

Temminck's Myotis

Myotis bocagii

Distribution: Rufous Myotis is known from eastern South Africa and eastern Zimbabwe, but further north it appears to be quite common in the equatorial regions from the DR Congo to West Africa; there are, however, only a few East African records (see map). Welwitsch's Myotis is recorded from a few localities in eastern South Africa and Zimbabwe, and more widely to the north. **Angolan Wing-gland Bat** is restricted to the far west, from the Northern Cape province through western Namibia to south-western Angola. **Lesueur's Wing-gland Bat** is only known from the Western Cape and adjacent parts of the Karoo, as well as Lesotho and marginally into adjoining areas of the Free State and KwaZulu-Natal. **Temminck's Myotis** is found along the southern and eastern areas of the region and from there north to East Africa.

Habitat: Welwitsch's, Temminck's and Rufous Myotis favour open woodland and savanna habitats, whereas the **Angolan Wing-gland Bat** favours more arid, semi-desert areas. **Lesueur's Wing-gland Bat** is strongly associated with montane grasslands over 1,500m and roosts in rock crevices. **Temminck's Myotis** is principally a cave-roosting species, preferring damp caves, whereas **Welwitsch's** and the **Rufous Myotis** prefer to roost in hollow trees and among leaves.

Behaviour: The *Myotis* bats are slow fliers and they usually hunt within 5m of the ground. **Temminck's Myotis** live in small colonies and are subject to some local migration. The **Rufous Myotis** is found singly or in pairs and is said to hunt its insect prey mainly over water. **Temminck's Myotis** roosts in caves in groups of up to 1,500 animals, moving between winter and summer roosts. Virtually nothing is known about the behavioural characters of the bats of these genera within their southern African range.

Food: They generally take a wide range of flying insects.

Reproduction: Temminck's Myotis is recorded as giving birth from October–November in the Western Cape, and November–December in KwaZulu-Natal. Young of this bat (a single young is the norm) are weaned after about 36 days. At least in the case of **Temminck's**, but possibly in other species as well, there is a period of delayed implantation and fertilization. **Lesueur's Wing-gland Bat** also seems to be an early summer breeder (October–December). Nothing is known about the reproduction of other species in the region. Mammae: 1 pair pectoral.

Longevity: Non-African *Myotis* bats have been recorded to live 2–19 years.

SEROTINE BATS   Genera *Eptesicus, Neoromicia, Pipistrellus*
(Subfamily Vespertilioninae)

The serotine bats are all small, short-eared species, usually with brown fur. When examined in profile the front of the skull is almost straight. With the exception of Rendall's and Aloe Serotine Bats, it is usually not possible to make a positive identification of the other species in the field. The commonest and most widespread species is the Cape Serotine Bat. In recent years, these small bats have been something of a taxonomic 'football' but, with more refined genetic techniques we are gaining a fuller, if more confusing, understanding of their relationships. Ongoing research is likely to reveal more species, especially in under-collected regions of the continent. The so-called Kruger Serotine Bat *(Neoromicia helios)* had not been described at the time of writing; it is very similar to the Cape Serotine Bat but has a different karyotype and is slightly larger. Within the region, it is only known from a few scattered records in the east. It is possible that more species will be described based on DNA investigations, but field identification will not be possible except perhaps by separating potential new species by their calls.

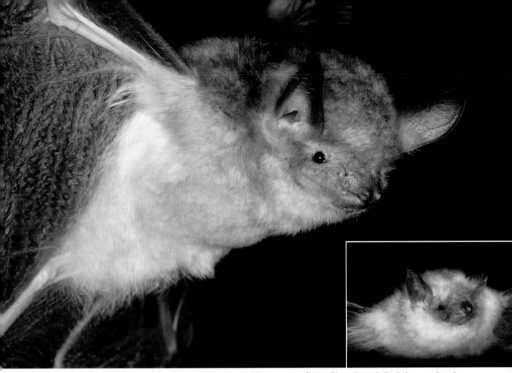

Temminck's Hairy Bat has reddish-brown upperparts and brown ears. **Inset:** Note the relatively long, pointed ears.

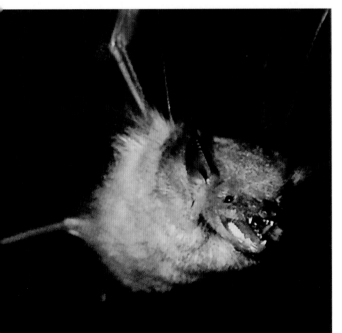

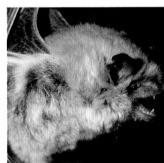

Rufous Hairy Bat

Kruger Serotine Bat

Rufous Hairy Bat favours open woodland habitats.

Eptesicus hottentotus

Neoromicia capensis

Neoromicia nanus

■ *Neoromicia rendalii*
■ *Neoromicia tenuipinnis*

Neoromicia zuluensis

Long-tailed Serotine Bat *Eptesicus hottentotus*
Total length 11.5cm; tail 4.9cm; forearm 5cm; wingspan 35cm; mass 16.6g.

Cape Serotine Bat *Neoromicia (Pipistrellus) capensis*
Total length 8.5cm; tail 3.2cm; forearm 3.3cm; wingspan 24cm; mass 6.5–7g.

Banana Bat *Neoromicia (Pipistrellus) nanus*
Total length 7.5cm; tail 3.6cm; forearm 3.2cm; wingspan 19cm; mass 4g.

Rendall's Serotine Bat *Neoromicia (Pipistrellus) rendalii*
Total length 9.5cm; tail 3.8cm; forearm 3.6cm; wingspan 25cm; mass 8.5g (4–9g).

Zulu (Aloe) Serotine Bat *Neoromicia (Pipistrellus) zuluensis*
Total length 8cm; tail 3.5cm; forearm 3cm; wingspan 22cm; mass 4.3g.
It is considered that some populations of the Zulu Serotine Bat are actually the Somali Serotine Bat *(P. somalicus)* but records are too few at this stage.

White-winged Serotine Bat *Neoromicia tenuipinnis*
Total length 6.4–8.7cm; tail 3.1cm; forearm 2.9cm; wingspan 21cm; mass 3–4g.

Identification pointers: Small size; relatively short ears; tail entirely enclosed by membrane; straight profile of head. See maps.

Description: With the exception of Long-tailed Serotine Bat, the serotine bats are quite similar in size, most average 8–9cm in total length. Rendall's Serotine Bat is easily recognized by the white wing-membranes, off-white interfemoral (tail) membrane and light brown ears. The wing-membranes of Zulu Serotine Bat are often edged with white. Long-tailed Serotine Bat can be distinguished by its larger size and, in the eastern parts of its range, its body fur is almost black but much lighter coloured in the west. All other species vary considerably, from light brown to dark brown, with slightly lighter underparts and dark brown wing-membranes. It is not possible to separate most of these species in the field. White-winged Serotine Bat has distinctive near-white wings, white fur along the edge of the body, and dark brown dorsal pelage.

Distribution: In the region, Rendall's Serotine Bat is only known from a few scattered records mainly in the east with most westerly records associated with the Okavango Delta, Botswana, but it occurs widely in East and West Africa. Long-tailed Serotine Bat has an apparently disjunct distribution with one population along the west and south coast of the region, and another in eastern South Africa, Zimbabwe and adjacent Mozambique (extending into Malawi and eastern Zambia). Zulu Serotine Bat is known from scattered localities in north-eastern South Africa, northern Botswana, north and west Namibia, Zimbabwe, with scattered records in Mozambique, Angola and Zambia. Cape Serotine Bats tend to be abundant and are found virtually throughout Africa but are absent from the Namib Desert. White-winged Serotine Bat only in a few locations in northern Angola.

Habitat: Serotine bats use a wide range of habitats, although Rendall's and Zulu Serotine Bats show a marked preference for open savanna woodland. They roost in a wide range of sites, including under bark and in roofs of buildings. Rendall's Serotine Bat also roosts in trees and bushes. Long-tailed Serotine Bat makes use of caves, old mine-shafts and rock crevices in outcrops. Banana Bat shows a preference for moister forested areas, particularly where banana and strelitzia plants are found; this bat often roosts in the curled leaves of these plants.

Long-tailed Serotine Bat roosting in a crevice

Long-tailed Serotine Bat

Cape Serotine Bat

Cape Serotine Bat

The Banana Bat has a mass of just 4g.

Rendall's Serotine Bat

Neoromicia helios is suspected to occur in Kruger National Park, South Africa.

Cape Serotine Bat

Banana Bat

Behaviour: The serotines roost in small numbers and, depending on the species, may be well hidden or hang in exposed clusters. The **Banana Bat** normally roosts in groups of 2–6 but solitary individuals are commonly encountered and **Cape Serotine Bat** may roost singly or in small groups but up to 100 individuals known. **Rendall's Serotine Bat** is a low flier, often less than 2m above the ground, whereas **Cape** and **Zulu Serotine Bats** are relatively high fliers (the former usually 10–20m). As with most other bats, little is known about their behaviour.

Food: Insects. All species seem to take a wide range of flying insects, but there may be seasonal variations, especially during times of abundance. The **Cape Serotine Bat** seems to be a general feeder but the **Banana Bat** appears to take mainly small beetles and moths.

Reproduction: Records indicate that some, and probably all, serotines give birth during the summer months (October–December). The **Cape Serotine Bat** may have single young, but twins are common (as they are in other serotine species), rarely triplets or quadruplets. The females of this serotine are known to store sperm from April–August, when fertilization takes place. Twins are also common in **Banana Bats,** and their young are weaned after about 56 days. Mammae: 1 pair pectoral; possibly more in some cases.

Longevity: Non-African species from 6 to almost 15 years.

Note: Within parts of the Namibian range of *Neoromicia zuluensis* it is believed that the species involved is the Somali Serotine Bat (*N. somalica*) but further research is required.

PIPISTRELLES   Genera *Hypsugo, Pipistrellus*
(Subfamily Vespertilioninae)

Five species of pipistrelle have been recorded from southern Africa. All are small and difficult to describe as they do not have outstanding features. They have tiny heads, the ears are not joined at the base (unlike in some of the free-tailed bats, see p.108) and, in all cases, the forearms are less than 4cm in length. Probably the most useful aid to separating the different species is the shape of the tragus, but this requires somewhat specialized knowledge.

Anchieta's Pipistrelle *Hypsugo (Pipistrellus) anchietae*
Total length 8.3cm; tail 3.6cm; forearm 3cm; mass 4.8g.

Dusk (African) Pipistrelle *Pipistrellus hesperidus*
Total length 8.2cm; tail 3.4cm; forearm 3.3cm; wingspan 23cm; mass 6g.

Rusty Pipistrelle *Pipistrellus rusticus*
Total length 7.3cm; tail 2.9cm; forearm 2.8cm; mass 4g.

Rüppell's Pipistrelle *Pipistrellus rueppelli*
Total length 9cm; tail 3.8cm; forearm 3.4cm; wingspan 26cm; mass 7g.

Dobson's Pipistrelle *Pipistrellus (Afropipistrellus) grandidieri*
Total length 8.5cm; tail 3.2cm; forearm 3.4cm; wingspan 25cm; mass 7.5g.

Identification pointers: Overall small size; Rüppell's Pipistrelle has pure white underparts; tail in all cases completely enclosed by interfemoral membrane; distribution maps should be consulted.

Hypsugo anchietae

■ *Pipistrellus hesperidus*
■ *Pipistrellus grandidieri*

Description: Anchieta's Pipistrelle is dark brown sometimes with a reddish tinge above and more greyish-brown underparts. Rüppell's Pipistrelle is the most easily distinguished of the group because it is the only pipistrelle with pure white underparts; its ears are dark brown and its upperparts are light brown; its tragus

The wing membranes of the Zulu Serotine Bat are often edged with white. **Inset:** Zulu Serotine Bat.

White-winged Serotine Bat

Anchieta's Pipistrelle

Dusk Pipistrelle

Rüppell's Pipistrelle

■ *Pipistrellus rusticus*
■ *Hypsugo crassulus*

Pipistrellus rueppelli

Note: The Broad-headed Pipistrelle *(Hypsugo crassulus)* has a very wide distribution across West, Central and East Africa. In the region apparently restricted to tropical moist lowland forest. Virtually nothing is known about this widespread bat.

is long, pointed and knife-shaped. **Dusk** and **Rusty Pipistrelles** are very similar, upperparts being fawn to reddish-brown and underparts paler. **Dusk Pipistrelle** underparts are sometimes off-white. The wing-membranes of both species are very dark brown to almost black, with a narrow white border around the margins in the **Dusk**. The tragus of the **Dusk Pipistrelle** is knife-shaped and that of the **Rusty Pipistrelle** is sickle-shaped. **Rusty Pipistrelle** takes its name from its pale rust-orange coat that is slightly paler on the underparts. **Dobson's Pipistrelle** has short, uniform light to medium-brown fur, but dark brown wings, interfemoral membrane and ears.

Distribution: Anchieta's Pipistrelle is limited to the extreme east of South Africa and a small number of localities in Zimbabwe, but outside of the region occurs in a broad swathe across Central Africa. The Dusk Pipistrelle has a very broad sub-Saharan distribution, but in southern Africa it is mainly restricted to the eastern seaboard, extending inland from northern South Africa and Zimbabwe. The **Rusty Pipistrelle** is found from north-eastern South Africa and northern Botswana north to Zimbabwe, Zambia and Angola; there is an apparently separate population in Sudan and Ethiopia. Rüppell's Pipistrelle is distributed from Zimbabwe and northern Botswana northwards to the Sahel zone and to Egypt along the Nile Valley. There are isolated records from the Northern Cape and Limpopo provinces of South Africa. Dobson's only recorded in a few scattered localities in Angola and Malawi but probably overlooked.

Habitat: Dusk Pipistrelles have a wide habitat tolerance, from oases in desert areas to the fringes of rainforests, but close proximity to open water may be a limiting factor. In southern Africa they seem to be mainly associated with riverine woodland and patches of forest. The **Rusty Pipistrelle** shows a preference for savanna woodland and Rüppell's Pipistrelle is largely restricted to riverine woodland. There are few habitat records for Anchieta's Pipistrelle but they may show a preference for well-wooded areas with open surface water and especially along rivers. Some, at least, roost behind the bark of trees and in narrow rock crevices.

Behaviour: Dusk Pipistrelles (and probably the other species) roost in small numbers, usually in groups of up to 10 or 12, but often fewer. All pipistrelles are slow but acrobatic fliers, emerging at dusk to hunt just a few metres above the ground or water. Very little is known about their behaviour.

Food: Insects. Although a variety of small aerial insects (such as moths, beetles, bugs and flies) are taken, **Rüppell's Pipistrelle** has been recorded taking insects off water surfaces.

Reproduction: The few records available indicate that most females drop twins, which are born during the warm, wet summer months (October–December). This seasonality in births probably applies to all pipistrelles in the region but may be less so in the north of southern Africa when insect prey is most abundant. Gestation is around 56 days for the **Rusty Pipistrelle**, excluding delayed implantation. Mammae: 1 pair pectoral.

Longevity: Non-African species have been recorded as living from 9 to almost 15 years; no records from the region.

The Dusk Pipistrelle roosts in rock crevices, as well as under roofs or loose bark. **Inset:** This bat has a tiny head, with ears that are not joined at the base.

Rüppell's Pipistrelle has pure white underparts.

Above: The Rusty Pipistrelle shows a preference for savanna woodland and occurs in northern South Africa and Zimbabwe.
Right and inset: The Rusty Pipistrelle has variably coloured fur on the upperparts.

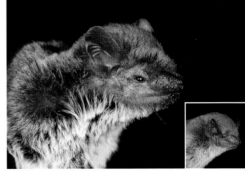

Glauconycteris variegata

■ *Glauconycteris argentata*
▨ *Glauconycteris beatrix*
■ *Glauconycteris machadoi*

Note: Machado's Butterfly Bat (*G. machadoi*), known from a limited area in Angola, is regarded by some to be a subspecies of Variegated Butterfly Bat.

Variegated Butterfly Bat *Glauconycteris variegata*
(Subfamily Vespertilioninae)

Total length 11cm; tail 4.7cm; forearm 4.5cm; wingspan 28cm; mass 13g.

Identification pointers: Overall pale yellow or fawn appearance; yellowish wing-membranes with numerous black lines forming a reticulated pattern. Resembles no other species across much of the region, so should not be mistaken for other species. Two other species, Common Butterfly Bat *(G. argentata)* and the Beatrix Butterfly Bat *(G. beatrix)*, occur only in the far north of Angola within the region and neither is as vividly marked as the Variegated Butterfly Bat. The former is known from very few records and the latter from just one specimen. Neither should be confused with the Variegated Butterfly Bat, as they are more uniformly coloured and lack distinctive markings.

Description: This is a very pretty bat and should not be mistaken for any other species. Its name derives from the reticulated pattern on the wing-membranes, which bears a fanciful resemblance to the veins of a butterfly's wings. The ground colour of the wing-membranes is yellowish-brown, overlaid with black lines. The upperparts range from nearly white to yellowish-fawn and the underparts are paler than the upperparts. The ears are small and similar in colour to the upperparts.

Distribution: In southern Africa it occurs in the north and east, extending down the east coast as far as KwaZulu-Natal.

Habitat: Bushveld and open savanna, as well as riverine and coastal forest. Roosts among leaves in trees and bushes and has been recorded in the thatch of abandoned huts.

Behaviour: Butterfly Bat leaves its roost early in the evening to hunt and is a high flier. It roosts singly or in pairs, or in very small numbers of 3–12 individuals.

Food: Insects, especially moths.

Reproduction: Nothing recorded for birthing periods but probably in early summer in the region. A single young is usual but twins have been recorded. Mammae: 1 pair pectoral.

Longevity: No records.

LONG-EARED BATS Genus *Laephotis* (Subfamily Vespertilioninae)

There are four small bats of the genus *Laephotis* in southern Africa. All are extremely rare, and information on their biology is either sparse or lacking entirely.

■ *Laephotis namibensis*
■ *Laephotis wintoni*
▨ *Laephotis angolensis*

Namibian Long-eared Bat *Laephotis namibensis*
Total length 10.5cm; tail 4.4cm; ear 2.4cm; forearm 3.8cm; mass 11g.

Botswana Long-eared Bat *Laephotis botswanae*
Total length 9.7cm; tail 4.2cm; ear 1.8cm; forearm 3.6cm; wingspan 26cm; mass 6g.

De Winton's Long-eared Bat *Laephotis wintoni*
Total length 10.4cm; tail 4.5cm; ear 2.2cm; forearm 3.9cm; mass 9g.

Angolan Long-eared Bat *Laephotis angolensis*
Total length 8.3cm; tail 3.7cm; forearm 3.5cm; mass 5–6g.

The Variegated Butterfly Bat has uniquely patterned wings, and is yellowish in colour.

Above: Botswana Long-eared Bat
Left: Variegated Butterfly Bat

Variegated
Butterfly Bat

Botswana
Long-eared Bat

Laephotis botswanae

Description: Long-eared bats have unusually long ears about one-third of the head-and-body length. The species can be separated on the shape of the tragus. The ears stand out sideways at an angle of 45° to the head and are not held almost vertically as in larger slit-faced bats (see p.76). All have short faces and lack facial decoration in the form of nose-leaves. General body colour is light to very light brown, with slightly paler underparts. Wing-membranes are light brown. It is generally not possible to separate the species in the field, although distribution should rule out confusion.

Distribution: The Namib and De Winton's Long-Eared Bats are each known only from a few localities in the region (see map). Botswana Long-eared Bat has been recorded from northern Botswana and Zimbabwe, and from South Africa (Punda Maria in Limpopo province, as well as two other records). There are scattered records also from Angola, Zambia and Malawi. Angolan Long-eared Bat is known only from a few specimens, three localities, in north-central Angola and elsewhere outside the region.

Habitat: Specimens of the Namib Long-eared Bat were taken in the wooded bed of the section of the Kuiseb River, which penetrates the Namib Desert, and along that desert's fringes, with an isolated record from South Africa's Cedarberg mountains to the south. In the region, De Winton's is known only from Lesotho and adjacent Free State at high altitude, but it is also known from East Africa to Ethiopia, also at high altitudes; the Botswana Long-eared Bat is associated with open woodland in the vicinity of rivers.

Behaviour: It is known that the Namibian Long-eared Bat shelters during the day in narrow rock crevices on sheer cliffs, in at least one location, and this probably also applies to the other three species.

Food: Insects. Based on a few records, small moths and beetles seem to make up the bulk of their diet.

Reproduction: Meagre records suggest a single young is born in early summer (November–December). Mammae: 1 pair pectoral.

Longevity: No records.

Scotoecus albofuscus

Thomas's House Bat *Scotoecus albofuscus* (Subfamily Vespertilioninae)

Total length 7–8.5cm; tail 3.2cm; forearm 3cm; mass 4.5g (one record 9.5g).
Identification pointers: Upperparts light buffy brown with off-white underparts. Wing membranes translucent to white.

Description: Upperparts light buffy brown and underparts light cream-brown to off-white. The translucent to white wing membranes are distinctive.

Distribution: Known from very few records in the far east of the region, but outside of the region has a very wide sub-Saharan range.

Habitat: Recorded from humid eastern coastal plain in the region, associated with large rivers and wetlands. Has been recorded roosting in palm leaves but little known.

The ears, held at an angle to the face, take up about one-third of the head-and-body length of long-eared bats, as depicted here by the Botswana Long-eared Bat.

De Winton's Long-eared Bat is known from only a few localities.

Thomas's House Bat

Behaviour: Nothing known.
Food: Mainly takes bugs (Hemiptera) but also some flies and small beetles.
Reproduction: Only 1 birth record from the region: twins dropped in November.
Mammae: Not recorded but probably 1 pair pectoral.
Longevity: No records.

---

*Scotoecus hindei,
Scotoecus albigula
& Scotoecus
hirundo*

Dark-winged Lesser House Bat *Scotoecus hindei/*
S. albigula (Subfamily Vespertilioninae)
Total length 9cm; tail 3.5cm; forearm 3.5cm; mass 9.5g.
The White-bellied Lesser House Bat (*S. albigula*) and Hinde's Lesser House Bat
(*S. hindei*) are currently lumped together as the Dark-winged Lesser House Bat
until such time as there is taxonomic clarity.
Identification pointers: Upperparts pale sandy-brown to somewhat darker
brown with contrasting white underparts.

Description: The pale sandy-brown to darker brown upperparts are clearly
separated from the white underparts, and the wing membranes are dark brown.
As with all members of this family, the face is plain and without any nose-leaves.
A third species, *S. hirundo*, may also be involved but information is lacking.
Distribution: They are known from very few localities in Mozambique, Malawi,
Zambia and Angola within the region. Known from a scattering of records through
Central and East Africa, as far as Sudan in the north and Nigeria in the west.
Habitat: In the region, most records are from areas of woodland savanna
associated with rivers and wetlands.
Behaviour: No information.
Food: Flying insects but no specific information.
Reproduction: No information but possibly same as Thomas's House Bat.
Longevity: No records.

Mimetillus thomasi

Thomas's Flat-headed Bat *Mimetillus thomasi* (Subfamily
Vespertilioninae)
Total length 9cm; tail 3.3cm; forearm 3cm.
Identification pointers: Overall coat colour dark brown; short, narrow wings.

Description: A sleek, short-furred bat with overall dark brown coat and light
brown wing membranes. Some authorities do not accept this as a full species and
believe it to be a subspecies of Moloney's Mimic Bat *(M. moloneyi)*, which has a
wide but sparse sub-Saharan range.
Distribution: Known from very few specimens. In the region, only recorded from
central Angola, Zambia and Zinave National Park in Mozambique.
Habitat: Most records are from miombo woodland. Specimens have been
collected from under tree bark. A very similar species has been found in thatched
roofs of huts and from under tree bark in West Africa.
Behaviour: No information.
Food: In East Africa, said to feed on small insects, such as termite alates.
Reproduction: In East Africa, said to have 2 birth seasons, coinciding with the
'big' and 'little' rains. No information for southern Africa. Mammae: Probably
1 pair pectoral.
Longevity: No records.

Dark-winged Lesser House Bat *(Scotoecus hindei)*

Dark-winged Lesser House Bat *(Scotoecus hirundo)*

Dark-winged Lesser
House Bat

Thomas's Flat-headed Bat

Schlieffen's Bat *Nycticeinops schlieffeni* (Subfamily Vespertilioninae)

Total length 7.5cm; tail 3cm; forearm 3.1cm; wingspan 18cm; mass 4.5–5.2g.
Identification pointers: Fawn or reddish-brown upperparts; dark brown wing-membranes; fairly large, rounded ears; very small.

Nycticeinops schlieffeni

Description: No outstanding features. Ears are large and rounded, wing-membranes dark brown and fur of upperparts is pale fawn to dark reddish-brown. Underparts lighter than upperparts. The individual hairs are unicoloured, unlike those of other pipistrelles. One of smallest bats in the region.
Distribution: Restricted to northern and north-eastern areas of region. It occurs very widely in sub-Saharan Africa.
Habitat: Open woodland, including areas dominated by mopane and along river courses. Roosts in crevices in hollow trees and buildings.
Behaviour: Hunts early in evening; flies jerkily. Roosts alone, in small groups or in large numbers.
Food: Feeds on a wide range of insects.
Reproduction: South African records show that mating occurs in June, fertilization is delayed and up to 3 young are born in November. Mammae: Possibly more than 1 pectoral pair but unknown.
Longevity: No records.

YELLOW HOUSE BATS Genus *Scotophilus* (Subfamily Vespertilioninae)

Solidly built bats, with bluntish heads and short ears; ear tragus is long and pointed. Fur is woolly and soft with a distinct sheen. Wide distribution in African tropics. It is possible that there are more species in the region than the four currently recognized.

Giant Yellow House Bat *Scotophilus nigrita*
Total length 18cm; tail 7.7cm; forearm 7.7cm; wingspan 58cm; mass 53–89g.

Yellow-bellied House Bat (African Yellow Bat)
Scotophilus dinganii
(It is believed that based on echolocation calls at least two species are named *S. dinganii*).
Total length 13cm; tail 5cm; forearm 5cm; wingspan 30cm; mass 26g.

Scotophilus nigrita

Green (Lesser Yellow) House Bat *Scotophilus viridis*
Total length 12cm; tail 4.6cm; forearm 4.8cm; wingspan 28–34cm; mass 20g.

White-bellied House Bat *Scotophilus leucogaster*
Total length 12cm; tail 5cm; forearm 5cm; mass 13–23g.

Identification pointers: Variable colouring but usually yellow or yellowish-brown on upperparts and often on underparts.

Scotophilus dinganii

Description: Body colour in this genus is not necessarily yellow. The **Yellow-bellied House Bat**, however, usually has distinctive yellowish or orange-yellow underparts although its upperparts are olive-brown to russet-brown. The **Green House Bat** has light or dark yellow-brown upperparts and white to grey-white

Schlieffen's Bat with young

Schlieffen's Bat

Giant Yellow House Bat

Schlieffen's Bat

Yellow-bellied House Bat

Scotophilus viridis

Scotophilus leucogaster

underparts, although some tend to light yellow with brighter colouring on the lower belly. **Giant Yellow House Bat** may be dark red-brown to yellow- or grey-brown above, and pale yellow to white (young) below. In all species wing-membranes are translucent dark brown. Best field criterion to separate **Yellow-bellied** and **Green House Bats** is the smaller size of the latter. **White-bellied House Bat** is pale to somewhat darker brown above and the underparts are white or creamish, with dark brown wing membranes.

Distribution: Giant Yellow House Bat has only been recorded from widely scattered locations in the far east of the region; Yellow-bellied House Bats in a broad swathe across the north and east of the region, with **White-bellied House Bat** being found in the north and **Green House Bat** restricted mainly to the east.

Habitat: Savanna woodland, with **Green House Bat** showing preference for riverine vegetation and high-rainfall areas. Yellow-bellied House Bat often roosts in buildings, as well as hollow trees. **Green** and **White-bellied** roost in hollow trees and roofs of buildings, changing roosting location every few days, perhaps to avoid predation. **White-bellied** often the commonest bat in tall mopane woodland in the region.

Behaviour: Very little known. The **Yellow-bellied House Bat** roosts in small groups of up to a dozen individuals, although several such groups may utilize the same roost. When roosting they crawl into crevices. They are fast, low fliers. At least the **Yellow-bellied** is a seasonal migrant in parts of its local range and this may apply to one, or more, of the other species.

Food: Insects. Beetles, including large specimens, seem to be very important in the diet of these bats, although they also take a wide range of other insects.

Reproduction: Yellow-bellied and Green House Bats give birth in early summer to litters of 1–3 young, usually 2. Probably all species have a delayed fertilization strategy. Mammae: Possibly more than 1 pair given the number of young in a litter.

Longevity: No records.

Kerivoula argentata

Kerivoula lanosa

■ known distribution

▨ presumed range limit

WOOLLY BATS Genus *Kerivoula* (Subfamily Kerivoulinae)

Immediately recognizable by their long, erect, soft, curly-tipped hair. (The long, erect hair of hairy bats, genus *Myotis*, p.88, is straight and not curled at the tips.) Woolly bats are also distinguished by a fringe of hair around the interfemoral membrane (fig. 1.8, p.108). There are only two species in southern Africa.

Damara Woolly Bat *Kerivoula argentata*
Total length 9.5cm; forearm 3.7cm; wingspan 25cm; mass 8g.

Lesser Woolly Bat *Kerivoula lanosa*
Total length 7.8cm; tail 3.8cm; forearm 3.1cm; mass 4.5–7g.

Identification pointers: Woolly, erect hair; noticeable fringe of short hair around margin of interfemoral membrane (fig. 1.8, p.18).

Description: Easily recognized by erect curly hair and characteristic fringe of stiff hairs that curve inwards at the tips, along edge of interfemoral membrane. Ears are funnel-shaped with long pointed tragus. Upperparts of **Damara Woolly Bat** are rich brown in colour and grey-flecked, and the underparts are greyish-brown. Upperparts of **Lesser Woolly Bat** are lighter brown but also have a grizzled appearance; underparts are very pale to white. In both species the wing-membranes are brown.

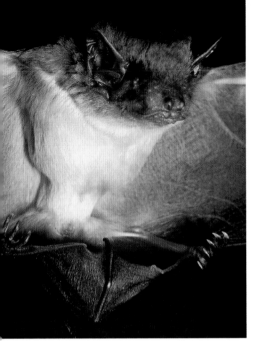

Yellow-bellied House Bat

The Yellow-bellied House Bat, also known as the African Yellow Bat, has a total length of about 13cm.

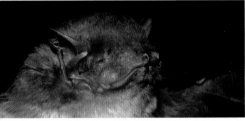

Yellow-bellied House Bat

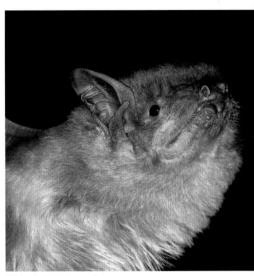

White-bellied House Bat

Green House Bat

Woolly bat skin, showing the fringe of hair around the tail membrane.

Damara Woolly Bat

Distribution: Damara Woolly Bat is only known in the region from the eastern areas, extending as far as western Zambia. The less abundant **Lesser Woolly Bat** is known from a few records in eastern and northern southern Africa and eastern Central Africa. Both species have a wide but sparse distribution in sub-Saharan Africa.
Habitat: Well-watered savanna woodland, including miombo and coastal forest, as well as riverine forest. Roost in clusters of dead leaves, under bark, under roofs and in deserted weaver-bird nests.
Behaviour: Roost singly, in pairs or in small groups. **Damara Woolly Bat** is a late-emerging species, with low, slow and erratic flight.
Food: Insects.
Reproduction: Nothing known for the region.
Longevity: Not known.

FREE-TAILED BATS Family Molossidae

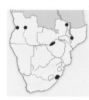

Otomops martiensseni

Also called mastiff or wrinkle-lipped bats, in reference to their dog-like faces and the heavily wrinkled upper lip in most species. Distinctive family character is the tail, of which only half or less is enclosed by the interfemoral membrane, the remainder projecting beyond the membrane (fig. 1.9, p.18). Ears are large, have a small tragus and are approximately equal in length and width. Hair is short, smooth and lies close to body. Most species are dark brown to reddish-brown. Members of the genus *Mops* have ears that are joined at the base, whereas those of the genus *Tadarida* are separate to the base. Most species have a distinctive pungent and even aromatic smell. They are far more mobile on the ground than any other bat group in the region and can be extremely vocal and readily heard by humans. Of the 15 species in region, nine are known from very few specimens or are considered to be rare. It is likely that some species may in fact be a complex of several species. Several are allocated to different genera by taxonomists.

Sauromys petrophilus

Large-eared Giant Mastiff Bat *Otomops martiensseni*
Total length 14cm; tail 4.2cm; forearm 6.4cm; wingspan 49cm; mass 33g.

Roberts's Flat-headed Bat *Sauromys petrophilus*
Total length 10.5cm; tail 3.8cm; forearm 4cm; wingspan 26cm; mass 9.5g.

Tadarida aegyptiaca

Giant Free-tailed Bat *Tadarida ventralis*
Total length 15cm; tail 5.8cm; forearm 6.2cm; wingspan 46cm; mass 43g.

Egyptian Free-tailed Bat *Tadarida aegyptiaca*
Total length 11cm; tail 3.8cm; forearm 4.8cm; wingspan 30cm; mass 15g.

Big-eared Free-tailed Bat *Tadarida lobata*
Total length 13cm; tail 5.3cm; forearm 6.3cm; wingspan 41cm; mass 26g.

Malagasy Free-tailed Bat *Tadarida fulminans*
Total length 15cm; tail 6cm; forearm 6cm; wingspan 40–50cm; mass 32g.

Ansorge's Free-tailed Bat *Chaerephon (Tadarida) ansorgei*
Total length 10cm; tail 3.8cm; forearm 4.6cm; wingspan 34.5cm; mass 21g.

■ *Tadarida ventralis*
■ *Tadarida lobata*

The woolly bats, here the Damara Woolly Bat, have distinctive long, curly-tipped hairs.

Lesser Woolly Bat

Large-eared Giant Mastiff Bat: each enlarged ear has a row of small spines along its forward edge. Note the gland on the upper chest.

Large-eared Giant Mastiff Bat skin

Large-eared Giant Mastiff Bat

Roberts's Flat-headed Bat

Tadarida fulminans

Chaerephon ansorgei

Chaerephon pumila

Little Free-tailed Bat *Chaerephon (Tadarida) pumila*
Total length 9cm; tail 3.2cm; forearm 3.8cm; wingspan 24cm; mass 10g.

Nigerian Free-tailed Bat *Chaerephon (Tadarida) nigeriae*
Total length 11.4cm; tail 4.2cm; forearm 4.8cm; mass 12–16g.

Pale (Chapin's) Free-tailed Bat *Chaerephon (Tadarida) chapini*
Total length 9.5cm; tail 3.6cm; forearm 3.8cm; wingspan 26cm; mass 8.4g.

Spotted Free-tailed Bat *Chaerephon (Tadarida) bivittata*
Total length 11cm; tail 3.9cm; forearm 4.9cm; wingspan 36cm; mass 18g.

Lappet-eared Free-tailed Bat *Chaerephon (Tadarida) major*
Total length 10cm; tail 3.4cm; forearm 4–5cm; mass 15g.

Angolan Free-tailed Bat *Mops (Tadarida) condylura*
Total length 11cm; tail 4cm; forearm 5cm; wingspan 36cm; mass 22g.

Midas Free-tailed Bat *Mops (Tadarida) midas*
Total length 14.5cm; tail 5cm; forearm 6.3cm; wingspan 45cm; mass 50g.

White-bellied Free-tailed Bat *Mops (Tadarida) niveiventer*
Total length 11cm; tail 3.5cm; forearm 4.5cm; mass 20g.

Identification pointers: All species have part of tail extending beyond limits of interfemoral membrane (fig. 1.9, p.18). Except for **Large-eared Bat** (whose long ears extend along face plane), the ears are large and rounded and may or may not be joined by flap of skin across forehead. Most have wrinkled upper lips. Males of two species have prominent crests on top of head.

Chaerephon nigeriae

■ *Chaerephon chapini*
■ *Chaerephon major*

Description: Large-eared Giant Mastiff Bat is easy to distinguish from other free-tailed bats by very long ears attached along length of face; no tragus or antitragus. Upperparts dark brown with paler band across shoulders; underparts also dark brown. Band of white hair runs along each side of body from shoulder to knee. **Roberts's Flat-headed Bat** characterized by its flattened head which enables it to crawl into narrow crevices. Largest species, **Midas Free-tailed Bat**, has white-flecked dark brown upperparts and slightly paler underparts. **Spotted Free-tailed** has tiny white spots scattered over head, shoulders and back. Bands of white hair run from forearm to thigh. **Angolan Free-tailed Bat** typically dark brown above, with tawny throat, grey-brown upper chest, and off-white abdomen. **Nigerian** and **Pale Free-tailed Bat** males have crests of erectile hair on top of head. The crest of the latter is longer, its wing-membranes are white and interfemoral membrane is dark brown. Tail and wing-membranes of **Nigerian Free-tailed Bat** are off-white. **Little Free-tailed Bat** is smallest and identified by band of white hair on wing-membrane from wing to thigh. **Egyptian Free-tailed Bat** is common and widespread. It has no outstanding features except that a pale neck yoke, present in most species, is absent. **White-bellied** has grey back, white underparts and black hair on top of head. The only certain way of identifying most free-tailed bats, however, is by detailed examination of teeth and genetic make-up, as well as calls.

Egyptian Free-tailed Bat is the most common and widespread of the free-tailed bats in the region. Most species are dark brown to reddish-brown, with short, smooth hair.

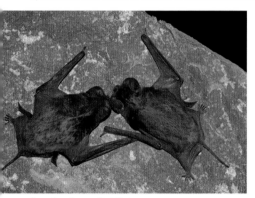

Egyptian Free-tailed Bat

Roberts's Flat-headed Bat

Malagasy Free-tailed Bat

Like most free-tailed bats, Ansorge's Free-tailed Bat has large, rounded ears. Their wrinkled upper lips and dog-like face have led to these bats also being called mastiff or wrinkle-lipped bats.

Little Free-tailed Bat

Midas Free-tailed Bat

111

Chaerephon bivittata

Mops condylura

Mops midas

Mops niveiventer

Distribution: See maps. Most species have extensive ranges to the north of the region covered by this book. In western Zambia Grandidier's Free-tailed Bat *(C. (T.) leucogaster)* may be present, based on analysis of echolocation calls.

Habitat: Usually associated with open woodland and riverine vegetation, but Egyptian and Little Free-tailed Bats occur in a wide range of habitats. Most species utilize natural roosts such as rock crevices, caves, hollow trees or behind loose bark of dead trees. Midas, Little and Egyptian Free-tailed Bats also use man-made structures, such as brickwork crannies or overlapping sheets of corrugated-iron roofing. They have the ability to withstand high temperatures (>40°C) for long periods, often roosting under metal roof-sheeting too hot for the human hand.

Behaviour: Usually gregarious. Angolan, Ansorge's and Midas Free-Tailed Bats form colonies of several hundred individuals, but Roberts's Flat-headed averages four and Spotted averages six. Although Little Free-tails and Angolan Free-tails may roost in small numbers, roosts running to thousands of individuals are known. In Kenya the Large-eared Giant Mastiff Bat has been recorded in cave roosts numbering many thousands. Unlike other bats, they prefer to move into cover when disturbed at the roost, rather than take to wing. They usually roost packed tightly together and the larger colonies can produce a considerable noise and give off a pungent, 'rubbery' smell. They have long, narrow wings and are high and rapid fliers. Several species, including the Egyptian Free-tailed Bat, undertake seasonal migrations in parts of their range but these are poorly understood.

Food: Insects. From the meagre information available, it seems that some species are generalists and take a wide range of insects, others are more specialized and take more moths (e.g. Large-eared Giant Mastiff), still others favour beetles (e.g. Midas Free-tailed).

Reproduction: All species give birth to a single young, with varying gestation periods, e.g. 60 days (Little), 90 days (Large-eared Giant Mastiff) and then 120 days (Egyptian). All species have a birth season in early summer (October–December) but a number of species have a second, and even a third, birth season in a year. In the tropics the Little Free-tailed may give birth five times within a 12-month period. Mammae: Probably 1 pair pectoral in all species.

Longevity: Nothing known for African species, but a South American free-tailed bat lived for 8 years.

BABOONS, MONKEYS & GALAGOS Order Primates
BABOONS & MONKEYS Family Cercopithecidae

SAVANNA BABOONS

■ *Papio cynocephalus*
■ *Papio ursinus*

Yellow Baboon *Papio cynocephalus*
Chacma Baboon *Papio ursinus*
Male: total length 120–160cm; tail 60–85cm; mass 25–45kg (average 32kg). (*P. c. kindae* race in Zambia smaller)
Female: total length 100–120cm; tail 50–60cm; mass 12–20kg (average 16kg).

Identification pointers: Fairly large size; long, dog-like snout in adults; uniform grey to grey-brown colour in Chacma Baboon; yellowish-brown in Yellow Baboon; males considerably larger than females; apparently 'broken' tail; nearly always in troops, very rarely solitary males.

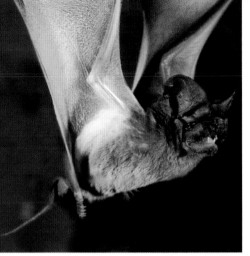

Pale Free-tailed Bat males have a distinct head crest.

Little Free-tailed Bat has a wingspan of about 24cm.

Little Free-tailed Bat

Angolan Free-tailed Bat

Nigerian Free-tailed Bat

The tail character that gives these bats their name.

Savanna Baboons

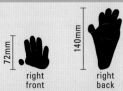

72mm

right
front

140mm

right
back

Note: The taxonomy of the African baboons is problematic but recent thinking now recognizes five species, of which two occur in the region. The blanket common name of Savanna Baboon is often used for the Yellow, Chacma and Olive Baboons. Three subspecies of the Chacma Baboon are generally recognized, the nominate race Cape *(P. u. ursinus)*, Grey-footed *(P. u. griseipes)* and the Ruacana *(P. u. ruacana)* but they are not recognized by some authorities. The Yellow Baboon has the Central nominate subspecies *(P. c. cynocephalus)* and the Kinda *(P. c. kindae)* from Zambia and adjacent areas of Angola. The Kinda Yellow Baboon is notably smaller than the other Yellow Baboon.

Description: The largest primate (other than man) in southern Africa. It is relatively slender and lightly built, although adult males have powerfully built shoulders and heads. When the baboon is on all fours the shoulders stand higher than the rump. The long, somewhat dog-like muzzle is particularly pronounced in the males. The body is covered by coarse hair, which may be light greyish-yellow, especially in the north of the region, through to dark grey-brown to almost grey-black in **Chacma**, but coat colour is variable, even within a troop. In the **Yellow Baboon** the overall coat colour is yellowish-brown. Only the male has a mane of long hair on the neck and shoulders, which is less pronounced in the **Yellow**. Hair on the upper surface of the hands and feet is dark brown to black in **Chacma**. Characteristic of the baboons is the posture of the long tail; the first third of the tail is held upwards and the remainder droops downwards, giving it a 'broken' appearance. Males have a single, hard pad of naked grey skin that extends across both buttocks, but the female has one smaller pad on each buttock. During gestation the skin around the female buttock pads is bright scarlet while at the onset of the menstrual cycle the skin distends enormously into rather unsightly swollen red protuberances.

Distribution: Occurs widely in southern Africa in suitable habitat. **Chacma Baboon** is mainly restricted to the area below the Cunene/Zambezi line but extends marginally into Zambia and Angola, with the **Yellow** extending northwards. There is an overlap region with interbreeding possibly taking place. In south-western Zambia within this zone a separate subspecies is sometimes recognized, *Papio ursinus griseipes*. The smaller *P. c. kindae* occurs across northern Zambia, adjacent Angola and DR Congo.

Habitat: Wide habitat tolerance but it requires rocky cliffs or tall trees to retreat to at night or when threatened. Drinking water is essential. It inhabits mountains, hill ranges and riverine woodland.

Behaviour: These are highly gregarious and social species that live in troops of 15 to sometimes 100 or more. Within a baboon troop all adult males are dominant over all females. Adult males have a strict rank order and only dominant males mate with oestrous or receptive females, although subordinate males do mate with young females and those that are not in oestrus. It is only in their fifth year that the males become dominant over the females. The dominant male determines when the troop will move. The females and infants remain closest to this male, with the non-breeding females staying close to the subordinate males. Youngsters and sub-adults move around the edges of the troop. Water sources are visited each day. Very vocal and the bark or 'bogom' of the adult male is a common day-time sound of the hills and savanna of southern Africa. Baboons are considered to be strictly diurnal, retreating to tree or cliff roosts before sunset. However, we have encountered baboons foraging on the ground at, or near, full moon, on several occasions, although they were never more than a few metres from roosts. This behaviour is the exception rather than the rule and may have something to do with seasonal food shortages and could be influenced by lack of baboon predators in a given area.

Food: Omnivorous. Digs for roots and bulbs, eats wild fruit, seeds, leaves and flowers, insects and other invertebrates. Raids cultivated crops. Will eat

A female Chacma Baboon and young; note the genital swelling

A young male Chacma Baboon on the lookout for predators.

A young male Chacma Baboon; note how the fingers are extended while walking

Female Yellow Baboon

Male Yellow Baboon

young antelope, hares, mice and birds if encountered but hunting is an almost exclusively male activity. In rocky areas a feeding baboon troop leaves a trail of overturned stones and small rocks.

Reproduction: A single young, weighing 600g–1.5kg (average 850g), born at any time of the year. When a female comes into oestrus the 'sexual skin' on the buttocks becomes red and considerably swollen. This is natural and is not a result of injury or sickness as is often thought. The gestation period is about 180 days (6 months). The newborn is black with a pink face and clings to its mother's chest for the first few weeks; as it grows older, it rides on her back. Mammae: 1 pair pectoral.

Longevity: Captive **Chacma** and **Yellow Baboons** are recorded as living for 27–45 years; although up to 45 years has been claimed in the wild, this seems unlikely.

■ *Chlorocebus pygerythrus*
■ *Chlorocebus cynosuros*

Vervet Monkey *Chlorocebus (Cercopithecus) pygerythrus*
Malbrouck's Monkey *Chlorocebus (Cercopithecus) cynosuros*

Male: total length 100–130cm; tail 60–75cm; mass 4–8kg (average 5.5kg).
Female: total length 95–110cm; tail 48–65cm; mass 3.5–5kg (average 4kg).

Identification pointers: Typical monkey appearance; grizzled grey hair on head, back and flanks; black face with rim of pale to white hair; long tail; lives in troops. Habitat usually separates these species from the Sykes's Monkey and other forest monkeys.

Note: Six of the previously recognized subspecies of the Vervet are now recognized as full species across its vast African range. In southern Africa, *Chlorocebus pygerythrus* occurs widely across the south and east, but *C. cynosuros* will be found in extreme northern Namibia, including across the Caprivi Strip, with marginal spillover into adjacent Botswana, and widely in Angola and across much of Zambia.

Description: A well-known animal with its grizzled grey, fairly long, coarse hair and typical monkey appearance. Its underparts are paler than its upperparts and are frequently white. The face is short-haired and black, with a rim of white hair across the forehead and down the sides of the cheeks. The hands and feet are black. Several subspecies occur in southern Africa, with some variation in colour: Animals from northern Namibia, Angola and Zambia *(C. cynosuros)*, usually have very pale feet and hands while the subspecies in northern Mozambique *(C. p. rufoviridis)* has a reddish back. The general hair colour varies from area to area but this monkey is unlikely to be confused with any other species. The adult male has a distinctive bright blue scrotum.

Distribution: Northern and eastern parts of southern Africa, extending along the southern coast as far west as Mossel Bay. It extends into otherwise inhospitable areas along rivers, including the Orange River as far west as its estuary, and along wooded streams in the Great Karoo. In recent years, small troops (up to 15 individuals) have established themselves in suitable locations in many parts of the Karoo, including near the authors' village; to get there, they must have crossed up to 20km of open plain, utilizing wooded watercourses. Closely related species are widespread throughout Central and East Africa with the exception of equatorial forest.

Habitat: These are monkeys of woodland savanna, riverine woodland and increasingly in isolated stands of trees and along river courses on the Great Karoo plateau of South Africa and elsewhere.

Behaviour: These monkeys live in troops of up to 20 or more. The formation of large groups will generally be associated with an abundant food source or water.

Female Yellow Baboon, race *P. c. kindae*, Zambia

Yellow Baboon female and young

A Vervet Monkey female and her dependent young

Vervet Monkeys commonly forage on the ground.

Vervet Monkey

55mm

right
front

85mm

right
back

They are completely diurnal and sleep at night in trees or more rarely on cliffs. A distinct 'pecking order' or hierarchy is well established in each troop. They forage in a well-defined home range, spending much of their time on the ground. They frequently raid crops and gardens and are in consequence heavily persecuted.

Food: Although these monkeys are mainly vegetarian, they also eat a wide range of invertebrates and small vertebrates such as nestling birds. Fruits, flowers, leaves, gum and seeds form the bulk of their food.

Reproduction: A single young, weighing some 300–400g, born after a gestation period of about 165 days, at any time of the year, although in some areas there seems to be a birth peak at certain times. Mammae: 1 pair pectoral.

Longevity: Up to 31 years in captivity; about 12 years in the wild, although up to 30 years has been claimed.

Red-tailed Guenon *Cercopithecus ascanius*

Total length (M) 100–150cm, (F) 85–130cm; tail length 55–90cm; mass 1.8->6kg (male larger than female).

Identification pointers: Relatively small to medium-sized; middle to tip of long tail rufous-red; nose patch usually white.

Cercopithecus ascanius

Description: A medium-sized monkey with dark greenish-olive dorsal coat tinged with red, and pale to white underparts. Tail mostly rufous-red. Nose has a distinctive pale to white (usual) spot, but some races have darker patches. Cheeks are white with dark stripe.

Distribution: Northern Angola and extreme north-western Zambia.

Habitat: Occupies a wide range of forest habitats, including lowland and riparian areas, as well as forest edges and adjacent cultivated lands.

Behaviour: Lives in troops averaging 7–35 individuals, usually with a single dominant male. It is strictly diurnal and predominantly arboreal but does descend to the ground to forage on occasion. Troops occupy a fixed home range, which is possibly defended against other troops. Readily mixes with monkeys of other species.

Food: Takes a wide range of plant foods – including leaves, flowers and fruits – as well as some invertebrates.

Reproduction: A single young, weighing an average 260g, may be born at any time but seasonal food abundance may influence mating. Mammae: 1 pair pectoral.

Longevity: Up to 22 years; to 28 years in captivity.

De Brazza's Monkey *Cercopithecus neglectus*

Total length (M) 110–140cm, (F) 95–110cm; tail 53–85cm; mass (M) 5–8kg, (F) 4–5kg.

Identification pointers: Stout, heavily built; relatively short, thick tail held arched or hanging down when walking; broad black and reddish bands above eyes; long, white beard; white thigh stripe.

Cercopithecus neglectus

Description: Easy to identify in the field, with its fairly stocky build and somewhat thickened tail. Overall coat colour is greenish-grey, but has a number of distinct, contrasting markings. It has a well-developed white beard that extends down the throat. A bright reddish-brown brow stripe, backed by a black band, runs on top of the head. A white stripe runs down the outer surface of the thigh. The tail is black.

The male Vervet Monkey has a distinctive bright blue scrotum.

Vervet Monkeys have a bright white band across the forehead.

Main and inset: The Red-tailed Guenon has a partly red tail. Most races have a white nose spot and white cheek whiskers.

Red-tailed Guenon

De Brazza's Monkey

119

Distribution: In the region, only in north-eastern Angola.
Habitat: Mainly swamp forest but montane and lowland associations.
Behaviour: Feeds readily in trees and on the ground. Troops of 15–35 may be encountered, but it also forms small family parties and solitary males are not unusual. Larger troops are led by a single adult male. Like other monkeys, they will flee from danger but will also freeze to avoid detection. Reportedly territorial and shy, avoiding other monkey species. They have a far-carrying, booming call. Reported to be good swimmers.
Food: Mixed diet, but mainly fruits and seeds, with some invertebrates.
Reproduction: In some areas births are seasonal. A single young, weighing 250–350g, is dropped after a gestation of around 182 days. Mammae: 1 pair pectoral.
Longevity: Possibly up to 30 years in captivity.

■ Cercopithecus albogularis
■ Cercopithecus albogularis erythrarchus
■ Cercopithecus albogularis labiatus
■ Cercopithecus mitis & moloneyi
■ Cercopithecus mitis mitis

Sykes's Monkey Cercopithecus albogularis
Blue Monkey Cercopithecus mitis

Male: total length 1.4m; tail 80cm; mass 8–10kg.
Female: total length 1.2m; tail 70cm; mass 4–5kg.

Identification pointers: Typical monkey appearance; much darker than Vervet Monkey, being black on legs, shoulders and last two-thirds of tail length; long hair on cheeks; brown (not black) face. Forest habitat usually separates it from the more open areas occupied by the Vervet Monkey.
Note: In South Africa, Sykes's Monkey is often referred to as the Samango, or Blue (now assigned full species status but only north of the Cunene/Zambezi line), Monkey. The name Sykes's Monkey is most extensively used in East Africa. Many subspecies/races have been described across its extensive African range, with several in the region. Several of these have now been assigned full species status.

Description: A fairly large forest species with dark brown face, and white only on lips and throat. Hair on legs and shoulders is dark brown or black, but rest of the back and sides is grizzled grey-brown, browner towards the tail. Long tail is black for the last two-thirds of its length. Long hair stands out on cheeks and forehead. Underparts are paler than upperparts, usually off-white with a suffusion of light brown.

Two subspecies are recognized from the southern part of the region: *C. albogularis erythrarchus* is restricted to the coastal forests of Maputaland in northern KwaZulu-Natal (north of the iMfolozi River), extending into Mozambique, Malawi and Zimbabwe, with isolated populations occurring in the Soutpansberg range and other Afromontane forests on the Eastern escarpment of Limpopo and Mpumalanga. *C. albogularis labiatus* is found in the forests of the Eastern Cape (from the vicinity of Pirie Forest) and northwards to the KwaZulu-Natal Midlands. The ranges of the two subspecies do not overlap, making for easy separation. *C. a. erythrarchus* has a black tail with patches of orange-red on the lower buttock area and around the anus. In *C. a. labiatus*, the tail is dark above but the basal third is paler to off-white below and there are no red hairs. Note that some races are now classified as a separate species, the **Blue Monkey** *(C. mitis)*, which has several subspecies that are sometimes placed as full species in their own right. **Blue Monkeys** lack a white throat patch and have black crowns. They occur to the north of the Cunene/Zambezi line.
Distribution: Isolated populations are found in forest and forest pockets extending from the Eastern Cape to KwaZulu-Natal, Mpumalanga and the

De Brazza's Monkey has a prominent white beard, bluish-pink snout and broad reddish and black bands across the front of the head.

A Sykes's Monkey in the Soutpansberg, clearly showing the white throat patch

Sykes's Monkey in northern KwaZulu-Natal

Sykes's Monkey

65mm

right
front

80mm

right
back

southern slopes of the Soutpansberg; also found in eastern Zimbabwe and Mozambique. Populations of **Blue Monkey** occur in western Angola and Zambia. A small isolated population of **Sykes's Monkey** was recently discovered in the Masebe River Gorge on the Makgabeng Plateau to the south of the Soutpansberg and Blouberg ranges. This riparian forest is very narrow and sided by steep cliffs and extends for just over 10km. Of interest is that these monkeys regularly use the cliffs and rock ledges to move between trees. Consult map.

Habitat: High forest, forest margins and riverine gallery forest; may forage in more open woodland but always close to forest.

Behaviour: Lives in troops up to 30 strong, although most are smaller than this. Each troop usually has a single adult male. Males disperse from the birth troop but females do not. More arboreal than Vervet Monkey. During the hottest hours of the day it rests in deep shade. Like most monkeys, the **Sykes's** and **Blue** are vocal species with a range of different calls. The males have a very loud, far-carrying bark sounding superficially like 'jack'. They also have distinctive alarm calls for aerial predators such as African Crowned Eagle, and ground-based predators such as Leopard. Calling and their crashing progress through trees is often all that is revealed of their presence, except where troops are habituated to the presence of humans. Although sometimes referred to as 'gentle' monkeys, recent research in South Africa's Soutpansberg range has shown that in clashes between troops, females from one troop will attack females from another, which can result in serious injuries, even death. Both the **Blue** and **Sykes's Monkeys** commonly mix with other monkey and guenon species.

Food: Feeds on a wide range of plants, including fruits, flowers, gum, leaves and seeds. Debarks young trees in softwood plantations, so is not popular with foresters. Sometimes eats insects; only rarely predates on birds and small mammals.

Reproduction: Normally single, almost black young, weighing about 400g, born during summer after a gestation of 120–140 days. Mammae: 1 pair pectoral.

Longevity: Up to 20 years in the wild recorded; to 27 years in captivity.

Miopithecus talapoin

Angolan Talapoin *Miopithecus talapoin*

Total length (M) 66–93cm, (F) 50–82cm; tail 26–53cm; weight 800g (male may reach 2kg).

Identification pointers: Smallest true monkey in region; large, rounded ears; facial mask dark to black with some dark hairs on muzzle; creamy white underparts contrasting with olive-green upperparts.

Description: By far smallest long-tailed monkey in the region, without striking markings or coloration. Face is dark to black (some with paler faces), with dark hairs on the muzzle, and the darker ears are large, rounded and prominent. Upperparts olive-green with an infusion of straw-yellow, contrasting with paler underparts.

Distribution: North-western Angola, extending down the coast and into adjacent interior with suitable habitat.

Habitat: Lowland swamp and coastal forest, including mangroves.

Behaviour: Forages in troops of 10–20 individuals but larger groups commonly observed. Smaller troops are believed to be made up of family units, within which, unusually, there seems to be no pecking order. Larger groups are made up of multiple male/multiple female combinations. They mix readily with other monkey species. Very active and agile, difficult to observe. Less vocal than most monkeys.

The forest-dwelling Sykes's, or Samango, Monkey has a very restricted distribution in southern Africa.

Sykes's Monkey

The male Sykes's Monkey has formidable canine teeth.

The Angolan Talapoin usually has a dark to black face.

Angolan Talapoin

Food: Wide range, including fruits, seeds, nuts, flowers, buds and leaves, as well as some insects and small vertebrates.
Reproduction: The only true monkey in which the female undergoes genital swelling during the oestrus cycle when she is sexually receptive. Single young, weighing 160g, said to be dropped from November–March, after a gestation of about 160 days. Mammae: 1 pair pectoral.
Longevity: To nearly 30 years in captivity; 28 years maximum in the wild.

Lophocebus opdenboschi

Black (Black-crested) Mangabey *Lophocebus opdenboschi*
Total length 93–126cm; tail 40–80cm; mass 5–12kg.
Identification pointers: Overall pelage colour black with glossy sheen; longish, pointed crest on top of head; long facial whiskers; tail usually held over back.

Description: Overall coat colour is black with some grizzling and with a glossy sheen. Prominent dark, pointed crest on top of head and long-haired cheek-patches. Tail often held erect, or curved over the back, when on the move. Relatively long snout compared to most other long-tailed monkeys.
Distribution: In the region, only north-eastern Angola.
Habitat: Lowland and gallery forests.
Behaviour: Lives in multi-male troops of 10–40 individuals. Agile climbers and most of their foraging is done in the trees. Home ranges tend to be small (often a few hundred hectares) but this will be determined by quality and quantity of food resources. Mix readily with other monkeys and guenons. They are very vocal and have a wide range of calls, with troop members often calling in chorus.
Food: Mainly fruits and seeds (their teeth are adapted to cracking even the hardest seeds); also take some insects.
Reproduction: Poorly known, but a single young dropped after a gestation of approximately 180 days. Mammae: 1 pair pectoral.
Longevity: Possibly 18–21 years in the wild.

Colobus angolensis

Angola Black and White Colobus *Colobus angolensis*
Total length 1.25–1.45m; tail 75cm; mass 9–16kg.
Identification pointers: Black, glossy coat; white hair patches (epaulettes) of variable length on shoulders; tail black, white or mixed; white facial whiskers long and erect.

Description: A large monkey with overall black glossy coat and contrasting long, white hair patches extending from the shoulders. The facial whiskers are long and erect, with a variably white brow line. The face is black and the tail may be white, black or a mix of the two. Newborns are white.
Distribution: Present in north-western Angola, north-western Zambia and northern Malawi. The Angolan populations have been greatly reduced in number as a result of hunting and habitat loss.
Habitat: They occupy a range of forest types, including woodland fringing forest.
Behaviour: Highly arboreal and only rarely come to the ground. Most troops number 10–25 individuals, each led by the dominant female but defended by a dominant male. Home ranges are relatively small but their size is a measure of the quality and abundance of available food. Territorial, but troop density can be quite high in some areas. Compared to other forest monkeys, colobuses can be

The Angola Black and White Colobus has long white epaulettes contrasting with the overall black coat.

Angola Black and White Colobus

Young male Black Mangabey

Black Mangabey

88mm right front

132mm right back

Angola Black and White Colobus

55mm right front

100mm right back

125

relatively easily observed when not disturbed, as they bask in the sun on exposed branches in the morning.

Food: Leaves make up about two-thirds of their diet, the remainder being fruits and seeds.

Reproduction: Little known in region but possibly not seasonal breeders. A single young, weighing around 450g, dropped after a gestation of about 180 days. The white newborns take on adult colouring after 2–3 months. Mammae: 2 pectoral.

Longevity: One captive lived 28 years.

POTTOS Family Lorisidae

Perodicticus potto

Potto Perodicticus potto
Total length 30–50cm; tail 5–8cm; mass 600–1,600g.
Identification pointers: Relatively stocky build; short tail; rounded, short head, superficially bear-like; thick, woolly fur; lowland forest habitat.

Description: A small, short-tailed and stoutly built primate with rounded, short-snouted face, small, rounded ears and well-developed hands and feet for grasping branches. Fur is thick and woolly and is usually greyish-brown and slightly paler on the undersides. The subspecies occurring in the region is *P. p. edwardsi*.

Distribution: Restricted to forests in northern Angola in the region.

Habitat: Restricted to areas of primary and secondary forests, especially where the undergrowth is dense and tangled.

Behaviour: Solitary, nocturnal and arboreal, rarely descending to the ground. In some areas it can occur at quite high densities. A study in Gabon, to the north, found that females occupied home ranges averaging about 7ha, and males some 12ha. The male Potto is territorial. Movements are slow and deliberate.

Food: A wide range of fruits and invertebrates, as well as small vertebrates, such as bats and birds. Quite high quantities of tree resins may also be eaten.

Reproduction: A single young, weighing about 35–50g, may be dropped at any time of year after a gestation period of about 190 days. Mammae: No records.

Longevity: 15–26 years in captivity; probably much less in the wild.

GALAGOS (BUSHBABIES) Family Galagidae

Otolemur crassicaudatus over entire range shown, with O. monteiri restricted to the miombo belt in the north of the region.

Thick-tailed (Greater or Brown) Galago Otolemur (Galago) crassicaudatus
Total length 70–80cm; tail 35–45cm; mass 1–1.5kg.
Identification pointers: Superficially cat-like when seen on the ground and tail usually held erect; uniformly grey to grey-brown; long, fairly bushy tail, same colour as body; large, thin ears and large eyes; harrowing and unnerving screaming call made at night; usually seen in trees. Silvery Thick-tailed Galago (O. monteiri) is now recognized as a full species and occurs in the same areas as O. crassicaudatus in the north of the region. Thick-tailed Greater Galago sometimes referred to as Large-eared Greater Galago, and Silvery Thick-tailed Greater Galago as Miombo Silvery Galago.

Description: Much larger than Southern Lesser Galago (see p.128), with which it is sometimes confused. On the ground somewhat cat-like, but hindquarters higher than shoulder region and long tail held high off ground, or erect. Hair

The Potto is strictly nocturnal and is easily overlooked in its forest habitat.

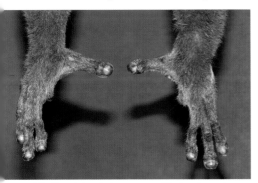

The Potto's hands have opposable thumbs and greatly reduced index fingers.

The round, short-snouted face and rounded ears of the Potto impart a somewhat bear-like appearance.

The second digit on each foot of the Potto has a long grooming claw.

Silvery Thick-tailed Galago walking on ground

Potto

Thick-tailed Galago

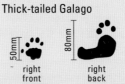

50mm
right front

80mm
right back

of upperparts and tail is woolly, fine and grey-brown. Underparts are lighter in colour than upperparts. Characteristic features are the very large, rounded, thin ears and large eyes, which shine red in torchlight. Silvery Thick-tailed Galago has a lighter-coloured coat and somewhat shorter ears.

Distribution: Restricted to the far eastern and northern parts of southern Africa, and occurs widely in East Africa. The Silvery is largely restricted to the extensive miombo woodland belt in the north and overlaps with Thick-tailed.

Habitat: Forest, woodland (sometimes dry) and wooded riverine margins. Also occupy forest and woodland on slopes of some mountain ranges.

Behaviour: Nocturnal, spending the day sleeping among dense vegetation tangles in trees or in self-constructed nests. Rest together in groups of 2–6 females; males sleep alone, apart from female groups. Usually forage alone at night. A group has a fixed home range of several hectares, within which are a number of resting-sites. Frequently forage on the ground. An obvious sign of their presence is a loud screaming call, like that of a baby in distress. They also use urine and gland secretions to communicate with other individuals. They urinate on the soles/palms of the feet and then transfer the urine to the ground or tree branches as they move. Both sexes have a scent-gland on the front of the chest, which is rubbed against branches and other individuals. May reach high densities in suitable habitat, up to 125 individuals in an area of 1km².

Food: Fruit and tree gum, particularly of acacias; also insects, reptiles, birds.

Reproduction: In the south give birth in November; in Zimbabwe and Zambia from August–September. Usually 2 young, each weighing 40–70g, are born after a gestation period of about 130 days. Mammae: 1 pair pectoral, 1 pair inguinal.

Longevity: Up to 14 years in captivity; one captive is claimed to have lived almost 19 years.

Galago moholi

Southern Lesser Galago (Bushbaby) *Galago moholi*

Total length 30–40cm; tail 20–25cm; mass 120–210g (average 150g).
Identification pointers: Small size with long fluffy tail; large, thin, mobile ears; large, forward-facing eyes; prodigious jumping ability and arboreal habits. Compare with Thick-tailed Galago where distributions overlap.
The name South African Galago is sometimes used for this species but, as it also occurs in Central Africa, we prefer to use Southern Lesser Galago, or Bushbaby.

Description: The Southern Lesser Galago is considerably smaller than the Thick-tailed Galago, with which it is frequently confused. The fine woolly, greyish to grey-brown hair extends onto the fluffy tail, which is slightly longer than the head and body. The ears are large, thin and rounded and extremely mobile. The eyes are very large, forward-pointing and ringed with black, and the head is small and rounded with a short snout.

Distribution: In our region this species is restricted to the northern and north-eastern parts. Closely related species are widely distributed in woodland areas of Central, East and West Africa but are absent from equatorial forests.

Habitat: Woodland savanna, particularly acacia and riverine woodland.

Behaviour: The Southern Lesser Galago is nocturnal and feeds mostly in trees but it does descend to the ground to forage. Family groups of 2–8 sleep together but they usually forage alone or in very loose association. Although they construct their own nests of leaves, they will also lie up in dense creeper tangles or in tree-holes. They are territorial and groups occupy home ranges of about 3ha, but this will vary according to food availability. Territories are marked by urinating on hands and feet and

The Thick-tailed Greater Galago forages in trees and on the ground. **Inset:** The foot of the Thick-tailed Greater Galago shows a large opposable big toe.

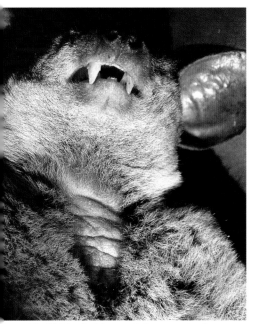

The Thick-tailed Greater Galago uses its chest gland to mark its territory.

The Thick-tailed Greater Galago has long, well-developed ears.

Southern Lesser Galago

28mm

right
front

29mm

right
back

transferring the urine to tree branches as they move around. They jump considerable distances from branch to branch and tree to tree. They are vocal animals with a wide range of calls, from low croaking to chittering and grunts. Like Thick-tailed Galago, in suitable habitat this small primate can reach very high densities.

Food: The gum or exuding sap of trees, particularly acacias, is very important in their diet but they also eat insects, which they catch with their hands, as well as other invertebrates and occasionally small vertebrates, such as geckos.

Reproduction: After a gestation period of slightly more than 120 days, 1 or 2 young are born. At birth they weigh about 9–12g, the eyes are open and they are well-haired. Females may have 2 litters a year, in early and late summer. The young are carried by the female in her mouth when she forages but are left clinging to branches while she moves about in the vicinity. Mammae: 1 pair pectoral, 1 pair inguinal.

Longevity: 14–17 years in captivity.

Galago granti

Grant's Galago *Galago granti*
Total length 37–42cm; tail 21–25cm; mass 165g.
Identification pointers: As for Southern Lesser Galago. It is sometimes considered a subspecies of Zanzibar Galago *(Galagoides zanzibaricus)* but call said to be distinctive.

Description: Slightly larger than Southern Lesser Galago and browner in colour. Calls differ from those of the last species.

Distribution: In the region, restricted to Mozambique coastal plain to an altitude of about 200m, extending inland to the eastern border with Zimbabwe.

Habitat: Coastal and low-altitude rainforest in region.

Behaviour: When jumping, lands with either the front feet, or all four feet, whereas Southern Lesser Galago normally lands hind feet first. The territorial male often lies up with one or two females, unlike Southern Lesser, where males sleep apart from females. The male's home range may cover the ranges of several female groups.

Food: Mainly insects, other invertebrates, small vertebrates and fruits; very rarely tree gum. In one study 70% of the diet was made up of animal food.

Reproduction: Probably similar to Southern Lesser Galago, with 2 birth seasons and a gestation of around 120 days. Only a single young (occasionally 2) recorded and female carries young in mouth to foraging grounds. Mammae: Probably the same as Southern Lesser Galago (p.128).

Longevity: No records.

DWARF BUSHBABIES

Galago demidovii

Demidoff's Dwarf Galago *Galago demidovii*
Total length 22–35cm; tail 15–20cm; mass 46–88g.

Thomas's Dwarf Galago *Galago thomasi*
Total length 27–39cm; tail 15–26cm; mass 55–149g.

Identification pointers: Small size; long, well-haired tail; prominent ears and forward-pointing eyes; nocturnal; in forest habitats.

Description: Demidoff's is the smallest African primate, followed closely by **Thomas's Dwarf Galago.** Demidoff's has ginger to grey-brown fur, with somewhat paler underparts and there is a white line that runs from between

The Southern Lesser Galago is extremely agile.

A Southern Lesser Galago youngster 'parked' by its mother

The Southern Lesser Galago has very large eyes and large, thin, mobile ears.

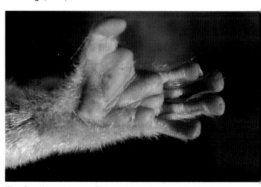

The Southern Lesser Galago has a large, opposable big toe.

Demidoff's Dwarf Galago

Grant's Galago

Demidoff's Dwarf Galago

131

Galago thomasi

the eyes and down the snout. **Thomas's** is similar in colour but in parts takes on yellowish tinge from skin secretions; the head is generally lighter in colour and there are prominent dark eye patches. Ears of **Thomas's** are larger than **Demidoff's** but both have pointed and upturned noses. Each has own distinctive calls. Both have distinctive rising, loud, 'crescendo' calls.

Distribution: Within the region, both species occur in northern Angola, touching on northern Zambia (see maps).

Habitat: Both species in tropical forested areas, including those of primary and secondary growth. Where the two species occur together, **Demidoff's** shows a preference for lower strata, whereas **Thomas's** generally remains within the canopy.

Behaviour: Commonly live in relatively large groups, with up to 10 recorded as sleeping together in **Demidoff's** and as many as 12 in **Thomas's**. Sex ratios may be equal in **Thomas's** but males establish a strict pecking order; **Demidoff's** males seldom share a home range. At least in the case of **Demidoff's**, only related females appear to share a home range but this may well also be the case in **Thomas's**. In ideal habitat both species may reach very high densities, with 50 to over 100 per square km in the case of **Demidoff's** and probably similar in **Thomas's**. Home range size is variable: up to 1.4ha in females and to 2.7ha in males. Both species usually sleep in self-constructed leaf nests, with as many as 10 individuals sometimes sharing a nest.

Food: Both dwarf galagos are mainly insectivores, eating large quantities of beetles, moths and caterpillars. Fruit and tree resin make up only a small percentage of intake.

Reproduction: Both species largely aseasonal but there are distinct birth peaks in some areas. Usually a single young (rarely 2), weighing 5–10g, born after an average 113-day gestation period. Mammae: Not recorded.

Longevity: 4–5 years in the wild; up to 13 years in captivity.

PANGOLINS Order Pholidota
Family Manidae

Smutsia temminckii

Ground Pangolin *Smutsia (Manis) temminckii*
Total length 70–140cm; tail 30–45cm; mass 5–16kg.
Identification pointers: Unmistakable; covered in large brown overlapping scales. Small head; heavy hindquarters and tail; small forelegs.

Description: This cannot be mistaken for any other species. Large, brown scales composed of agglutinated hair cover the upperparts, sides and tail. Smaller scales cover outer sides of legs and top of head. Underparts sparsely covered with hair. Head disproportionately small and pointed. It has powerfully built hind legs, short forelegs and a long, heavy tail. Walks on hind legs, occasionally using tail and forelegs for balance.

Distribution: Wide distribution in the region north of the Orange River, South Africa.

Habitat: Habitats range from low- to high-rainfall areas, including open grassland, woodland and rocky hills, but excluding forest and true desert but present throughout the Kalahari sand country.

Behaviour: Solitary and mainly nocturnal, although occasionally diurnal. May try to run away when threatened but usually curls into a ball to protect the head and underparts. May dig own burrows, but readily uses those dug by other species, or simply curls up among dense vegetation.

Demidoff's Dwarf Galago

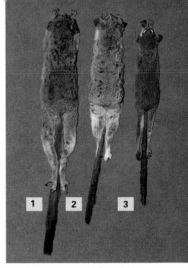

1. *Galago senegalensis* (possibly present in north-east Zambia); 2. *G. moholi*; 3. *G. demidovii*

Pangolins are also known as scaly anteaters. **Inset:** Pangolins curl into a ball for protection when they feel threatened.

Ground Pangolin

60mm

right front

60mm

right back

133

Food: Only eats certain species of ants and termites. Scratches superficially into nests close to the surface, under plant debris and animal dung.
Reproduction: Single young, weighing 330–450g, apparently normally born in winter after a gestation of about 140 days. Mammae: 1 pair pectoral.
Longevity: Never survive long in captivity; no records from the wild.

African White-bellied Tree Pangolin *Phataginus (Manis) tricuspis*
Total length 80–100cm; tail 50–62cm; mass 2–3kg.
Identification pointers: Large, brown, overlapping scales; tiny head; heavy hindquarters.

Phataginus tricuspis

Description: The covering of large, brown, overlapping scales is diagnostic, as is the long, scale-covered, prehensile tail, small, pointed head and well-developed hind legs. Separated from Ground Pangolin by habitat and arboreal lifestyle.
Distribution: In the region, found only in northern Angola.
Habitat: Rainforest, secondary growth.
Behaviour: Arboreal and rarely descends to the forest floor, although some reports indicate they descend to forage where disturbance is low. Mainly crepuscular and nocturnal. Very little known but probably solitary, except when female accompanied by single young, which clings to her tail base. Females hold territories that are smaller than those of males, with the latter overlapping those of several females.
Food: Mainly ants and termites, but also other insects.
Reproduction: A single young, weighing about 100g, is dropped after a gestation of about 150 days. They breed throughout the year. Mammae: 1 pair pectoral.
Longevity: No records.

HARES & RABBITS Order Lagomorpha
Family Leporidae

Three species of hare and five species of rabbit occur naturally in southern Africa. The European Rabbit *(Oryctolagus cuniculus)* occurs on a number of small offshore islands in South Africa, to which it was introduced by man.

Cape Hare *Lepus capensis*
Total length 45–60cm; tail 7–14cm; mass 1.4–2.5kg.

Scrub Hare *Lepus saxatilis*
Savanna Hare *Lepus microtis (victoriae)*
Total length 45–65cm; tail 7–17cm; mass 1.5–4.5kg.

Lepus capensis

The **Cape Hare**, **Scrub Hare** and **Savanna Hare** vary considerably in size from area to area, although **Scrub Hare** is generally larger than the other two.

Identification pointers: The three species have long ears, and the hind legs are much longer than the forelegs. The tail is black above, white below. See also distribution maps and habitat requirements. The exact range boundaries of the **Scrub Hare** and **Savanna Hare** are not known and they are impossible to separate in the field.

African White-bellied Tree Pangolins are almost exclusively arboreal.

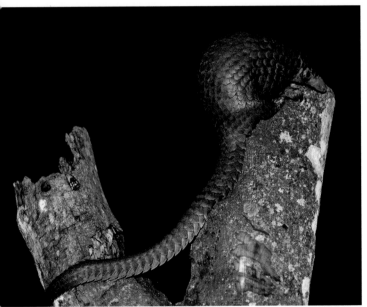

The Long-tailed Tree, or Black-bellied, Pangolin *(Uromanis tetradactyla)* occurs in the Cabinda enclave of Angola and may well occur in the north of that country.

An adult and juvenile African White-bellied Tree Pangolin

African White-bellied Tree Pangolin

Cape Hare

300mm running track

left back

right back

left front

right front

135

■ *Lepus saxatilis*
■ *Lepus microtis*
■ Overlap

Description: The three species of hare have long ears, long, well-developed hind legs and a short fluffy tail. The body hair is fine and soft. Overall appearance of the Scrub Hare and Savanna Hare is very similar but the latter averages smaller but otherwise indistinguishable in the field and range boundaries remain unknown.

	Cape Hare	Scrub Hare/ Savanna Hare
Upperparts	Variable; light brown and black-flecked; whitish-grey in north and west	Brown-grey to grey; black-flecked
Underparts	Chest not white; abdomen white; in north may be completely white	White throughout
Face	Yellowish on nose and cheeks; pale grey in northern animals	Lighter (whitish or buff) on sides of face and around eyes
Nuchal patch (on nape of neck behind ears)	Brownish-pink; pale grey in northern animals	Reddish-brown

Distribution: Cape Hare has a wide distribution in the western and central areas of southern Africa with isolated populations in the north (Botswana) and east (Limpopo province and southern Mozambique). Its northernmost range in the north-west appears to be south-western Angola. If one accepts the validity of Savanna Hare in southern Africa then it occurs across much of the north and east of the region, with Scrub Hare occurring in the western sector of South Africa, extending in to southern Namibia.

Habitat: Cape Hare prefers drier, open habitat; Scrub Hare and Savanna Hare occur in woodland and scrub cover with grass. Scrub Hare is commonly seen in cultivated areas. Normally the Scrub Hare and Savanna Hare are not seen in completely open grassland and the Cape Hare is not found in dense scrub or woodland; there is some overlap, however.

Behaviour: The three species are mainly nocturnal but some early morning and late afternoon activity may occur, especially when cool and overcast. They lie up in 'forms' (shallow indentations in the ground made by the body), with those of Scrub and Savanna Hares being in more substantial cover. They rely on their camouflage when approached, only getting up and running off at the last minute. Normally zigzag, often at high speed.

Food: Predominantly grazers but will feed on other plants, especially new growth.

Reproduction: Young born at any time of the year. Cape Hare may have as many as four litters per year. The Savanna Hare may have up to eight litters in any given year. Gestation period about 42 days; 1–3 leverets are born fully haired and with open eyes and can move about soon after birth. Scrub Hare has 1–3 leverets, weighing about 115g average. Mammae: 3 pairs, abdominal/inguinal.

Longevity: No African records but related species 7–12 years for captives, 3–5 years in the wild.

Cape Hare upperparts are whitish-grey in the north-west.

Cape Hares in the south of their range are darker than those in the north; this individual is from the Nuweveld.

Most, but not all, Scrub Hares have a white forehead spot.

The Savanna Hare is very similar to the Scrub Hare.

Scrub Hare in typical alert stance

Above left and right: Undersurfaces of hare and rabbit feet are covered in dense mats of hair.

RED ROCK RABBITS Genus *Pronolagus*

Four species occur in the region. Based on DNA sequencing, Hewitt's Red Rock Rabbit is recognized as occurring in the Western and Eastern Cape, but cannot be separated from Smith's Red Rock Rabbit in the field; specimens of Hewitt's seen by the authors in the wild appear to be darker in coat colour than Smith's but this may well vary from area to area.

Pronolagus randensis

Jameson's Red Rock Rabbit *Pronolagus randensis*
Total length 48–63cm; tail 6–13cm; mass 1.8–3kg.

Natal Red Rock Rabbit *Pronolagus crassicaudatus*
Total length 50–67cm; tail 3–11cm; mass 2.4–3kg.

Hewitt's Red Rock Rabbit *Pronolagus saundersiae*
Smith's Red Rock Rabbit *Pronolagus rupestris*
Total length 43–65cm; tail 5–11cm; mass 1.3–2kg.

Identification pointers: Different red rock rabbits can be identified from distribution maps, except where there is overlap. They can also be separated from the three hare species and Riverine Rabbit by their much shorter ears, especially in the case of the rock rabbits.

Pronolagus crassicaudatus

Description: All rabbit-like and all are similar in appearance. The distribution ranges of three species only overlap marginally, however, and therefore use of distribution maps is very important. Coloration can be variable but usually the back and sides are reddish-brown, grizzled with black. Underparts of all species range from pinkish-brown to reddish-brown.

■ *Pronolagus saundersiae*
■ *Pronolagus rupestris*

	Jameson's	Natal	Smith's
Rump and back legs	Lighter than back and sides	Bright red-brown	Bright red-brown
Tail	Red-brown, black tip	Uniform red-brown; no black tip	Dark to red-brown; black tip
Face and neck	Head light grey, brown-flecked	Grey-white band from chin along lower jaw and to back of neck	Sides of face greyish

Distribution: See distribution maps.
Habitat: Rocky habitats from isolated outcrops to mountain ranges, in high- and low-rainfall areas but absent from true desert.
Behaviour: Essentially nocturnal, but may forage on overcast days. Normally rest up in rock crevices or in dense vegetation cover but frequently sun bask in early morning and late afternoon, especially during cold weather. Usually single animals encountered, but in suitable habitat may reach quite high densities. They make regular use of dung middens and these are a sure way of identifying their presence.
Food: Predominantly grazers, but at least Jameson's eats leaves of woody plants. In more arid areas, such as rock outcrops on the Karoo plateau and along the Namib Desert fringe, herbaceous plants and succulents are of considerable importance.

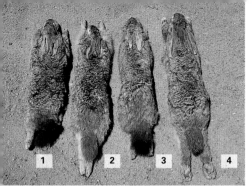

Red rock rabbit skins: 1. Smith's; 2. Natal;
3. Jameson's; 4. Riverine Rabbit

'Latrine' sites with heaps of lozenge-shaped
pellets are characteristic of areas inhabited by
red rock rabbits.

Jameson's Red Rock Rabbitt, one of the few known
photographs of this little-known species. Note the
dark-coloured tail.

Smith's Red Rock Rabbit usually has a distinctive
red tail.

Juvenile Smith's Red Rock Rabbit

In some areas Hewitt's Red Rock Rabbit is darker
than Smith's Red Rock Rabbit.

Red Rock Rabbits

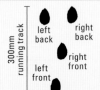

300mm running track

left back   right back

right front

left front

Reproduction: After a gestation of about 38 days, 1 or 2 young, weighing 40–50g, are born hairless and helpless in a cup-shaped nest lined with soft hair from the female's underparts. In at least **Smith's** most births September–February, with up to 3 litters per season, although evidence indicates that **Jameson's** may breed throughout the year. Mammae: 3 pairs abdominal/inguinal.
Longevity: No records but probably rarely more than 5 years.

*Bunolagus
monticularis*

Riverine Rabbit *Bunolagus monticularis*

Total length 52cm; tail 9cm; mass ±1.5–1.9kg.

An endangered species, but numbers probably not as low as previously thought, certainly to the low thousands and not the low hundreds as claimed by some. Scattered populations, mainly in the districts of Victoria West, Fraserburg and Beaufort West; also recently discovered near Touwsrivier and in Little Karoo, including the Anysberg.

Identification pointers: Similar to red rock rabbits, but ears much longer, upperparts drab grey; differs from the two hares in having a more or less uniformly coloured grey-brown tail, not black and white. Dark brown stripe along lower jaw towards ear base only found in this species; white eye-ring.

Description: Similar to the red rock rabbits but has longer, more hare-like ears. White ring around eye and dark brown stripe down the side of the lower jaw, extending to ear base. Upperparts grizzled grey; nuchal patch deep red-brown; tail short, fluffy and grey-brown, somewhat darker towards the tip. Shares habitat with Scrub Hare but black-and-white tail of that species clearly separates it.

Distribution: Central districts of Karoo and its southern fringes, South Africa. Critically Endangered due to loss of habitat – as a result of land clearing for cultivation and overgrazing by livestock – and hunting by humans and dogs.

Habitat: Dense but low riverine bush in arid areas. These are seasonal rivers and only flow during good rains.

Behaviour: Little known but home range about 10–15ha, those of males perhaps to 20ha. Mainly nocturnal but can be flushed during the day. They will sun bask after cold nights and the authors have seen one foraging on an overcast day.

Food: Mainly browse, but also grass when fresh.

Reproduction: Apparently 1 (rarely 2) 40–50g young born in nest in shallow burrow from August–May, after an estimated 35 day gestation. Mammae: Not known.

Longevity: Not known.

Smith's Red Rock Rabbit varies greatly in pelage colour: an animal at Augrabies (**left**), and one from Goegap, near Springbok (**right**).

The Riverine Rabbit is seriously endangered.

The facial markings of the Riverine Rabbit are diagnostic.

The Riverine Rabbit is the only lagomorph in the region that digs a burrow.

Riverine Rabbit

RODENTS Order Rodentia

Rodents are characterized by the pair of large, chisel-like, continuously growing incisors in both jaws. Currently, 140 species have been recorded from the region (four introduced), ranging in size from the 6g Pygmy Mouse to the >20kg Cape Porcupine. Ongoing genetic work is likely to increase this species list but will make little difference to field observations, as externally it will not be possible to differentiate most newly described species, except where there are distinct distributional boundaries, or where specimens are collected for genetic work.

SCALY-TAILED SQUIRRELS Family Anomaluridae

Anomalurus derbianus

Lord Derby's Scaly-tailed Squirrel *Anomalurus derbianus*
Total length 50–65cm; tail 22–28cm; mass 450–1,000g.
Identification pointers: Relatively large size; extensive hair-covered gliding membrane linking the feet and tail; two rows of overlapping scales on underside of tail towards base.

Description: A large gliding squirrel (it is in fact not a true squirrel) with a hair-covered membrane that extends between front and hind limbs, hind limbs to tail. Extends the limbs when moving from tree to tree, spreading the membrane and then gliding up to and beyond 100m. The long, well-haired tail is used as a rudder. It has large ears and eyes, with long facial whiskers. Overall dorsal coloration is dark grey, brown or reddish-brown, with lighter coloured hairs scattered through the coat giving a grizzled appearance. Underparts are paler to white. The tail usually has a distinctive tip. The under-surface of the tail towards the base has two rows of overlapping scales that are used to prevent slipping when landing on smooth, vertical tree trunks.
Distribution: Occurs in a broad swathe across northern Angola and Zambia.
Habitat: Usually associated with closed-canopy forest but in Zambia mainly found in tall miombo woodland.
Behaviour: They are almost exclusively arboreal, being very clumsy on the ground, and either crepuscular or nocturnal. Variously reported to be solitary and live in small groups, and may reach high densities in prime habitat. They spend the day in tree-holes.
Food: A variety of plants and parts, including tree bark, fruit, leaves and flowers.
Reproduction: Outside the tropical forest belt they may be seasonal breeders. Usually 1 but up to 3 fully haired and well-developed young are dropped but gestation length is not known. Young only leave the nest when they are almost adult size. Mammae: 2 pairs, location uncertain.
Longevity: A captive lived for 5 years and 1 month.

A very similar species, Beecroft's Anomalure/Scaly-tailed Squirrel *(A. beecrofti)* is known from very few records in northern Angola and possibly also north-western Zambia. In Beecroft's the tail is bushy and greyish, whereas that of Lord Derby's is darker and black towards the tip. Nothing is known about Beecroft's in the region.

Despite its relatively large size, Lord Derby's Scaly-tailed Squirrel is seldom seen as it is largely nocturnal and elusive.

In this photograph of Lord Derby's Scaly-tailed Squirrel one can clearly see the sharp-pointed scales on the underside of the tail pressing into the bark.

Two rows of pointed scales on the underside of the scaly-tailed squirrels' tails prevent slipping when landing on smooth tree trunks.

Lord Derby's Scaly-tailed Squirrel

Of the 14 species in the region, 12 are arboreal and two terrestrial. The Grey Squirrel is an alien introduced from North America via the United Kingdom to the south-west of South Africa.

GROUND-DWELLING SQUIRRELS

Xerus inauris

Southern African Ground Squirrel *Xerus inauris*
Total length 40–50cm; tail 19–25cm; mass 500–1,000g (average 650g).
Identification pointers: Terrestrial, lives in burrows; white stripe down each side; long, bushy tail; very small ears. Nearly impossible to distinguish from Damara Ground Squirrel where ranges overlap, but incisors of the latter are orange; those of Ground Squirrel are white. Occasionally confused with the Suricate (p.254) but that species lacks the bushy tail or side stripes.

Description: Easily identifiable species, being entirely terrestrial yet typically squirrel-like. Upperparts usually cinnamon-brown, some animals more grey-brown. Single white stripe runs along each side of body from shoulder to thigh. Underparts are white tinged with light brown in mid-belly. Coarse hair; white incisors.
Distribution: Endemic to the arid areas of southern Africa. There has been a steady westward spread of this rodent on the Great Karoo plateau over the past few decades as grass density has increased, possibly as a result of climate change and lower stocking rates on some farms. This same pattern can be discerned with the Springhare, with which it shares much of its range.
Habitat: Open areas with sparse cover and usually a hard substrate, such as calcrete, but also in sandy ground.
Behaviour: Gregarious diurnal species occurring in groups of 5–30. It excavates extensive burrow systems with several entrances. Females and young remain in close proximity to the burrows but males live in separate burrow systems, moving from colony to colony. Frequently stands on its hind legs to enhance its view of the surrounding area. Its bushy tail is often held over the body and head when the squirrel feeds, to act as a sunshade. Burrow systems often shared with Suricate and Yellow Mongoose.
Food: Grass, roots, seeds and bulbs; also insects, particularly termites.
Reproduction: After a gestation of ±45 days, 1–3 naked, helpless young, weighing ±20g, born any time of year, in a burrow from which they emerge at about 6 weeks. Mammae: 2 pairs inguinal.
Longevity: One captive lived 6 years; probably 3–5 years in the wild.

Xerus princeps

Damara Ground Squirrel *Xerus princeps*
Total length 46–48cm; tail 24cm; mass probably similar to last species but few weights known.
Identification pointers: Similar to Southern African Ground Squirrel; three black bands (not two) on longer basal tail hairs; yellow-orange incisors; rocky habitats.

Description: Very similar to Southern African Ground Squirrel in appearance but incisor teeth are yellow, not white. Difficult to tell apart where ranges overlap, but habitat preference often useful.

Northern animals are often greyer than those in the south.

Southern African Ground Squirrel

This is the more usual brown form of Southern African Ground Squirrel; note the tail being used as a shade.

The Damara Ground Squirrel is mainly restricted to the pro-Namib escarpment.

Southern African
Ground Squirrel

soft
ground   24mm   60mm

right
front

right
back

Damara Ground
Squirrel

Distribution: Occurs in a broad belt along the pro-Namib Desert zone and adjacent interior from south-western Angola, through Namibia at least to South Africa's Northern Cape province border. Recent records indicate it also occurs on the south bank of the Orange River in the Richtersveld, and possibly as far south as the Kamiesberge and eastwards in the Orange River broken veld. These records need to be confirmed.

Habitat: Closely associated with rocky hills and broken mountain country, within a rainfall range of 100–250mm. Unlike the Southern African Ground Squirrel, it seldom ventures into open, flat country and avoids sandy soil.

Behaviour: Unlike the other ground squirrel, which lives in groups, the Damara is largely solitary, lives in pairs or a female with young. Burrows are dug under rocks, among boulder clusters and only very rarely in more open areas. When alarmed, will not always head straight for a burrow but may take shelter under vegetation or among rocks. Not as strictly terrestrial as its cousin, but will climb readily into bushes to feed. Strictly diurnal.

Food: A variety of plants and plant parts, including seeds and succulents, but also takes some insects.

Reproduction: After an estimated 48-day gestation period, 1–3 young are dropped during the cooler winter months. Mammae: 2 pairs inguinal.

Longevity: Not known but probably similar to previous species.

TREE-DWELLING SQUIRRELS

Mutable Sun Squirrel *Heliosciurus mutabilis*
Total length 40–55cm; tail 20–30cm; mass 300–480g.

Identification pointers: One of the largest arboreal squirrels in the region; variable in colour but usually grizzled light brown; bushy, narrowly banded tail. Compare with Red Bush Squirrel (see p.152).

Heliosciurus mutabilis

Description: One of the largest indigenous, arboreal true squirrels occurring in southern Africa. Varies considerably in colour but the upperparts are usually grizzled light brown. In parts of Zimbabwe, it can be black above while in other areas it is reddish. The underparts are pale fawn to white. The tail has a series of narrow, indistinct whitish bands.

Distribution: Restricted in southern Africa to the forests of eastern Zimbabwe and Mozambique, eastern Zambia and Malawi. It is widely, if patchily, distributed in East Africa and westwards through the equatorial forest areas into West Africa.

Habitat: Forested areas at both high and low elevations, including riverine forest.

Behaviour: Diurnal, occurring singly or in pairs. Most activity is restricted to early morning and late afternoon. It is often observed basking in the sun, stretched out on branches. Tree-holes are used for shelter. In areas where its distribution overlaps with the Red Bush Squirrel, it tends to utilize the higher canopy zone. As is common with most arboreal squirrels, it is quite vocal, giving vent to clucking calls accompanied by frequent tail-flicking.

Food: It takes a wide range of plant food but it will also eat insects and possibly smaller vertebrates such as lizards and birds.

Reproduction: All that is known with any certainty is that litters consist of 1–4 young and are probably produced in summer. The young are dropped and raised in tree-holes. Mammae: Not known.

Longevity: A closely related species, *H. rufobrachium*, lived for 8 years 9 months in captivity.

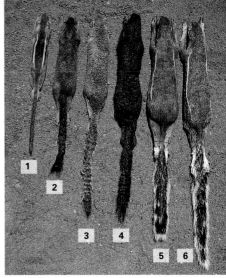

The Mutable Sun Squirrel is active in the morning and late afternoon hours.

Key to squirrel skins:
1. Striped Tree Squirrel
2. Tree Squirrel
3. Red Bush Squirrel
4. Mutable Sun Squirrel
5. Southern African Ground Squirrel
6. Damara Ground Squirrel

Skins of arboreal tree squirrels (**left to right**): Mutable Sun Squirrel (two colour phases); Red Bush Squirrel (p.152); Striped Tree Squirrel

Mutable Sun Squirrel

Heliosciurus gambianus

Gambian Sun Squirrel *Heliosciurus gambianus*
Total length 43–46cm; tail 23.5cm; mass 210–330g.
Identification pointers: Overall colour variable; tail has black rings and tip.

Description: There is considerable colour variation in this squirrel, even within the same species, and it is generally believed that several species may be involved. Overall somewhat duller and paler than other squirrels within its range. The dorsal pelage may be fawn to richer brown with paler to white underparts. The tail has black rings and tip. Hind feet are paler to off-white above.
Distribution: In the region, across much of north-central Angola and northern Zambia.
Habitat: Shows strong preference for dense woodland and usually in savanna woodland associations but also into tall tropical forest.
Behaviour: Little is known, but seems to be solitary and uses tree-holes for resting and for females to drop young.
Food: Mixed feeders, taking a variety of plant parts and insects.
Reproduction: Apparently two breeding peaks, in July–August and December–January. 1–5 young per litter. Nothing else is known. Mammae: Not known.
Longevity: A single captive lived for 8 years 11 months.

Funisciurus congicus

Striped Tree Squirrel *Funisciurus congicus*
Total length 30cm; tail 17cm; mass 110g.
Identification pointers: Small size; white side stripe; only found in northern Namibia and in Angola. Could be confused with Tree Squirrel but the latter does not have white body stripe. Tail held over back. Also called Congo Rope Squirrel.

Description: Smallest squirrel in region. Upperparts pale yellow-brown; underparts paler or off-white. Single white stripe runs down side from neck to base of long bushy tail. A darker stripe runs below the white stripe. When on the move, tail held curled over back.
Distribution: Restricted to north-western Namibia but extending widely in western Angola and through much of Congo Basin.
Habitat: Dense woodland, near watercourses and rocky outcrops in the region.
Behaviour: Diurnal and arboreal, but descends frequently to the ground to forage. It lives in small family groups. Resting-sites (winter) are in tree-holes, and its nest ('drey' (summer) is constructed from leaves and twigs in the fork of a branch. Only indigenous squirrel to construct a drey.
Food: A wide range of plant food but also insects. Said to bury seeds and other plant parts for later consumption.
Reproduction: Two young are born in a tree-hole or drey with most births taking place either at the onset or at the end of the rains. Mammae: 2 pairs inguinal.
Longevity: No records.

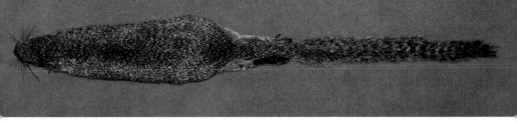

Gambian Sun Squirrel

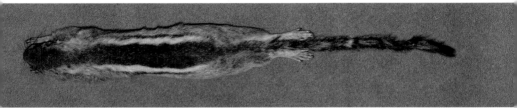

Striped Tree Squirrel

Striped Tree Squirrel

Gambian Sun Squirrel

Striped Tree Squirrel

149

Funisciurus bayonii

Funisciurus
pyrropus

Lunda Rope Squirrel *Funisciurus bayonii*
Total length 38–45cm; tail 20cm; mass 135g.

Fire-footed Rope Squirrel *Funisciurus pyrropus*
Total length 34cm; tail 15cm; mass 150–200g.
Note that the measurements of both species are based on few specimens.

Identification pointers: Small size; pale lateral body stripes and red legs of **Fire-footed**.

Description: Relatively small tree squirrels. Single pale to white stripe runs along each side, fur is soft and ears are short and rounded (those of *Paraxerus* are noticeably longer). **Fire-footed** has red legs and head, with noticeably elongated snout. Both species notably darker in colour than Striped Tree Squirrel. Neither should be mistaken for other species within their range.
Distribution: Lunda Rope Squirrel occurs in north-eastern Angola; **Fire-footed** Rope Squirrel occurs to the north-west.
Habitat: Lunda occupies moist lowland forests, moist woodland savanna and plantations; **Fire-footed** occurs in moist woodland savanna and various forest associations.
Behaviour: Both appear to be mainly solitary. Much time is spent foraging on the ground, particularly in the case of **Fire-footed**, which commonly nests in fallen logs and in burrows excavated by other species. Males have larger home ranges than females, with average areas of slightly greater than 5ha and as little as 1ha.
Food: Fruits and seeds make up as much as 80% of their diet with insects making up the remainder, particularly termites and ants.
Reproduction: Poorly known, but litters of 1 or 2 usual and probably aseasonal. Mammae: 2 pairs inguinal.
Longevity: No records.

Paraxerus cepapi

Tree Squirrel *Paraxerus cepapi*
Total length 35cm; tail 16cm; mass 100–260g.
Identification pointers: Small size; uniformly greyish or yellowish-brown upperparts; no distinctive markings. Most widespread of the region's tree squirrels.

Description: Variable in size and colour. In general, animals from western areas are greyer and eastern animals are more yellow-brown. Underparts range from fawn to white. Body has a generally grizzled appearance; bushy tail similar colour to body.
Distribution: Occurs widely in north-eastern parts of southern Africa and in a broad swathe extending westwards into northern Namibia and adjacent southern Angola.
Habitat: A wide variety of woodland habitats but not true high forest.
Behaviour: Although it is usually seen singly or in mother/young groups, a number of animals, average 5, live in loose association. The adult male or males in a group will defend a territory against incursions by other squirrels. Like other squirrel species, it is very vocal, with harsh, chattering scold accompanied by vigorous tail-flicking. Group members remain bonded by regularly marking each other, and objects, with secretions from the anal gland. Average group territory size is about 4ha but this no doubt varies between habitats. Equally at home foraging in trees and on the ground. Natural and bird-excavated tree-holes are used as night-time retreats and for raising the young.

Skins of Lunda Rope Squirrel (**left**) and Fire-footed Rope Squirrel (**right**)

Tree Squirrels (**top and above**) are equally at home in trees or foraging on the ground.

The Tree Squirrel is the most commonly seen arboreal squirrel within its range.

Lunda Rope Squirrel

Tree Squirrel

soft ground

25mm

right front

46mm

right back

Food: A wide variety of plant food and also insects. Will cache surplus food.
Reproduction: After a gestation period of about 55 days, 1–3 young, each weighing about 10g, are born in a leaf-lined tree-hole, mostly in summer. Mammae: 1 pair each abdominal, inguinal and pectoral (which may or may not be developed).
Longevity: Similar-sized squirrels in genus *Funisciurus* have lived 5–9 years in captivity.

Paraxerus palliatus

Red Bush Squirrel *Paraxerus palliatus*

Total length 35–40cm; tail 17–20cm; mass 200–380g.
Identification pointers: Dark grey to black upperparts; underparts and tail reddish or yellowish. Compare with Mutable Sun Squirrel where range overlaps.

Description: The upperparts are grizzled dark grey to black and the underparts, sides of face, feet and tail are usually reddish or yellowish. As one of the most brightly coloured of the region's squirrels, it should not be mistaken for any other.
Distribution: Largely confined to Mozambique and extreme eastern parts of Zimbabwe, but there are two small isolated populations in KwaZulu-Natal and it also occurs throughout Malawi. Beyond the region it extends into East Africa.
Habitat: Forest habitats, including coastal dune and montane forests.
Behaviour: Diurnal, usually solitary except when female is accompanied by young. A male, female and small young may be observed in a loose association. Very vocal species with a range of different calls, usually accompanied by tail-flicking. In one study in the region, males were found to have larger home ranges than females (3.2–4.2ha and 1.2–2.2ha) and there may be considerable overlap of ranges, especially where there is a rich food resource. Interestingly, unlike most arboreal squirrels, they will readily seek shelter in fallen logs on the forest floor and not always flee into treetops when alarmed.
Food: It takes a wide range of plant food, including fruits, berries and some insects.
Reproduction: 1 or 2 young, each weighing about 13–14g, born in a tree-hole lined with leaves, after a gestation period of 60–65 days. As with other squirrel species, the young are born hairless and blind. Births occur mainly during the wet season but it is possible that a female has more than 1 litter in a season. Mammae: 2 pairs inguinal, 1 pair pectoral not always developed.
Longevity: Not known.

Paraxerus vincenti

Vincent's Bush Squirrel *Paraxerus vincenti*

Found only in the forests on Mount Namuli in central Mozambique north of the Zambezi River, at altitudes of 1,200–1,850m. Some believe it to be an isolated subspecies of *Paraxerus palliatus*. Threatened by habitat clearing.

The Tree Squirrel *(Paraxerus cepapi)* is the most abundant and widespread of southern African tree-dwelling species.

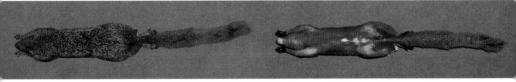

The Red Bush Squirrel has a distinctive coat and its range is mainly limited to the eastern seaboard.

Red Bush Squirrel

Paraxerus flavovittis

Striped Bush Squirrel *Paraxerus flavovittis*

Total length 35cm; tail 17.5cm; mass 120-200g.
Identification pointers: The only tree squirrel in the north-east (northern Mozambique and southern Malawi) with pale to white lateral stripes.

Description: Overall dorsal colour dark grey to olive-brown; this is variable and is believed to be related to the squirrel's age and not seasonal. Has white to yellowish lateral line on either side of back, pale and darker facial lines, and white underparts.
Distribution: Occurs over much of Mozambique north of the Zambezi River, south-eastern Malawi and extending northwards through Tanzania and into southern Kenya.
Habitat: Shows a preference for moist savanna woodland, thickets and plantations.
Behaviour: Very little known but probably similar to other species in this genus.
Food: Mainly plant food, including fruit and seeds, but some insects are included in its diet. Said to favour fruits of the sugar plum (*Uapaca* spp.) tree.
Reproduction: Nothing known; probably similar to other squirrels in this genus.
Longevity: Not known.

Paraxerus boehmi

Boehm's Bush Squirrel *Paraxerus boehmi*

Total length 25-27cm; tail 13-15cm; mass 40-100g.
Identification pointers: Small squirrel with four black dorsal stripes.

Description: Cannot be mistaken for any other squirrel within its very limited southern African range. Its small size and the four black dorsal stripes, separated by three paler stripes, is distinctive. There are also dark and light facial stripes. It closely resembles the chipmunks *(Tamias)* of North America and eastern Asia.
Distribution: Only north-eastern Zambia on the Mwera-Wantipa Flats but widespread through eastern DR Congo and South Sudan.
Habitat: Tropical moist lowland forests, montane forest and wooded savanna.
Behaviour: Little is known about this attractive squirrel. It apparently shows a preference for dense undergrowth and spends much time foraging here and in the lower forest storey. Said to be mainly solitary, although sightings of two or three individuals sometimes made.
Food: Mainly fruits, seeds and other plant material but also includes some insects in its diet.
Reproduction: Breeds throughout the year and litters consist of a single young. Mammae: Not known.
Longevity: No records.

Paraxerus lucifer

Black and Red Bush Squirrel *Paraxerus lucifer*

Total length 38-58cm; tail 16-26cm; mass 650g.
Identification pointers: Reddish underparts contrasting with dark back.

Description: An attractive, fairly large squirrel with light reddish upperparts and a broad, darker dorsal patch.
Distribution: In the region, restricted to northern Malawi and possibly the adjacent strip of Zambia. Their range is centred on the Misuku

Boehm's Bush
Squirrel

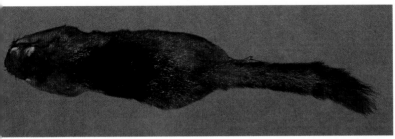

Black and Red
Bush Squirrel

The Black and Red Bush Squirrel is known to occur only in northern Malawi in the region.

Striped Bush Squirrel

Boehm's Bush
Squirrel

Black and Red Bush Squirrel

155

Hills and the Nyika Plateau of Malawi at an altitude of around 2,000m. It occurs in the Nyika National Park.

Habitat: Montane forest and adjacent wooded grassland.

Behaviour: Like all African tree squirrels, it is diurnal and mainly arboreal but the few records indicate that it will come to the ground to forage. Generally noisy; calling is accompanied by vigorous tail flicking. Said to flatten itself against branches when disturbed, rather than fleeing.

Food: Takes a mix of plant food, including leaves, buds, fruits and seeds. Eats some insects, especially termites.

Reproduction: Poorly known but the few records indicate it may be a seasonal breeder, with 2 or more litters in a season. Mammae: Not known.

Longevity: Not recorded.

African Giant Squirrel *Protoxerus stangeri*

Total length 47–70cm; tail 25–38cm; mass about 650g.

Identification: Relatively large size; sparsely haired to almost hairless underparts; hair coarse and colour variable from olive-straw to almost black; high forest.

Protoxerus stangeri

Description: The largest arboreal squirrel in the region (also see Lord Derby's). Hair relatively coarse and colour ranges from olive-straw to almost black and usually somewhat grizzled; hair cover on underparts relatively sparse and lighter to white. Head colour lighter than upperparts, pale cheeks. The long, bushy tail may, or may not, be clearly banded. Ears short and rounded.

Distribution: Occurs patchily in northern Angola with isolated populations on the Angola Escarpment.

Habitat: Areas of tropical forest.

Behaviour: Mainly arboreal but does sometimes forage on the forest floor. Diurnal, sheltering at night in tree-holes.

Food: Seeds, nuts and fruits; in some areas, feeds extensively on oil palm nuts, hence alternative name Oil Palm Squirrel.

Reproduction: Usually 3 or 4 young dropped in leaf-lined tree-hole. In the east of their range, may be seasonal breeders.

Mammae: Not recorded.

Longevity: One captive lived for 5 years and 1 month.

Eastern Grey Squirrel *Sciurus carolinensis* (Introduced)

Total length 38–52cm; tail 15–25cm; mass 540g.

Identification pointers: Restricted to south-western Cape, where it is the only squirrel. Uniform grey-brown or silvery-grey upperparts, white underparts.

Sciurus carolinensis

Description: This large squirrel has a summer coat that is generally brownish-grey, but after the moult the winter coat is silvery-grey. The underparts are white to off-white. The tail is long and bushy.

Distribution: Native to eastern North America. In the region it is restricted to alien pine plantations and oak trees in extreme south-western South Africa.

Habitat: Oak woodland, pine plantations and suburban gardens.

Behaviour: Normally solitary or in mother/young family groups but several may be seen feeding in close proximity. Makes use of tree-holes but also constructs dreys. Although arboreal, it spends large amounts of time on the

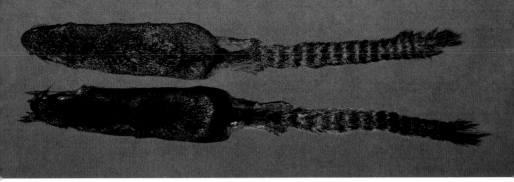

The African Giant Squirrel is also known as the Oil Palm Squirrel.

The Eastern Grey Squirrel is an exotic imported into South Africa's Western Cape. **Inset left:** Eastern Grey Squirrels feed readily on pine cone seeds. **Inset right:** These squirrels construct leaf nests known as dreys.

African Giant Squirrel

Eastern Grey Squirrel

ground foraging. It is a scatter-hoarder, like many squirrel species, and buries numerous food items for later retrieval. A pest species.

Food: Acorns, pine nuts, cultivated fruits, fungi, insects, young birds, birds' eggs.

Reproduction: All year round but birth peaks in August and January in South Africa's Western Cape. After a gestation of 45 days, 1–4 (rarely up to 8) young born, each weighing about 15g. Mammae: 2 pairs pectoral, 1 pair abdominal, 1 pair inguinal.

Longevity: Most die before the end of their first year but up to 12 years 5 months in the wild; one captive lived 23 years 6 months.

DORMICE Family Myoxidae

Graphiurus microtis

Graphiurus monardi

■ *Graphiurus ocularis*
■ *Graphiurus platyops*
　 Graphiurus rupicola
■ *Graphiurus johnstoni*
■ *Graphiurus angolensis*

As many as 11 dormouse species occur in the region, but the **Lesser Savanna Dormouse** is sometimes considered by authorities to be merely a smaller form of the Woodland Dormouse. Because of their bushy tails they are sometimes mistaken for squirrels but they differ in being much smaller in size and nocturnal in habit.

The smaller savanna-dwelling dormice are very similar and in large part difficult, or impossible, to tell apart in the field. These include **Angolan Dormouse** (*G. angolensis*); **Johnston's African Dormouse** (*G. johnstoni*), which is known only from southern Malawi; **Small-eared Dormouse** (*G. microtis*); **Monard's Dormouse** (*G. monardi*) – consult the maps to narrow down the species occurring in a given area. An additional species, **Lorraine's African Dormouse** (*G. lorraineus*), may occur in extreme north-western Zambia (no map). It is very similar to the other small African dormice.

Spectacled Dormouse *Graphiurus ocularis*
Total length 25cm; tail 10cm; mass 80g.

Rock Dormouse *Graphiurus platyops*
Stone Dormouse *Graphiurus rupicola*
Total length 18cm; tail 7cm; mass 45g.

Woodland Dormouse *Graphiurus murinus*
Total length 16cm; tail 7cm; mass 30g.

Lesser Savanna Dormouse *Graphiurus kelleni*
Total length 14cm; tail 6cm; mass <30g.

Identification pointers: See distribution maps and habitat descriptions. Distinct black-and-white facial markings and larger size distinguish **Spectacled Dormouse**; **Rock** and **Stone Dormice** distinguished by flattened skull and rocky habitat; the **Woodland** and **Lesser Savanna Dormice** the smallest and most frequently seen. All generally greyish in colour with bushy, squirrel-like tails.

Description: Dormice have bushy, squirrel-like tails, fairly short muzzles, small ears and soft fur. Hair colour is grey to silvery-grey. **Spectacled Dormouse** is most distinctive, not only because of its relatively large size but also its black, white and grey facial markings. A dark ring surrounds each eye (the 'spectacles'), and a dark line runs from the sides of the muzzle onto the shoulders. Lips, cheeks, underparts and upper-surfaces of the hands and feet are white. Tail is usually rimmed and tipped with white. **Rock** and **Stone Dormice** also have a dark facial pattern but much less distinct than **Spectacled Dormouse**. The bushy pale grey tail is usually white-tipped. The underparts are grey. An interesting feature of these dormice is the somewhat flattened skull, an adaptation to living in narrow

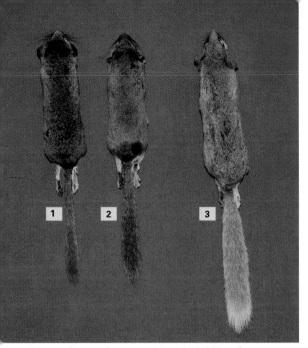

1. Lesser Savanna Dormouse; 2. Lorraine's African Dormouse; 3. Woodland Dormouse

1. Woodland Dormouse; 2. Rock Dormouse; 3. Spectacled Dormouse

Spectacled Dormouse has distinct facial markings.

Spectacled Dormouse

Lesser Savanna Dormouse

■ *Graphiurus murinus*
■ *Graphiurus kelleni*

rock crevices. Although **Woodland Dormouse** lacks distinctive facial markings, cheeks, lips and underparts are either white or greyish-white but many individuals have brown or reddish 'staining' of these white areas; tail may or may not be white-tipped. **Lesser Savanna Dormouse** is very similar to **Woodland Dormouse**.

Distribution: Spectacled Dormouse is restricted to western South Africa. The Rock Dormouse occurs in north-east South Africa and Zimbabwe, with the Stone Dormouse in north-west South Africa and Namibia. The Woodland Dormouse has a wide distribution in eastern South Africa and narrowly along the southern coastal belt; it is difficult to separate from the **Lesser Savanna Dormouse** where ranges overlap (see distribution maps).

Habitat: Both the Spectacled, Rock and Stone Dormice are associated with rocky habitats but the Spectacled Dormouse also utilizes trees and buildings. The Woodland Dormouse is a woodland savanna and bush species, as are many other species, but it is also frequently found in association with man-made structures.

Behaviour: All are nocturnal and are agile climbers. Woodland Dormouse may construct substantial nests of grass, leaves and lichen and may become quite tame where it lives in close association with man. Both **Spectacled** and **Rock Dormice** appear to be solitary but several **Woodland Dormice** may share the same nest. Northern hemisphere dormice hibernate in winter; local species appear either to hibernate or, at least, become more sluggish during cold periods; this probably does not apply in more tropical parts of the region, although they may be less active during the dry season when food availability is limited.

Food: Seeds, other plant material, insects and other invertebrates. Few studies show insects as most important component in the diet. Nests of the **Woodland Dormouse** often cluttered with inedible insect fragments, such as beetle elytra.

Reproduction: Virtually nothing is known about this aspect of dormouse biology, but indications are that young are born during summer. **Spectacled Dormouse** has litters of 4–6 young every 6 months under optimum conditions. One **Rock Dormouse** from Zambia was recorded carrying 5 foetuses in February and with small young in November–December. **Woodland Dormouse** has litters of 2–4 pups, weighing about 3.5g, dropped after a 24-day gestation. Mammae: **Woodland** has 4 pairs.

Longevity: One captive **Woodland** lived 5 years 9 months.

SPRINGHARES Family Pedetidae

Pedetes capensis

Southern African Springhare *Pedetes capensis*

The East African Springhare population, now known to be a separate species, *P. surdaster*, differs from the South African species in relatively minor anatomical and cytogenic details; but, unlike its southern relative, it occupies communal burrow systems.

Total length 75–85cm; tail 35–45cm; mass 2.5–3.8kg.

Identification pointers: Kangaroo-like appearance; long, powerful hind legs; long, well-haired tail with black tip; ears and eyes fairly large. Nocturnal and found in habitats with sandy soils.

Description: A true rodent despite its name. Kangaroo-like, with long, powerfully built hind legs and short, lightly built forelegs. Hind feet have three large nails and forefeet have five long, pointed claws for digging. Progresses by hopping; forelegs used only while digging and feeding. Tail long, bushy and black towards tip. Ears long and pointed; eyes large. General colour of upperparts is yellowish or reddish-fawn and underparts are off-white to pale fawn.

Woodland Dormouse male

Note the orange staining on the throat of this Woodland Dormouse.

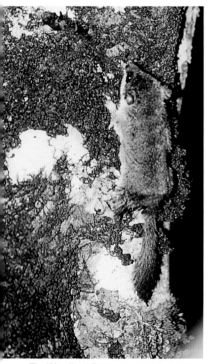

A young Small-eared Dormouse just out of the nest.

The Woodland Dormouse uses lichen to construct its nest.

The Southern African Springhare's long tail has a bushy black tip.

Southern African Springhare

38mm

left back

38mm

right back

Distribution: Widespread, although absent from Western Cape and Namibian coastal belt, as well as the extreme north-eastern parts of southern Africa. In recent decades there has been a westward spread of the Southern African Springhare on the Great Karoo plateau, presumably as a result of climate change, changing grazing patterns and an increase in densities of grass, which is their principal food. Absent from the Rift Valley of Central Africa but a closely related species occurs in East Africa.

Habitat: Compacted sandy soils with short vegetation cover, although often with seasonally long grass. It will colonize sandy areas along river-banks where these pass through unsuitable habitat.

Behaviour: Nocturnal, terrestrial and apparently not territorial. Although several burrows, housing several individuals, may be situated in close proximity, each burrow is occupied by a single animal or a female with young. Two types of hole are dug: a sloping one with a fan-shaped ramp of excavated sand around it, which is most frequently used, and a vertical escape-burrow, which has no fan of sand. Burrows may be blocked with sand if the Southern African Springhare is in occupation. In areas of prime habitat, Southern African Springhares can occur in large numbers and can become a problem in grazing and cultivated lands. In some areas they are heavily hunted as a food resource by man. Their eyes shine brightly in torchlight.

Food: Grass, grass roots and other plants. Cultivated crops.

Reproduction: After a gestation of about 79 days, a single young, weighing approximately 250–300g, may be born at any time of the year, but there are distinct seasonal peaks. Young is fully haired at birth and the eyes open fully within 2–3 days. Juvenile emerges from the burrow for the first time at 6–7 weeks after birth. Mammae: 1 pair pectoral.

Longevity: Up to 8 years in captivity.

RODENT MOLES (MOLE-RATS) Family Bathyergidae

■ *Bathyergus suillus*
■ *Bathyergus janetta*
■ *Heliophobius argenteocinereus*

At least 13 species of mole-rat occur in southern Africa, two of which are restricted to the extreme west of South Africa. Like many other groups, the mole-rats are in taxonomic flux, especially in the northern reaches of the region. Many species previously falling into the genus *Cryptomys,* based on genetics now divided in to 5 species are now placed in *Fukomys*, with several new species having been described in recent years. These include *Fukomys vandewoustijneae* from the Ikelenge pedicle in north-western Zambia; **Zambian Mole-rat** *(F. amatus)*; **Bocage's Mole-rat** *(F. bocagei)* from Angola and northern Namibia; **Ansell's Mole-rat** *(F. anselli)*; **Kafue Mole-rat** *(F. kafuensis)*; **Mechow's Mole-rat** *(F. mechowi)* from Angola and Zambia. Several of the new species have very localized ranges (consult maps). It is likely that several more species will be identified in the future. All are easily recognized as mole-rats.

Cape Dune Mole-rat *Bathyergus suillus*
Total length 32cm; tail 5cm; mass 650–890g (>2kg exceptional).

Namaqua Dune Mole-rat *Bathyergus janetta*
Total length 25cm; tail 4cm; mass 340–470g.

Common (African) Mole-rat *Cryptomys hottentotus*
Total length 15cm; tail 2cm; mass 100–150g.

Damara Mole-rat *Fukomys (Cryptomys) damarensis*
Total length 15cm; tail 2cm; mass 100–150g.

The Southern African Springhare has powerful hind legs and short forelegs.

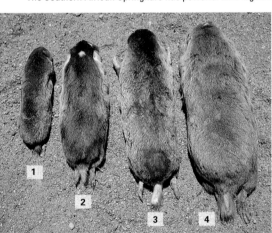

Mole-rat skins: 1. Common Mole-rat; 2. Cape Mole-rat; 3. Namaqua Dune Mole-rat; 4. Cape Dune Mole-rat

Mechow's Mole-rat is one of the largest species outside South Africa.

Silvery Mole-rat

Cape Dune Mole-rat

Damara Mole-rat

163

Mashona Mole-rat *Fukomys (Cryptomys) darlingi*
Mass 64g.

Cape Mole-rat *Georychus capensis*
Total length 20cm; tail 3cm; mass 180g.

Silvery Mole-rat *Heliophobius argenteocinereus*
Total length 11–24cm; tail 1.5–4cm; mass 160g.

■ *Cryptomys hottentotus*
□ *Fukomys damarensis*
■ *Fukomys darlingi*
■ *Fukomys anselli*
□ *Fukomys mechowi*

Identification pointers: Large size distinguishes **Cape Dune Mole-rat** and **Namaqua Dune Mole-rat**; small size and uniform colouring of **Common Mole-rat**; **Cape, Damara** and **Mashona Mole-rats** nearly always have white patch on top of head but **Cape** also has other black-and-white head markings and is larger, and can be separated on range. Consult the distribution maps.

Georychus capensis

Description: All have soft fur, short tails, large, rounded heads, well-developed and prominent incisors, and tiny eyes and ears. Legs are short and forefeet each carry four long claws for digging. Snouts are flattened and somewhat pig-like. **Cape Dune Mole-rat** the largest, with cinnamon to pale fawn upperparts, grey underparts and white chin and muzzle. **Namaqua Dune Mole-rat** differs from **Cape Dune Mole-rat** in having dull to silvery-grey fur with broad, darker band extending down back from base of neck to rump. There is usually a white ring around the eyes. Tail brown above and white below. **Common Mole-rat** variable but usually greyish-fawn to dark brown without any distinguishing markings. **Cape Mole-rat** is easily distinguished from the other species because of black-and-white markings on head; general body colour brown to reddish-brown with greyish underparts. The **Silvery Mole-rat** has a particularly soft and light-coloured coat. Some authorities do not accept the designation *Fukomys* to replace *Cryptomys*.

Distribution: See distribution maps. **Mashona Mole-rat** restricted to northern Zimbabwe and probably adjacent Mozambique. Similar to **Damara Mole-rat**.

Habitat: Sandy soils but **Common Mole-rat** also occupies a wide range of other soils with the exception of heavy clay; although this species frequently occurs in hilly and mountainous country where there is sufficient soil between the rocks.

Behaviour: Fossorial, digging extensive underground burrow systems marked on the surface by mounds of earth. Digging is undertaken by well-developed incisors, then the feet are used to shovel loosened earth out of the way. Most digging follows rain. Within burrow systems of most, if not all, species, there are usually chambers that serve for food storage. All mole-rats in the region are believed to live in small to large colonies. Some, such as the **Damara Mole-rat** and **Mashona Mole-rat**, have a complex social system that may be similar to that of the **Naked Mole-rat** of East Africa. A reproductive pair is dominant over the colony and these animals are larger than other group members. Colony size of the **Damara** may reach almost 40 individuals, with the breeding male being dominant over all other animals in the colony. The activity patterns do not seem to be tied to day or night but with active and resting periods spread through 24 hours, although the **Damara** is said to be mainly diurnal. Activity patterns may be influenced by season and temperature levels within the burrow systems. **Common Mole-rats** live in summer colonies with an average of five animals, but up to 17 individuals have been recorded. Both the **Cape** and **Namaqua Dune Mole-rats** are solitary burrow-dwellers, only coming together to mate.

The Cape Dune Mole-rat is the largest of the mole-rat species.

Namaqua Dune Mole-rat has dull to silvery-grey fur.

Common Mole-rat

Mashona Mole-rat has a large rounded head, well-developed incisors and tiny ears and eyes.

Cape Mole-rat has black-and-white markings on the head.

This Silvery Mole-rat has unusually dark pelage; most are much paler.

Cape Mole-rat

Silvery Mole-rat

Food: Vegetarian, eating mostly roots, bulbs and tubers. A nuisance in gardens and agricultural areas.

Reproduction: Damara Mole-rats are aseasonal breeders and the dominant female only produces 2 or 3 young per litter, weighing 8-9g, after a gestation period of 78-92 days. Cape Mole-rats have 4-10 pups per litter, weighing 5-12g, in summer. Namaqua Dune Mole-rats have a gestation said to be just 52 days but this could be an underestimate, with 2-7 pups born from August-November. Cape Dune Mole-rats have litters of 1-6 pups, each weighing on average 34g, after an estimated gestation of 60-65 days. Common Mole-rat has 2-6 pups, weighing about 9g, October-February, after a gestation of 55-66 days. Mammae: Namaqua Dune Mole-rat 1 pair pectoral, 2 pairs inguinal.

Longevity: Cape Mole-rat up to 3 years; one Common Mole-rat in captivity 9 years 7 months; one Silvery Mole-rat lived 3 years and 1 month in captivity.

PORCUPINE Family Hystricidae

Hystrix africaeaustralis

Cape Porcupine *Hystrix africaeaustralis*

Total length 75-100cm; tail 10-15cm; mass 10-24kg.

Identification pointers: Unmistakable with body-covering of long quills banded in black and white. Confusion sometimes arises between this species and the Southern African Hedgehog (p.48) but the latter is much smaller, is brown rather than black and white, and has very short spines.

Description: By far the largest rodent occurring in southern Africa; unmistakable with its protective covering of long quills banded in black and white. The sides, neck, head and underparts are covered in dark, coarse hair. A crest of long, erectile, coarse hairs extending from the top of the head, down the neck and onto the shoulders, is raised when the animal is alarmed or angry. The head and snout are broad, with small eyes and short, rounded ears. Legs are short and stout, with heavily clawed feet. Quills are easily detached and are frequently found lying on trails and pathways. The tail is short and carries a number of hollow, open-ended quills, which act as warning rattles when vibrated together.

Distribution: Occurs virtually throughout region, except Namib Desert.

Habitat: Wide range but preference for more broken country.

Behaviour: Solitary porcupines are most commonly seen but pairs and family parties will also be encountered. Porcupines form monogamous pairs and are territorial. This exclusive territory lies within a larger non-exclusive home range, within which other porcupines may move and forage. Home range sizes in one study ranged from about 140-200ha or more, but this varies according to habitat and food abundance. It is nocturnal and during the day it lies up in caves, among rocks, in burrows (either its own or those of other species) or even among dense vegetation. A common feature of well-used porcupine shelters is the accumulation of gnawed bones. It is generally believed that the Cape Porcupine gnaws these bones both for their mineral content and to sharpen the long incisors and prevent overgrowth. Within its home range, it makes use of regular pathways, along which are numerous shallow excavations exposing plant roots and bulbs. Although several related porcupines may share a shelter, foraging is usually a solitary activity.

Food: Roots, bulbs, tubers and the bark of trees, as well as cultivated crops such as potatoes and pumpkins. It has been recorded as eating from animal carcasses, and it is often caught in traps baited with meat set to catch carnivores.

The heavily quilled Cape Porcupine is the largest rodent in the region. **Inset:** This is the view a predator will have of an alarmed porcupine.

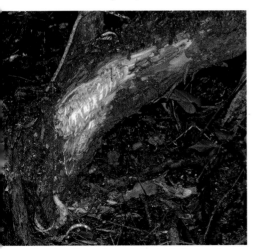

The Cape Porcupine eats the bark of several tree species.

The Cape Porcupine has a prominent crest on the head and neck.

Cape Porcupine

62mm

right
front

81mm

right
back

Reproduction: After a gestation of about 94 days, 1–4 (usually 1 or 2) young, weighing 100–300g (rarely to 450g), are born, usually in summer. They are well developed at birth and move around within a few hours but remain in the burrow until about their ninth week, when they have a full complement of hardened, protective quills and spines. Mammae: 2 pairs pectoral, pointing to the sides.
Longevity: 12–15 years in the wild; at least 20 years in some captives.

CANE-RATS Family Thryonomyidae

Two species of cane-rat occur in southern Africa.

Thryonomys swinderianus

Greater Cane-rat *Thryonomys swinderianus*
Total length 65–80cm; tail 15–20cm; mass 3–5kg.

Lesser Cane-rat *Thryonomys gregorianus*
Total length 40–60cm; tail 12–18cm; mass 1.5–2.5kg.

Identification pointers: Large size; dark brown speckled hair; short tail; stout appearance. **Lesser Cane-rat** has a very limited distribution in southern Africa (see 'Habitat' and maps).

Thryonomys gregorianus

Description: Large, coarse-haired, stockily built rodents with short tails. Two species differ only in size and in positioning of grooves on incisor teeth: grooves of **Greater Cane-rat** run close to inner edge of teeth; those of **Lesser Cane-rat** more evenly spaced over front surface of incisors. Upperparts and sides are generally dark speckled brown, underparts range from off-white to greyish-brown. The body hair falls out readily if an animal is handled. On the face, a fleshy pad, used in aggressive butting bouts, extends beyond the nostrils.
Distribution: Both widely distributed in Africa, but in the region mainly restricted to the east.
Habitat: Occurs in reed beds and dense vegetation near water; **Lesser Cane-rat** utilizes drier habitats.
Behaviour: Predominantly nocturnal although also crepuscular. Tend to forage alone, but live in loosely associated groups, with a male and two or more females and their young making up a family group. Distinct runs are formed within feeding areas and these are characterized by small piles of cut grass or reed segments along their length and small piles of distinctive, grooved droppings. Despite their bulky appearance, they can run rapidly and swim well. Hunted for their meat and regarded as a delicacy.
Food: Mostly roots, leaves, stems and shoots of grasses, reeds and sedges. **Greater Cane-rat** can be a problem in sugar-cane areas.
Reproduction: Greater Cane-rats give birth to 2–4 (up to 8) young, weighing 80–190g, August–December, after a gestation of about 154 days. The pups are born fully haired and with eyes open, and can soon follow the mother. Nothing is known about the reproduction of the **Lesser Cane-rat**. Mammae: **Greater** has 3 pairs pectoral/abdominal extending from sides of body.
Longevity: One captive lived 4 years 4 months.

The Greater Cane-rat is a coarse-haired, stockily built rodent.

Head of Greater Cane-rat, showing the brown and rust-speckled coat, as well as the distinctive nose-pad.

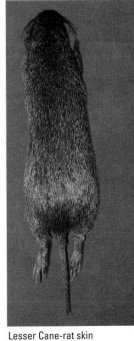

Lesser Cane-rat skin

Greater Cane-rat

40mm
right front

80mm
right back

Lesser Cane-rat

DASSIE RAT (NOKI) Family Petromuridae

These rodents are neither dassies nor rats, so their common name is unfortunate. Efforts should be made to rather use the local Khoikhoi name, Noki.

Petromus typicus

Dassie Rat *Petromus typicus*

Total length 25–30cm; tail 14cm (12–17cm); mass 100–250g.
Identification pointers: Squirrel-like appearance; tail very hairy but not bushy; general colour brown; rocky habitat; diurnal.

Description: Somewhat squirrel-like in appearance but although its tail is hairy, it is not bushy. Grizzled grey-brown to brown with hindquarters usually being more uniformly brown. Underparts vary from off-white to yellowish-brown. Head is somewhat flattened and ears are small and rounded.
Distribution: Largely restricted to the Namibian escarpment but the range extends southwards into the north-west of South Africa and northwards, marginally into Angola.
Habitat: Restricted to rocky areas, including isolated rock outcrops, even within the pro-Namib, where annual rainfall may be less than 100mm.
Behaviour: Pairs or family groups live in rock crevices, and occupied home ranges are defended against other Noki. The Noki is active by day although much of its activity is restricted to early morning and late afternoon; it will, however, move about in shade even during the hottest part of the day. It is frequently observed basking in the early-morning sun, much like its namesake, the dassie (hyrax). When feeding, it usually plucks a leaf or twig and takes it to shelter to feed. Like dassies, the Noki urinates at specific sites, which become stained yellowish-white. When handled, they readily and easily shed substantial tufts of hair. This may be a way to escape predators that do not take a firm grip.
Food: The Noki is vegetarian and eats a wide variety of plant food, with a preference for leaves and flowers; seeds and fruits to a lesser extent. At least in some parts of their range they favour grasses when these are available.
Reproduction: 1–3 fully-haired young, weighing on average 15g, born after a 90-day gestation. The well-developed young are dropped in rock crevices, mainly in summer but also at other times of year. Mammae: 3 pairs, 2 thoracic just behind shoulders, 1 pair abdominal, all projecting outwards along sides. Longevity: No records.

RATS & MICE Family Muridae

At least 99 species of rats and mice, all belonging to the Muridae, are recorded as occurring in southern Africa. Ongoing evolution of taxonomic research will certainly add to this impressive species total. The five species below are characterized by wholly or partially white tails; the first four have short tails.

Zelotomys woosnami

Woosnam's Desert Mouse *Zelotomys woosnami*

Total length 24cm; tail 11cm; mass 55g.
Identification pointers: Tail and upper surface of feet white; tail slightly shorter than head-and-body length. Range does not overlap with White-tailed Mouse, which is similar but has much shorter tail. See Pouched Mouse (p.174).

Description: Easily identifiable with its pale grey, black-flecked upperparts, paler sides and creamy-white underparts. Tail and top of feet are white.

The Dassie Rat's tail is hairy, but not bushy.

The Dassie Rat has a flat head, an adaptation that allows it to enter narrow rock crevices.

A Dassie Rat midden with dried urine and droppings

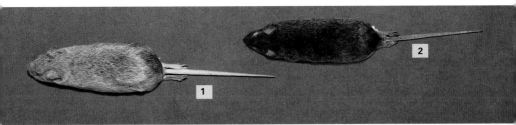

Two *Zelotomys* species occur in the region: 1. Woosnam's Desert Mouse, and 2. Hildegarde's Broad-headed Mouse.

Dassie Rat

Woosnam's Desert Mouse

171

Distribution: North-central and north-western areas; endemic to southern Africa.
Habitat: Arid areas with sandy soil and sparse vegetation.
Behaviour: Nocturnal and mainly solitary but small numbers may be found in close proximity. Makes own burrows or uses those dug by other species, especially those excavated by gerbils of the genus *Gerbilliscus*. Said to be mainly terrestrial but are adept climbers in bushes and low trees.
Food: Mainly seeds but also insects and possibly small vertebrates.
Reproduction: Litters of up to 11 young, usually less, are born in summer (November–April). Mammae: 3 pairs pectoral, 2 pairs inguinal.
Longevity: Not known.

---

*Zelotomys
hildegardeae*

Hildegarde's Broad-headed Mouse *Zelotomys hildegardeae*

Total length 18–23cm; tail 8–12cm; mass 40–80g.
Identification pointers: Tail shorter than head-and-body length; no distinguishing markings other than fairly light-coloured tail and rather broad, somewhat flattened muzzle.

Description: Overall dorsal coloration varies from greyish to grey-brown, or darker grey-brown and paler flanks with underparts usually lighter than upperparts. Tail generally lighter in colour than upperparts and shorter than head-and-body length. Muzzle somewhat flattened, hence this species' common name.
Distribution: In the region, found only in Angola, Zambia and Malawi.
Habitat: Wide range, including moist forests, savanna and lowland grassland, as well as seasonal floodplains, but often where there are tall grasses.
Behaviour: Probably similar to Woosnam's Desert Mouse but poorly known. Solitary. Said to emit loud whistles. Although mainly nocturnal, some crepuscular activity has been recorded. Occurs at low densities over much of its range.
Food: Believed to be mainly an insect predator but some seed also taken.
Reproduction: Possibly an aseasonal breeder in the region, but very few records; has litters of 3–7 pups. Mammae: 3 pairs pectoral, 2 pairs inguinal.
Longevity: Not known.

*Mystromys
albicaudatus*

White-tailed Mouse *Mystromys albicaudatus*

Total length 16–24cm (22cm); tail 6–7cm; mass 75–110g (130g maximum recorded).
Identification pointers: Grey-brown body and short white tail. See Woosnam's Desert Mouse (p.170), but latter has proportionately longer tail. Pouched Mouse has short tail but not pure white.

Description: Most characteristic feature is short, white tail. Upperparts grey to grey-brown flecked with black; underparts greyish-white. Upper surfaces of feet white.
Distribution: Swaziland, Lesotho, southern and eastern South Africa.
Habitat: Grassland and heath but also Karoo vegetation, as well as rocky terrain with good grass cover.
Behaviour: Nocturnal and lives in burrows and cracks in ground. Almost nothing known.

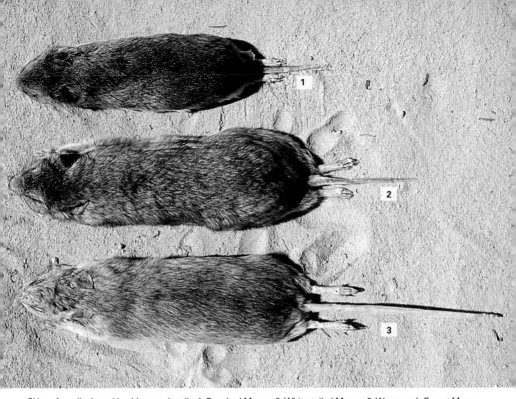

Skins of small mice with white or pale tails: 1. Pouched Mouse; 2. White-tailed Mouse; 3. Woosnam's Desert Mouse.

White-tailed Mouse has grey-white upperparts.

Hildegarde's Broad-headed Mouse

White-tailed Mouse

173

Food: Seeds, green plant material and insects.
Reproduction: Litter of 2–5 young, weighing about 6.5g, dropped after gestation period of 37 days. Young remain attached to nipples for up to 21 days. Breeds throughout the year, although in Lesotho pregnant females found only October–February. Mammae: 2 pairs inguinal; in litter of 5 young, they will take turns to feed.
Longevity: About 2.5 years.

Saccostomus campestris

Pouched Mouse *Saccostomus campestris*
Total length 15–26cm; tail 5cm; mass 45g.
Identification pointers: Dumpy appearance (similar to the domestic hamster); short tail; large cheek-pouches for food transport.

Description: Round, fat body, with soft, silky-grey or greyish-brown fur. Underparts and lower face white. Tail length is much less than head-and-body length. Variable in size and colour.
Distribution: Widespread in southern Africa, absent from true desert.
Habitat: Wide habitat tolerance but prefers soft, particularly sandy soils. Can be found in open or dense vegetation and in rocky areas. Occurs in areas with annual rainfall of 250->1,200mm.
Behaviour: It leads a generally solitary existence, although it may live in loose colonies. It digs its own burrows but also utilizes burrows excavated by other species. Where other shelter is not available, it will use termitaria, logs and rock piles. One of the principal characters of this species is its ability to carry large quantities of food in the cheek-pouches. The food is carried in these pouches to the shelter or burrow, where it can be eaten in relative safety from predators. Compared with most other rodents, it is slow-moving and quite easy to catch by hand. It is nocturnal and terrestrial.
Food: Chiefly seeds, small wild fruits; occasionally insects, depending on season.
Reproduction: 2–10 fully haired young, each weighing less than 3g, are born mainly in the wet summer months (October–April), after a gestation period of about 20 days. Females may transport young in the cheek-pouches. Mammae: 3 pairs pectoral, 2 pairs inguinal.
Longevity: <3 years in the wild; one captive just short of 4 years.

Cricetomys gambianus

Gambian Giant Pouched Rat *Cricetomys gambianus*
Southern African populations sometimes classified as Southern Giant Pouched Rat *(Cricetomys ansorgei)* but range limits and validity of this species designation still in question.
Total length 80cm; tail 42cm; mass 1–3kg.
Identification pointers: Large size; long, naked tail which is white towards tip; dark ring around eye and long, thin ears. The superficially similar House Rat is smaller and lacks white on the tail.

Description: Largest 'rat-like' rodent in region. Distinctive long, whip-like tail that is white for slightly less than half of its length towards the tip. Upperparts grey to grey-brown; underparts lighter. Hair around eyes is dark. Ears are large, thin and mobile.
Distribution: North-east and northern areas of region but isolated populations occur in, among others, the Soutpansberg and southern Zimbabwe. This large

Above: Pouched Mouse has a round, fat body.
Right: Foot of Gambian Giant Pouched Rat

The Gambian Giant Pouched Rat has a dark ring around the eye.

Pouched Mouse

Gambian Giant Pouched Rat

20mm
right
front

<50mm
right
back

175

rat genus has a very wide sub-Saharan range, occurring right across West Africa and large swathes of Central and East Africa, but absent from the equatorial forest belt. However, recent taxonomic thinking indicates that four species of giant rat should be recognized. A very similar species, Emin's Giant Pouched Rat *(Cricetomys emini)* occurs in far northern Angola. Records indicate that it does not occur in areas receiving less than 800mm of rain a year.

Habitat: Forest and woodland but occasionally urban areas.

Behaviour: Mainly nocturnal but if undisturbed can be diurnal. Digs own burrow but also makes use of holes, hollow trees and piles of plant debris. Surplus food is carried in cheek-pouches to store. When a burrow is occupied, it is usually closed from the inside. Placid and generally harmless. Because of this, they have been trained and used to detect landmines in countries such as Mozambique, as well as in laboratories to detect certain types of cancer and TB. They are mainly solitary, with each occupying its own burrow system, with chambers that serve as nest, food storage and defecation locations. Small heaps of dung pellets often concentrated in vicinity of burrow entrance. Home ranges recorded cover from about 2ha to more than 11ha, with size differences probably an indication of food availability.

Food: Fruits, roots and seeds (including cultivated crops); occasionally insectivorous.

Reproduction: 2–4 young, each weighing about 20–30g, are born in summer. The gestation period is about 28–36 days (some authors have noted that it may be as much as 42 days). Unusually for rodents, the young remain in the burrow for at least 40 days before beginning to forage, and leave the nest for good at about 80 days. Mammae: 2 pairs pectoral, 2 pairs inguinal.

Longevity: Probably up to 4 years in the wild; one captive 7 years 10 months.

POUCHED (HAMSTER) RATS Genus *Beamys*

Long-tailed Pouched Rat *Beamys hindei*
Total length 28–33cm; tail 10–15cm; mass to 150g.
Identification pointers: Grey to grey-brown pelage with white underparts; tail naked and white tipped; has cheek-pouches, but smaller than Gambian Giant Pouched Rat *(Cricetomys gambianus)* and tail longer than in Pouched Mouse *(Saccostomus campestris)*.

Beamys hindei

Description: Typical rat-like appearance; upperparts grey to greyish-brown; underparts white. Tail naked, generally pale and white-tipped. Has cheek-pouches, in which it carries food.

Distribution: Only in north-west Mozambique and patchily in eastern Zambia, extending into coastal East Africa.

Habitat: Various forest types and damp woodlands; soft and sandy soils near water.

Behaviour: Nocturnal and mainly terrestrial but said to be able to climb well. Excavates fairly extensive burrow systems with side passages that serve as nest, defecation and food storage locations. Seeds and fruits are harvested and carried back to the chambers in the cheek-pouches.

Food: Seeds and fruits.

Reproduction: Breeding may coincide with the rainy season in the region. Litters of 4–7 pups, each weighing just over 3g, born after a gestation period of about 23 days. Mammae: Not known.

Longevity: 2–3 years in the wild.

The Gambian Giant Pouched Rat has a long, partially white tail.

The Long-tailed Pouched Rat is restricted to a small area of Mozambique, Malawi and north-eastern Zambia. **Inset:** Examples of museum skins of Long-tailed Pouched Rats.

Long-tailed Pouched Rat

Steatomys pratensis

FAT MICE Genus *Steatomys*

Fat Mouse *Steatomys pratensis*

The slightly larger *S. bocagei* is sometimes considered to be a sub-species of *S. pratensis*, and occurs on the central plateau of Angola and extending across the north-east of that country. Female has an additional pair of mammae.

Total length 13cm; tail 5cm; mass 26g.

Tiny Fat Mouse *Steatomys parvus*

Total length 12cm; tail 4cm; mass 18g.

Krebs's Fat Mouse *Steatomys krebsii*

Total length 13cm; tail 5cm; mass 24g.

Identification pointers: Quite small size; dumpy appearance; short tail; white to off-white below; upper surface of feet white.

Steatomys parvus

Steatomys krebsii

Description: All four species of fat mice show considerable size and colour variation. The **Fat Mouse** itself is usually rusty-brown above and white below; its tail is darker above than below. The **Tiny Fat Mouse** is rufous-grey above with off-white underparts. In the Botswana part of its range, the tail is pure white but, in the separate KwaZulu-Natal population, it is brown above and white below. **Krebs's Fat Mouse** is ochre-yellow above and white below, with a similar colour division on its tail. The upper-surfaces of the feet in all four species are white, although the hind feet of **Krebs's Fat Mouse** are yellowish-buff.

Distribution: All four species have patchy distributions, with ranges that overlap in some areas. The only species occurring in south-western and southern South Africa is **Krebs's Fat Mouse**. The **Fat Mouse** occurs widely south of the Sahara but the other two species are more restricted in their distribution. The range of *Steatomys bocagei* (the species awaiting resolution) overlaps partly with that of **Krebs's Fat Mouse** on the Angolan Plateau in north Angola.

Habitat: Usually found over sandy substrates in a range of habitats, including wooded grassland and moist savanna. Sometimes in cultivated lands.

Behaviour: Nocturnal, terrestrial and apparently live singly or in pairs, in burrows that they dig themselves. An interesting character of the fat mice is their ability to lay down very thick fat deposits under the skin and around the body organs. This makes them a sought-after item in the diet of some African peoples. They are also able to reduce the body temperature and decrease food intake. This has obvious advantages during droughts and other times of food shortage. Unlike Pouched Mouse, the fat mice do not have cheek-pouches, but they do carry food to the burrow in the mouth.

Food: The fat mice are primarily seed-eaters but they have also been recorded as digging up and eating bulbs. Insects are also eaten occasionally.

Reproduction: Little known. The **Fat Mouse** apparently gives birth during summer (October–April). Although litters of 1–9 young have been recorded, litters of 3 or 4 are more usual, and birth weight is about 1.5g. Reproduction features are probably similar in all four species. Mammae: **Fat Mouse**, 8 pairs arranged along length of body; **Krebs's Fat Mouse** and **Tiny Fat Mouse**, 2 pairs pectoral, 2 pairs inguinal, up to 8 pairs.

Longevity: One **Fat Mouse** lived to 3 years in captivity.

In some parts of its range, the Fat Mouse population can reach large numbers when conditions are optimal.

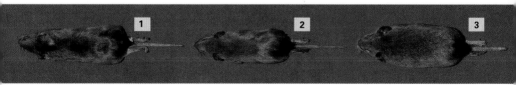

1. Krebs's Fat Mouse; 2. Tiny Fat Mouse; 3. Fat Mouse

Fat Mouse

Tiny Fat Mouse

Krebs's Fat Mouse

CLIMBING MICE Genus *Dendromus*

Dendromus nyikae

At least five species of climbing mice occur in the region; it is possible that at least three of these species constitute complexes of undescribed species, but they could almost certainly not be differentiated in the field. Vernay's Climbing Mouse *(D. vernayi)* is known only from one location in central Angola.

Nyika Climbing Mouse *Dendromus nyikae*
Total length 16cm; tail 9cm; mass 15g.

Dendromus melanotis

Grey Climbing Mouse *Dendromus melanotis*
Monard's Climbing Mouse *(D. leucostomus)* from Angola sometimes recognized as separate from *D. melanotis*.
Total length 15cm; tail 8cm; mass 4–15g (8g).

Brants's Climbing Mouse *Dendromus mesomelas*
Kivu Climbing Mouse *(D. nyasae)* from one locality in Zambia/Malawi border region sometimes recognized as separate from *D. mesomelas*.
Total length 17cm; tail 10cm; mass 9–14g.

■ *Dendromus mesomelas*
■ *Dendromus vernayi*

Chestnut Climbing Mouse *Dendromus mystacalis*
Total length 15cm; tail 8cm; mass 6–10g (8g).

Identification pointers: In all cases the tail is longer than the head-and-body length and a dark dorsal stripe is present.

Description: All species have a dark, diffused, dorsal stripe and a long, thin tail. Grey Climbing Mouse has ash-grey fur with browner tinge on head and shoulder region; others are reddish-brown to chestnut-coloured. Underparts are white to off-white.

Dendromus mystacalis

Distribution: See maps.
Habitat: Tall grass and rank vegetation; some species favour reed beds.
Behaviour: Nocturnal. Good climbers with semi-prehensile tails and toes adapted for clinging to grass-stalks. **Grey** and **Chestnut Climbing Mice** build small, ball-shaped nests of fine grass just above ground, and use burrows dug by other species. Although some species are quite abundant in suitable habitat, little is known, in part because they seldom enter traps.
Food: Seeds and insects.
Reproduction: Litters of 2–8 born in summer; more than 1 litter in a season is probable. Mammae: **Grey**, 2 pairs pectoral, 2 pairs inguinal.
Longevity: In the wild, <1.5 years; between 3 years 3 months and 4 years recorded for captive members of this genus.

Malacothrix typica

Large-eared (Gerbil) Mouse *Malacothrix typica*
Total length 11cm; tail 3.5cm; mass 15–20g.
Identification pointers: Dark patterning on back and head; large ears; very short tail. Should not be confused with any other species.

Description: Characterized by dark patterning on the back and head, and by large ears. Upperparts pale grey to reddish-brown; underparts grey or white.
Distribution: Drier central and western areas of the region, within the 150–500mm rainfall range.
Habitat: Short grass habitats over hard soils.

Grey Climbing Mouse has greyish hindquarters with a browner tinge on the head and shoulders.

Like all *Dendromus* species, Chestnut Climbing Mouse has a dark dorsal stripe.

Brants's Climbing Mouse in a typical habitat

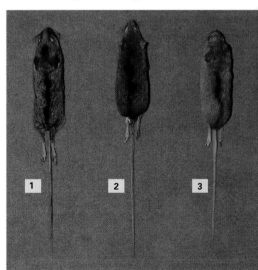

1. Grey Climbing Mouse; 2. Brants's Climbing Mouse; 3. Chestnut Climbing Mouse

Nyika Climbing Mouse; Grey Climbing Mouse; Brants's Climbing Mouse; Chestnut Climbing Mouse

Large-eared Mouse

Behaviour: Nocturnal, sheltering by day in deep, self-excavated burrows. Can be easily caught by hand in torchlight and will not attempt to bite but gives a loud buzzing (dzizz-dzizz) call when handled.
Food: Green plant material as well as seeds; occasionally eats insects, especially termites.
Reproduction: Litters of 2–8 (usually 4), weighing 1g each, born in summer (August–March) after a gestation of 23–27 days. Mammae: 4 pairs from pectoral to inguinal region.
Longevity: Captives up to 2.5 years.

Gerbils Subfamily Gerbillinae

Eleven species in three genera occur in southern Africa.

Desmodillus auricularis

Cape Short-tailed Gerbil *Desmodillus auricularis*
Total length 20cm; tail 9cm; mass 50g (40–70g).
Identification pointers: Tail shorter than head and body and relatively thick; diagnostic white patch at base of each ear. Soles of feet hairy.

Description: Dumpy appearance and only gerbil with tail shorter than head-and-body length. Upperparts vary from reddish-brown to grey-brown and underparts clean white, but species is easily distinguishable by prominent white patch at base of ear.
Distribution: Widespread in the drier south-western areas.
Habitat: Hard ground with grass or karroid bush. Not sandy soils as with other gerbils.
Behaviour: Nocturnal. It digs its own burrows and lives singly or in pairs. It digs two types of burrow, a normal sloping one with small fan of excavated soil at the entrance, and a vertical burrow with no debris, which is used as an escape or bolt-hole. Distinct pathways link the various burrow entrances.
Food: Seeds, mostly of grasses and of *Tribulus* species; some green plant parts. Also insects, especially termites.
Reproduction: Year-round litters consisting of 1–7 young (usually 4), weighing some 3.6g, born after a gestation of about 21 days. As with most rodents and many other mammals, birth weight is usually dependent on the number of young in a litter. Mammae: 2 pairs pectoral, 2 pairs inguinal.
Longevity: Up to 3 years in captivity.

Gerbillurus paeba

HAIRY-FOOTED GERBILS Genus *Gerbillurus*

Pygmy Hairy-footed Gerbil *Gerbillurus paeba*
Total length 20cm; tail 11cm; mass 25g.

Brush-tailed Hairy-footed Gerbil *Gerbillurus vallinus*
Total length 20cm; tail 12cm; mass 35g.

Dune Hairy-footed Gerbil *Gerbillurus tytonis*
Total length 22cm; tail 12cm; mass 27g.

Setzer's Hairy-footed Gerbil *Gerbillurus setzeri*
Total length 23cm; tail 12cm; mass 38g.

Large-eared or Gerbil Mouse has dark patterning on the head and back, large ears and a short tail.

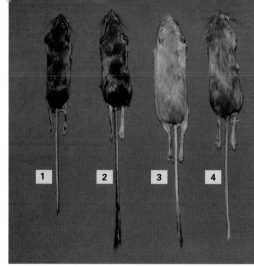

1. Pygmy Hairy-footed Gerbil; 2. Brush-tailed Hairy-footed Gerbil; 3. Setzer's Hairy-footed Gerbil; 4. Dune Hairy-footed Gerbil

Cape Short-tailed Gerbil

The upperparts of the Cape Short-tailed Gerbil vary in colour from reddish-brown to grey-brown.

Pygmy Hairy-footed Gerbil is reddish-brown.

Cape Short-tailed Gerbil

Brush-tailed Hairy-footed Gerbil

Setzer's Hairy-footed Gerbil

183

■ *Gerbillurus vallinus*
■ *Gerbillurus setzeri*

Gerbillurus tytonis

Identification pointers: Fairly small size; long tail – three species with tufts of longish hair at tip; large hind feet with hairy soles; **Setzer's** and **Dune** with white patches above eyes and at ear bases.

Description: Pygmy Hairy-footed Gerbil has small tuft of long hair at tail-tip; **Brush-tailed Hairy-footed Gerbil** has a prominent tassel. Colour variable but **Pygmy Hairy-footed Gerbil** commonly reddish-brown or greyish-red; **Brush-tailed Hairy-footed Gerbil** reddish-brown to dark grey-brown. Both have white underparts but **Brush-tailed Hairy-footed Gerbil** also has white forelegs. **Setzer's** and **Dune Hairy-Footed Gerbils** have white spot just above eye and behind ear. Both have tufts of longish hair at tip of tail. Soles of hind feet hairy, unlike naked soles of *Gerbilliscus (Tatera)* gerbils.
Distribution: See maps.

Habitat: Sandy soils in arid areas, although **Pygmy Hairy-footed Gerbil** extends into moister environment of southern coastal zone but always where sandy soils present.

Behaviour: All species probably nocturnal, excavate their own burrows. Burrow entrances are usually at least partially hidden among vegetation, but ramps of loose sand usually give them away. In the Namib Desert, and possibly elsewhere, gerbils will use spots where larger mammals have urinated to start excavating burrows, as the sand is compacted. Home range size varies greatly from <1ha to >4ha and is probably a measure of food abundance. **Brush-tailed Hairy-footed Gerbil** lives in colonies, **Pygmy Hairy-footed Gerbil** apparently in smaller groups. They frequently dust-bath and the resulting small depressions are a common feature where these gerbils are abundant.

Food: Omnivores mainly, taking seeds, green plant material and insects. All species hoard food, both in chambers within the burrow system and buried within the home range.

Reproduction: Pygmy Hairy-footed Gerbil has a litter of 2–5 young, dropped after a 21-day gestation; the young first leave the nest on their 19th day. Birth mass for all species 2–3g. **Pygmy Hairy-footed**, and probably others, may breed at any time of the year. Mammae: All 1 pair pectoral, 2 pairs inguinal.
Longevity: More than 2 years in captivity.

Gerbilliscus leucogaster

THE TATERA GROUP Genus *Gerbilliscus (Tatera)*

Bushveld Gerbil *Gerbilliscus (Tatera) leucogaster*
Total length 28cm; tail 15cm; mass 70g.

Cape Gerbil *Gerbilliscus (Tatera) afra*
Total length 30cm; tail 15cm; mass 100g.

Highveld Gerbil *Gerbilliscus (Tatera) brantsii*
Total length 28cm; tail 14cm; mass 80g.

Gorongoza Gerbil *Gerbilliscus (Tatera) inclusa*
Total length 32cm; tail 16cm; mass 120g.

Savanna Gerbil *Gerbilliscus validus*

Boehm's Gerbil *Gerbilliscus boehmi*
Both **Savanna** and **Boehm's Gerbils** fall within the range of measurements for the genus. Refer to maps for distribution.

Setzer's Hairy-footed Gerbil has large hind feet.

The Brush-tailed Hairy-footed Gerbil has a tuft of longish hair at the tip of the tail.

The Highveld Gerbil is greyish-brown underneath.

Bushveld Gerbil

Gorongoza Gerbil

185

Identification pointers: Fairly large size; tails about same length as head and body; well-developed hind legs and feet; ears greater length than width; eyes quite large. Soles of feet are naked (see *Gerbillurus* p.182).

Description: All have white underparts, but eastern form of **Highveld Gerbil** is greyish-white underneath. **Bushveld Gerbil** has distinct dark line along upper side of tail and tip is never white. Its upperparts are most commonly reddish-brown, bright and silky. Many **Highveld Gerbils** have white-tipped tails. **Cape Gerbil's** long, woolly hair is usually pale fawn and mottled with brown; has a grizzled appearance. Its tail is uniform in colour. **Gorongoza Gerbil** dark brown; tail dark brown above, white underneath; some have white tip to tail.

■ *Gerbilliscus afra*
■ *Gerbilliscus brantsii*
▨ *Gerbilliscus boehmi*

Distribution: See maps. **Cape Gerbil** is the only species occurring in the south-west of South Africa.

Habitat: All species are found on sandy soils with the two widespread species occurring in a wide variety of habitats. All favour areas of wooded and more open grassland, including areas of cultivation.

Behaviour: Nocturnal; dig own burrows and live in loosely knit colonies. In one study, **Highveld Gerbil** males occupied home ranges of <0.5ha and females <0.2ha. Colonies of all species may be extensive and have been measured as up to 70ha in the **Highveld Gerbil** and 10ha in the **Cape Gerbil**. Although burrow entrances are usually located under a bush or grass clump, this is not always the case. **Cape Gerbil** burrows are often in open, cleared areas with only low grass and herbaceous growth.

■ *Gerbilliscus inclusa*
■ *Gerbilliscus validus*

Food: Grass-seed but also other plant food. Partly insectivorous.

Reproduction: Litter sizes of the **Highveld Gerbil** vary from 1–5 (usually 3); the **Bushveld Gerbil** has 2–9 with an average of 5, weighing on average 2.8g, after a 28-day gestation. **Bushveld** and **Highveld Gerbils** breed throughout the year, although in some areas there are distinct summer peaks, but **Cape Gerbil** only after the wet winter months. **Cape Gerbil** has litters of 3–5 young, each weighing about 4g. **Highveld Gerbil's** gestation said to be 22 days. Mammae: **Cape** and **Bushveld Gerbils** have 2 pairs pectoral, 2 pairs abdominal/inguinal.

Longevity: Closely related *Tatera* spp. from Asia lived 7 years in captivity.

SPINY MICE Genus *Acomys*

Least Spiny Mouse *Acomys spinosissimus*
Total length 17cm; tail 8cm; mass 24g.

Cape Spiny Mouse *Acomys subspinosus*
Total length 17cm; tail 8cm; mass 22g.

■ *Acomys spinosissimus*
■ *Acomys subspinosus*

Identification pointers: Spiny hairs on back; white underparts.

Description: Unmistakable with their dorsal covering of erectile spiny hairs. Upperparts of **Least Spiny Mouse** are reddish-grey and those of **Cape Spiny Mouse** are dark grey-brown. Both species have white underparts. Populations of *Acomys spinosissimus* are now split to include *Acomys selousi* in south of range but exact range boundaries are not defined. It cannot be seperated in the field. Many specimens have partly missing tails, which may indicate a predator escape mechanism; they also easily shed their skin, which rapidly regrows.

Distribution: In the region, **Spiny Mouse** restricted to north-eastern parts. **Cape Spiny Mouse** only occurs in Western Cape. **Least Spiny Mouse** range extends into Tanzania.

Gerbil skins: 1. Cape Gerbil; 2. Highveld Gerbil; 3. Bushveld Gerbil; 4. Short-tailed Gerbil; 5. Brush-tailed Hairy-footed Gerbil; 6. Pygmy Hairy-footed Gerbil

Bushveld Gerbil has variably coloured upperparts, usually reddish-brown to yellow-brown.

Cape Gerbil has long, woolly hair.

Cape Gerbil burrow

Least Spiny Mouse has a covering of spiny hairs.

Cape Spiny Mouse has grey-brown upperparts.

Least Spiny Mouse

Cape Spiny Mouse

Habitat: Rocky habitats but also woodland and other associations in the case of the **Least Spiny Mouse**. **Cape Spiny Mouse** found only within mountainous and hill country in the Cape fynbos, or heathland, vegetation zone.

Behaviour: Nocturnal, but can be active in early morning and late afternoon in shadows cast by rocks. Live singly or in small groups. It is possible that they have complex social lives but this has not been studied in these two species.

Food: Seeds and green plant material; also insects, millipedes and snails. Although the **Cape Spiny Mouse** is said to feed exclusively on nutlets of *Restio* species, the authors have examined stomach contents that also contained the remains of insects and unidentified seeds. Captives readily took termites, small grasshoppers and green leaves.

Reproduction: **Least Spiny Mouse** litters of 2–5 (average 3) are born during summer (October–April). **Cape Spiny Mouse** gives birth from August–October but probably more extensive than limited records show; birth weights average just over 3g with young well developed at birth compared to similar-sized mice. Mammae: **Cape Spiny Mouse**, 2 or 3 pairs.

Longevity: Other *Acomys* spp. have lived 3–5 years in captivity.

■ *Micaelamys namaquensis*
■ *Aethomys kaiseri*

ROCK MICE   Genera *Aethomys* and *Micaelamys*

As many as nine species occur in southern Africa; the Selinda Rock Rat is known from very few specimens collected in eastern Zimbabwe. This species group is genetically complex and it is possible that additional species will 'emerge' over time. Although some species have been designated as *Micaelamys*, it is still not clear whether all should remain as *Aethomys*. The following four species occur north of the Cunene/Zambezi line: Kaiser's Rock Rat *(Aethomys kaiseri)* – Angola, Zambia, Malawi; Bocage's Rock Rat *(A. bocagei)* – Angola; Nyika Rock Rat *(A. nyikae)* – Malawi, Zambia; Thomas's Rock Rat *(A. thomasi)* – Angola. Refer to the distribution maps.

Namaqua Rock Mouse   *Micaelamys (Aethomys) namaquensis*
Total length 26cm; tail 15cm; mass 50g.

Grant's Rock Mouse   *Micaelamys (Aethomys) granti*
Total length 20cm; tail 10cm; mass 40g.

Red Veld Rat   *Aethomys chrysophilus*
Total length 28cm; tail 15cm; mass 75g.

Tete Veld Rat   *Aethomys ineptus*
Total length 29cm; tail 16cm; mass 75g.

Selinda Rock Rat   *Aethomys silindensis*
Total length 35cm; tail 18cm.

Identification pointers: Nondescript; typically rat-like; long, well-scaled tail; underparts lighter than upperparts. See distribution maps.

Description: Both Namaqua Rock Mouse and Red Veld Rat have a tail that is longer than the head-and-body length; Grant's Rock Mouse has a tail equal in length to that of the head and body. The tail of Red Veld Rat is shorter, thicker and more heavily scaled than that of Namaqua Rock Mouse. Coloration is very variable but in general Grant's Rock Mouse is dark grey-brown above and grey below with a

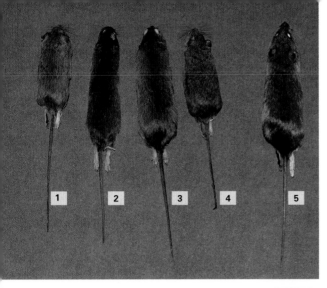

1. Namaqua Rock Mouse
2. Nyika Rock Rat
3. Kaiser's Rock Rat
4. Grant's Rock Mouse
5. Selinda Rock Rat

Namaqua Rock Mice pull sticks and other plant debris into the entrances of their rock crevice shelters.

A Namaqua Rock Mouse female with nipple-clinging young

Namaqua Rock Mouse (yellow-fawn form)

Namaqua Rock Mouse (reddish-brown form)

Grant's Rock Mouse

Red Veld Rat

189

■ *Micaelamys granti*
■ *Aethomys ineptus*
■ *Aethomys silindensis*
■ *Aethomys nyikae*
■ *Aethomys thomasi*

■ *Aethomys chrysophilus*
■ *Aethomys bocagei*

dark tail. **Namaqua Rock Mouse** has reddish-brown to yellowish-fawn upperparts, often pencilled with black, and the underparts are white to greyish-white. As its name implies, **Red Veld Rat** is usually reddish-brown, but is also pencilled with black; the underparts are grey-white. **Tete Veld Rat** is very similar to **Red Veld Rat** but is overall paler, with brighter underparts.

Distribution: **Grant's Rock Mouse** is restricted to the central Karoo of the Northern Cape province and may be found together with **Namaqua Rock Mouse**. The latter is widely distributed in southern Africa mainly below the Cunene/Zambezi line. **Red Veld Rat** is also widespread, as is **Tete Veld Rat** *(A. ineptus)* (see map) in north-east South Africa, but is absent from southern and western areas of that country.

Habitat: **Namaqua** and **Grant's Rock Mice** largely restricted to rocky habitats. **Red Veld Rats** are found in a wide range of habitats, from grassland to savanna woodland and including rocky outcrops.

Behaviour: Nothing is known about the behaviour of **Grant's Rock Mouse**. The other species are nocturnal. **Namaqua Rock Mouse** lives in small colonies and a character of its communal shelters are the large accumulations of dry grass and other plant material dragged into the entrances of rock crevices, probably a deterrent to predators such as snakes. It is also known to dig burrows at the base of bushes. **Red Veld Rat** appears to be more solitary or to live in pairs. Home range sizes of all species vary greatly and are largely dictated by food availability.

Food: All species eat grass- and other seeds, with some insects being eaten.

Reproduction: **Red Veld Rat** breeds throughout the year; **Namaqua Rock Mouse** gives birth in warmer months. Both species usually have 3–5 young per litter, with those of **Red Veld Rat** weighing slightly more than 4g and Namaqua 2.5g. **Tete Veld Rat** has a maximum of 3 young in a litter. Young of both species nipple-cling until about 16–21 days. All species commonly have more than one litter per year. Mammae: **Red Veld Rat** and **Namaqua Rock Mouse** 1 pair pectoral, 2 pairs inguinal.

Longevity: In the wild, <2 years.

Arvicanthis niloticus

African Grass (Kusu) Rat *Arvicanthis niloticus*

Total length 24–36cm; tail 9–16cm; mass 50–180g.

Identification pointers: Overall appearance similar to the *Otomys* species; tail shorter than head-and-body length and darker above than below; stocky build and blunt snout; ears reddish-russet; wide range of habitats from wet grasslands to dry thickets. It should be noted that some authorities believe this species in Zambia is *A. abyssinicus*.

Description: Rather stocky build, with round head and blunt snout, and a tail less than half the total length. Coat is rather coarse and stiff; grizzled yellowish-dark brown overall; there may be a darker band running down the back from head to tail base, but not as distinct as a stripe. Underparts off-white to pale grey. Ears and eye-rings orange. Tail darker above, lighter below.

Distribution: In the region, the only known populations are centred on the Kafue and Bangweulu floodplains in Zambia.

Habitat: In Zambia, occur on grassed seasonal floodplains and fringes of miombo woodland.

Behaviour: Apparently live in colonies, constructing their own burrows, or among vegetation tangles, with multi-male and -female groups defending territories against intruders. Home ranges are larger in the wet season than in the dry.

The Tete Veld Rat (**above**) is paler than the Red Veld Rat (**inset**), with a clean white belly.

Grant's Rock Mouse is dark grey above and lighter below.

Red Veld Rat is reddish-brown above with grey-white underparts.

African Grass (Kusu) Rat

Populations may increase dramatically when conditions are ideal. Said to be both nocturnal and diurnal but at least in areas known to the authors, daylight activity is most common.

Food: Seeds and green plant material, including grasses. They can become a nuisance in cultivated areas.

Reproduction: Drops 5 or 6 (up to 11) pups after a 22-day gestation, with several litters per season. In Zambia, breeding may be seasonal but this is not certain. Mammae: 3 pairs.

Longevity: In the wild, 2.5–3 years; up to 6 years, or more, in captivity but most captives die in their second year.

Dasymys incomtus

African Marsh Rat *Dasymys incomtus*

Recent revision of the species indicates that as many as eight genetically distinct species may occur in the region, for example, Cape Marsh Rat *(D. capensis)* in the south-west; Roberts's Marsh Rat *(D. robertsi)* in eastern South Africa and adjacent Zimbabwe; Shortridge's Marsh Rat *(D. shortridgei)* and West African Marsh Rat *(D. rufulus)*; Angolan Marsh Rat *(D. nudipes)* in a broad swathe mainly north of the Cunene/Zambezi line; Crawford Cabral's Shaggy Rat *(D. cabrali)* in a very limited area of Angola. This could explain the disjunct nature of its range. All very similar in appearance and impossible to separate in the field except by comparing distributional ranges, which are often widely separated, and genetic structures.

Total length 30–35cm; tail 14–18cm; mass 100–220g.

Identification pointers: Similar to vlei rats (p.216) but longer tail; dark, long, shaggy fur and white claw bases, which contrast with the dark feet. Flat, disc-like face with small eyes. Incisors not grooved.

Description: Similar in appearance to vlei rats but has longer tail. Hair is relatively long and shaggy and dark grey-black colour with brown flecks. Underparts are paler. Ears are large and rounded and the usually dark feet contrast with the white bases of the claws.

Distribution: African Marsh Rat occurs along the southern coastal belt and in the east, then extensively north of the Cunene/Zambezi line.

Habitat: Well-vegetated and wet habitats.

Behaviour: Like vlei rats, African Marsh Rat uses distinct runways and in fact probably shares them with those species. It swims well and takes readily to water. Mostly diurnal, but crepuscular and nocturnal to some extent. They dig relatively shallow burrows with a series of surface trails leading to feeding-grounds. Alongside the trails are small heaps of droppings, as well as piles of cut grass and reeds accumulated while feeding. Good swimmers.

Food: A variety of reeds, grasses and other plants but also insects.

Reproduction: After a gestation period of about 29 days, 5 young are born; although 3 is the norm in some areas and as many as 9 have been recorded. Young are born in the summer months, although in some areas the breeding season may be more extensive. Several litters may be dropped in a season. Mammae: 1 pair pectoral, 2 pairs inguinal.

Longevity: No records.

African Grass (Kusu) Rat is known from only two areas of Zambia within the region.

African Marsh Rat is also called Shaggy Rat.

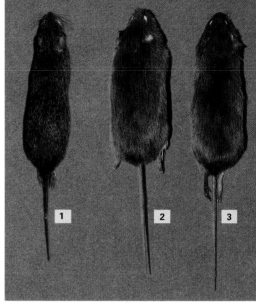
1. African Grass (Kusu) Rat; 2. & 3. African Marsh Rat

The Cape Marsh Rat is possibly a species in its own right and distinct from the African Marsh Rat.

African Marsh Rat

Rhabdomys pumilio
& R. dilectus

Four-striped Grass Mouse *Rhabdomys pumilio*
Mesic Four-striped Grass Mouse *Rhabdomys dilectus*

This widespread mouse may consist of a complex of perhaps four, as yet undescribed species but all would be easily recognizable as belonging to this group and separation would depend largely on genetic analyses. Contrasts between the two currently recognized species are given below but measurements are similar.

Total length 18–26cm; tail 8–13cm; mass 30–85g.

Identification pointers: Four dark stripes down the back. Cannot be confused with any other species in the region. The **Mesic** species usually darker reddish-brown along the back, sides lighter and legs dark grizzled.

Description: These mice are easily distinguished from all other species as they have four distinct longitudinal stripes running down the back. General colour is variable and ranges from dark russet-brown to almost grey-white. Similarly, the underparts vary from off-white to pale grey-brown. The backs of the ears (and often the snout) are russet to yellowish-brown. There are considerable variations in size from different regions.

Distribution: Four-striped Grass Mouse occurs widely in the region but only patchily in Zambia, Zimbabwe, Mozambique and Botswana. The **Mesic** species occupies areas of higher rainfall, whereas **Four-striped Grass Mouse** occupies a wider range of habitats but especially more arid areas. Range limits have not been fully established for these species and it is possible that in some areas they may occur together.

Habitat: Wide-ranging, from desert fringe to high-rainfall montane areas. The only consistent requirement is the presence of grass. From sea-level to 2,700m.

Behaviour: Principally diurnal and crepuscular but also often active at night. Dig own burrows with the entrances well hidden by vegetation, from which radiate numerous runways. Within the range of Bush Karoo Rat they dig burrows under the considerable stick nests constructed by that species. Often around houses and farmsteads. The **Mesic** species is apparently solitary, whereas **Four-striped Grass Mouse** is social over much of its range; but evidence from some areas indicates they may also be solitary on occasion.

Food: Mainly seeds, but also other plant parts; insects.

Reproduction: Litters of 2–9 (usually 5 or 6) young, weighing about 2.5g, born after a gestation period of about 22–25 days, usually in summer (September–April). However, breeding recorded in all months throughout its range and several litters dropped in a season. Mammae: 2 pairs pectoral, 2 pairs inguinal.

Longevity: Mean in the wild just 45 days; captives up to 2 years 11 months.

Lemniscomys
rosalia

Single-striped Grass Mouse *Lemniscomys rosalia*

Total length 20–30cm (27cm); tail 12–15cm; mass 60g.

Identification pointers: Single dark stripe runs down centre of back; the climbing mice also have single dark dorsal stripes but they are much smaller than this species.

Description: The upperparts vary in colour from pale grey-brown to orange-brown and a single dark brown or black stripe runs down the middle of the back. The underparts are white, often russet-tinged. Muzzle and backs of ears usually russet-orange.

Four-striped Grass Mouse is diurnal and is commonly seen, often in association with human habitation.
Inset: The Four-striped Grass Mouse has reddish-brown ears.

Striped Grass Mouse skins:
1. Single-striped Grass Mouse;
2. Four-striped Grass Mouse

The Mesic Four-striped Grass Mouse

Four-striped Grass Mouse

Single-striped
Grass Mouse

195

Distribution: Has a wide range in the east of the region, extending westwards to southern Angola and northern Namibia.

Habitat: Grass cover is essential but in associations varying from dry scrub to savanna woodland or even around agricultural land.

Behaviour: A diurnal species that excavates its own burrows. Runways lead out from the burrows to the feeding-grounds but usually under dense grass cover so not always visible. Burrows occupied by solitary individuals, pairs or family groups.

Food: Grass- and other seeds, green plant material, some insects.

Reproduction: Litters of 2–11 (average 5) pups, weighing about 2.6g, born September–March. Mammae: 2 pairs pectoral, 2 pairs inguinal.

Longevity: In the wild usually less than 1 year; captives average 2 years, one reached exceptional 5 years.

■ *Lemniscomys griselda*
■ *Lemniscomys roseveari*

Three other species of grass mouse *(Lemniscomys)* occur within the region: **Typical Striped Grass Mouse** *(L. striatus)* in northern Angola and north-eastern Zambia; **Griselda's Striped Grass Mouse** *(L. griselda)* in central to north-eastern Angola and north-western Zambia; **Rosevear's Striped Grass Mouse** *(L. roseveari)* known from only two localities in western Zambia. All characterized by numerous white or buff lines of dots (sometimes joined) running from behind head to tail base on back and sides. Overall body colour ranges from light to dark brown; tail darker above than below. Underparts off-white to grey-brown. Ears and snout often russet coloured. Although they occupy a wide range of habitats, the presence of grass seems to be the common denominator.

Hybomys univittatus

Peters' Striped Mouse *Hybomys univittatus*

Total length 17–28cm; tail 8–13cm; mass 30–70g.

Identification pointers: Similar to *Arvicanthis* species but more slender appearance and near-naked tail; dark to black dorsal stripe usually present. In region, occurs only in far north-western Zambia and adjacent area of Angola.

Description: Typical rat-like appearance, usually with a soft coat that is brown to almost black, with a narrow, darker dorsal strip running from nape to tail base. Underparts paler and range from yellowish to off-white. Thinly haired tail dark to black.

Distribution: In region, only far north-western Zambia and adjacent area of Angola.

Habitat: Forest, dense thickets and often associated with cultivated fringes but nearly always in close association with rivers, swamps and other wetland types.

Behaviour: Diurnal, spending nights in burrow systems. Home ranges of males do not overlap and intruders are fought and driven off, although a male range will overlap those of one or more females. Activity apparently a solitary affair.

Food: Said to be mainly a fruit eater but also take insects.

Reproduction: Possibly breeds throughout the year but this may depend on food abundance. After a gestation period of 29–31 days, litters of 1–4 (usually 3) pups are dropped. Mammae: Not recorded.

Longevity: Probably <2 years in the wild; to 4 years in captivity.

The Single-striped Grass Mouse is characterized by a dark to black line running from the nape to the base of the tail.

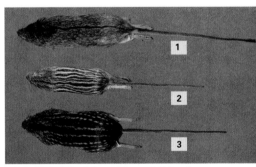

1. Griselda's Striped Grass Mouse; 2. Zebra Grass Mouse; 3. Typical Striped Grass Mouse

The Zebra Grass Mouse is not yet recorded from the region but may occur in Zambia adjacent to Tanzania.

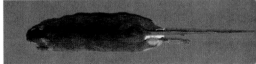

Peters' Striped Mouse has a narrow, dark dorsal stripe.

Peters' Striped Mouse

African Water Rat *Colomys goslingi*

Total length 26–32cm; tail 14–18cm; mass 50–80g.
Identification pointers: Fur soft and velvet-like; upperparts cinnamon- to darker brown, with contrasting bright white underparts; tail sparsely haired; always near fresh water.

Colomys goslingi

Description: Fur is soft; cinnamon to darker brown upperparts with contrasting bright white underparts extending from under chin to tail base. Hair on back usually darker towards rump than rest of dorsum. There is usually a pale to white spot at the base of the ear. Tail clearly scaled and nearly hairless. Ears quite long, rounded and naked.
Distribution: Wide tropical range but in the region known only from north-western Zambia and north-eastern Angola.
Habitat: Moist lowland and montane forest, wooded floodplains and savanna mosaic. Usually associated with small, shallow, flowing streams and pools in forest.
Behaviour: Nocturnal and apparently solitary. They excavate shallow burrows in soil banks. Expert swimmers and catch much of their prey while wading in shallow water.
Food: A range of aquatic invertebrates (no doubt some taken on land) and some small vertebrates; small quantity of plant food.
Reproduction: Possibly seasonal breeders but nothing known from the region. Litter numbers 1–3 pups but nothing else known. Mammae: 4 pairs.
Longevity: Not known.

Big-eared Swamp Rat *Malacomys longipes*

Total length 23–40cm; tail 12–22cm; mass 50–140g.
Identification pointers: Slender appearance; long, slender, hairless tail; very soft coat, brown above, contrasting white below; large, naked, rounded ears.

Malacomys longipes

Description: A slender, medium-sized rat with a long, thin tail, large rounded ears. Very soft fur that is coloured brown above with some grey grizzling contrasting with the clean white to pale grey underparts. Reddish-yellow fur to greater or lesser extent along sides.
Distribution: Wide range in the tropics but only extreme north-eastern Angola and north-western Zambia in the region.
Habitat: Moist lowland forests and closely associated with stream edges and muddy pools.
Behaviour: Mainly nocturnal but little is known about them, although they are believed to be solitary and to construct nests among tree roots and crevices.
Food: A mix of invertebrate (including crabs) and plant food.
Reproduction: Nothing known of season, but in Zambia pregnant females observed in August. Litters of 1–5 pups but usually 3. May have several litters each year. Mammae: 3 pairs.
Longevity: Not known.

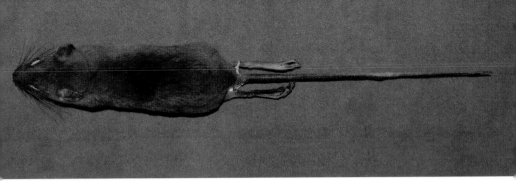

Skin of African Water Rat with typical cinnamon-coloured coat

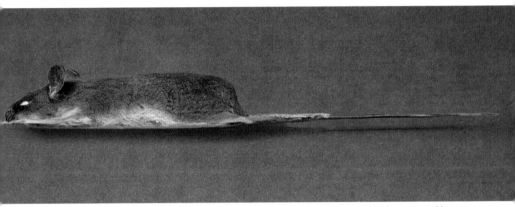

Side view of Big-eared Swamp Rat skin; note the contrasting colours of upper- and underparts, and large, naked ears

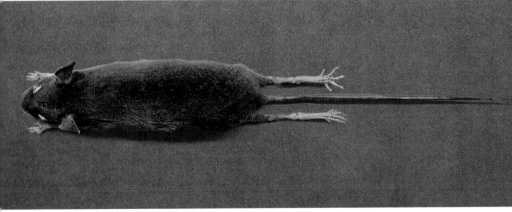

The Big-eared Swamp Rat has relatively long hind feet.

African Water Rat

Big-eared
Swamp Rat

Mus setzeri
Mus triton
Mus orangiae

Mus indutus
Mus minutoides

Mus neavei
■ confirmed range
■ presumed range

PYGMY MICE Genus *Mus (Nannomys)*

At least six species of pygmy mice are recorded as occurring in southern Africa. The taxonomy of these minute mice is unresolved – some taxonomists believe more species are involved, some believe far fewer. Even within a single species there are regional differences in their genetic make-up. Although the distribution maps will aid in narrowing down the choices, they must only be seen as a guide.

Setzer's Pygmy Mouse *Mus (Nannomys) setzeri*
Total length 9cm; tail 4cm; mass 7g.

Grey-bellied Pygmy Mouse *Mus (Nannomys) triton*
Total length 10cm; tail 4.5cm; mass 10g.

Desert Pygmy Mouse *Mus (Nannomys) indutus*
Total length 10cm; tail 4cm; mass 6g.

Pygmy Mouse *Mus (Nannomys) minutoides*
Total length 10cm; tail 4cm; mass 6g.

Neave's Pygmy Mouse *Mus (Nannomys) neavei*
Total length 10cm; tail 4cm.

Free State Pygmy Mouse *Mus (Nannomys) orangiae*
Total length 10cm; tail 3.8cm.

Identification pointers: Very small; tail shorter than head-and-body length; only **Grey-bellied** does not have white underparts; **Desert Pygmy Mouse** has patch of white hair at base of each ear. Pygmy mice can be distinguished from the climbing mice (*Dendromus* spp.), see p.180, by their much shorter tails and lack of dark dorsal stripe.

Description: Small, with tails shorter than length of head and body. All but **Grey-bellied Pygmy Mouse** have white underparts. Upperparts range from greyish-brown to reddish-brown even within the same species. Tail of **Desert Pygmy Mouse** is white below while in **Pygmy Mouse** it is pale brown; the former also has a small patch of white hair at the base of the ear.
Distribution: See maps. **Pygmy Mouse** most widespread. **Desert Pygmy Mouse** is found in Botswana and north-eastern Namibia, and in the north shares habitat with **Setzer's Pygmy Mouse**. **Free State Pygmy Mouse** known only from a limited area of Free State (Viljoensdrift) and adjacent Lesotho.
Habitat: **Pygmy Mouse** from Cape fynbos to savanna grassland and woodland. **Desert Pygmy Mouse** in arid scrub savanna but also Okavango. **Setzer's** occupies areas within the 400–1,000mm annual rainfall range. **Neave's** has been collected in rocky terrain with sandy soils. **Grey-bellied** has been found in relatively high-rainfall areas in damp grassland and on swamp fringes.
Behaviour: Nocturnal and at least some species partly diurnal; terrestrial, and usually occur solitarily, in pairs or in family parties. Although they will dig their own burrows in soft soils, they usually make use of burrows dug by other species, or shelter under dead vegetation, rocks and the debris of human occupation. **Pygmy Mouse** and **Desert Pygmy Mouse** are subject to population explosions in the more arid parts of their range following good rains and food abundance.
Food: Seeds, but these mice also feed on green plant food and insects, especially termites.
Reproduction: **Pygmy Mouse** has a gestation period of 19 days and births take

Note: Callewaert's Pygmy Mouse *(Mus callewaerti)* known from a few locations in Angola, is similar to Grey-bellied Pygmy Mouse, but information on genetic makeup unknown and it may not be a distinct species.

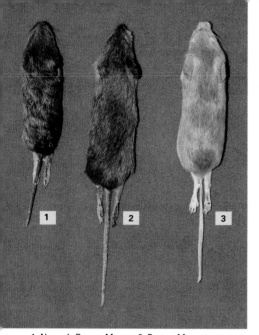

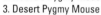

1. Neave's Pygmy Mouse; 2. Pygmy Mouse;
3. Desert Pygmy Mouse

Desert Pygmy Mouse has white underparts.

Neave's Pygmy Mouse

The tiny Pygmy Mouse has a tail that is shorter than its body length.

Grey-bellied
Pygmy Mouse

Pygmy Mouse

201

place in summer; a typical litter consists of 4 young (1–7), each weighing less than a gram at birth. **Desert Pygmy Mouse** probably has young throughout the year with peaks in summer. Five young is the usual litter size. Both male and female, in at least two species, care for and defend the young in the nest. **Mammae: Pygmy Mouse** has 2 pairs pectoral, 1 pair abdominal, 2 pairs inguinal. **Longevity:** One captive >3 years, much less in the wild. Several captives kept by the authors from birth to death ranged from 6 months to just over 2 years.

Mus musculus

House Mouse *Mus musculus* (Introduced)
Total length 16cm; tail 9cm; mass 18g.
Identification pointers: Nondescript; associated with human dwellings. Larger than the pygmy mice and has light-brown to greyish-brown, not white, underparts. Could be confused with *Mastomys* group (p.208), but smaller and lighter.

Description: The upperparts are grey-brown with the underparts being slightly lighter in colour. The tail is lighter brown below than above. No distinctive markings.
Distribution: This introduced species with worldwide distribution is strongly tied to human settlement and therefore has a patchy but wide distribution. It is widely distributed in South Africa but is also known to occur in most, probably all, other southern African countries.
Habitat: Human settlements, including isolated farmsteads.
Behaviour: Nocturnal and lives in pairs or family parties. Untidy nests are constructed from a wide range of man-made and natural materials. Can reach high densities when conditions are optimal.
Food: Omnivorous. It can be extremely destructive in food stores.
Reproduction: Breeds throughout year, giving birth to 1–13 (usually 5 or 6) young per litter; gestation about 19 days; first litters at the age of 6 weeks.
Mammae: Apparently variable; 4 or 5 pairs, 3 pairs pectoral, 2 pairs inguinal.
Longevity: Wild 12–18 months; captives average 2 years but up to 4 and 6 years recorded.

■ *Thallomys paedulcus*

■ *Thallomys shortridgei*

Acacia Rat *Thallomys paedulcus*
Black-tailed Tree Rat *Thallomys nigricauda*
These two rats are very similar in appearance and occur over much of the same range, but have been shown to be genetically distinct.
Total length 30cm; tail 17cm; mass 100g.
Identification pointers: Arboreal habits; tail longer than head-and-body length; dark ring around eye and extending onto muzzle; prominent ears.

Description: Both species characterized by having a tail longer than the head-and-body length, prominent ears and a dark ring around the eyes. Upperparts usually pale grey tinged with fawnish-yellow; underparts white; tail usually dark.
Distribution: Widely distributed in northern parts of the region, largely absent in Lesotho and areas south of Orange River. Both species apparently occur in the same areas in some parts of their range, particularly Botswana, but the **Black-tailed** is the only species in the arid west. A third species, *T. shortridgei*, occurring to the south of the Orange River, is recognized by some but cannot be specifically identified in the field and overlaps with the **Black-tailed**.

The House Mouse is common and widespread.

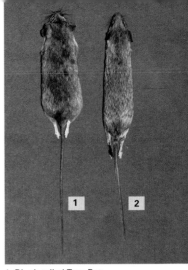

1. Black-tailed Tree Rat;
2. Acacia Rat

The Black-tailed Tree Rat has a tail that is longer than the head and body, and a dark ring around the eyes.
Inset: The Acacia Rat is arboreal and nocturnal.

House Mouse

Acacia Rat
Black-tailed Tree Rat

203

Thallomys nigricauda

Habitat: Savanna woodland – particularly areas dominated by acacias.
Behaviour: Nocturnal and arboreal. Lives in holes in trees but may also make use of large birds' nests to which it adds finer plant material. They will also construct their own untidy domed twig-nests in the fork of a tree, usually no more than a few metres above the ground. Nests may be occupied by a family group or several adults.
Food: Green leaves, especially those of *Vachellia* and *Senegalia* (formerly *Acacia*) tree species, fresh seeds and seed-pods but also insects. Although some food may be eaten where harvested, much is carried back to the nest.
Reproduction: Litters of 2–5 young (each weighing between 2.5 and 2.8g) are dropped mainly during the summer (August–April). Mammae: 2-3 pairs.
Longevity: One captive up to 3 years 6 months.

Grammomys dolichurus

■ *Grammomys cometes*
■ *Grammomys ibeanus*

Woodland Thicket Rat *Grammomys dolichurus*
Total length 27cm; tail 17cm; mass 30g.

Mozambique Woodland Thicket Rat *Grammomys cometes*
Total length 30cm; tail 18cm.

Identification pointers: Long, thin tail; white underparts clearly separated from grey-brown or reddish-brown upperparts. Forest and woodland habitat. A third species, **Macmillan's Thicket Rat** *(G. macmillani)*, is believed to occur in eastern Zimbabwe and adjacent Mozambique, although it is possible that this may be a case of mistaken identity. Ruwenzori Thicket Rat *(G. ibeanus)* is known from Malawi and adjacent area of Zambia. Shining Thicket Rat *(G. kuru)* is known from two locations in far northern Angola. This is another group of small rodents that need extensive taxonomic revision as several more species may well be involved.

Description: The thicket rats have long tails well over half their total length. Colour of the upperparts may be reddish-brown with a grey tinge or much more grey-brown; underparts white. Ears are large and prominent. Mozambique Woodland Thicket Rat sometimes has white patch at base of ear.
Distribution: Both found in woodland habitats along eastern coastal plain, extending inland to the eastern Zimbabwe highlands, with Woodland Thicket Rat having a wide range through Zambia and Angola.
Habitat: Forest and dense woodland; Woodland Thicket Rat sometimes found in more open woodland.
Behaviour: Nocturnal and arboreal. The Woodland Thicket Rat constructs nests of grass and other fine plant material in vegetation tangles up to 2m from the ground. It will also make use of holes in trees and even weaver-bird nests.
Food: Green plant material, wild fruits and seeds, and some insects.
Reproduction: Woodland Thicket Rat has 2–5 pups, weighing about 4g, after a gestation of about 24 days. Young are born throughout the year, with a possible peak in summer but this is less clearly defined as one moves northwards. Mozambique Thicket Rat has litters of 2–5 (average 3) pups, weighing >4g, after a gestation of 24 days. Young are also born throughout the year, with a peak in summer. Pups may cling to the female's nipples for up to 26 days. Mammae: No records.
Longevity: Woodland Thicket Rat has lived for >4 years 5 months in captivity.

Black-tailed Tree Rats inhabit acacia woodland.

1. Woodland Thicket Rat; 2. Ruwenzori Thicket Rat;
3. Macmillan's Thicket Rat

Woodland Thicket Rat eats green plant material,
fruits and seeds.

The Woodland Thicket Rat (also called Woodland Mouse) inhabits forests and woodlands along the eastern
coastal plain, and in the far north of the region.

Woodland Thicket Rat

Mozambique Woodland
Thicket Rat

Pelomys fallax

Creek Groove-toothed Swamp Rat *Pelomys fallax*

Total length 22–36cm; tail 12–18cm; mass 100–170g.
Identification pointers: Similar in appearance to the vlei rats (p.216), but distinguished by much longer tail; tail dark above, lighter below. Face not as blunted as vlei rats. Usually indistinct dark band down back. Strong association with wet habitats. Two similar species, **Least Groove-toothed Swamp Rat** (*P. minor*) and **Bell Groove-toothed Swamp Rat** (*P. campanae*), occur in Angola.

■ *Pelomys minor*
■ *Pelomys campanae*

Description: The upperparts vary from reddish-brown to yellow-brown and the rump may be more reddish than the rest of the body. An indistinct dark band is usually present down the mid-back. The tail is dark above and pale below. An interesting feature of the fur on the back is that in certain light conditions it has a distinct greenish-blue sheen. Not a field character but incisors grooved.
Distribution: Has a wide range in the north of the region, extending southwards into southern Mozambique and the Okavango Delta in Botswana.
Habitat: The fringes of vleis, swamps, reed beds and river-banks; although they penetrate wet areas to feed, the burrows are on the drier edges, unlike those of vlei rats (*Otomys* spp.).
Behaviour: Mainly nocturnal, although has been noted foraging in the day, and excavates its own burrows. In East Africa, said to construct surface nests in dense tussocks but this may be a result of confusion with the similar vlei rats.
Food: Green plant food such as young reed shoots; seeds.
Reproduction: 2–7 pups, weighing an average 2.8g, born mostly in summer months but births may occur any time of the year. Mammae: 4 pairs.
Longevity: Not recorded.

Mylomys dybowskii

Mill Rat (African Groove-toothed Rat) *Mylomys dybowskii*

Total length 22–36cm; tail 10–18cm; mass 46–190g.
Identification pointers: Relatively long, glossy coat; upperparts yellowish-brown and pencilled with darker hairs; underparts off- to greyish-white; quite large, rounded ears; usually high-altitude grasslands.

Description: Stocky build, moderately long tail and fairly large, rounded ears. Quite long, glossy coat with upperparts usually yellowish-brown but heavily pencilled with darker hairs; underparts off- to greyish-white.
Distribution: In region, known only from Nyika Plateau area in northern Malawi.
Habitat: High-altitude moist grasslands in region.
Behaviour: Apparently mainly diurnal but also nocturnal. It does not burrow but constructs nests on the surface.
Food: Grass stems and leaves.
Reproduction: Nothing known from region. Litters of 2–6 young possibly dropped throughout the year. Mammae: 4 pairs.

Longevity: Not known.

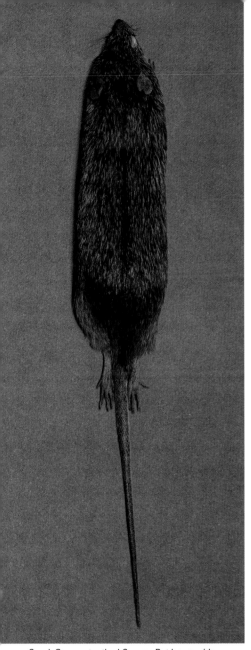

Creek Groove-toothed Swamp Rat has a wide distribution in the north of the region.

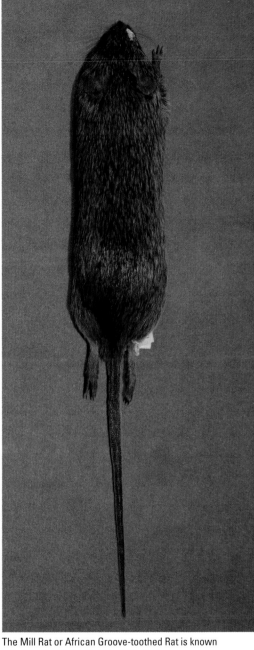

The Mill Rat or African Groove-toothed Rat is known only from the Nyika Plateau in Malawi.

Creek Groove-toothed
Swamp Rat

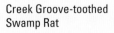

Mill Rat

Rudd's Mouse (White-bellied Brush-furred Rat)
Uranomys ruddi
Total length 14–20cm; tail 5cm; mass 40–55g.
Identification pointers: Back hairs, especially towards rump, fairly long with stiffish appearance. No distinguishing characters, except short tail.

Uranomys ruddi

Description: Upperparts variable, from dark grey to grey-brown, to dark brown, with lighter underparts. Bristle-like rump hairs somewhat springy and diagnostic when in the hand. Upper surfaces of hands and feet off-white to buffy-white.
Distribution: In region, found only in Mozambique and adjacent area of far eastern Zimbabwe, and through Malawi. Has a wide sub-Saharan range outside the region.
Habitat: Floodplains and fringing grasslands of rivers and streams.
Behaviour: Nocturnal and terrestrial. Excavate their own burrows occupied by single animals or pairs, with a nest chamber lined with dried vegetation.
Food: Little recorded but one study found only insect remains in stomachs. Its dentition suggests it may be a specialist invertebrate predator, but it is likely that some plant material is eaten.
Reproduction: Little recorded but litters of 2–6 pups; number of pups in a litter may vary seasonally, and in at least some regions breed throughout the year. Mammae: Mammae: 6 pairs.
Longevity: Not known.

MASTOMYS GROUP   Genera *Mastomys, Praomys* and *Myomyscus*

Seven species fall within this group, two of which, the Multimammate Mouse and the Natal Multimammate Mouse, are impossible to tell apart in the field. These small mice are referred to as soft-furred rats in other parts of their ranges. Additional species in the region include Angolan Multimammate Mouse *(Myomyscus angolensis)*; Delectable Soft-furred Mouse *(P. delectorum)* and Jackson's Soft-furred Mouse *(P. jacksoni)*. The *Myomyscus* species are sometimes referred to as meadow mice.

Mastomys natalensis

Natal Multimammate Mouse   *Mastomys natalensis*
Total length 24cm; tail 11cm; mass 60g.

Southern Multimammate Mouse   *Mastomys coucha*
Total length 20cm; tail 11cm; mass 50g.

Shortridge's Mouse   *Mastomys shortridgei*
Total length 22cm; tail 10cm; mass 45g.

Verreaux's White-footed Mouse   *Myomyscus verreauxii*
Total length 25cm; tail 14cm; mass 40g.

■ *Mastomys coucha*
■ *Mastomys shortridgei*

Identification pointers: Typical mouse-like appearance; underparts paler than upperparts; females of Natal Multimammate Mouse and Southern Multimammate Mouse have up to 12 pairs of nipples; Verreaux's Mouse has darker facial markings, white upper-surfaces to feet and is the only member of this group that occurs in extreme south-west of South Africa. Shortridge's Mouse is very dark above with greyish-white underparts.

Description: Range in colour from pale grey through grey-brown to almost black, with paler sides and grey underparts. Tail is finely scaled, with sparse hair covering. All species have soft, silky hair. **Southern Multimammate Mouse** females unique

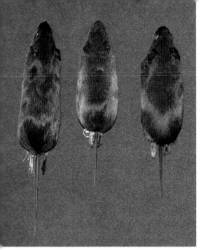

Rudd's Mouse skins showing slight differences in pelage

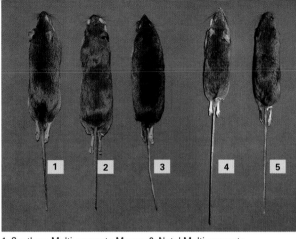

1. Southern Multimammate Mouse; 2. Natal Multimammate Mouse; 3. Shortridge's Mouse; 4. Angolan Multimammate Mouse; 5. Verreaux's White-footed Mouse

Southern Multimammate Mouse and Natal Multimammate Mouse are identical in appearance.
Inset: Shortridge's Mouse has dark fur.

Rudd's Mouse

Shortridge's Mouse

Verreaux's White-footed Mouse

209

■ *Myomyscus*
  verreauxii
■ *Myomyscus*
  angolensis

with 8–12 pairs of nipples. **Shortridge's Mouse** has much darker fur and greyish-white underparts; females have 5 pairs of nipples. **Verreaux's White-footed Mouse** has a dark band running between the ears and onto the muzzle, with dark hair around the eyes; upper-surfaces of its feet are white, as is under-surface of the tail.
Distribution: See maps; the multimammate mice are liable to be confused and cannot be separated in the field.
Habitat: Multimammate mice have wide habitat tolerance. Some species favour wet habitats and relatively dense vegetation.
Behaviour: Nocturnal and terrestrial. Often around houses. They are common reservoir hosts for a range of diseases that affect humans, including Q-fever, Lassa fever and Congo-Crimean haemorrhagic fever. Multimammate mice are subject to periodic population explosions following good rains and resulting food abundance. All species excavate their own burrow systems but the multimammate mice will also shelter among debris, both natural and human-generated.
Food: Seeds and fruit but also substantial quantities of insects and other invertebrates. **Verreaux's White-footed Mouse** is a pollinator of several ground-hugging protea species when it seeks out nectar, but it also takes seeds and many insects. Its diet probably varies seasonally.
Reproduction: **Southern Multimammate Mouse** most fecund of all southern African mammals, 22 foetuses having been recorded in a single female; 6–12 is a more usual litter size. Gestation 23 days; newborn young weigh only 2g. **Southern** and **Natal Multimammate Mice** breed throughout the year. Mammae: **Natal** and **Southern** 12 pairs from pectoral to inguinal region.
Longevity: A West African species in captivity lived for more than 5 years; certainly much less in the wild for all species.

Hylomyscus carillus

Hylomyscus denniae

Angolan Wood Mouse *Hylomyscus carillus* –
North-central Angola.
Total length 22cm; tail 13cm.

Montane Wood Mouse *Hylomyscus denniae* –
West-central Angola and northern Zambia.
Total length 23cm; tail 14cm; mass 30g.

Identification pointers: Soft fur, grey to grey-brown upperparts, lighter underparts; very long tail; prominent ears. Compare with the thicket rats.

Description: Rather nondescript small mice with a very long tail (may be more than 25% longer than head-and-body length), large rounded ears and soft pelage. Colour of coat variable from grey to grey-brown upperparts, and lighter to white underparts.
Distribution: Restricted to north of region.
Habitat: Both species occur in forest associations and dense woodland.
Behaviour: Little known but are nocturnal and both arboreal and terrestrial.
Food: A wide range of plant (leaves, fruits, seeds) and insect food.
Reproduction: Montane Wood Mouse has litters of 3–7 pups, several times per year. Possibly aseasonal breeders. Mammae: 4 pairs. Angolan Wood Mouse – Mammae: 3–4 pairs.
Longevity: Not known.

Verreaux's Mouse has dark facial markings and white feet.

Several subspecies of the Montane Wood Mouse are sometimes recognized, here *H. d. anselli*, which has a limited range in Zambia and Tanzania.

Despite its name, the Montane Wood Mouse occurs in mainly non-mountainous habitats within the region.

Angolan Wood Mouse
Montane Wood Mouse

Oenomys
hypoxanthus

Common Rufous-nosed Rat *Oenomys hypoxanthus*

Total length 24–42cm; tail 13–20cm; mass to 120g.
Identification pointers: Moderate size and long tail; long-haired coat and reddish snout, or reddish hair along side of face; only in northern Angola.

Description: Medium-sized, long-tailed rat with soft underfur and a much longer outer coat (25–30mm long). Underparts are white, sometimes creamy, and upperparts variable from olive-grey to straw-brown and rump with a reddish-brown tinge. It takes its name from the reddish-coloured hairs on the snout and/or the sides of the face.
Distribution: Northern Angola.
Habitat: Forest clearings with dense undergrowth.
Behaviour: Said to be both nocturnal and diurnal. They are both arboreal and terrestrial, nesting in tunnels, among debris and in tree forks. Apparently solitary.
Food: Mainly green plant material but also some insects.
Reproduction: Nothing known from the region but outside of the region breed throughout the year. Litters number 1–6 pups (usually 2–4). Mammae: 2–4 pairs, usually 3 pairs.
Longevity: Not known.

■ *Lophuromys
flavopunctatus*
■ *Lophuromys
sikapusi*

Yellow-spotted Brush-furred Rat *Lophuromys flavopunctatus*
Rusty-bellied Brush-furred Rat *Lophuromys sikapusi*

Total length 20–30cm; tail 7–10cm (many tails damaged/broken); mass 45–110g.

Identification pointers: Chunky build; relatively short legs; many with damaged tails and ears; coat has 'brush-like' feel to it; coloration ranges from light to dark brown, whitish underparts; **Yellow-spotted** with sprinkling of pale spots.

Description: Rather chunky build with quite short legs; coat rather coarse; feels like a soft brush. Upperparts vary from lighter to dark brown, with underparts usually lighter but variable in colour. **Yellow-spotted** has scattering of yellowish to white flecks over the coat. This is a complex group with many species and it is believed many more will be described.
Distribution: **Rusty-bellied** only in northern Angola but **Yellow-spotted** in scattered locations in north-east Angola, Zambia, Malawi and Mozambique.
Habitat: Wide range of habitats but permanent water and grass seem to be essential. Not present in areas prone to periodic drought.
Behaviour: Solitary and apparently territorial judging by the number of animals that have torn ears and damaged tails. They may dig shallow burrows but usually construct nests among deadfalls, rocks and vegetation tangles. They are mainly diurnal and crepuscular. Not studied in the region.
Food: Take considerable quantities of animal food, mainly insects, but also some plant material.
Reproduction: Both seasonal and aseasonal breeders in different parts of their range. Gestation about 30 days, with **Yellow-spotted** litter sizes averaging 2 pups, weighing 5–8g, and 2–5 in **Rusty-bellied**.
Longevity: Up to 3 years in captivity.

The Common Rufous-nosed Rat takes its name from the reddish colour on its snout and sides of the face.

Subspecies of the Yellow-spotted Brush-furred Rat, *L. f. aquilus*, occurs in Zambia and Tanzania.

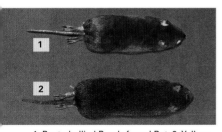

1. Rusty-bellied Brush-furred Rat; 2. Yellow-spotted Brush-furred Rat

Rusty-bellied Brush-furred Rat *(L. s. verhageni)*

Common Rufous-nosed Rat

Yellow-spotted Brush-furred Rat
Rusty-bellied Brush-furred Rat

Rattus rattus

House Rat *Rattus rattus* (Introduced)
Total length 37cm; tail 20cm; mass 150g.

Brown Rat *Rattus norvegicus* (Introduced)
Total length 40cm; tail 19cm; mass 300g.

Identification pointers: Brown Rat – large size; heavy tail, slightly shorter than head and body; restricted to coastal towns. House Rat – large size; tail longer than head and body; large, naked ears; associated with human settlements.

Rattus norvegicus

Description: House Rat more slender than Brown Rat. Large feet; tail prominently scaled and longer than head and body. Ears large, thin and naked. Upperparts grey-brown to black; underparts white to grey. Brown Rat is bulkier, with shorter tail and smaller ears; usually greyish-brown.
Distribution: Brown Rat restricted to coastal settlements and adjacent areas; House Rat is widespread but patchy. Both occur worldwide.
Habitat: Around human settlements, but House Rat less so.
Behaviour: Nocturnal. Active diggers; swim well. House Rat adept at climbing. Live in family groups and build large, untidy nests from a wide range of materials.
Food: Omnivores, taking a wide range of foodstuffs. Destructive to stored food.
Reproduction: Has several litters of 5–10 per year after a gestation of 3 weeks. Mammae: House Rat 5 pairs (rarely 6); Brown Rat 6 pairs (1 pair pectoral, 2 pairs abdominal, 3 pairs inguinal).
Longevity: In the wild, both species rarely live beyond the first year; similar in captivity but individuals have lived for 3–4 years.

Parotomys, Otomys and Myotomys groups

These are all fairly large, short, stocky rats with blunt faces and rounded ears. The fur is quite long and shaggy and the tail length is usually less than the head-and-body measurement. With the exception of Littledale's Whistling Rat, all species have grooved upper incisors. The cheek-teeth are laminated.

WHISTLING RATS Genus *Parotomys*

Two species of whistling rat occur in southern Africa.

Parotomys brantsii

Brants's Whistling Rat *Parotomys brantsii*
Total length 18–24cm; tail 10cm; mass 100–200g.

Littledale's Whistling Rat *Parotomys littledalei*
Total length 25cm; tail 10cm; mass 100–180g.

Identification pointers: See description. Both species, as their name implies, give a sharp whistling call and this is diagnostic for *Parotomys*. Open sandy country is favoured. See 'Behaviour' on p.216.

Parotomys littledalei

Description: Like other members of this group, the whistling rats are stockily built, with tails shorter than the head-and-body length. Body colour is very variable and ranges from pale reddish-yellow with white underparts to a brownish or greyish yellow with grey underparts. The tail may be similar in colour to the upperparts or dark above and pale below. Littledale's Whistling Rat tends to be somewhat darker on the back. The only sure way to differentiate between the two

The alien Black, or House, Rat is widespread around the world.

Skins of house rats showing some of the colour variations

The alien Brown Rat is large, with a heavy tail.

Vlei rat and whistling rat skins:
1. Brants's Whistling Rat
2. Littledale's Whistling Rat
3. Saunders's Vlei Rat
4. Bush Karoo Rat
5. Sloggett's Rat
6. Angoni Vlei Rat
7. Vlei rat
8. Angola Vlei Rat

The tail of the Brown Rat is noticeably shorter than that of the House Rat.

House Rat

Brown Rat

Littledale's
Whistling Rat

215

species is to examine the upper incisors. Those of **Littledale's Whistling Rat** are not grooved, but the upper incisors of **Brants's Whistling Rat** are grooved.
Distribution: Whistling rats are restricted to the arid western areas and are found only in southern Africa. Large, loosely tied colonies of **Brants's Whistling Rat** can be observed in Kgalagadi Transfrontier Park and Goegap Nature Reserve, South Africa.
Habitat: Arid, sandy environments. **Brants's** occurs mainly in areas receiving less than 300mm of rain per annum, whereas **Littledale's** favours even drier areas with under 200mm of rain but this does not form a strict barrier. **Littledale's** occurs along the extremely arid Namib Desert coastline, from which **Brants's** is absent.
Behaviour: Largely diurnal but some crepuscular and nocturnal activity, especially at brightest moon phases, and completely terrestrial. **Brants's Whistling Rats** commonly live in colonies, but do not share burrows; may live solitarily. **Littledale's** is apparently often solitary and its burrow entrances are usually located at the base of a bush or grass tussock. Large **Brant's** colonies stand out on the landscape because they are generally stripped of most vegetation. When alarmed they stand on their hind legs, in close proximity to the burrow, and then give shrill whistling calls before disappearing down the burrow. They occasionally feed at the food site, but more commonly they bite off pieces of vegetation and carry them back to eat at the burrow entrance, into which they can rapidly retreat if danger threatens. Vegetation debris and droppings may accumulate around burrow entrances. When feeding, they stand on the hind legs, using the front feet to hold and manipulate the food.
Food: They are vegetarian, eating the leaves of succulents and other green plant food, as well as seeds and flowers.
Reproduction: Littledale's Whistling Rat has up to 4 litters, with 1–3 young each, in a good wet season. **Brants's Whistling Rat** gives birth to 1–4 young, mainly during late summer and gestation lasts some 38 days. The young cling to the female's nipples, and are dragged along when she goes out to feed. Mammae: 2 pairs inguinal.
Longevity: Probably <2 years in the wild.

VLEI RATS Genera *Otomys* and *Myotomys*

Possibly as many as 12 species of *Otomys* and *Myotomys* are recognized as occurring in southern Africa. Of these, six species are poorly known: the Angola Vlei Rat (*O. anchietae*) and Cuanza Vlei Rat (*O. cuanzensis*) from Angola, and the Tanzanian Vlei Rat (*O. lacustris*) that may be found to occur in northern Malawi. Dent's Vlei Rat (*O. denti*), Tropical Vlei Rat (*O. tropicalis*) and Ethiopian Vlei Rat (*O. typus*) have been recorded from, or in the vicinity of, the Nyika Plateau, Malawi/Zambia. Vlei rats are sometimes known as African swamp rats or groove-toothed rats.

▪ *Otomys laminatus*
▪ *Otomys anchietae*
▪ *Otomys cuanzensis*
▪ *Otomys lacustris*

Laminate Vlei Rat *Otomys laminatus*
Total length 30cm; tail 10cm; mass 190g.

Angoni Vlei Rat *Otomys angoniensis*
Total length 30cm; tail 8–12cm (8cm); mass 100–250g.

Saunders's Vlei Rat *Otomys saundersiae*
Total length 25cm; tail 9cm; mass 100g.

Southern African Vlei Rat *Otomys irroratus*
Total length 24cm; tail 9cm; mass 120g.

Sloggett's Rat *Myotomys (Otomys) sloggetti*
Total length 20cm; tail 6cm; mass 130g.

Above and right: Brants's Whistling Rat can vary in colour from pale reddish-yellow to brownish or greyish-yellow.

Above and inset: Littledale's Whistling Rat often tends to be darker on the back than Brants's.

Angoni Vlei Rat may sometimes be almost black.

Sloggett's Rat has thick grey-brown fur.

Laminate Vlei Rat

Sloggett's Rat

Otomys angoniensis

Bush Karoo Rat *Myotomys (Otomys) unisulcatus*

Total length 17–29cm (24cm); tail 7–11cm (9cm); mass 78–176g (125g).

Identification pointers: All species have robust, stocky appearance, short tails, blunt muzzles, rounded ears and grooved upper incisors. Use distribution maps and habitat preferences to assist identification, but only examination of teeth and skull can usually give positive identification. Confusion could arise with African Marsh Rat (p.192) but its tail is more or less equal in length to that of head and body, and there are no grooves on upper incisors.

Otomys saundersiae

Description: Measurements above subject to variation. Coloration can also vary and there is a degree of colour overlap between the different species. Only certain way to distinguish between different species is to examine skull and cheek-teeth, and genetic makeup. Distribution maps can be used to eliminate species that should not be present in given area. All species are densely furred and usually grizzled grey-brown, although **Southern African Vlei Rat** and **Angoni Vlei Rat** may be almost black. **Sloggett's** and the **Bush Karoo Rats** both tend to be brown to grey-brown, but former has particularly short tail.

Distribution: Southern African Vlei Rat and Angoni Vlei Rat are the most widespread but only former occurs widely south of the Orange River. Bush Karoo Rat only found in south-west. Sloggett's Rat is found in east-central parts of South Africa and in Lesotho, even on the summits of the Drakensberg. Large Vlei Rat *(Otomys maximus)* is now considered to be a subspecies of Angoni Vlei Rat.

Otomys irroratus

Habitat: Despite the common name 'vlei rat', only Vlei Rat and Angoni Vlei Rat are commonly associated with moist, marshy habitats, but even they can also be found in drier habitats – grassy hillsides in the case of the former and open savanna for the latter. Sloggett's Rat is the only species that is associated with rocky habitats at high altitudes, although Saunders's Vlei Rat is recorded as occurring in the mountains in close association with sedge meadows in heathland and Southern African Vlei Rat occurs up to 2,400m. Only the Bush Karoo Rat is found in arid areas.

Behaviour: Predominantly diurnal, live singly, in pairs or small family parties. Several species construct nests of grass and other vegetation in dense grass tussocks and vegetation tangles. **Sloggett's Rat** lives in rock crevices and among boulders. Runs are marked by small piles of discarded grass, reed and leaf segments and small cylindrical droppings. **Bush Karoo Rat** constructs large stick lodges up to 2.3m in diameter and to a height of 70cm. Sticks often supplemented with bones, sheep wool, animal droppings and human litter. On West Coast, lodges are 'tiled' with mussel shells. Each lodge is occupied by up to 11 rats, and is usually built around a bush, with platforms for defecating, sunning and feeding. **Bush Karoo Rats** climb readily into low bushes to sun themselves and to harvest greenery.

Myotomys sloggetti

Food: Shoots and stems of grass, sedges, reeds and other plants. Bush Karoo Rats usually carry plant food back to the safety of the lodge.

Reproduction: No reproduction information is available for most species. Angoni Vlei Rat gives birth to 2–5 young, weighing just over 11g on average, August–March after gestation of about 37 days. Only Southern African Vlei Rat has been studied in detail; its litters of 1–4 young are born, usually in summer but at any time of year, after a gestation of about 40 days. A female may have as many as 7 litters in a season. Bush Karoo Rat breeds throughout the year in the Karoo, has litters of 2–5 (usually 2 or 3) pups, weighing 10–14g, after a gestation of about 38 days. Sloggett's breeds October–March, with 2–5 pups, weighing 10–12g, born after a gestation of about 38 days. Mammae: 2 pairs inguinal in Bush Karoo Rat, Angoni Vlei Rat, Southern African Vlei Rat and Sloggett's. Nipple-clinging in at least some species.

Longevity: Sloggett's <2 years in the wild; probably similar for other species.

Myotomys unisulcatus

Bush Karoo Rats forage alone but frequently sunbask in small family groups.

Bush Karoo Rat constructs lodges from twigs and sticks.

Bush Karoo Rat occurs mainly in arid western areas.

Bush Karoo Rat

PYGMY ROCK MICE Genus *Petromyscus*

Petromyscus collinus

Pygmy Rock Mouse *Petromyscus collinus*
Total length 19cm; tail 10cm; mass 20g.

Barbour's Pygmy Rock Mouse *Petromyscus barbouri*
Total length 16cm; tail 8cm; mass 15g.

Brukkaros Pygmy Rock Mouse *Petromyscus monticularis*
Total length 15cm; tail 7cm.

Shortridge's Pygmy Rock Mouse *Petromyscus shortridgei*
Total length 18cm; tail 9cm; mass 12–30g.

Identification pointers: Small size; well-scaled tail; prominent ears and facial whiskers; rocky habitat.

Petromyscus barbouri

Description: Pygmy Rock Mouse is small with grey-yellow to brownish-yellow upperparts; the underparts and upper surface of the feet are greyish-white. The tail is heavily scaled and sparsely haired. Prominent ears; long facial whiskers. Barbour's Pygmy Rock Mouse has dull grey upperparts with indistinct brownish grizzling. Underparts pale grey to off-white, with upper foot surfaces dirty white. Tail scales much smaller than those of **Pygmy Rock Mouse**. Coarse hairs sparse on tail but more numerous towards tip. Brukkaros Pygmy Rock Mouse is, on average, slightly smaller than other species, and the ears are shorter. Fur brownish-yellow above, underparts are grey. Upper surfaces of the feet are white. Shortridge's Pygmy Rock Mouse has dark greyish upperparts and an overall grizzled appearance. Underparts and throat are both grey.

Petromyscus monticularis

Distribution: Consult the distribution maps, but all are restricted to the arid south-west of southern Africa. Range limits are not exactly known.

Habitat: All species are associated with rocky habitats. These range from continuous mountain ranges to broken hill country and isolated rock outcrops. In the Namib Desert, the **Pygmy Rock Mouse** reaches quite high densities on rocky inselbergs (island mountains) that are completely isolated from other outcrops.

Behaviour: As far as is known, all four species are nocturnal. Only the **Pygmy Rock Mouse** has been studied in the wild. During the hottest summer period in the Namib Desert it is known to aestivate. They are solitary foragers but several individuals may occupy the same rock crevices. These crevices are also often occupied by Namaqua Rock Mice, Rock Dormice and the rock-dwelling sengis within their range. Their tiny size presumably allows them to occupy the deepest areas of such crevices. Barn Owls and Spotted Eagle-Owls are known to prey on them.

Petromyscus shortridgei

Food: They are predominantly seed eaters, but **Barbour's** collected on the western escarpment of South Africa included some green plant material in their diet. They are also known to forage on rock hyrax (dassie) dung middens (crevices often shared), possibly for undigested seeds and other material. Pygmy Rock Mouse eats some insects and this may well apply to other species as well.

Reproduction: Pygmy Rock Mouse in the Namib breeds in the summer months, producing litters of 2 or 3 young weighing just over 2g at birth. Unusually for small rodents, they only produce one litter per season. **Shortridge's** is recorded as producing 2 or 3 young per litter. Pregnant females have only been collected in May, but the season is likely to be longer. Nothing is known about the other two species. Mammae: **Pygmy** and **Shortridge's** 2 pairs inguinal, but an additional pair pectoral sometimes carried by the latter.

Longevity: Not recorded but probably averages less than 1 year in the wild.

The Pygmy Rock Mouse is grey-yellow to brownish-yellow above, with greyish-white underparts.
Inset: 1. Barbour's Pygmy Rock Mouse; 2. Pygmy Rock Mouse; 3. Brukkaros Pygmy Rock Mouse

Barbour's Pygmy Rock Mouse, like the Pygmy Rock Mouse, occurs in the arid west of the region.

Pygmy Rock Mouse

Vulpes chama

Cape Fox   *Vulpes chama*

Total length 86–97cm; tail 29–39cm; shoulder height 30cm; mass 2.5–4kg.
Identification pointers: Typically fox-like appearance; long, bushy tail; greyish-grizzled back and sides; light-coloured legs; muzzle generally light in colour; ears 'normal' in size. Compare with Bat-eared Fox, which has black legs and muzzle and disproportionately long ears. Cape Fox normally seen singly or in pairs; Bat-eared Fox usually in pairs or small groups.

Description: Only 'true' fox in the region. Back and sides grizzled silvery-grey and neck, chest and forelegs pale tawny-brown to almost white. Throat usually white. Tail long and bushy and usually darker than rest of body. Ears long and pointed, brown at back and fringed with white hair at front.
Distribution: Restricted to the region.
Habitat: Open areas, such as grassland and arid scrub. Also wheatlands and Cape fynbos vegetation zone in the Western Cape, South Africa.
Behaviour: Mainly nocturnal but in undisturbed areas active in cooler daylight hours. Usually alone or in pairs but hunting is a solitary activity. During the day it lies up in holes or dense thickets but will readily sun bask at mouth of den. They may dig their own den or modify the burrow of another species, such as Springhare. Hunting ranges extend up to 5km². Pups begin to forage on their own from the 16th week but remain with the mother until in their fifth month. In some areas they reach quite high population densities despite heavy persecution in some small livestock-farming regions. Numbers tend to be lower in those areas where the Black-backed Jackal is abundant.
Food: Mainly insects, other invertebrates and rodents; also reptiles, birds, carrion and wild fruit. Rarely newborn lambs.
Reproduction: 1–5 (usually 3) pups born in spring (August–November) after a gestation of 50–52 days. Two females may raise their litters in the same den. Mammae: 1 pair inguinal, 2 pairs abdominal.
Longevity: Probably 6–9 years but information lacking.

Otocyon megalotis

Bat-eared Fox   *Otocyon megalotis*

Total length 75–90cm; tail 23–34cm; shoulder height 35cm; mass 3–5kg.
Identification pointers: Jackal-like appearance; disproportionately large ears; bushy, silvery-grey coat; black legs; bushy tail – black above and at tip; face black below eyes, paler above eyes.

Description: This small, jackal-like carnivore has slender legs, a sharp-pointed, fairly long muzzle and disproportionately large ears. The ears may reach a length of 14cm and are dark at the back, particularly at the tip; the insides of the ears are white or light in colour. The body is covered in fairly long, silvery-grey hair with a distinctly grizzled appearance and the legs are black. The tail is bushy and black above and at the tip. Although the front of the face is generally black, a light or white band runs across the forehead to the base of the ears.

Cape Fox pups suckling. **Inset:** Cape Foxes in the Namib often scavenge around campsites.

Cape Fox is the only true fox in southern Africa.

Bat-eared Fox

Cape Fox

  38mm 36mm

right
front

right
back

Bat-eared Fox

  35mm 32mm

right
front

right
back

Distribution: Widespread in central and western areas below Cunene-Zambezi line. Its presence in far northern Zambia needs to be confirmed but it is known to occur in adjacent areas of Tanzania.

Habitat: Open country, such as short scrub and grassveld and sparsely wooded areas. Absent from mountains, dense woodland and forest.

Behaviour: Both diurnal and nocturnal activity is recorded but it lies up during the hotter hours of the day. An active digger, and will excavate its own burrows, although frequently modifies those dug by other species. Regularly lies up in the shade of a low, dense bush. Normally in groups of 2–6 individuals. As pairs mate for life, groups usually comprise a pair and their offspring. Occasionally more may be seen but such groupings are temporary, perhaps associated with an abundant, localized food source. The authors have seen up to 26 loosely associated foxes feeding in a field where irrigation was flushing large numbers of crickets and other insects. When foraging, it appears to wander aimlessly, stopping periodically with ears turned to the ground; when food is located, digs shallow holes with the forepaws.

Food: Mostly insects (particularly harvester termites) and a variety of beetle species; also reptiles, rodents and wild fruits.

Reproduction: After gestation of 60–70 days, 2–6 pups (usually 2–4), weighing 100–150g, born in burrow September–November. Pale grey at birth, with eyes closed. Populations rise and fall in poorly understood cycles. Mammae: 2 pairs inguinal.

Longevity: 13 years in captivity; probably much less in the wild.

Canis mesomelas

Black-backed Jackal *Canis mesomelas*

Total length 71–130cm; tail 26–40cm; shoulder height 30–48cm; mass 6–12kg.
Identification pointers: Dog-like appearance; dark, white-flecked 'saddle' on back; black tail; fairly large, pointed, reddish-backed ears. See Side-striped Jackal where distributions overlap.

Description: Medium-sized, dog-like carnivore with characteristic black saddle, which is broad at neck and shoulders, narrowing to base of tail. Saddle liberally sprinkled with white hair. Face, flanks and legs reddish-brown; underparts usually paler. Lips, throat and chest are white. Fairly large pointed ears, reddish on back surface and lined with white hair on inside. Black bushy tail but paler towards base. Male overall larger than female.

Distribution: Very widely distributed in the region but absent from parts of the north and north-east and reduced by farmers in other areas. In recent years this jackal has reoccupied most areas from which it was eliminated up to the 1980s within South Africa.

Habitat: Wide habitat tolerance, from the coastal Namib Desert to the moist Drakensberg. Unlike Side-striped Jackal, however, it prefers drier areas.

Behaviour: Mainly nocturnal when in conflict with man, but in protected reserves frequently seen during the day. Normally solitary or in pairs but also occurs in family parties. Pairs form long-term pair-bonds, with both the male and the female marking and defending a territory, which varies considerably in size, depending on the availability of food and competition with other jackals. It is well known for its wariness and cunning and is generally able to avoid all but the most sophisticated of traps. When resting, it may lie up in a burrow dug by other species, or under a bush or other vegetation. Its call is characteristic and has been described as a screaming yell, finished off with three or four short yaps. Calling is more frequent during the winter months when mating takes place. Home range sizes vary considerably and are influenced by factors such as food availability,

Bat-eared Fox has very large ears and contrasting black-and-white facial markings. **Inset:** Bat-eared Fox pairs mate for life.

Black-backed Jackal. **Inset:** Black-backed Jackal may rest at any point within its home range.

Black-backed Jackal

54mm

right
front

43mm

right
back

competition and general jackal density, from as little as 9km² for young animals to 18km² for mated pairs in the high-rainfall Drakensberg range. In excess of 500km² has been recorded for sub-adult home ranges in the Kalahari.

Food: It takes an extremely wide range of food items, from young antelope, rodents, hares, birds, reptiles and insects to wild fruits and berries. It also feeds on carrion; in fact, there is little that it has not been recorded eating. Unfortunately, it has proved to be a problem in sheep- and goat-farming areas, but only certain individuals take to stock-killing, not all.

Reproduction: Seasonal breeder with 1–8 (usually 3 or 4) pups being born July–October. Gestation approximately 60 days. Newborn dark brown pups are helpless, weigh 150–200g, and are born in burrows dug by other species. Both male and female bring food to the young, as do 'helpers', sub-adults from the previous breeding season. Pups start to forage with the parents when they are about 14 weeks old. Mammae: 2–4 pairs abdominal/inguinal.

Longevity: Up to 14 years in captivity; rarely more than 7 years in the wild.

Note: Black-backed Jackal is one of three carnivore species that occur in two widely separated populations, one in southern Africa and the other in East Africa. The other members of this 'club' are Bat-eared Fox and Aardwolf.

Canis adustus

Side-striped Jackal *Canis adustus*
Total length 96–120cm; tail 30–40cm; shoulder height 40–48cm; mass 7.5–12kg.

Identification pointers: Overall grey appearance with a light-and-dark stripe along each side; lacks dark, silver-mottled saddle typical of the Black-backed Jackal; tail usually with white tip; ears fairly large but smaller and less pointed than those of Black-backed Jackal. Habitat can be a useful aid to identification. Also see distribution maps of the two jackals.

Description: From a distance this jackal has a uniform grey appearance but at close quarters a light-coloured band, liberally fringed with black, can be seen along each flank. These side-stripes give the jackal its name. The underparts and throat are paler than the upperparts. The tail is quite bushy, mostly black and usually has a white tip.

Distribution: Only found in the northern and eastern areas of southern African region, but has a wide distribution outside of the region in sub-Saharan Africa, excluding the equatorial forest zone, although present in Gabon.

Habitat: It shows a preference for well-watered wooded areas, but not forest.

Behaviour: Although it is mainly nocturnal, it may be seen in the early morning and late afternoon. Most sightings are of single animals, although pairs and family parties are often encountered. Home range and defended territory occupied by a mated pair; ranges seem to be well spaced and in one study they averaged 18–19km², larger than those of Black-backed Jackals living in the same area. Call has been likened to an owl hoot, quite unlike the long, drawn-out howl of the Black-backed Jackal.

Food: It is an omnivorous species taking a wide variety of food items ranging from small mammals, birds, reptiles, insects and carrion to wild fruits. Will also feed on cultivated maize, pumpkin and groundnuts.

Reproduction: 3–6 pups, weighing about 200g, born after gestation of 57–60 days, August–January, in the abandoned burrows of other species. Both male and female will either regurgitate food for the young, or carry it back in the mouth, once they start regularly eating solid food. Mammae: 2 pairs inguinal.

Longevity: 10–12 years in captivity; probably less in the wild.

The Black-backed Jackal is easily identified by its dark 'saddle' flecked with white hair.

Facial colour varies from pale to rich reddish-brown, while the throat, lips and chest are white.

Above and inset: The Side-striped Jackal has a light-and-dark stripe along each side and a white-tipped tail.

Side-striped Jackal

43mm

right
front

47mm

right
back

Lycaon pictus
- ■ present range
- ■ historic range

African Wild Dog *Lycaon pictus*

Total length 105–150cm; tail 30–40cm; shoulder height 60–75cm; mass 20–30kg (17–25kg).

Identification pointers: Heavily blotched black, white and yellow-brown; slender body, long legs; normally white-tipped tail; large, dark, rounded ears; black muzzle and stripe from between eyes over top of head.

Description: Unmistakable; similar in size to a domestic German Shepherd dog. It has large, rounded ears, long legs and a bushy, white-tipped tail. Body irregularly blotched with black, white, brown and yellowish-brown. Muzzle is black, with black continuing as line from muzzle to between the ears. Forehead on either side of the black line is pale fawn to white.

Distribution: In South Africa, African Wild Dog occurs permanently only in the Kruger National Park (±320 individuals) but a number of animals have been introduced to the Hluhluwe/iMfolozi complex in KwaZulu-Natal, also Madikwe and Pilansberg game reserves in the north-west of South Africa, as well as Greater Addo and Kwandwe. In the other southern African countries it only survives in the larger reserves and uninhabited areas. One of largest populations in the region in Niassa, north Mozambique. African Wild Dogs previously occurred widely in Africa outside the equatorial forests, but have been greatly reduced in numbers by man. Rarest large carnivore in the region.

Habitat: As it hunts by sight it is usually associated with open country. It avoids dense woodland, forest and extensive areas of tall grass.

Behaviour: It is a highly specialized hunter, living in packs usually numbering from 10–15 animals, although smaller and larger groups have been observed. It is predominantly diurnal, most of its hunting taking place in the cooler morning and late afternoon hours. Hunting is undertaken by the pack, which moves slowly towards the intended prey at first, increasing the pace as the quarry starts to move away. Once an individual has been singled out, the pack rarely deviates from its goal and a chase may continue for several kilometres. Smaller prey may be pulled down immediately but larger prey is bitten and torn while on the move until it weakens from shock or loss of blood and can be overpowered. Despite its reputation as a wanton killer, African Wild Dog kills only for its immediate needs. During hunts it is able to reach speeds of over 50km/h. When pups begin to eat solids, the adults regurgitate meat at the den for the pups, as well as for the adults that remained to guard the young and any sick animals unable to take part in the hunts.

African Wild Dogs do not establish territories but have very large home ranges. The average home range size in Kruger National Park has been estimated at 450km², but in arid areas home ranges are considerably larger. It is a very vocal species with a wide range of calls. Normally, only a single female comes into oestrus at any one time and she is mated by the dominant male. Packs include several related adult males, and one or more related adult females originating from different packs.

Food: African Wild Dogs hunt a wide range of mammals, ranging in size from Steenbok to Buffalo. They also take rodents, hares and birds. Impala is the most important prey species in the Kruger National Park, with Springbok being very important throughout much of the African Wild Dogs' range in Botswana.

Reproduction: Young are born during the dry winter months (March–September) when grass is short and hunting conditions are best. Between 2 and 10 (usually 7–10) pups, weighing about 365g, are born after a gestation period of 69–73 days. The young are born in the abandoned burrows of other species; for the first three months of their life they remain in close proximity to the den. Mammae: 6–8 pairs.

Longevity: 10–11 years in the wild; up to 15 years in captivity.

Once found throughout sub-Saharan Africa, Wild Dogs are extinct as a viable breeding species in many countries, with most populations restricted to conservation areas. The total population estimates for Africa range from 3,000–5,750 animals.

The endangered African Wild Dog, Africa's largest canid, is characterized by its patterned coloration and rounded ears. **Inset:** The African Wild Dog's muzzle is always black.

African Wild Dog

76mm
right
front

68mm
right
back

■ *Aonyx capensis*
■ *Aonyx congicus*

Cape Clawless Otter *Aonyx capensis*

The Congo (Cameroon) Clawless Otter *(A. congicus)* is sometimes recognized as a separate species but is very similar to the Cape Clawless.

Total length 110–160cm; tail 50cm; shoulder height 35cm; mass 10–21kg (max 25kg).

Identification pointers: Quite large size; dark brown coat (appears black when wet) with white lips, chin, throat and upper chest. Finger-like digits. On land, ambles along with back arched. Larger than Spotted-necked Otter and lacks neck spots. Unlike the latter, Cape Clawless Otter may be found away from permanent water. Occasionally confused with much smaller Water Mongoose (p.248).

Description: Larger of two otter species occurring in the region. Soft dark brown coat, with lips, chin and throat being silvery-white; white coloration sometimes extends to upper part of chest. Legs short and stout and tail long, heavy at base and tapering towards tip. On land it walks and runs with back arched. Toes distinctively finger-like, but lack claws, although there are small, flat, rudimentary nails on some digits of hind feet.

Distribution: Absent from most of the dry interior of the region.

Habitat: Rivers, marshes, dams and lakes; also dry stream-beds in most terrain if pools of water exist. May wander several kilometres from water. Also utilizes the coastal intertidal zone.

Behaviour: Active during early morning and late afternoon but may hunt at any time of day or night. Lies up in cover or shade during hotter hours. Will make use of rock overhangs, dense bush and reed beds but will dig own burrows (holts) in sandy riverbanks. It is said that they require dense riparian vegetation for cover, however, where such habitats are scarce, such as in several localities in the Great Karoo, they use shallow rock overhangs, mainly facing south. Several lying-up sites, or couches, occur within any single home range. In general, they tend to have linear home ranges strongly tied to aquatic habitats but regular forays are made away from this range, sometimes up to 5km. Occurs singly, in pairs, or small family parties. 'Latrine' areas with numerous droppings made up largely of crushed crab-shell are a useful indication of its presence. Otters crush and eat the entire crab; Water Mongoose usually leaves carapace, pincers and legs of larger crabs. Cape Clawless Otter will hunt by sight, but much prey is found by feeling with fingers, and it therefore thrives in water with poor visibility. (Compare Spotted-necked Otter.)

Food: Freshwater crabs, but also fish and frogs. Takes molluscs, small mammals, birds and insects. Crabs are almost entirely consumed, in contrast to those eaten by the Water Mongoose, where the carapace and legs of larger crabs are generally discarded. Both species will dig crabs out of mud. Freshwater mussels are dug out with the fingers and smashed against a rock or hard object to break the shell, and the meat eaten. In coastal waters takes fish, crabs, urchins and octopus. Can become a nuisance by hunting poultry, and will often kill more than it requires.

Reproduction: Usually 1–3 (1 or 2 most common) cubs per litter, each weighing about 200g; gestation 60–65 days. Most births March–August in the region but few records. Mammae: 2 pairs abdominal.

Longevity: One captive lived 15 years.

The Cape Clawless Otter hunts readily in water and on land.

The Congo Clawless Otter is sometimes considered to be a separate species from the Cape Clawless Otter.

Cape Clawless Otter inhabits rivers, marshes and dams.

The Cape Clawless Otter has finger-like digits.

Cape Clawless Otter

70 (106) mm

right front

108mm

right back

Hydrictis
maculicollis

Spotted-necked Otter *Hydrictis maculicollis*
Total length <100cm; tail 30–50cm; mass 3–6.2kg.
Identification pointers: Upperparts uniform brown to dark brown;
underparts lighter with pale blotching on throat and upper chest and
occasionally between hind legs. Considerably smaller than Cape Clawless
Otter; closer in size to Water Mongoose (p.248) but lacks the long hair of the
latter. Closely associated with water and rarely seen far from it.

Description: Smaller of two otter species occurring in the region. Body slender
and long, with somewhat flattened tail. Feet fully webbed and toes clawed. Coat
uniform dark brown to reddish-brown, with throat and upper chest mottled or
blotched with creamy-white. Appears black when wet.
Distribution: Patchy distribution in the south but more widespread north of
the Cunene and Zambezi rivers. Declining in numbers perhaps because of soil
erosion, consequent muddy rivers and poor visibility for otter.
Habitat: Larger rivers, or those with large permanent pools, as well as lakes,
dams and well-watered swamps. More closely tied to water than Cape Clawless
Otter; not associated with estuaries or coastal environment.
Behaviour: Diurnal. Normally in groups of 2–6, but sometimes larger groups
or single. Prey usually taken to bank to eat but also eaten in the water. It is
quite vocal, with whistles being most frequently heard, probably as a means of
maintaining group contact. In water they dive and 'porpoise' in much the same
way as a dolphin and can be very playful, chasing each other and rolling in the
water, while communicating with whistle and twittering calls. Uses latrine sites
close to water's edge. Droppings are smaller than those of Cape Clawless Otter
and similar in size to those of Water Mongoose. Those of the latter species,
however, usually contain greater quantity of mammal hair and are rarely so white.
Food: Mostly fish but also crabs, frogs, birds and insects.
Reproduction: 2 or 3 cubs probably born in summer, although some evidence
indicates it may be year-round. Gestation 60 days. Mammae: 2 pairs abdominal.
Longevity: Up to 8 years recorded in wild-living animals; one captive lived 23 years.

Mellivora capensis

Honey Badger (Ratel) *Mellivora capensis*
Total length 90–100cm; tail 18–25cm; shoulder height 30cm; mass 8–14kg.
Identification pointers: Stocky build and short legs; silver-grey upperparts
including top of head; black underparts and legs; short, bushy black tail –
often held erect when walking. Cannot be confused with any other species.

Description: Unmistakable animal, with its thickset form, silver-grey upperparts
and black underparts and legs. Top of head and upper neck usually paler than
rest of upperparts. Tail short, bushy and black and often held erect when
walking. Ears are small and barely noticeable. Spoor distinctive with clear
impressions in prints left by long, heavy claws of forefeet (see opposite).
Distribution: Widespread in the region, but apparently absent from much of the
Free State and Lesotho.
Habitat: Found in most major habitats, but absent from coastal Namib Desert.
Behaviour: Tough and aggressive; records of attacks on Elephant and Buffalo and
also humans when threatened. Usually seen singly, but pairs and family groups may
also be observed. Nocturnal in areas with high human populations, but where not
disturbed will be active in early morning and late afternoon; as an adaptation to

The Spotted-necked Otter is entirely reliant on clear waters, as it hunts mainly by sight.

Spotted-necked Otter has well-developed claws.

The throat and chest mottling of this otter is very variable.

The Honey Badger's ears are barely noticeable.

Spotted-necked Otter

58mm

right front

70mm

right back

Honey Badger

70mm

right front

81mm

right back

temperature extremes, become mainly nocturnal in summer and diurnal in winter. Largely terrestrial but can climb well. They readily excavate their own burrows but will also modify those dug by other species. Home ranges may be very large, as for example in the Kalahari, where they may cover areas of 100km² to almost 550km², with those of males being considerably larger.

Food: Wide range of food items but insects, other invertebrates and rodents are the most important. Much of their prey is obtained by digging with the powerful front claws. Reptiles, birds, other small mammals, wild fruit and carrion are also eaten. In coastal areas, such as in the Western Cape, individuals frequently forage along the high-tide line. Common name is derived from their tendency to break into beehives (both natural and man-made) to eat honey and larvae. 'Rogue' individuals may take to killing poultry, sheep and goats but this is extremely rare.

Reproduction: Young may be born at any time of year, with 1–4 (usually 1 or 2) born after a gestation period of about 62–74 days, in a grass- and leaf-lined burrow but only 1 pup is usually successfully reared. Birth weights are approximately 180g. They stay with the mother for up to 20 months and development is very slow. Mammae: 2 pairs inguinal.

Longevity: One captive lived for 26 years, another lived 30 years. Estimates for the Kalahari are just 6–8 years.

Poecilogale albinucha

African Striped Weasel *Poecilogale albinucha*

Total length 40–50cm; tail 12–16cm; shoulder height 5–7cm; mass 220–350g.
Identification pointers: Long, thin body; fairly long, bushy white tail and very short legs; overall colour black with white cap on head and four white to yellowish stripes running from neck to base of the tail. Often confused with Striped Polecat (p.236), but the latter has much longer hair and white patches on the face.

Description: This is a long, slender carnivore, with short legs. The overall colour is black with four off-white to yellowish stripes running from the neck to the base of the tail, combining into a white cap on the top of the head. The tail is quite bushy and white but the body hair is coarse and short.

Distribution: It has a wide distribution in the eastern and northern areas of southern Africa, with a few records from Namibia, Botswana and Mozambique, and recent extension into the south-western extreme of South Africa, in Western Cape.

Habitat: It has a wide habitat tolerance but most of the records are from grassland areas. Recent records in fynbos/farmland mosaics in the south-west.

Behaviour: Occasionally sighted during the day but predominantly nocturnal. Although usually solitary, pairs and family parties may be observed. When it walks or runs, the back has an arched appearance. It is an efficient digger in soft soil but probably uses rodent-burrows as well as its own for shelter. Like the Striped Polecat, it can eject a strong-smelling fluid from the perineal glands when threatened, but it is not as pungent, or as unpleasant.

Food: It hunts small, warm-blooded prey, particularly rodents. Food may be hoarded or carried to the shelter to be eaten. Its build is well adapted for the pursuit of rodents in their burrows.

Reproduction: Most records of births are in the summer months, November–March. Litters consist of 1–3 young, each with a mass of about 4g; the gestation period is about 32 days. At birth the young are almost hairless and their eyes are closed; they open after about 52 days. Mammae: 1 pair abdominal, 1 pair inguinal; a second pair of inguinal sometimes present.

Longevity: 4–6 years in captivity.

The Honey Badger is extremely tough and shows little fear; they are mainly nocturnal and, to a lesser extent, crepuscular.

The African Striped Weasel has a long, thin body and a bushy white tail. **Inset:** These skins show the difference in size between 1. Striped Weasel and 2. Striped Polecat.

African Striped Weasel

18mm

right
front

15mm

right
back

Ictonyx striatus

Striped Polecat *Ictonyx striatus*

Total length 57–67cm; tail 26cm; shoulder height 10–15cm; mass 0.5–1.4kg.
Identification pointers: Small size and long white and black hair; white hair in four stripes down back; white patch between eyes and one at base of each ear. (See African Striped Weasel, p.234.)

Description: Conspicuous black-and-white markings warn would-be predators that they can expect a squirt of foul-smelling liquid from its anal glands. Long body hair is shiny black with four distinct white stripes extending from top of head to base of tail along back and flanks. White patch on forehead between eyes and larger white patch at base of ear. The tail is predominantly white but black shows through.
Distribution: Throughout the region except for Namib Desert coast.
Habitat: Found in all the major habitat types, including agricultural lands. Occur from sea level to about 1,500m.
Behaviour: Strictly nocturnal; usually solitary, but also in pairs and family parties. Shelter is sought in other species' burrows, on rocky outcrops, among matted vegetation and even under the floors of buildings; can dig own burrow. If threatened it adopts threat posture, with rump towards aggressor, back arched and tail held erect. If threat persists, it squirts foul-smelling fluid at aggressor. Under extreme threat they will sham death.
Food: Mostly insects, rodents and other small animals.
Reproduction: After gestation of 36 days, litter of 1–3 young (up to 5) born in summer, each weighing 10–15g. Most litters dropped in summer months. This carnivore is a marathon copulator, with sessions lasting over 100 minutes. Mammae: 1 pair inguinal, 1 pair abdominal.
Longevity: Up to 5.5 years in captivity.

MONGOOSES Family Herpestidae

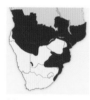

Mungos mungo

Banded Mongoose *Mungos mungo*

Total length 50–65cm; tail 18–25cm; shoulder height 18–20cm; mass 1–1.6kg.
Identification pointers: Small size; usually with 10–12 dark brown to black transverse stripes on grey to grey-brown back. Superficially similar to Suricate but the banding is much more distinct and tail is bushier. Also occurs in groups. Compare the distribution maps and habitat preferences.

Description: This small, very distinctive mongoose has 10–12 dark brown to black transverse bands on back, from behind shoulders to base of tail. Colour varies from grizzled grey to grey-brown. Tail bushy and usually darker in colour towards tip. Head relatively long and pointed. Compare with Suricate where ranges overlap in the west.
Distribution: It is restricted to eastern and northern areas of southern Africa and mainly absent from the drier central and western regions. In recent years there have been sightings of small bands of this mongoose in the Kgalagadi Transfrontier Park, including two observations by the authors. It is unlikely that this is an isolated population, but originates with animals that have followed dry watercourses from either the northern or eastern ranges.

The Striped Polecat has four distinct white stripes on the back and a bushy black-and-white tail.
Inset: Some individuals have yellow-white stripes, others have clean white stripes.

Banded Mongooses frequently sit on their hind legs, remaining on the alert for predators.

This mongoose is gregarious and lives in troops.

Striped Polecat

22mm
right
front

22mm
right
back

Banded Mongoose

26mm
right
front

29mm
right
back

Habitat: Wide habitat tolerance but absent from desert, semi-desert and rainforest but usually in areas receiving >500mm of rain annually. Preference for woodland with adequate ground cover.

Behaviour: Highly gregarious and social species, strictly diurnal; troops number 5–30 or more. When foraging, they maintain contact with constant soft calls. Troop's home range will include several shelters, usually in termitaria. Size of home range depends on number of pack members and availability of food, from 80ha to over 4km². Frequent marking with anal gland secretions is performed on rocks and logs, as well as individuals within the troop. Encounters between different troops may result in conflict but apparently they do not defend territories.

Food: Insects and other invertebrates are the most important food items but they also take reptiles, amphibians, birds and their eggs, carrion and probably small rodents. To crack open birds' eggs they use the front feet to throw the eggs between the hind legs against a rock or other hard object.

Reproduction: Usually 2–6 (up to 8) young, each weighing about 20–50g, are born after a gestation period of approximately 60 days. Breeding usually synchronized within a troop and most litters dropped fOctober–February, the wet summer months. The young suckle from any lactating female, not just the mother, and all the adults perform guard duty over the young animals. Juveniles begin following the troop about 5 weeks after birth. Mammae: 3 pairs abdominal.

Longevity: 11 years in captivity; <10 years in the wild.

Ansorge's Cusimanse *Crossarchus ansorgei*

Total length 45–76cm; tail 15–32cm; shoulder height 18–20cm; mass 450–1,500g (tend towards lower measurements).
Identification pointers: Medium-sized; proportionately short tail; elongated snout; shaggy, dark brown coat; social; forest habitat.

Crossarchus ansorgei

Description: A medium-sized mongoose, with a relatively short tail that tapers towards the tip, elongated snout and short, rounded ears. The coat has a shaggy appearance and is usually dark brown, sometimes with a glossy sheen. Head colour usually lighter than rest of body.

Distribution: Southernmost portion of the Dembos Forest, north of the Cuanza River in north-west Angola. It may have been overlooked elsewhere but forest destruction indicates it may no longer survive there.

Habitat: Lowland rainforest.

Behaviour: Lives in troops of 10–20 individuals and in many ways is the forest equivalent of the Banded Mongoose. Apparently they are very mobile and have no fixed den except when breeding. Although mainly diurnal, some nocturnal activity has been recorded.

Food: Invertebrates, small vertebrates and some wild fruits.

Reproduction: Believed to be aseasonal breeders with more than 1 litter per year. Litter size averages 4 young, dropped after a gestation of about 70 days. Mammae: Not known.

Longevity: The closely related *C. obscurus* has lived to 9 years in captivity.

Banded Mongoose. **Inset:** Skins of Banded Mongoose (**top**) and Suricate (**bottom**), showing the variations in banding on the back.

Banded Mongooses readily dig for invertebrates and other prey.

Banded Mongooses mating

Banded Mongoose with young

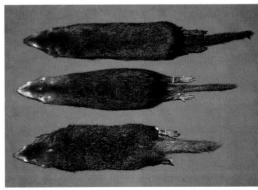

The members of the cusimanse mongoose group are all very similar and are characterized by short, bushy tails.

Ansorge's Cusimanse

Rhynchogale melleri

Meller's Mongoose *Rhynchogale melleri*

Total length 60–98cm; tail 30–39cm; mass 1.7–3kg.
Identification pointers: May have black, brown or white tail; individuals with white tails may be confused with White-tailed Mongoose (p.252) but are smaller with a blacker overall appearance than the latter. May also be confused with smaller Selous's Mongoose (p.242). The crest-like parting on the neck, although difficult to see, is a useful identification aid. The distribution ranges of White-tailed, Meller's and Selous's mongooses overlap in the far north-eastern areas of the region.

Description: Hair shaggy. Upperparts vary from light to dark brown; underparts lighter. At close quarters upperparts appear grizzled. Tail colour often aids identification but in this species is variable. Near base it is usually brown, towards the tip it may be black, brown or white; dark brown to black, however, is the most usual. Legs are black. Useful distinguishing character is a distinct crest-like parting in the hair on either side of the neck. Head quite short; muzzle swollen appearance.
Distribution: Patchy distribution in north-eastern parts of southern Africa, extending northwards across Zambia and into Tanzania.
Habitat: Open woodlands but extends marginally into grassland savanna, nearly always in the vicinity of dense ground cover and water. Has been recorded in vicinity of rocky hills and inselbergs lying in woodland savanna.
Behaviour: Nocturnal and usually solitary. The least known of all mongoose species in the region.
Food: Mainly termites. Also other invertebrates, reptiles, amphibians and wild fruit.
Reproduction: 2 or 3 young born in summer in burrows or rock crevices. Mammae: Not known.
Longevity: Not recorded.

Bdeogale crassicauda

Bushy-tailed Mongoose *Bdeogale crassicauda*

Total length 65–72cm; tail 23–30cm; mass 1.5–2.1kg.
Identification pointers: Overall black appearance; should not be confused with any other mongoose species occurring in southern Africa but see habitat-restricted Water Mongoose.

Description: Overall body and tail colour appears black, but at close quarters appears grizzled. Legs and long-haired bushy tail are jet-black.
Distribution: Apparently very rare in the region and seldom seen. Restricted to extreme northern and eastern Zimbabwe and northern Mozambique, northwards in eastern Zambia and Malawi.
Habitat: Open woodland with grass, often in rocky outcrops, in areas up to 1,500m. A number of sightings in the region were on river floodplains with dry woodland associations but always in vicinity of rock outcroppings.
Behaviour: Apparently solitary and nocturnal, although day-time sightings have been made. Unlike most mongoose species, when captured it is calm and docile. Little is known of the way of life of this mongoose.
Food: Insects, other invertebrates, but more rarely rodents, reptiles and amphibians. Ants and termites said to be particularly important.
Reproduction: The few records indicate that only a single young is born, probably in the wet summer months. Mammae: 2 pairs abdominal.
Longevity: A closely related species *(B. nigripes)* lived 15 years 10 months in captivity.

Meller's Mongoose varies in colour from light to dark brown.

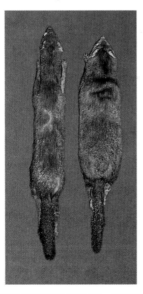

Meller's Mongoose

Far left: Meller's Mongoose skin
Left: Bushy-tailed Mongoose skins
Above: The rare Bushy-tailed Mongoose is
solitary and nocturnal.

Meller's Mongoose

25mm | 32mm

right
front

right
back

Bushy-tailed Mongoose

33mm | 31mm

right
front

right
back

241

Selous's Mongoose *Paracynictis selousi*

Total length 63–90cm; tail 28–43cm; mass 1.4–2kg.
Identification pointers: Smaller and more slender than White-tailed Mongoose (p.252). Tail only white towards the tip, whereas in White-tailed Mongoose it is white for three-quarters of its length. See Yellow Mongoose from northern Botswana (p.252).

Paracynictis selousi

Description: The overall body colour of this mongoose is pale speckled grey to tawny-grey but head usually slightly lighter; the lower legs are brown to black and short haired. The fairly long-haired tail is usually light fawnish-grey to grey-white but only white towards the tip. Claws on the front feet quite long and curved, an adaptation for digging.
Distribution: Restricted to north-east and far north of the region, extending into Angola, Zambia and Malawi.
Habitat: Savanna grassland and woodland, within an annual rainfall range of 400–1,000mm, and usually where the substrate is sandy.
Behaviour: Nocturnal and usually solitary, but pairs and females with young are not uncommon. It digs its own burrows but will use those excavated by other species when under stress. The self-excavated burrows can be complex and are usually occupied by a single individual, except when a female has young. This mongoose is probably overlooked due to its relatively small size and its nocturnal habits.
Food: It feeds mainly on invertebrates but also takes a wide range of small rodents, amphibians, reptiles and birds.
Reproduction: Litters of 2–4 born August–March. Mammae: Not known.
Longevity: Not recorded.

Small Grey Mongoose (Cape Grey Mongoose) *Galerella (Herpestes) pulverulenta*

Total length 55–76cm; tail 20–34cm; mass 0.5–1.25kg.
Identification pointers: Small size; uniform grey colouring; only marginally overlaps distribution range of Slender Mongoose in north-west of South Africa (p.244). It lacks the latter's black tail-tip and holds tail horizontally when running, whereas Slender Mongoose holds tail vertically or curved slightly over the body. Much smaller than Large Grey Mongoose which, in any case, has black tail-tip.

Galerella pulverulenta

Description: Uniform light to dark grey above, appearing grizzled at close quarters. In north-west some animals may appear more brown. Legs darker than rest of body. Head quite long and muzzle pointed. Tail long, bushy and uniformly grizzled grey.
Distribution: Small Grey Mongoose occurs widely south of the Orange River and extends through the southern Free State, Lesotho and marginally into KwaZulu-Natal and southern Namibia.
Habitat: It has a very wide habitat tolerance, from forest to open scrub, wherever there is some cover. Particularly common in the southern coastal areas and adjacent interior.
Behaviour: Active by day, although tends to lie up during the hottest part of the day in summer. Usually solitary but pairs and family parties are occasionally seen (maximum 5, usually 3). It makes use of regular pathways within home range. Commonly seen crossing roads. Home ranges, recorded from 5–92ha, overlap considerably and although this species marks with glandular secretions, it is not known whether it is territorial.

Selous's Mongoose is nocturnal and usually solitary. It is small in size with uniformly grey colouring.

Small Grey Mongoose is common throughout southern South Africa. **Inset:** These skins show colour variants of Small Grey Mongoose.

Selous's Mongoose

25mm · 31mm

right front · right back

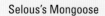

Small Grey Mongoose

25mm · 28mm

right front · right back

Food: Invertebrates (mainly insects) and small rodents; also carrion, birds, reptiles, amphibians and wild fruits. One observed standing on hind legs and eating grapes in vineyard.
Reproduction: From 1–3 young are born in holes, among rocks or in dense vegetation, from about August–December in the south. Mammae: 3 pairs abdominal.
Longevity: One captive lived 8 years 8 months; one wild marked animal lived at least 4 years.

Galerella flavescens

Kaokoland Slender Mongoose *Galerella (Herpestes) flavescens*
Total length 69cm; tail 34cm (males slightly larger than females).
Based on aspects of morphology and some behaviour differences, an additional species may be recognized, *G. (H.) nigrita*.
Identification pointers: *G. (H.) nigrita* appears black in the field but 'in hand' dark brown, with darker to black stripe down back. Should not be confused with any other mongoose in range. Kaokoland Slender Mongoose overall grizzled brown-yellow and similar to Slender Mongoose.

Description: In Black Mongoose *(G. (H.) nigrita)* overall coat colour appears black at distance but in fact dark brown, lacking grizzling of Kaokoland Slender Mongoose, with a darker to black stripe running from snout to tip of tail. Last third of tail black. Legs and flanks dark brown but former marginally lighter in colour. In Kaokoland Slender Mongoose the coat is brown-yellow with a distinctive grizzled appearance, with a contrasting black tail-tip.
Distribution: Limited to narrow belt in the north, along the north-south running western escarpment, extending into Kaokoland, across the Cunene River into Angola.
Habitat: Seems to be restricted to rocky areas in semi-arid country and both are independent of water.
Behaviour: Apparently mainly solitary but pairs and groups of 3 observed and several seen in close proximity to a rotting Greater Kudu carcass.
Food: Takes a wide range of prey items, especially insects but also reptiles, and birds (including nestlings) up to the size of Helmeted Guineafowl recorded. Scavenges flies, larvae and pupae from game carcasses.
Reproduction: Nothing known.
Longevity: Not known.

Galerella sanguinea

Slender Mongoose *Galerella (Herpestes) sanguinea*
Total length 50–65cm; tail 23–30cm; mass (M) 500–800g, (F) 370–560g.
Identification pointers: Small size and slender body; colour grey, brown or chestnut-orange; short legs and fairly bushy tail with black tip - raised or vertical but with forward curve when running; compare with Small Grey Mongoose (p.224) where range overlaps, but the latter lacks black-tipped tail. (According to some taxonomists, more than one species is involved, others believe only one is involved, with no subspecies.)

Description: Body colour of this slender species varies from grizzled yellow-brown to rich red-brown; with the latter colour most frequently encountered in the western areas of the region. In central and northern Namibia usually dark brown but reddish-brown specimens also occur. Tail bushy and black-tipped. When

The Black Mongoose is considered by some to be a distinct species.

The Slender Mongoose comes in many colour forms.

The reddish form of the Slender Mongoose is common in the Kalahari.

The Slender Mongoose is a solitary hunter that takes a wide range of prey.

Kaokoland Slender Mongoose

Slender Mongoose

23mm   25mm

right front   right back

the animal runs, tail typically held well clear of the ground and often vertical, but curving forward over back and not rigidly upright as in the Suricate (p.254). *Galerella (H.) flavescens* and *G. (H.) nigrita* (see previous account) are sometimes given full species recognition.

Distribution: Widespread in the region north of the Orange River, with an extensive sub-Saharan range. It is possible that several species are involved given its near Pan-sub-Saharan distribution.

Habitat: It is found in areas of high and low rainfall, and from forest to open savanna, as long as there is adequate cover.

Behaviour: Terrestrial but climbs well. Usually solitary. One of most commonly seen small carnivores within its range, particularly along roads, and almost exclusively diurnal. They occupy fixed home ranges (one study 50–100ha) within which several individuals may have contact in overlapping ranges. Males will form long-lasting coalitions. Will shelter in dense thickets and under debris but will dig their own burrows and will also share those dug by Southern African Ground Squirrels where ranges overlap, with no apparent conflict.

Food: Insects and other invertebrates; also takes reptiles, small rodents, birds and amphibians as well as wild fruits.

Reproduction: Litter size 1 or 2, sometimes 3, born in summer (October–February). Gestation period approximately 45 days. Mammae: 2 or 3 pairs abdominal.

Longevity: Estimate for wild, 4–6 years.

Large Grey Mongoose *Herpestes ichneumon*

Total length 100–112cm; tail 45–58cm; mass 2.5–4kg.

Identification pointers: Large size; long grey-grizzled body hair; black tail-tip and black lower legs. Much larger than Small Grey Mongoose, which has a completely grey tail and no black at tip; much bigger than Slender Mongoose, which also has black-tipped tail.

Herpestes ichneumon

Description: As its name indicates, this is a large grey mongoose, with overall grizzling. The tail is prominently black-tipped and the lower parts of the legs are covered with short black hairs. The body hair is very long, particularly towards the hindquarters. Tail hair is long, becoming shorter towards the black tip. When walking, the tail is held in a shallow curve with tip angled upwards.

Distribution: Occurs in a narrow belt along the southern and west coast from close to Cape Town, then northwards into KwaZulu-Natal. It is fairly widely distributed in the eastern areas of southern Africa and extensively in the north. Records from the 1950s indicated that it occurred only as far as Knysna in South Africa, but by the 1970s it had spread to the Caledon and Bredasdorp districts. Since then, it has steadily expanded its range westwards up the West Coast to Lambert's Bay and, in 2006, was observed at Kleinzee, just 120km south of the Orange River estuary. It is also widespread in other parts of Africa, although absent from much of the equatorial forest zone and from the desert regions.

Habitat: Riverine vegetation and around lakes, dams, marshes and coastlines. When foraging, however, it may wander several kilometres from its usual habitat but rarely far from fresh water.

Behaviour: Mainly diurnal, although nocturnal activity has been recorded. It is usually seen solitarily or in pairs, but family parties are not uncommon. Such parties may walk in a line, nose to anus, giving the group a snake-like appearance. It frequently stands on its hind legs to view the surrounding area. Droppings are

The Slender Mongoose is an active hunter and takes a wide range of small prey.

The Large Grey Mongoose has a grey-grizzled coat but the legs and tail-tip are black.

Large Grey Mongoose

42mm

right
front

44mm

right
back

deposited at regular latrine sites and it also marks objects within its home range with anal gland secretions. Home range size varies but in one regional study individuals and family parties moved over 300–450ha.

Food: Small rodents are very important in its diet but it also eats other small mammals, reptiles, birds, amphibians and a wide range of invertebrates, as well as wild fruits. It is known to eat snakes, including fairly large puff-adders.

Reproduction: Young are probably born in the summer months but there is no information available for southern Africa. Litter size has been recorded as 2–4, born after a gestation period of about 75 days (some references give 60 days). Young remain with the parents until at least the end of their first year. Mammae: 2 (rarely 3) pairs abdominal.

Longevity: One captive lived 17 years 5 months, another is claimed to have exceeded 20 years; records to 12 years in the wild.

Atilax paludinosus

Water (Marsh) Mongoose *Atilax paludinosus*

Total length 80–100cm; tail 30–40cm; shoulder height 22cm; mass 2.5–5.5kg.
Identification pointers: Large; generally uniform dark brown; associated with water. Sometimes confused with the two otter species, but much smaller than Cape Clawless Otter, and lacks the pale markings found on throat and neck of the Spotted-necked Otter (both p.232). The head is long and pointed and typically mongoose-like.

Description: Large, usually uniformly dark brown, shaggy-haired animal, but may appear black when wet. Short hair on feet and face. Some are reddish-brown or almost black. The relatively long toes leave distinctive splayed tracks in mud.

Distribution: Widespread in the region but absent from arid interior. It penetrates the Karoo along the length of the Orange River to the west coast and many annual streams that penetrate the Great Karoo plateau. Occurs throughout sub-Saharan Africa, wherever habitat is suitable.

Habitat: The Water Mongoose is usually associated with well-watered areas, along rivers and streams, and around dams, lakes, estuaries and swamps wherever there is cover. It utilizes temporary stream-beds where there are pools and may wander some distance from water.

Behaviour: This mongoose is active mainly at night but is also crepuscular (active at dusk and dawn). It is probably territorial and sightings are mostly of single animals, although pairs and females with young are occasionally seen. The home ranges tend to be linear, in that they follow rivers and streams or the perimeters of other bodies of water. Droppings accumulate at latrine sites, which are usually situated near the water's edge; these latrines are not, however, as dispersed as those of otters and the droppings are usually darker in colour. When foraging, it follows regular pathways. It swims readily. Usually spends the day lying up in dense reed beds, vegetation tangles, and sometimes burrows dug by other species. In the Great Karoo, will lie up in rock crevices and boulder tumbles.

Food: Mainly crabs and amphibians but also small rodents, birds, fish, insects, reptiles and occasionally wild fruits. Aquatic food hunted in shallows where feet are used to dig in the mud and explore under rocks. It smashes freshwater mussels by throwing them against rocks with front feet between hind legs. It forages along beaches and in rock-pools in coastal areas. To avoid skin toxins of toads, they flip them on the back and eat from the belly, discarding the back skin. Large crabs are disabled by removing pincers and carapace, which are discarded. Compare with Cape Clawless Otter (p.230).

The Water, or Marsh, Mongoose is usually associated with marshes, lakes, estuaries, dams and other bodies of water.

The Water Mongoose has a shaggy coat and naked toes.

Water Mongoose cubs weigh about 120g at birth.

Water Mongoose

41mm

right front

36mm

right back

Reproduction: Most of the young probably born August– December, after about a 74-day gestation. There are usually 1–3 young, each weighing about 120g at birth, and they are born in burrows, rock crevices or among dense vegetation. Mammae: 2 or 3 pairs abdominal.

Longevity: One captive lived to 17 years 5 months; it's claimed that a wild individual lived for 19 years but most probably rarely survive long beyond their tenth year.

Helogale parvula

Dwarf Mongoose *Helogale parvula*

Total length 30–40cm; tail 14–20cm; shoulder height 7cm; mass 220–350g.
Identification pointers: Very small size; uniform dark brown, glossy coat; always in troops.

Description: Dwarf Mongoose is the smallest carnivore occurring in the region. Its body is a uniform dark brown and from a distance appears to be almost black. The fur is glossy and has a slightly grizzled appearance at close quarters.

Distribution: Dwarf Mongoose is restricted to the northern and eastern regions of the southern African region. Outside of the region in Africa it extends into East Africa to as far north as Somalia and Ethiopia.

Habitat: Open woodland and grassland savanna. It is absent from very dry areas and forest but is often associated with rocky areas, even in mountain ranges such as the Soutpansberg.

Behaviour: A strictly diurnal mongoose usually living in troops of up to 10 individuals, although as many as 30 have been recorded. They occupy a fixed home in a range that is usually no greater than 50ha (2–30ha). Will frequently occupy termitaria, but also den in burrows (dug by other species or self-excavated) as well as among rocks. Several, up to 20, suitable dens are used within a home range. Dwarf Mongoose troops have a rigid social system with a dominant male and female, the rest of the members falling into a 'pecking order'. Usually only the dominant female breeds, and apart from suckling the young, she leaves their care to the other troop members. When disturbed, Dwarf Mongooses will dive for cover but they are inquisitive and will soon re-emerge, standing on their hind legs to look around. They frequently mark objects, and each other, within the home range with secretions from anal and cheek glands. Droppings are deposited at midden sites within the home range. When foraging, troop members keep contact with a constant 'chatter' call.

Food: Insects and other invertebrates are by far the most important prey items but they will also eat reptiles, birds and birds' eggs. Several troop members may co-operate to overpower larger prey.

Reproduction: 2–4 (1–7) young are born in the summer months (October–March) after a gestation period of some 50–54 days. The young are covered with hair at birth and the eyes are closed. Mammae: 3 pairs abdominal.

Longevity: Up to 7 years in the wild; two captives lived 12 years 3 months, and 10 years.

The social Dwarf Mongoose often lives in large termite mounds.

Above and inset: The Dwarf Mongoose's coat ranges in colour from very dark brown to grey-fawn. Paler animals are more frequently seen in the north and east of the region.

Dwarf Mongoose

16mm
right
front

16mm
right
back

Ichneumia albicauda

White-tailed Mongoose *Ichneumia albicauda*

Total length 90–150cm; tail 35–48cm; mass 3.5–5.2kg.
Identification pointers: Large size; white tail, dark body and legs. The superficially similar Selous's Mongoose (p.242) is smaller and its tail is only white towards the tip. When walking, the head is held lower than the rest of the body.

Description: This very large mongoose has a coarse, shaggy coat and distinctively long, white tail. Tail generally darker towards the base. The body and the long legs are brown-grey to almost black but the head is usually somewhat lighter in colour, and distinctly grizzled. When it walks, its hindquarters appear to be higher than the shoulder region.

Distribution: Found in the eastern and northern parts of the southern African region. Further north, it occurs widely in central and East Africa, extending as far north as Egypt, and also occurs through the savannas of West Africa to Senegal. Also present in southern Arabia.

Habitat: Woodland savanna but marginally in forest, particularly in well-watered areas. Largely absent from equatorial forest and desert, but penetrates drier savanna areas along watercourses.

Behaviour: Nocturnal and usually solitary but occasionally pairs or family parties may be seen. It lies up in burrows dug by other species, or in rock crevices and among dense vegetation. In a study outside the region, home ranges covered between 23–29ha. Both sexes are territorial, although 2 or 3 females and their young of the season may live in loosely knit clans. They defecate at den sites and also elsewhere within the home range. Little is known about the biology of this mongoose.

Food: Insects and other invertebrates are by far the most important food but it also takes rodents, amphibians, reptiles, birds and wild fruits. It is recorded as catching mammals up to the size of hares and cane-rats.

Reproduction: The young are probably born in spring and early summer (October–February). There are 1 or 2, rarely 3 or 4, young per litter. Mammae: 3 pairs abdominal.

Longevity: One captive lived 12.5 years, but up to 14 years has been claimed.

Cynictis penicillata

Yellow Mongoose *Cynictis penicillata*

Total length 40–60cm; tail 18–25cm; shoulder height 15–18cm; mass 450–900g.
Identification pointers: Small size; yellowish body and tail; white tail-tip; in parts of northern range, specimens are greyer, lacking white tail-tip (see Selous's Mongoose p.242); pointed face.

Description: Usually reddish-yellow to tawny-yellow with prominent white tip to tail. However, in northern parts of range, particularly Botswana, it is more grey and usually lacks white tip to tail. Could be confused with Selous's Mongoose in that part of range. Tail quite bushy. Chin, throat and upper chest paler than rest of body and eyes are orange-brown. Tail held parallel to the ground when walking, and at 45° to the ground when running. Compare with Slender Mongoose (p.244) and Suricate (p.254).

Distribution: Western and central areas of the region, extending as far east as north-western KwaZulu-Natal and Limpopo provinces, South Africa. A southern African endemic.

Above and inset: The large White-tailed Mongoose has a coarse shaggy coat and a long, white tail.

The White-tailed Mongoose is mainly a savanna species but in some areas it is found in more rugged country. Some individuals have black tails, as here.

The reddish-yellow form of the Yellow Mongoose is the most widespread.

Over much of its range the Yellow Mongoose has a white tip to the tail but in the far north this may be absent. **Inset**: These Yellow Mongoose skins show the extent of the white tail-tip.

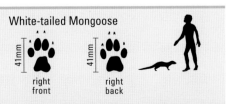

White-tailed Mongoose

41mm
right front

41mm
right back

Yellow Mongoose

25mm
right front

25mm
right back

Habitat: This is a mongoose of open habitats, such as short grassland and semi-desert scrub, but it also occurs in the more open areas along the coast. It is absent from forest, dense vegetation and the coastal Namib Desert.

Behaviour: Diurnal species and, although usually seen alone, it lives communally in warrens of 5–10 (sometimes as many as 20 but this based on one record) individuals. It may dig its own burrows but will readily occupy those dug by Suricate or Southern African Ground Squirrels, sometimes with all three species living in the same burrow systems. Each morning the Yellow Mongoose colony disperses along regularly used pathways to forage. The droppings are deposited in latrines in close proximity to the entrances to the burrows. Males occupy larger home ranges than females.

Food: Mostly insects and invertebrates, but also takes small rodents, amphibians and reptiles and occasionally carrion.

Reproduction: In the southern parts of its distribution range, litters of 2–4 (rarely 5) young are born after a gestation of 60–62 days, October–January, but in the north this extends through to March. It is possible that births also occur at other times of the year as well, and often 2 litters dropped per season. The only mongoose known to bring larger food items to young at den. Mammae: 3 pairs abdominal.

Longevity: One captive lived 15 years 2 months; 2 years fairly common, probably less in the wild.

Suricata suricatta

Suricate (Meerkat) *Suricata suricatta*

Total length 45–55cm; tail 20–24cm; shoulder height 12cm; mass 620–960g.
Identification pointers: Small size; pale body colour with several irregular transverse bands on the back; thinly haired tail, usually with darker tip, and often used as a fifth 'leg' when standing on hind legs and held rigidly vertical when running. Occurs in groups. Could be confused with Banded Mongoose (p.236) but ranges only overlap marginally (see maps) and banding much more distinct in that species. Habitat preferences also differ.

Description: The body is fawn to silvery-grey with a number of darker, irregular transverse bars running from behind the shoulders to the base of the tail. The tail is thin, tapering and short-haired; not bushy. The head is broad at the back and the muzzle is pointed. Frequently stands on hind legs and the tail is used for support. When running, tail held vertically (see Slender Mongoose, p.244). The front claws are very long and are used when digging for prey and excavating burrow systems.

Distribution: Widely distributed in the central and western parts of the region south of the Cunene-Zambezi line, extending marginally eastwards. Marginally enters south-west Angola.

Habitat: Open, arid, lightly vegetated country.

Behaviour: Completely diurnal in habit, and lives in groups numbering 5–40 individuals, but usually 8–15. They have a complex and rather fluid social system, living in multi-male, multi-female groups, and occupying home ranges that average some 500ha (maximum 1,500ha). It will dig its own burrow complexes (warrens) but also makes use of those dug by Southern African Ground Squirrels and Yellow Mongooses, often living in harmony with both species. There may be two or three burrow systems within a troop's home range but with many others that are used as bolt-holes when danger threatens. As with Yellow Mongoose, principal warren sites become raised above the surrounding ground as soil is excavated over long periods.

Suricates are highly social, living in multi-male, multi-female troops.

Suricates frequently stand on their hind legs, using the tail as a 'fifth leg' for balance.

Young female Suricate

Suricate on guard

Suricate (Meerkat)

20mm

right front

23mm

right back

When foraging or on the move, they maintain communication with a constant soft grunting. During foraging, at least one individual stands guard, alert for predators, often climbing into a low bush or on a rock or termite mound to increase the area visible. Although area dependent, over much of their range Suricates deposit droppings in latrine sites near the warrens. Scent marking is frequent.

Food: Predominantly insects and other invertebrates, but will also eat reptiles and birds. Much of the food is obtained by digging with the long claws of the forefeet.

Reproduction: After a gestation period of 73 days, 2–5 young, weighing 25–36g, mainly born in summer (October–March), but records throughout the year. All troop members care for the young; dominant female often produces most litters. Mammae: 3 pairs abdominal.

Longevity: Up to 12 years or more in captivity.

GENETS & CIVETS Family Viverridae

Recent thinking identifies four species of genet found in southern Africa: Small-spotted *(Genetta genetta)* with a wide range; **South African Large-spotted** *(G. tigrina)*, found along the coastal plain of South Africa; **Common Large-spotted** *(G. maculata)*, found widely to the north-east; and **Angolan** *(G. angolensis)* from northern parts of the region. However, there is no finality on the range limits of the different species, nor on their taxonomic standing. We suspect these problems will be revisited many more times in the future.

Genetta genetta

Small-spotted Genet Genetta genetta
Total length 86–100cm; tail 40–50cm; mass 1.5–2.6kg.

Angolan Genet Genetta angolensis
Total length 82–91cm; tail 38–43cm; mass 1.3–2kg.

Common Large-spotted Genet Genetta maculata
Total length 85–110cm; tail 40–50cm; mass 1.5–3.2kg.

South African Large-spotted Genet Genetta tigrina
Total length 85–110cm; tail 40–50cm; mass 1.5–3.2kg.

■ *Genetta angolensis*
■ *Genetta tigrina*

Identification pointers: All genets have long, slender bodies and tails; Small-spotted Genet has a white tail-tip, smaller dark to black spots, and a crest of longish hair along back that is only raised when alarmed. This latter character is also found in Angolan Genet. Large-spotted genets usually have a black tail-tip, larger, rusty-brown spots, and no crest along the back. Compare distribution maps and habitat requirements. Sometimes confused with African Civet (p.260), but very much smaller.

Description: Genet species have long, slender bodies and tails, and short legs. The ears are long, rounded and thin. Small-spotted Genet is usually off-white to greyish-white, spotted with dark brown to almost black spots and bars. The tail is black-ringed and usually has a white tip. A crest of fairly long, black-tipped hair runs along the back and is raised when the animal is frightened or angry. Angolan Genets have overall reddish-grey to dark grey coats liberally sprinkled with small brown spots and five rows of elongated spots or stripes along sides of neck. Only other genet with an erectile dark dorsal crest (to 60mm) that can be raised when angry or frightened. In Large-spotted Genets, the spots are generally larger and rusty-brown in colour and the legs are usually paler. There is no prominent crest

Genetta maculata

The tail of the Suricate is well haired but not bushy. **Inset:** These skins of Banded Mongoose (**top**) and Suricate (**bottom**) show the variations in banding on the back.

Small-spotted Genet has prominent black-and-white facial markings. **Inset:** Detail of the spots of the Small-spotted Genet.

Genets

22mm

right
front

20mm

right
back

down the back and the hair is shorter and softer. The tail-tip is usually dark brown to black. The black-and-white facial markings are usually more prominent in **Small-spotted** and **Angolan Genets** than in **South African** and **Common Large-spotted Genets**; the chin of the former is dark and the latter usually white. The claws are retractile like those of the cats.

It should be noted that the systematics of the various species of African genet, including the southern African species, have not yet been fully clarified. There are enormous variations in colour and patterning, and all intermediate grades between the two large-spotted may be encountered.

Distribution: Small-spotted Genet is widespread in southern Africa but absent from much of Mozambique, northern and eastern Zimbabwe; occurring marginally in KwaZulu-Natal. Also occurs widely in southern Angola and the extreme west of Zambia. It is absent from much of Central Africa but a separate population extends from Tanzania northwards to Sudan and through the Sahel to West Africa, North Africa, the Middle East and parts of Europe (sometimes referred to as *G. felina*). Common Large-spotted Genet is chiefly restricted to the eastern and northern areas of southern Africa. **South African Large-spotted Genet** occurs in a narrow belt along the south coast of South Africa. **Common Large-spotted Genet** also occurs widely in the rest of sub-Saharan Africa.

Habitat: Small-spotted Genet has a very wide habitat tolerance, ranging from desert margins to areas with high rainfall. This includes woodland, riverine margins and even isolated rocky outcrops on open plains. **South African** and **Common Large-spotted Genets** are more associated with well-watered areas and fairly dense vegetation. Small-spotted and the two large-spotted occur together in some areas of southern Africa. In the region, the **Angolan Genet** is largely restricted to the miombo woodlands in Angola, Zambia and northern Mozambique.

Behaviour: Genets are mainly nocturnal, lying up under cover during the day. Dens may be in animal burrows, vegetation tangles, among rocks, hollow logs and not uncommonly in roofs of human habitation. They are excellent climbers although much of their foraging is done on the ground. Normally solitary, pairs are occasionally seen, or a female accompanied by young. Droppings are deposited at latrine sites and these are usually in open or conspicuous places. Radio-tracking of **Common Large-spotted** in Kenya showed male average home range of 590ha and female 280ha. In a South African study, home ranges measured 50–100ha for the **South African Large-spotted**.

Food: Genet species have a similar diet. Invertebrates, particularly insects, are very important sources of food, as are small rodents. Reptiles, amphibians, birds and other small mammals are taken, as well as wild fruits. Genets can be a problem to poultry-owners; if they gain access to a poultry-run or hen-house, they will often kill far more than they require.

Reproduction: Young are born in the summer months (September–March) in holes, rock crevices or among dense vegetation; 2–4 young (up to 5 have been recorded for the **South African** and **Common Large-spotted Genets**) are born after a gestation period of about 70 days, weighing 50–80g. The eyes are closed at birth. Mammae: 2 pairs abdominal.

Longevity: 9–14 years in captivity; Small-spotted Genet 13 years; record captive 21 years 6 months.

The Common Large-spotted Genet has a very wide distribution in the north and east of the region.
Inset: In areas with higher rainfall this genet tends to have a darker coat.

South African Large-spotted Genet has large, usually rusty-brown, spots, and a dark-brown or black-tipped tail.

Civettictis civetta

African Civet *Civettictis civetta*

Total length 120–140cm; tail 40–50cm; shoulder height 40cm; mass 9–15kg (rarely to 20kg).

Identification pointers: Large size; white, black and grey facial markings; grey body heavily marked with black spots, blotches and irregular stripes; black legs; black-and-white neck bands; bushy tail with white bands below and black tip; walks with back arched and head held low. Sometimes confused with genets but is much larger, with shorter tail. See the genets (p.256).

Description: Long-bodied, heavily built and long-legged – about the size of a medium-sized dog. When moving, it holds its back in an arched position and its head low. Hair long and coarse. Forehead light-grey, muzzle white, and broad black band runs horizontally between forehead and muzzle and extends round head onto throat. Distinct light band extends from ear base towards chest. Greyish to grey-brown overall with many black spots, blotches and bands covering the body but varies between individuals. Spotting is less distinct on, or may be absent from the shoulder and neck. Legs black. Ridge of dark hair along spine to tail is erected when African Civet is threatened or under stress. Ears small with black tip. Bushy tail banded white and black below; upper side and tip black.

Distribution: Restricted to the northern and eastern parts of the region. Recent records outside the African Civet's natural normal distribution range have been noted in parts of the southern Free State, and south-eastern Namibia. At this stage, we have no explanation why this expansion is taking place, but it may have something to do with changing agricultural or farming practices.

Habitat: Fairly wide habitat tolerance but preference for more densely vegetated areas, for example, open woodland; near permanent water.

Behaviour: Mainly nocturnal but often active in early morning and late afternoon. Solitary or in pairs. Regular latrine sites known as 'civetries', usually in hollows or depressions. Marks points within its range with secretions from anal glands and these are repeatedly revisited. Several individuals may use the same civetries and marking points.

Food: Insects, other invertebrates, wild fruits, small rodents, reptiles, birds and carrion. Largest prey recorded are hares and guinea-fowl.

Reproduction: Litter 2–4, cub weighing about 300g, usually born in summer (August–January), in burrows excavated by other species, in rock crevices, or in dense vegetation. Gestation period 60–65 days. Mammae: 2 pairs abdominal.

Longevity: One captive lived 15 years (unconfirmed 28 years); probably <10 years in the wild.

PALM CIVET Family Nandiniidae

Nandinia binotata

African Palm Civet *Nandinia binotata*

Total length 87–97cm; tail 45–50cm; mass 1.5–3kg.

Identification pointers: Previously called Tree Civet; also called Two-spotted Palm Civet. Long, fairly slender body and tail; generally dark appearance in the field, but at close quarters seen to be lighter brown with numerous darker, irregular spots. Forest habitat. Compared with the genet species (p.256), African Palm Civets have a more limited distribution in southern Africa. See distribution map.

The heavily built African Civet is strictly terrestrial. This civet has distinctive facial markings. **Inset:** This photograph shows the coarse hair and spots close-up.

The African Civet is sometimes mistaken for the much smaller and shorter-legged genets.

African Palm Civet

African Civet

50mm

right
front

48mm

right
back

African Palm Civet

33mm

right
front

33mm

right
back

Description: Similar to but stouter than genets. Head rounder with short ears. At a distance appear uniformly dark brown but at close quarters, upperparts noticeably spotted with small, irregularly shaped, dark brown, almost black spots, on a lighter-brown background. More or less visible white or yellowish spot above each shoulder-blade. Sides and lower parts of limbs not spotted. Hair soft and woolly on body and quite long on the long tail.

Distribution: In the region, occurs only in eastern Zimbabwe and adjacent areas of Mozambique, and Malawi, and across much of northern Angola. Widespread in the equatorial forest zone.

Habitat: Found in areas of high forest or Afromontane rainforest with an annual rainfall of 1,000mm or more.

Behaviour: It is nocturnal, solitary and largely arboreal. Usually moves in the taller trees but does descend to the ground.

Food: Its principal food is wild fruit, although it also feeds on birds, rodents and insects. It has also been recorded as catching and eating fruit-bats. Carrion is eaten and they may take to raiding poultry-runs.

Reproduction: Virtually nothing is known about its biology in southern Africa but it seems likely that it may breed at any time of the year. Usually 2, but up to 4, young, weighing an average 56g, are born in tree-holes after a gestation period of about 64 days. Mammae: 2 pairs.

Longevity: More than 16 years in captivity; one lived to 16 years 5 months.

HYAENAS Family Hyaenidae

Crocuta crocuta
■ present range
▨ historic range

Spotted Hyaena *Crocuta crocuta*
Total length 120–180cm; tail 25cm; shoulder height 85cm; mass 60–80kg.
Identification pointers: Large size; shoulders higher than rump; short-haired, fawn-yellow to dirty grey coat with numerous dark brown spots or blotches; lacks the long hair and pointed ears of Brown Hyaena (p.264). Characteristic repertoire of whooping, giggling and cackling calls.

Description: Unmistakable. Heavily built forequarters stand higher than rump. Large head with prominent rounded ears; black muzzle. Body usually fawn-yellow to grey-fawn with scattering of dark brown spots and blotches, less distinct in old animals. Head, throat and chest not spotted. Short tail has coarse hair covering and held erect or curved over back during certain social interactions. Short erect mane along neck and shoulders.

Distribution: Formerly occurred as far south as Cape Town. Now only found in the northern and eastern parts of region but reintroduced to a number of parks within former range in the south.

Habitat: Open country but also rocky areas and in open woodland. Absent from forest and the Namib coastal belt but penetrates this desert along seasonal riverbeds. Requires access to drinking water.

Behaviour: Usually live in family groups or 'clans' led by a female. Clan members share the same range and dens and may number from 3 or 4, to 15 or more individuals. Territories are defended against other clans and are marked with anal gland secretions, urine and the distinctive bright white droppings – usually deposited in latrine sites. Mainly nocturnal but frequently seen during the day. Very vocal with whoops, groans, grunts, whines, yells and giggles. Dens may be holes in the ground, or complex warren system associated with rocky outcrops and caves. Den use most critical when there are cubs. Clan territories in the Kalahari may exceed 1,000km².

The African Palm Civet is a tree-dweller but does occasionally operate on the ground.

Spotted Hyaena

Spotted Hyaena, the best-known of Africa's three hyaena species, has an extensive range south of the Sahara.

Spotted Hyaena

96mm right front

89mm right back

Clan members consist of related females, their young, and unrelated males that remain with a clan for varying lengths of time (up to several years in some cases). The highest-ranking female dominates all other members, including the dominant male.
Food: In the past regarded as a cowardly scavenger, now known to be an efficient and regular hunter. Hunts singly, in small groups or in packs, depending on type of prey taken. Diet ranges from insects to large game such as zebra, wildebeest and giraffe. Scavenges and will chase other predators from their kills. Raids dustbins and rubbish-heaps at campsites.
Reproduction: 1 or 2 cubs is usual, very rarely more, each weighing about 1.5kg; largely an aseasonal breeder although seasonal peaks can be discerned in some regions. Gestation about 110 days. Two or more females may keep young in same burrow for several months but each exclusively suckles its own young. Uniform dark brown at birth with lighter heads. Mammae: 2 pairs abdominal.
Longevity: More than16 years recorded in the wild; 12–25 years in captivity; one lived for 41 years 1 month.

Hyaena brunnea

Brown Hyaena   *Hyaena brunnea*

Total length 130–160cm; tail 17–30cm; shoulder height 80cm; mass (M) 47kg, (F) 42kg; 35–58kg range.
Identification pointers: Large size with shoulders higher than the rump; long dark brown hair, lighter in colour on neck and shoulders; large head with long pointed ears; long-haired tail. Spotted Hyaena has shorter hair, a spotted coat to lesser or greater extent, and has shorter, more rounded ears.

Description: Brown Hyaena is higher at the shoulder than at the hindquarters; shoulders and chest are heavily built. The body is covered in a long, shaggy coat, with a dense mantle of hair on the back and shoulders. The mantle is lighter in colour than the rest of the body. Body colour varies from light to dark brown and the legs are striped black and light brown. The tail is short, bushy and dark. Ears are long, erect and pointed.
Distribution: Brown Hyaena used to occur widely in south of region but today are only seen occasionally south of the Orange River, although recently reintroduced to a number of parks and reserves within its former range. It is most frequently encountered in the Kalahari and along the coastline of southern Namibia, but wanderers may turn up far outside their main range. Sightings are becoming more frequent in South Africa's Eastern Cape province and along the south-western coastal plain within its historical range. Marked individuals have been recorded covering distances in excess of 600km, thus explaining why this hyaena may turn up in areas where it has not been seen for many years.
Habitat: Although it is now found mainly in the drier parts of southern Africa, even occurring along the arid Namib Desert coastal belt, its past distribution shows that it has a potentially wide habitat tolerance.
Behaviour: Brown Hyaenas are mainly nocturnal and solitary, usually seen singly. However, several animals (up to 14) may share a territory, although foraging tends to be an individual activity. Territory size varies considerably, from about 19km² in one study to 235–480km² in the southern Kalahari. Animals sharing a territory are apparently an extended family unit, or clan, consisting of 4–6 individuals, all of whom assist in raising cubs. Clan territories in the Kalahari are roughly 30,000–40,000ha in extent and they are actively defended by clan members. However, in the north-east of South Africa, territories are found to

Spotted Hyaena with cub. **Inset:** Young Spotted Hyaenas develop spots in their fourth month.

The Brown Hyaena is distinguished by its long shaggy coat and pointed ears. **Inset:** Brown Hyaena anal gland pasting on grass stalk

Brown Hyaena

85mm

right
front

66mm

right
back

be much smaller, probably a measure of food availability. Some males become nomadic and may mate with receptive females in several clans. Territories are marked with droppings deposited at middens and secretions of the anal glands. Unlike the Spotted Hyaena, the Brown Hyaena is not particularly vocal.

Food: Brown Hyaenas are mainly scavengers but they also eat a wide variety of small vertebrates, insects and fruits. Hunting and killing of large prey is rare, although on occasion it has been recorded as killing sheep and goats in farming areas. Surplus food may be hidden in holes or under vegetation.

Reproduction: Nomadic males overlap the territories of several groups and mate with receptive females, while alpha males resident within the groups also mate. After a gestation of 90–97 days, 2 or 3 (1–5) cubs are born and weigh about 1kg. The eyes are closed at birth and open after 2 weeks. Young are mainly born August–January. Mammae: 2 pairs abdominal.

Longevity: Up to at least 12 years in the wild; one captive >29 years.

Note: The coastline of the Namib Desert offers a reasonable chance of observing this hyaena. Good locations are the vicinity of Lüderitz, especially Grosse Bucht, the campgrounds north of Swakopmund and Cape Cross; also Kleinzee in South Africa's Northern Cape province, the site of a large fur seal colony. Brown Hyaenas are especially attracted during the seal pupping season, from November to early December.

Proteles cristatus

Aardwolf *Proteles cristatus*

Total length 84–100cm; tail 20–28cm; shoulder height 50cm; mass 6–11kg.
Identification pointers: Hyaena-like appearance; prominent mane of erectile long hair down neck and back; pale buff background colour with dark vertical body stripes, with black bands on upper part of legs; feet, muzzle and much of distal part of tail black; long, pointed ears. Much smaller than the two hyaenas.

Description: The Aardwolf is a medium-sized carnivore that is higher at the shoulders than at the rump. The hair is quite long and coarse, with a long mane of erectile hair down the neck and back, raised only when the animal is frightened or threatened. The general background colour varies from pale tawny to yellow-white and there are several vertical black stripes on the body and black bands on the upper parts of the legs. The muzzle and feet are black. At its base the bushy tail is yellow-fawn but the remainder is black. The ears are large and pointed.

Distribution: Aardwolf is very widely distributed in the region and extends into southern Angola and marginally into Zambia. It is largely absent from Central Africa but there is a population in East Africa that extends north along the Red Sea to southern Egypt.

Habitat: This carnivore has a very wide habitat tolerance, occurring in regions of both low and high rainfall. It shows a marked preference for open habitats and avoids wooded or forested areas. Its distribution is dictated by the availability of termites, its principal food.

Behaviour: Although mainly active at night, it may be seen during the early morning and late afternoon, as well as on overcast days. It occurs singly, in pairs or in family parties. A home range may be occupied by two or more animals. Although it will dig its own burrows, it mainly uses and modifies burrows dug by other species, especially those of Springhares. Droppings are usually deposited at a number of latrine sites within the home range and grass-stalks are marked with a secretion from the anal glands. Aardwolf is socially monogamous, with

The front legs of the Brown Hyaena are boldly ringed with black.

The Brown Hyaena is a largely solitary forager.

The Aardwolf has a naked black muzzle and large pointed ears.

Aardwolf

60mm
right front

53mm
right back

a mated pair occupying a territory with their current young, but both male and female will mate with other individuals. Male and female mark the territory and will chase off intruders. Territories cover 100–600ha, size being dependent on termite abundance.

Food: Mostly termites, but it will occasionally take other insects. Despite the frequent claim that it kills and eats sheep, there is no evidence of this. Although the canine teeth are well developed, the cheek-teeth (p.432) are greatly reduced in size and are not capable of dealing with flesh. Aardwolf feed almost exclusively on harvester termites of the genus *Trinervitermes*. In a single night, an individual Aardwolf can consume up to 300,000 termites, with a combined weight of about 1.2kg. In one study, it was estimated that a single Aardwolf may consume an astounding 105 million termites in one year, which would amount to 420kg. A farmer's friend indeed!

Reproduction: 1–4 young, weighing about 450g, are born in a burrow after a gestation period of about 90 days. Although most young are dropped October–February in the region, they have also been recorded at other times of the year. Pups remain in the den for their first month, and at 9–12 weeks of age they accompany an adult on foraging expeditions up to 100m from the den. From 7 months they will forage alone and at 12 months they are independent of their parents. Mammae: 2 pairs inguinal.

Longevity: One captive lived to 15 years, another to 18 years 11 months.

Note: There is controversy as to whether the Aardwolf belongs to the hyaena family (three species), or its own family (single species). There are characters that indicate that the Aardwolf is, in fact, a highly specialized hyaena, both anatomically and behaviour-wise and it is generally classified as such today.

CATS Family Felidae

Felis silvestris cafra

African Wild Cat *Felis silvestris cafra*
Total length 85–100cm; tail 25–37cm; shoulder height 35cm; mass 2.5–6kg (one record 8.2kg).
Identification pointers: Very similar in appearance to domestic cat but distinguishable from it by the rich reddish-brown colour of back of ears, over belly and on back of hind legs. Vertical body stripes are present but range from very distinct to very faint.

Description: Similar in appearance to domestic cat but larger with proportionately longer legs. Colour ranges from pale sandy-brown in drier areas to light or dark grey in wetter parts of region. Two subspecies have been recognized on this basis but much overlap and variation. Body marked with more or less distinct dark vertical stripes. Relatively long tail dark-ringed with black tip. Chin and throat white and chest usually paler than rest of body. Belly usually reddish. Back of each ear coloured rich reddish-brown. Dark rings, to lesser or greater extent, on legs. Interbreeds readily with domestic cats and resulting hybrids can cause confusion.

Distribution: Throughout the region, but absent from Namib Desert coastal belt, with wide Pan-African range, into Europe and Asia.

Habitat: Wide habitat tolerance but requires cover. In the region, from sea-level to some 2,400m; all rainfall areas above 100mm per annum but even penetrate desert areas along seasonal watercourses.

The Aardwolf is distinguished by its dark, vertical body stripes and long, pointed ears. **Inset:** The footpads are similar to those of the other hyaenas, in that the rear edge of the main pad is angled.

An African Wild Cat sprays urine to serve as a territorial marker. **Inset:** Domestic cats are significant predators of small vertebrates and readily interbreed with the African Wild Cat.

African Wild Cat

36mm
right
front

36mm
right
back

Behaviour: Solitary, except when mating or when female is tending kittens. Droppings usually buried in the same way as domestic cat but they also establish small latrines where droppings accumulate. Use a variety of dens from rock outcrops, holes dug by other mammals, dense vegetation and will lie up in trees, in areas such as in the Kalahari. Establish marked territories, primarily using urine and possibly tree scratchings, and are defended by both sexes.

Food: Mainly small rodents but they also eat other small mammals, birds, reptiles, amphibians, insects and other invertebrates. The largest recorded prey items are hares, springhares and birds up to the size of guineafowl.

Reproduction: 1–5 kittens, weighing 40–50g, are born following a gestation of 56–65 days, mainly in summer (September–March) among dense vegetation cover, rocks or in burrows dug by other species. Mammae: 3 or 4 pairs abdominal.

Longevity: Up to 15 years in captivity.

Small Spotted Cat *Felis nigripes*

Total length 50–63cm; tail 16cm; shoulder height 25cm; mass 1.3–2.5kg.
Identification pointers: Small size; pale body colour well covered with smallish dark brown to black spots; white chin and throat; back of ears same colour as body. Smaller and more distinctly marked than African Wild Cat, also lacks reddish-ginger colour at back of ears; can be distinguished from genets (p.256) by short tail and typical short, cat-like face.

Felis nigripes

Description: Also called Black-footed Cat. This is the smallest cat species occurring in the region. Colour ranges from reddish-fawn in southern parts of range to much paler in the north. Numerous black (red-brown in north) spots and bars on body, legs, head and tail. Tail is short, black-ringed and -tipped. Chin and throat are white but there are two or three distinct dark bands on the throat. Back of ear is usually same colour as rest of body but lacks markings.

Distribution: Small Spotted Cat is restricted to the more arid southern and central parts of southern Africa. Only recently found to occur on the west coast and south-western interior of the Western Cape province. Within annual rainfall range of 100–500mm.

Habitat: Open, dry habitats with some vegetation cover, especially grass and low Karoo scrub. A single record from Lesotho was at an altitude of 2,000m.

Behaviour: Small Spotted Cat is nocturnal and rarely seen. Usually leaves den after sunset and returns before sunrise. Hunting takes place throughout the night with foraging distances from 4.5–16km. Female home ranges cover 500–1,500ha and ranges of both sexes are marked by urine spraying, scent marking and scratching. Droppings are scattered at random throughout the range. It is nowhere common and little is known about its behaviour. Most sightings are of solitary animals and it lies up in burrows dug by other species and in hollow termite mounds. For this reason, it is sometimes called the 'Anthill Tiger'.

Food: Mostly small rodents, but also takes reptiles, birds and insects. The largest recorded prey item is a Southern African Ground Squirrel, but there are also records of Cape Hare. Largest bird prey recorded is Karoo Korhaan. Scavenging is also known.

Reproduction: A litter of 1–3 kittens (rarely 4) is born in the summer months after a gestation period of about 68 days. Mean birth mass 78g. Most litters born in summer months (possibly August–April), but captives breed throughout the year. Mammae: 2 pairs abdominal, 1 pair inguinal.

Longevity: In the wild, 4–8 years; in captivity, up to 16 years.

African Wild Cat

The African Wild Cat has a pale-reddish belly.

The Small Spotted Cat, the smallest in the region, has numerous spots and bars on the body, legs, head and tail.

Kittens of this size stay in close proximity to the den.

A Small Spotted Cat female and her kitten

Small Spotted Cat

24mm
right front

22mm
right back

Leptailurus serval
■ present range
▨ historic range

Serval *Leptailurus serval*

Total length 96–120cm; tail 25–38cm; shoulder height 60cm; mass 8–13kg.
Identification pointers: Pale, usually yellowish-fawn coat, black-spotted and black-barred; large, rounded ears each with two black bands separated by white patch at back; short, black-banded and black-tipped tail, long legs. Much smaller than either the Cheetah (p.276) or Leopard (p.280), with a proportionately shorter tail and large ears.

Description: Slender, long-legged, spotted cat with short tail and large, rounded ears. Body colour very variable but usually yellowish-fawn with scattered black spots and bars. Black bars and spots on neck; black bands extend down legs. Underparts paler but usually also spotted. Back surface of large, rounded ears has black band, separated from black tip by white patch. Tail banded with black and has black tip. Servals in parts of Zambia are reported to have much smaller spot patterning than is typical for this cat and they are sometimes referred to as Servalines.
Distribution: North and east of the region; formerly along south coast. Recent reintroductions have been made to conservation areas within their former coastal South African range. Widespread outside of the region in Africa.
Habitat: Usually environments with water, adjacent tall grassland, reed beds or rank vegetation fringing forest. Also seems to thrive in areas where sugarcane is grown, possibly because of abundance of rodents. Mainly in higher-rainfall areas from sea-level to higher grassed slopes of mountain ranges (e.g. Drakensberg).
Behaviour: Usually nocturnal but sometimes active in early morning and late afternoon. Usually solitary but also in pairs and family groups. Mainly terrestrial but a good climber. Male and possibly female territorial. Home range size varies from as little as 150ha to 3,000ha. Although female home ranges barely overlap those of males, may overlap those of two or more females. When foraging, tend to follow regularly used pathways and roads.
Food: Small mammals (particularly vlei rats, but up to hares and cane-rats), birds, reptiles and insects. Perhaps young of smaller antelope species.
Reproduction: Most young are born in summer after a gestation of 68–73 (79) days. Usually 1–3 (up to 5) kittens, each weighing about 200g, are born in burrows dug by other species or in dense vegetation. Mammae: 2 pairs abdominal, 1 pair inguinal.
Longevity: 13–20 years in captivity; a captive female that last bred at 14 years lived to 19 years 9 months.

Caracal caracal

Caracal *Caracal caracal*

Total length 70–110cm; tail 18–34cm; shoulder height 40–45cm; mass 7–19kg (exceptional 32kg from Free State, South Africa).
Identification pointers: Hindquarters slightly higher than shoulders; general reddish-fawn coloration; short tail; pointed ears with tuft of black hair at tip and black at back sprinkled with white hairs.

Description: A robustly built cat, its hindquarters slightly higher than its shoulders. Coat thick but short and soft; colour varies from pale reddish-fawn to a rich brick-red. Underparts off-white with faint spotting or blotching. Long, pointed ears with tuft of longish black hair at the tip are characteristic. Backs of ears are black, liberally sprinkled with white hairs. Face prominently marked with black-and-white patches, notably around eyes and mouth. Short reddish tail.

The Serval has very long legs and in some ways resembles a small Cheetah.

The Serval has distinct black-and-white markings on the backs of the ears. **Inset:** A Serval sub-adult

The Caracal has long, pointed ears with a black tuft on the tips. **Inset:** A two-month-old Caracal kitten

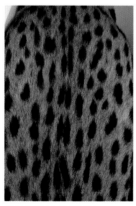

Above left: Serval neck spotting and stripes.
Above right: Rump spotting

The Caracal's rump stands higher than the shoulder region.

Serval

47mm · 44mm

right front · right back

Caracal

47mm · 55mm

right front · right back

Distribution: Widespread in the region but absent from parts of KwaZulu-Natal and the Namib coastal strip. Occurs widely in the rest of Africa, but absent from equatorial forest, and extends into Middle East and as far east as India.

Habitat: Semi-desert to savanna woodland; hilly country to coastal forests; sea level to mountain ranges over 2,000m.

Behaviour: Mainly nocturnal, but partly diurnal if undisturbed. Solitary, except when mating or females accompanied by kittens. Stalks its prey as close as possible and then relies on a direct pounce or short, fast run. Male is territorial, with home range that may overlap that of two or more females. Home ranges of females overlap, but contact probably avoided by olfactory signals, such as from urine, droppings, as well as tree scratchings. Depending on food abundance, home ranges can be as small as 400ha to as large as 10,000ha or more.

Food: The Caracal hunts mainly small to medium-sized mammals, ranging from mice to antelope (up to the size of Bushbuck ewes). It also catches birds and reptiles. In some small-stock farming areas it is considered to be a major problem because of its depredations on sheep and goats.

Reproduction: Litters of 1–3 kittens may be born at any time of the year, although there is a summer peak. The gestation period is about 79 days and the birth mass is around 250g. Kittens may be born in burrows excavated by other species, in rock crevices or among dense vegetation. Mammae: 3 pairs abdominal.

Longevity: Up to 18 years or more in captivity; rarely to 10 years in the wild.

Golden Cat *Caracal aurata*
Total length 1.7–1.35m; tail 35–45cm; shoulder height 38–50cm; mass 8–16kg.
Identification pointers: Medium size; ears rounded; colour reddish-brown to dark brown, grey; tropical forest habitat.

Caracal aurata

Description: Robust and medium-sized cat, with dark-backed, rounded ears. Colour is commonly overall red-brown but in some areas may be dark brown or grey. Dark spots are present to a greater or lesser extent on the underparts and sides, occasionally over the entire body. Underparts and inside of legs usually white to buffy-white, with some barring on the legs. Genetically, closely related to the Caracal and Serval, the Golden Cat is placed in its own genus *Profelis* by some.

Distribution: Only in far northern Angola within forest in the region.

Habitat: Tropical and montane forests.

Behaviour: Solitary; males are known to be territorial. Urine scrapes and scat are possible territorial markers as these are frequently encountered on forest trails. They are both terrestrial and partly arboreal, and both nocturnal and diurnal.

Food: Take a wide range of small prey, including rodents, small forest duikers and birds. Records also of monkeys, but these may be scavenged as they are said to feed from animals caught in snares.

Reproduction: Litters of 1 or 2 kittens, weighing 180–235g, born after gestation of some 75 days. Mammae: Not recorded.

Longevity: Up to 12 years in captivity.

Caracal are normally solitary except when a female is accompanied by young.

The Golden Cat is a solitary species.

The Golden Cat has shorter ears than the Caracal and lacks the prominent ear tufts of that species.

Golden Cats come in several different colour forms, including red-brown (**above**) and grey (**inset**). All forms of Golden Cat are spotted to a greater or lesser extent.

Golden Cat

Acinonyx jubatus
■ present range
▣ historic range

Cheetah *Acinonyx jubatus*

Total length 1.8–2.2m; tail 60–80cm; shoulder height 80cm; mass 40–60kg.
Identification pointers: Large size; slender, greyhound-like build; long, spotted white-tipped tail, black-ringed towards tip; spotted coat – single, rounded, black spots; rounded face with a black line from inner corner of eye to corner of mouth ('tear-mark'). Leopard (p.280) has a heavier build; its spots form rosettes, it has no black lines on the face and it usually frequents different habitats. Serval (p.272) is much smaller, with a disproportionately short tail.

Description: The Cheetah, sometimes referred to as the 'greyhound of cats', is arguably the most elegant member of the cat family. It is tall and slender, with long legs and a short muzzle with a rounded head. The body colour is off-white to pale fawn and is liberally dotted with black, rounded spots more or less uniform in size. A clear black line (the 'tear-mark') runs from the inner corner of each eye to the corner of the mouth. Numerous small black spots are present on the forehead and top of the head. The tips of the ears are white. The long tail is black-ringed with a white tip. A short, erectile crest is situated on the back and sides. The Cheetah is the only cat that does not have fully retractile claws and the impressions of the claws can be seen in their tracks. The well-publicized 'King Cheetah' is merely an aberrant colour form, albeit an attractive one.

Distribution: Although formerly widespread in southern Africa, it is estimated that only 4,000–6,000 survive here. It is still widespread in Botswana and Namibia and has been reintroduced to KwaZulu-Natal and other parts of South Africa but is nowhere common. It is difficult to establish accurate Cheetah numbers; South Africa has just 350 in major reserves, of which some 200 are found in Kruger and Kgalagadi national parks. A further 300 are sparsely distributed in the northern reaches of Limpopo, North-West and Northern Cape. There are no recent estimates for Angola, Zambia and much of Mozambique. Cheetahs still occur widely but patchily throughout much of Africa, except in the equatorial forest regions, although in greatly reduced numbers. Previously it occurred as far east as India, where it is now extinct, but small numbers survive in parts of Iran.

Habitat: Open savanna and light woodland, but also hilly country on occasion. The availability of drinking water is not essential.

Behaviour: Normally seen singly, in pairs or small family parties consisting of female and cubs. It is principally diurnal, but tends to hunt in the cooler hours. Adult males move singly or in bachelor groups (usually brothers) and females establish territories from which they will drive other females. Males are apparently often non-territorial and may move over areas held by several females. Cheetahs roam over large areas; home ranges of females larger than those of males. Favoured lying-up spots are usually raised above the surrounding area and are urine-marked by both males and females. When hunting, Cheetahs stalk to within a short distance of their intended prey and then sprint in for the kill. Although they may top speeds of well over 70km (>100km reported) per hour, this can only be sustained for a few hundred metres.

Food: Normally Cheetahs hunt medium-sized mammals up to a mass of ±60kg, although if two or more cheetah hunt together, larger prey may be overpowered. Antelope are the principal prey items. In Kruger National Park, Impala is the most important prey. It also catches birds up to the size of Ostrich.

Reproduction: Cheetahs have a long, drawn-out courtship. The litters of 1–5 (usually 3) young may be born after gestation of some 92 days, at any time of

Cheetahs hunt mainly small to medium-sized antelope. In the Kalahari, Springbok are the Cheetah's most important prey.

The sleek, long-legged Cheetah is built for speed.

Above: The black tear-mark running from the Cheetah's eye to its mouth is distinctive.
Left: The so-called 'King Cheetah' is merely an aberrant colour form, albeit an attractive one.

Cheetah

84mm

right front

80mm

right back

the year. The cubs are blind and helpless and weigh 250–300g at birth. For the first 6 weeks they are usually hidden in dense plant cover, thereafter following the mother. Mammae: 4 pairs abdominal/pectoral.
Longevity: 9–12 years in the wild; 17–21 years in captivity.
Note: Cheetahs used to be tamed and used for hunting, particularly in Asia. The 16th century Indian Mogul emperor, Akbar the Great, was said to have kept a 'stable' of 1,000 Cheetahs.

Panthera leo
■ present range
▨ historic range

Lion *Panthera leo*

Male: total length 2.5–3.3m; tail 1m; shoulder height 1.2m; mass 150–225kg.
Female: total length 2.3–2.7m; tail 1m; shoulder height 1m; mass 110–152kg.
Identification pointers: Large size; usually uniform tawny colour; males with long mane; dark-tipped tail. Cannot be confused with any other species.

Description: Largest of the African cats and adult males and females are easy to tell apart. Body colour ranges from reddish-grey to pale tawny with lighter underparts. Although faint spots are present on the sides of cubs, these are usually lost by adulthood. Tail is short-haired and same colour as rest of body but has a dark tip. Only the adult male carries a mane of long hair, extending from the sides of the face onto the neck, shoulders and chest. Mane colour ranges from pale tawny to black. 'White' lions from the South African Lowveld are not true albinos but are genetic variants with strongly reduced pigmentation.
Distribution: In the recent past, Lion occurred throughout the region but are now found only in the northern and eastern areas, largely restricted to the major conservation areas. Of the ±2,500 Lions occurring in the wild in South Africa, some 2,000 are found in the Kruger National Park, while the Kgalagadi Transfrontier Park has ±450 Lions; both naturally occurring populations. Reintroduced to the Hluhluwe/iMfolozi complex in KwaZulu-Natal, Madikwe and Pilanesberg in North-West province, also Karoo, Mountain Zebra and Addo national parks in South Africa. The only large population in Mozambique occurs in and around Niassa National Park on the Tanzanian border, with smaller numbers adjacent to South Africa's Kruger and remnant populations elsewhere. The first Lions in 20 years in Malawi were reintroduced in 2013 to Majete Wildlife Reserve. The situation in Angola is poorly known but in Zambia they are centred on Kafue and the Luangwa conservation areas. Lions once occurred widely in parts of Europe, Asia, the Middle East and throughout most of Africa. They now have a patchy distribution in Africa and are only found south·of the Sahara, excluding the equatorial forest regions.
Habitat: The Lion has a very wide habitat tolerance, from desert fringe to woodland or open savanna, but is absent from equatorial forest.
Behaviour: It is the most sociable member of the cat family, living in prides of 3–30 individuals. Pride size varies according to the area and prey availability. In Botswana prides usually 6 or fewer individuals, whereas average pride size in Kruger National Park is about 12. Prides normally consist of from 1–4 adult males, several related adult females (one of which is dominant) and a number of sub-adults and cubs. A pride area or territory is defended against strange Lions by both the males and females but some prides and solitary males are nomadic. Territories are marked by urine, droppings and by earth-scratching. The mighty roars of the Lion, audible over several kilometres, also serve to indicate that an area is occupied. Most of their activity takes place at night and during the cooler

Above and inset: The extent and coloration of the male Lion's mane is variable.

The Lioness does not carry a mane but confusion could still arise as individual males may also lack a mane.

Lion

128mm

right
front

121mm

right
back

daylight hours. The females undertake most of the hunting, and despite the fact that the males play little part in most kills, they may feed before the females. Cubs compete for what remains once the adults have finished their meal.

Food: Although Lion mainly hunts medium-sized to large mammals, particularly ungulates, it will take anything from mice to young Elephants as well as a wide range of non-mammalian prey. It also scavenges, and often chases other predators from their kills.

Reproduction: No fixed breeding season; 1–4 (occasionally up to 6) cubs each weighing about 1.5kg are born after gestation of 110 days. Lioness gives birth under cover, returning to the pride once the cubs are strong enough (1 or 2 months). Any lactating lioness allows any pride cub to suckle. Pride females often conceive at approximately the same time, ensuring that maximum food and maternal care are available to cubs. Cubs may remain with their mother for 2 years or longer. Mammae: 2 pairs abdominal.

Longevity: 13–15 years in the wild; average 13 years in captivity but 30 years recorded.

Note: Unless provoked, Lions will rarely attack humans, but it is useful to know the warning signs: an angry Lion will drop into a crouch, flatten its ears and give vent to growls and grunts, meanwhile flicking its tail-tip rapidly from side to side. Just prior to a charge the tail is usually jerked up and down.

Panthera pardus
■ present range
■ historic range

Leopard *Panthera pardus*

Total length 1.6–2.1m; tail 68–110cm; shoulder height 70–80cm; mass (M) 20–90kg, (F) 17–60kg.

Note: Leopards from the mountain ranges of the Western Cape are generally much smaller than those from further north; however, in all areas, the males are considerably larger than the females.

Identification pointers: Large size; rosette spots on body, solid black spots on legs, head, sides and hindquarters; lacks the black facial lines of Cheetah and is more heavily spotted (see Cheetah, p.276). Size, long tail and different form of spots make for easy differentiation from Serval.

Description: An elegant, powerfully built cat, with a beautifully spotted coat. The basic body colour varies from almost white to orange-russet, with black spots on the legs, flanks, hindquarters and head. The spots on the rest of the body consist of rosettes or broken circles of irregular black spots. The tail is about half of the total length, with rosette spots above and a white tip. The ears are rounded and white-tipped. The underparts are usually white to off-white. Cubs have dark, woolly hair and less-distinct spots.

Distribution: Extremely widely distributed in southern Africa, but now absent from the sheep-farming areas of central South Africa. Widely distributed in the rest of sub-Saharan Africa, the Middle East and through Asia into China. By far the most successful of the large cats.

Habitat: It has an extremely wide habitat tolerance, from high mountains to coastal plain, from low- to high-rainfall areas. South of the Orange River it has been eradicated from all but the more mountainous and rugged areas but in recent years there have been range extensions into parts of the arid interior, west coast and South Africa's Eastern Cape. Although drinking water is not essential, cover is an important requirement.

Behaviour: Normally solitary except when a pair comes together to mate or when a female is accompanied by cubs. Although it is mainly active at night, in areas where it is not disturbed it can be seen moving during the cooler daylight

A Lion scenting where the Lioness has just urinated.

Cubs are spotted to a greater or lesser extent, especially on the legs and belly.

Mane development in male Lions is usually complete in their fourth to fifth year.

The Leopard's face is heavy and, unlike the Cheetah, it has no 'tear-mark'.

Leopard

92mm

right
front

92mm

right
back

hours. Although it is mainly terrestrial, it is a good climber and swimmer. Males mark and defend a territory against other males, and a male's territory may overlap that of several females. Territories are marked with urine, droppings and tree-scratching points. Home ranges may be as small as 10km² or cover areas of several hundred square kilometres, the size being largely dependent on the availability of food. Normally silent, the Leopard does have a characteristic call that has been likened to the sound of a coarse saw cutting wood. Leopards stalk and pounce on their prey and do not rely on running at high speed like the Cheetah.

Food: A broad diet, ranging from insects, rodents and birds to medium-sized and occasionally large antelope. In some rocky and mountainous areas hyrax (dassies) make up an important part of the diet. It will on occasion kill more than its immediate needs, the surplus being stored for later use. Kills may be dragged under dense bush, among rocks or, in some areas, into trees out of reach of other predators. Leopard readily feed from rotten carcasses.

Reproduction: Litters of 2 or 3 cubs, each weighing around 500g, are born in dense cover, rock crevices or caves after a gestation of about 100 days. There is no fixed breeding season. Mammae: 2 pairs abdominal.

Longevity: Possibly 9–14 years in the wild; up to 23 years in captivity.

Note: Although Leopards may take to man-eating, this has not apparently been recorded for southern Africa. Trapped, wounded or threatened, Leopard can be extremely dangerous, but under normal circumstances it is shy and withdraws from disturbance.

AARDVARK Order Tubulidentata
Family Orycteropodidae

Orycteropus afer

Aardvark *Orycteropus afer*
Total length 1.4–1.8m; tail 45–60cm; mass 40–70kg.
Identification pointers: Unmistakable; large size; elongated, pig-like snout; tubular ears; generally heavy build; walks with back arched.

Description: The Aardvark resembles no other mammal occurring in southern Africa, with its long, pig-like snout, elongated tubular ears, heavily muscled kangaroo-like tail and very powerful, stout legs, which terminate in spade-like nails. It has only a sparse covering of hair and the skin is grey-yellow to fawn-grey. The hair at the base of the tail and on the legs tends to be quite dark. Normally, however, an Aardvark will be of a colour similar to the soil in the area in which it lives. The back is distinctly arched.

Distribution: This strange mammal is found throughout southern Africa with the exception of the coastal Namib Desert. It is widespread in Africa south of the Sahara.

Habitat: The Aardvark is found in a wide range of habitats and the limiting factor is probably the availability of suitable food. It shows a preference for open woodland, sparse scrub and grassland. This is one of the few species that has benefited from man's overstocking of areas with domestic stock. As they trample the grass, domestic stock make it more accessible to the termites on which the Aardvark feeds.

Behaviour: It is rarely seen during the day, most of its activity taking place at night. During the winter months, activity and foraging may begin early

The undersurface of the Leopard's tail-tip is clean white.

The Leopard's spots take the form of rosettes.

Leopards are agile climbers, readily taking to trees to rest or observe.

Leopards are masters of camouflage.

With its long, pig-like snout and elongated ears, the Aardvark cannot be mistaken for any other animal.

Aardvark

100mm

right front

90mm

right back

in the afternoon. This may well be because their termite prey moves deeper underground during the coldest night hours. Periods of drought, and hence shortage of their prey, cause Aardvark to become active during daylight hours. During one severe drought in north-western Namibia in the late 1980s, Aardvark were commonly seen foraging throughout the daylight hours; many Aardvark and Ground Pangolin died of starvation at that time. Although normally solitary, females may be accompanied by a single young; they excavate extensive burrow systems. Males usually dig quite shallow burrows to lie up in during the day and are greater wanderers than the females. Occupied burrows are often characterized by numerous small flies in the entrance-way. Aardvarks may walk several kilometres to feeding-grounds each night, where they appear to wander aimlessly, nose close to the ground. When they locate an ant or termite colony they rip into it with the massive claws on the front feet. In areas where the Aardvark is present, numerous termitaria have holes excavated at their bases. It is generally unpopular with farmers because it excavates holes in roads and dam walls.

Food: Mainly ants and termites. Termites dominate the diet in the rainy season and ants during the dry season. Once a colony has been opened up, the long, sticky tongue probes for the small insects, their larvae and eggs. It occasionally eats other insects and the fruit of the wild cucumber.

Reproduction: There are very few records of births but it is probable that its single young is born during the rainy season; it has a mass of almost 2kg and the gestation period is about 7 months. A baby Aardvark will start following its mother in its third week. Mammae: 1 pair abdominal, 1 pair inguinal.

Longevity: 18–24 years in captivity.

Note: Although they are, in the main, protected, Aardvark are persecuted by farmers because their excavations undermine dam walls and burrow under jackal-proof fences. This level of hunting has little impact on their numbers and, although seldom seen, they remain relatively common.

ELEPHANT Order Proboscidea
Family Elephantidae

Loxodonta africana
■ present range
▥ historic range

African (Bush) Elephant *Loxodonta africana*
Male: tail 1.5m; shoulder height 3.2–4m; mass 5,000–6,300kg.
Female: tail 1.5m; shoulder height 2.5–3.4m; mass 2,800–3,500kg.
Identification pointers: Massive size; long trunk; usually carries tusks; large ears. Cannot be mistaken for any other species.

Description: Apart from its vast size, the Elephant is characterized by its long trunk, large ears and the (normal) presence of tusks. The trunk is extremely mobile and is almost as efficient as the human hand. The large ears serve a display function but also assist in cooling the body. The backs of the ears are well supplied with blood vessels and, as the ears are flapped, the blood is cooled. Elephants may also squirt water behind the ears to cool the blood. Tusks are characteristic of most elephants, although some individuals and even populations may be tuskless. The heaviest pair of tusks on record, weighing 102.3kg and 97kg, came from a Kenyan elephant. Tusks continue to grow throughout life but, because of continuous wear and breakages, they never reach their full potential length.

In profile, the Aardvark's characteristic humped back and kangaroo-like tail can clearly be seen. Animals from tropical forest areas tend to be virtually hairless; this individual was photographed in Gabon. **Inset:** A termite mound opened up by an Aardvark in search of its preferred food.

Elephant cows providing shelter for a resting calf.

Elephants frequently use their trunks to touch each other.

African Elephant

500mm

right front

520mm

right back

Distribution: Once occurring virtually throughout southern Africa but now restricted to the northern and north-eastern areas. An isolated, natural population is present in the Greater Addo National Park in the Eastern Cape, while two or three individuals may survive in the forests near Knysna in the south-western Cape. Widely reintroduced in conservation areas within its former South African range. It still occurs widely in Africa south of the Sahara but the populations are becoming increasingly isolated and numbers are being reduced by poaching.

Habitat: African Elephants have an extremely wide habitat tolerance as long as sufficient food, water and shade are available.

Behaviour: Live in small family groups, each led by an older cow, the matriarch, together with her offspring, and may include related cows with their young. A number of family groups may come together to form larger herds, not infrequently numbering several hundreds. The family group retains its identity during these gatherings and normally the smaller groups move off on their own. These large congregations gather at water sources or when food is abundant, but there are no reproductive or social benefits. If left uncontrolled, large herds may destroy their habitat, not only for themselves but for other species as well, making culling inevitable. Adult bulls usually join the family herds when cows are in breeding condition, leaving for bachelor groups afterwards. A cow may mate with several bulls during oestrus. Although Elephants are active by both night and day, they usually rest in shade during the heat of the day. Elephants are normally peaceful but can be dangerous when wounded, sick, or defending a small calf.

Food: A very wide variety of plants. Although not specialized feeders they do show a marked preference for certain species, for which they will travel long distances. During the rains, green grass forms a large percentage of their diet. An adult Elephant may eat as much as 300kg per day.

Reproduction: A single calf, weighing approximately 90–120kg, is dropped after a 22-month gestation period. Calves may be born at any time of the year but in some areas there is a peak in births that coincides with the rainy season. The calf is pinkish-grey and hairier than the adults. Cows are very protective of calves. Mammae: 1 pair pectoral.

Longevity: Up to 60–70 years in the wild.

Note: Elephants are threatened by ivory poaching and human encroachment on their traditional areas. When confined to limited areas, they can inflict considerable damage to vegetation, particularly riparian woodland. Evidence of this can be seen in the Kruger National Park, South Africa, and Botswana's Chobe National Park.

DASSIES (HYRAX)   Order Hyracoidea
Family Procaviidae

Although, at first sight, hyraxes appear rodent-like, their evolutionary relationships lie with Elephant, Manatee and Dugong. Three species occur in southern Africa: two of which are associated predominantly with rocky habitats, while the third, Southern Tree Dassie (p.292), lives in forested areas.

There is considerable scientific debate over the taxonomy of the Rock Dassie, or Hyrax *(Procavia capensis)*. It has a vast range that extends over large areas of suitable habitat across Africa, extending into the Arabian Peninsula. Many subspecies have been described, as well as a number of species, not all of which can be separated in the field. Identification of many of these has therefore been based on pelage coloration, which is a dubious character at best. Recent genetic

Access to water is vital, as an adult elephant requires an average of 160 litres of water daily.

Large tuskers are now mostly restricted to well-protected conservation areas. **Inset:** African Elephant lower molar

work is starting to identify the possibility that at least two species are located in South Africa, with several more across the continent. However, the average observer will be unable to distinguish these 'potential' species, as identity relies primarily on genetic differentiation.

Rock Dassie (Hyrax) *Procavia capensis*
Total length 40–60cm; shoulder height 15–22cm; mass 2.5–5kg; .

Kaokoveld Rock Dassie (Hyrax) *Procavia capensis welwitschii*
Total length 36–50cm.

Procavia capensis & P. c. welwitschii

Yellow-spotted Rock Dassie (Hyrax) *Heterohyrax brucei*
Total length 32–56cm; ; shoulder height 15–20cmmass 1.3–3.6kg (one record to 4.5kg).

Identification pointers: Small, but stocky build; no tail; small rounded ears; rocky habitat; where Rock Dassie overlaps with the other species, the colour of the erectile hair in the middle of the back is the most certain character – black in Rock Dassie; white to off-white or yellowish in the other species and one subspecies.

Heterohyrax brucei

Description: The two species of Rock Dassie, or Hyrax, are small, stoutly built, tail-less animals with short legs and small, rounded ears. Hair colour varies considerably in both species. Both species have a patch of erectile hair overlying a glandular area in the centre of the back, the colour of which is a very important character for distinguishing the different species and subspecies, as indicated in the table below. The taxonomic standing of the population of Kaokoveld Rock Dassie and that of the Yellow-spotted Rock Hyrax in Angola should be interesting.

	Rock Dassie	Kaokoveld Rock Dassie	Yellow-spotted Rock Dassie
General colour	Yellow-fawn to dark brown	Yellow-fawn to dark brown	Grey to dark brown
Dorsal gland hairs	Black	White or yellowish	White or yellowish
Underparts	Slightly pale; never white	White to off-white	White to off-white
Other	Inconspicuous fawn-buff patch above eye and at ear base	Off-white patch at ear base	Conspicuous white patch above eye

Distribution: The Rock Dassie is the most widespread of the two rock-dwelling hyraxes occurring in southern Africa. However, it is absent from the north and north-central areas, the Namib Desert coastal belt and most of Mozambique. The Kaokoveld subspecies is restricted to north-western Namibia and south-western Angola. Yellow-spotted Rock Dassies occur in the north-eastern parts of southern Africa with an isolated population in western Angola.
Habitat: Rocky areas, from mountain ranges to isolated rock outcrops. Rock Dassie and Yellow-spotted Rock Dassie frequently occur together where ranges overlap. Rock Dassie generally favour dry areas but are also found in higher-

Three Rock Dassies (**right**) and a single Yellow-spotted Rock Dassie subspecies *H. b. ruddi*), photographed in the Tuli region of south-eastern Botswana.

The Rock Dassie frequently climbs into bushes and low trees to feed and can be confused with the Tree Dassie.

Young Rock Dassies suckling. They are perfectly proportioned miniatures of the adults and able to move about soon after birth. Gestation averages about 210 days, but the timing of the birth season varies from region to region.

Rock Dassie (Hyrax)

40mm

right
front

50mm

right
back

rainfall areas. They may be found living in holes in erosion gulleys (dongas), or among the roots and leaves of sisal, prickly pear and spekboom.

Behaviour: The behaviour of all the rock-dwelling hyrax species is similar. They are predominantly diurnal but on warm, moonlit nights they may emerge to feed. Normally they only become active after sunrise when they lie for some time on the rocks in the sun to warm up before moving off to feed. While the group basks in the sun, an adult male or female keeps watch for predators. If disturbed, the 'guard' gives a sharp cry and the dassies scuttle for cover among the rocks. Groups usually number from 4-8, but larger groups may live together, depending on the available habitat. Each group or colony has a dominant male and female and the other animals fit into a hierarchy or pecking order. During the mating period, males may fight fiercely.

Most feeding is done in the morning and late afternoon and they retreat to the shelter of rocks during the hotter hours. They usually feed close to the shelter although they will move up to several hundred metres to feeding areas. If a food shortage develops, a hyrax colony will migrate to a more favourable area. **Rock Dassies** readily climb into trees and bushes to feed and, because of this, are often thought to be Southern Tree Dassie.

Hyraxes deposit their droppings at fixed latrine sites and accumulations of their pellets may become very large. Hyrax urine leaves white and brown streaks on rocks and often serves as an indication of their presence.

Food: Grazers and browsers, with quantities of each varying according to the season. Feeding usually takes place on the ground but they will climb trees to feed on leaves, bark and fruits. They eat a very wide range of plants. Both feed in bushes but **Yellow-spotted** more so.

Reproduction: Both give birth to precocious young: fully haired, with eyes open and able to move about soon after birth. They are perfectly proportioned miniatures of the adults. There is a distinct birth season in the **Rock Dassie** but the timing varies considerably in different regions. In south-western South Africa, births normally occur September –October, and in Zimbabwe in March–April. In the lower Orange River area of the north-west of South Africa, with its extremely hot summer temperatures, the young are dropped in the cooler months of June and July; 1–4 young may be born but 2 or 3 is usual. Birth weight varies according to the size of the litter and may range from 150–300g. The **Kaokoveld** subspecies gives birth during February–March to 2 or 3 young, rarely 4. **Yellow-spotted Rock Dassie** apparently give birth at any time of the year to litters with an average of 2 offspring, each weighing approximately 200g. Mammae: 1 pair pectoral, 2 pairs inguinal.

Longevity: Rock Dassie 4–8.5 years in the wild; 12 years in captivity; **Yellow-spotted Rock Dassie** female in the wild to 11 years (average about 5 years); more than 10 years in captivity.

Note: Rock Dassie comprise the main diet of Verreaux's (Black) Eagle, between 70 and 90 per cent in most areas. Crowned Eagles also take substantial numbers of both Rock and Southern Tree Dassies. In many mountain and hill ranges, such as the Cedarberg and Soutpansberg, as well as Zimbabwe's Matobos, Leopards are important predators of hyraxes. In the Karoo hills, the Caracal is a significant hyrax predator, with African Wild Cat taking substantial numbers of young.

Hyrax usually have favoured sunning spots that become stained white with their urine.

Hyrax urine leaves characteristic white and brown streaks on rocks and overhangs, which can be seen from a considerable distance.

A Yellow-spotted Rock Hyrax *(H. b. ruddi)* photographed in Tuli, south-eastern Botswana

Yellow-spotted Rock Hyrax (note distinctive pale dorsal spot); in some areas they are darker and in South Africa this form is represented by *H. b. granti.*

A Yellow-spotted Rock Hyrax defecating at a midden site.

Dendrohyrax arboreus

Southern Tree Dassie (Hyrax) *Dendrohyrax arboreus*

Total length 42–52cm; mass 2–3.5kg.

Identification pointers: Similar in size to rock hyrax species; hair quite long and woolly in appearance; upperparts grey-brown, flecked with white or brown; white to creamy underparts and dorsal gland; forest or dense bush habitat; distinctive, nocturnal screaming call.

Description: Similar in size to the rock hyraxes but body hair is much longer and has a woolly appearance. Upperparts vary from grey flecked with white to grey-brown. Underparts are white to creamy white, as is the long hair around the dorsal gland in the centre of the back. No external tail.

Distribution: Their distribution is limited to suitable habitat. They occur along the coastal plain in the Eastern Cape and extend into KwaZulu-Natal. Another isolated population occurs in south-central Mozambique. Outside of the region, they are found in Zambia, eastern Congo and throughout the western parts of East Africa. Its forest and densely bushed habitats are generally in decline in South Africa, but substantial populations probably survive in Amatole, Pirie and Alexandria forests in the Eastern Cape, as well as Oribi Gorge and Vernon Crookes nature reserves in KwaZulu-Natal. The status of populations in Mozambique is unknown, but it is common in parts of Zambia, Angola and Malawi. However, habitat destruction could greatly reduce these populations in future.

Habitat: Southern Tree Dassie inhabit suitable forest and bush areas, including coastal dune forest. Fairly dense cover is an essential habitat requirement.

Behaviour: Solitary, arboreal and nocturnal, but may bask in the sun, particularly in the early morning. Although a solitary hyrax, in some areas they occur at quite high densities. Based on call rates, the authors once estimated more than 30 individuals in a relatively small forest pocket on the lower slopes of Mount Kenya. Southern Tree Dassiees are largely arboreal, but they descend to the ground when moving between trees and it is not unusual for them to forage on the ground. Like their Rock Dassie relatives, they will also dust bathe if the substrate is suitable. Although they are rarely seen, their hair-raising screaming call at night is characteristic. For those unfamiliar with this bloodcurdling shriek, it can be a disturbing experience. Droppings accumulate on lower branch forks and particularly at the base of trees.

Food: Mainly a browser but will feed on grasses and herbaceous plants. They are generally selective feeders, with favoured species varying from location to location. For example, in Pirie Forest in the Eastern Cape, Yellowwood foliage is important, and in Alexandria Forest to the west of Port Alfred, Bush Boerbean makes up a significant part of their diet.

Reproduction: It probably breeds throughout the year, with 1–3 young, weighing 150–300g, being born after a gestation period of about 210 days. Mammae: 1 pair pectoral, 2 pairs (sometimes 1 pair) inguinal.

Longevity: One captive lived more than 12 years.

Note: Apart from *D. arboreus*, there are two other species of tree hyrax. *Dendrohyrax dorsalis* occurs from Uganda westwards to Senegal, also in the Angolan Cabinda enclave north of the Congo River, while the much more localized *D. validus* (its taxonomic standing sometimes questioned) is restricted to a few montane areas in East Africa and the islands of Unguja and Pemba (Zanzibar). However, not all are tree-dwellers; a population of tree dassie *(D. a. ruwenzorii)* found in the upper reaches of the Ruwenzori Mountains (straddling the Uganda/DR Congo border) lives in colonies among rocks, and is partly diurnal. In the lower forested areas, however, the tree dassie reverts to type and is arboreal, solitary and nocturnal.

A young Tree Hyrax; these nocturnal animals inhabit suitable forest and bush areas, seeking dense cover.

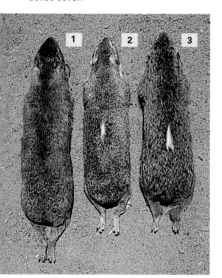

Dassie skins: 1. Rock Hyrax; 2. Kaokoveld Rock Hyrax; 3. Tree Hyrax

The Tree Hyrax has white underparts.

Tree Hyrax (Dassie)

Equus zebra zebra
■ present range
■ historic range

■ *Equus zebra hartmannae*

Cape Mountain Zebra *Equus zebra zebra*
Hartmann's Mountain Zebra *Equus zebra hartmannae*

Cape subsp.: Total length 2.7m; shoulder height 1.3m; tail 40cm; mass 250–260kg.
Hartmann's subsp.: Total length 2.7m; shoulder height 1.5m; tail 40cm; mass 250–350kg.

Identification pointers: Black-and-white stripes without shadow stripes; legs striped to the hooves; grid-iron pattern on rump; throat with dewlap. Range of **Hartmann's** overlaps marginally with that of **Plains Zebra** in north-western Namibia. **Hartmann's** introduced to farms and reserves outside normal range. Some authorities believe that the two mountain zebras warrant full species status.

Description: The two subspecies of mountain zebra are similar in appearance but **Hartmann's** is slightly larger, with some variations in striping on the hindquarters. Both, however, are white with black stripes, the legs being striped to the hooves; underparts are white. No shadow stripes (see opposite page) and over the top of rump above the tail there is a series of transverse black stripes forming a grid-iron pattern characteristic of the species. Tip of muzzle is black with orange-brown hair extending a short way towards eyes. An erect mane runs from the top of the head to the shoulders. A dewlap is present on the throat; this feature is diagnostic of the species and does not occur in other zebras.

Distribution: Cape Mountain Zebra was once widespread in the mountains south of the Orange River, but is now restricted to a small group of conservation areas. **Hartmann's** is restricted to the montane escarpment of Namibia but occurs marginally in south-western Angola, and a population has crossed the Orange into the Richtersveld in recent times. **Hartmann's** has also been introduced onto several game farms and nature reserves inside and outside its natural range, including Augrabies Falls National Park.

Habitat: Mountainous and broken hill country, but makes frequent use of upland plateaux and adjacent flatland.

Behaviour: Breeding herds consist of an adult stallion with mares and their foals and usually number 4 or 5 but occasionally more. In the dry season, however, **Hartmann's** may congregate in loose associations of up to 40. Non-harem-holding stallions form bachelor groups, which may include young mares and weaned foals of both sexes. Stallions do not defend territories, but keep other stallions away from mares, although submissive males are tolerated.

Food: Predominantly grazers but also browse occasionally.

Reproduction: A single foal (±25kg) is born after gestation of about 360 days. **Cape Mountain Zebra** may drop young at any time of year but with a summer peak; most **Hartmann's** births recorded in northern Namibia take place in summer. Mammae: 1 pair inguinal.

Longevity: Up to at least 24 years in the wild; one captive up to 28 years 9 months, most to 26 years.

Cape Mountain Zebras have no shadow stripes and striping does not extend onto the belly. **Inset:** Skin showing the grid-iron pattern on the rump of Cape Mountain Zebra

The rump of the Plains Zebra lacks the grid-iron pattern of the mountain zebras.

Hartmann's Mountain Zebra occupies arid and semi-desert areas of western southern Africa. **Inset:** The grid-iron pattern of the two mountain zebra species differs in the detail.

Cape Mountain Zebra
Hartmann's Mountain Zebra

100mm

right
front

100mm

right
back

Plains Zebra *Equus quagga*

Total length 2.3–3m; shoulder height 1.3m; tail 45cm (43–56cm); mass 290–340kg.
Identification pointers: Stocky and horse-like; black-and-white stripes with shadow stripes superimposed on white stripes; stripes extend onto underparts; lacks dewlap on throat.

Equus quagga
■ present range
■ historic range

Description: Plains Zebra shows considerable variation in coloration and patterning but is usually striped in black and white with a fainter 'shadow' stripe superimposed on the white stripe, particularly on the hindquarters. No grid-iron pattern on rump and striping extends onto underparts. Long, erect mane extends from top of head to shoulders. Striping may or may not extend to the hooves. Ears noticeably shorter than those of mountain zebras. Throughout much of southern Africa, Plains Zebra has 'shadow' stripes over the white stripes, whereas shadow stripes are not usually present in the populations north of the Cunene-Zambezi line.
Distribution: North and east of region but widely introduced and reintroduced.
Habitat: Grassland plains and open grassed woodland, with access to water.
Behaviour: Plains Zebras associate in family herds consisting of an adult stallion, plus a number of mares and their foals; other stallions form bachelor herds or run alone. Family units normally number 4–6. Larger herds usually consist of numerous smaller herds coming together temporarily. Most populations are seasonal migrants, such as those in Etosha and over their Botswana range. In South Africa's Lowveld there are both migratory and sedentary populations, ranging over home ranges of 4,900->56,000ha. Their characteristic call has been likened to a bark, 'kwa-ha-ha'; it was also the call of the extinct Quagga, hence the name. Frequently mixes with other game species, such as Blue Wildebeest and Red Hartebeest.
Food: Grazers but they do occasionally browse.
Reproduction: Single foal, weighing 30–35kg, born in summer (November–February) after a gestation period of 375 days. Mammae: 1 pair inguinal.
Longevity: Up to 20 years in the wild (average 9 years); up to 40 years in captivity.

RHINOCEROSES Family Rhinocerotidae

Hook-lipped (Black) Rhinoceros *Diceros bicornis*

Total length 3.5–4.3m; shoulder height 1.6m; tail 70cm; mass 800–1,100kg.
Record front horn length 1.359m (East Africa), 1.05m (KwaZulu-Natal).
Identification pointers: Large size but smaller than Square-lipped Rhinoceros; lacks neck hump present in Square-lipped; characteristic pointed upper lip; shorter head than Square-lipped (see p.300); two horns on face.

Diceros bicornis
■ present range
■ historic range

Description: Frequently called Black Rhinoceros, this species is more appropriately known as Hook-lipped Rhinoceros, as the triangular-shaped prehensile upper lip is characteristic. Dark grey with slightly lighter underparts. Body colour influenced by its habit of wallowing in dust and mud. Sparse scattering of body hair. No raised hump on neck, unlike the Square-lipped Rhinoceros. Two horns on face, one behind other, the front horn usually being the longer. Rhino horn is composed of numerous, matted, hair-like filaments, which are attached to the skin, not to the bone; it is not a sheath-like covering to

Plains Zebra from northern Namibia, showing the shadow stripes characteristic of the southern races, with striping that extends onto the belly. **Inset:** Plains Zebra north of the Cunene-Zambezi line usually lack shadow stripes.

Crawshay's race of the Plains Zebra lacks shadow stripes and occurs in eastern Zambia, Malawi and northern Mozambique.

Some populations of Plains Zebra have weak striping on the rump.

Plains Zebra

77mm

right front

83mm

right back

a bony core as is the case with antelope horns. The spoor (footprint) is rounded at the back, whereas that of Square-lipped Rhinoceros is sharply indented. **Distribution:** Once widely distributed throughout the region, but now occurs naturally only in some KwaZulu-Natal reserves, north-western Namibia, the Zambezi Valley, and possibly in parts of southern Mozambique. Reintroduced to Greater Addo National Park and the Great Fish River Conservation Area in Eastern Cape and Karoo and Mokale national parks in the Western and Northern Cape. There are more than 3,500 Hook-lipped Rhinoceroses in southern Africa, making up a large percentage of the world total for the species. Previously common throughout Central and East Africa, extending into West Africa, but has been brought to the verge of extinction over much of its former range through relentless poaching.

Habitat: The Hook-lipped Rhinoceros requires areas with shrubs and trees reaching to a height of about 4m, with dense thickets for resting. Although it requires water for drinking and wallowing, it may go several days between visits to water in arid areas. It occupies a wide range of habitats where these basic requirements are met, from the arid plains of Kaokoland to the rich savanna woodland of the KwaZulu-Natal game reserves.

Behaviour: Hook-lipped Rhinoceroses are solitary animals although groups may come together temporarily at water. Bulls and cows only come together for mating and cows are often accompanied by calves. Serious fighting may take place when bulls compete for a receptive cow. During the heat of the day they usually lie up in dense thickets, feeding in the early morning and late afternoon but also after dark. The dung may be dropped in latrine or midden areas or at random through the home range. Bulls kick the dung vigorously with the hind feet at the latrine sites leaving distinct grooves in the ground. Apart from being smaller, the dung balls can be distinguished from those of the Square-lipped Rhinoceros by their content of light-coloured, coarse woody material. The Square-lipped Rhinoceros, being a grazer, has much finer, darker material in the dung. Hook-lipped Rhinoceroses are notoriously bad-tempered, this being particularly true of bulls associating with receptive cows, and of cows with calves. Despite their cumbersome appearance they are surprisingly fast and agile; they rely on their hearing and sense of smell to locate a threat as their eyesight is poor.

Food: The Hook-lipped Rhinoceros uses its pointed, mobile upper lip to grasp twigs and shoots, which are either snapped off or cut through by the cheek-teeth. It is a selective feeder and tends to reject dry plant material. During the rains it will on occasion take grass.

Reproduction: There is no fixed breeding season but there are seasonal peaks, and a single calf, weighing about 40kg, is born after a gestation period of about 450 days. It is able to walk and suckle within 3 hours of birth. The calf either walks alongside or behind the mother, the reverse of the situation with Square-lipped Rhinoceros. Mammae: 1 pair inguinal.

Longevity: Probably over 40 years in the wild; captives up to 45 years 10 months.

General: The rapid decline in numbers of both African rhinoceros species is a result of the demand for their horns. Until recently most of the horns found their way to Yemen, where they were carved into dagger handles for tribesmen, and to the Far East where they are used in the production of traditional medicines. Although South Africa is still the stronghold for both rhinoceros species, since 2010 there has been a massive escalation in poaching in that country.

The Hook-lipped Rhinoceros is smaller than the Square-lipped Rhinoceros. **Inset:** The dung of this rhinoceros contains coarse woody material.

The triangular prehensile upper lip of the Hook-lipped Rhinoceros is ideally suited for browsing selected shoots.

The Hook-lipped Rhinoceros favours dense bush.

Hook-lipped Rhinoceros

In this species the calf walks alongside or behind the cow.

200mm

right front

190mm

right back

299

Ceratotherium
simum
■ present range
■ historic range

Square-lipped (White) Rhinoceros *Ceratotherium simum*

Total length 4.5–4.8m; shoulder height 1.8m; tail 1m; mass (M) 2,000–2,300kg, (F) 1,400–1,600kg.
Record front horn length (southern Africa) 1.58m.
More than 20,000 Square-lipped Rhinoceroses are dispersed across national parks, nature reserves and private game farms in southern Africa. The largest national southern African 'herd' is located in Kruger National Park, followed by that of the Hluhluwe/iMfolozi complex in KwaZulu-Natal.
Identification pointers: Large size; broad, square muzzle; hump on neck; large, pointed ears; two horns on face. See Hook-lipped Rhinoceros (p.296).

Description: The Square-lipped Rhinoceros, also known as the White Rhinoceros, is much larger than the Hook-lipped Rhinoceros. The skin colour is grey but this is often influenced by the colour of the mud and dust in which it rolls. A large, distinctive hump is present on the neck. The head is long and carried low, frequently only a few centimetres above the ground, and terminates in a broad, square muzzle – hence the common name. There are two horns on the face, the front one usually being the longer. The ears are large and pointed.

Distribution: Restricted by the beginning of the 20th century to the iMfolozi Game Reserve in KwaZulu-Natal, the southern subspecies of the Square-lipped Rhinoceros was strictly protected and, over time, spread naturally into the adjacent Hluhluwe Game Reserve; it has since been widely reintroduced and introduced to other reserves and game farms throughout the region. The Square-lipped Rhinoceros once had a very wide distribution, with the northern subspecies occurring in Sudan, Chad, Uganda and the DR Congo, and the separate southern subspecies in South Africa, Mozambique, Zimbabwe, Botswana, Namibia and Angola. More than 20,000, despite recent upsurge in poaching in South Africa.

Habitat: This species shows a preference for short-grassed areas, with thick bush cover and water. Where adequate food and water is available, it will occupy a wide range of open woodland associations.

Behaviour: The Square-lipped Rhinoceros is much more sociable than the Hook-lipped Rhinoceros. Territorial bulls occupy clearly defined territories, which they will defend against neighbouring bulls; subordinate bulls may be allowed to remain within a territory if they remain submissive. The home range of cows may overlap with the territories of several territorial bulls but when a cow is receptive for mating, the bull will attempt to keep her within his area. Family groups usually number 2–5 individuals, although larger numbers may come together for short periods. The home ranges and territories are only left when water is not readily available. When they move to watering points they follow the same paths each time. Feeding takes place during the cooler morning and afternoon hours but they are also active at night. Bulls usually have a number of fixed latrine sites within their territories.

Food: Square-lipped Rhinoceroses are grazers, with a preference for short grass. A reliable source of drinking water is an essential requirement.

Reproduction: Calves, weighing about 40kg, are dropped at any time of the year after a gestation period of approximately 480 days. The cow moves away from the rhinoceros group to give birth and remains separated with her newborn calf for several days. In contrast to the Hook-lipped Rhinoceros, the calf of the Square-lipped Rhinoceros walks in front of the mother. Mammae: 1 pair inguinal.

Longevity: 50 years in captivity; probably similar in the wild.

Square-lipped Rhinoceros cow and calf at waterhole. **Inset:** Fine plant remains in Square-lipped Rhino dung

Square-lipped Rhinoceros bull dung midden clearly showing grooves cut by hind feet

The Square-lipped Rhinoceros has a broad, squared-off muzzle.

Square-lipped Rhinoceros

In this species the calf walks or runs ahead of the cow.

250mm

right front

242mm

right back

Hippopotamus *Hippopotamus amphibius*

Total length 3.4–4.2m; shoulder height 1.5m; tail length 30–50cm; mass (M) 1,000–2,000kg, (F) 1,000–1,700kg.

Identification pointers: Large size; barrel-shaped body and short legs; massive head with broad muzzle; most often found in water by day.

Hippopotamus amphibius
■ present range
▨ historic range

Description: Large, rotund animal with smooth, naked skin, short, stocky legs and a massive, broad-muzzled head. Mouth is equipped with an impressive set of tusk-like canines and incisors. Short, flattened tail is tipped with a tuft of black hair. Body colour greyish-black with pink tinge at the skin folds, around eyes and ears, while underparts are pinkish-grey. Four-toed feet leave a characteristic track.
Distribution: The Hippopotamus is restricted to the northern and eastern parts of southern Africa. At the present time, the most southerly natural population is in northern KwaZulu-Natal but they previously occurred in the vicinity of Cape Town, along the southern coastal belt and along the entire length of the Orange River, until hunted out by colonial settlers. It has a patchy distribution over the rest of sub-Saharan Africa but is widespread. There are reintroduced populations in, among others, Addo Elephant National Park and Great Fish River Conservation Area in South Africa.
Habitat: Hippopotamus requires sufficient water in which to submerge and shows a preference for permanent waters with a sandy substrate. This includes rivers, dams and lakes. Surrounding areas must have enough suitable grass for feeding.
Behaviour: This semi-aquatic mammal spends much of the day lying in water, emerging at night to move to feeding-grounds. It also lies up on sand- or mud-banks in the sun, particularly during the winter months. Although it normally occurs in herds or schools of 10–15 animals, larger groups and solitary bulls are not uncommon. Schools are usually composed of cows and young of various ages with a dominant bull in overall control. Territories are narrow in the water but broaden out towards the feeding-grounds. Dominant bulls mark their territories by scattering their dung, with a vigorous sideways flicking of the tail, onto rocks, bushes and other objects. Territoriality is apparently strongest closer to the water but virtually absent in the feeding-grounds. Fixed pathways are used and these are characterized by a 'double' trail – each one made by the feet of one side. Exceptionally, they may travel up to 30km to reach feeding areas, depending on the availability of food. An adult Hippopotamus can remain under water for up to six minutes. Skin glands secrete a reddish fluid which is frequently mistaken for blood but probably acts as a skin lubricant and moisturizer. Hippopotamus is extremely vocal and its deep roaring grunts and snorts constitute one of the typical sounds of Africa. Provoked, it can be extremely dangerous, particularly solitary bulls or cows with calves.
Food: Hippopotamus is a selective grazer. In areas with high populations, considerable damage can be done to grazing areas near water.
Reproduction: Mating takes place in the water; after a gestation period of 225–257 days a single calf is born weighing 25–55kg (usually about 30kg). The cow gives birth on land in dense cover and she and the calf remain separated

The Hippopotamus is characterized by a massive barrel-shaped body, heavy, broad-muzzled head, and short, stocky legs.

Hippopotamuses spend much of the day submerged.
Inset: A Hippopotamus displaying its tusk-like canines

Hippopotamus bulls mark territories by flicking dung with their short, stubby tail.

Hippopotamus

250mm

right
front

210mm

right
back

from the school for about 2 weeks. Calves may be produced at any time of the year but there is some evidence of a seasonal peak (October–March). Mammae: 1 pair inguinal.

Longevity: One individual to 62 years in captivity; 41 years in the wild.

PIGS & HOGS Order Suiformes
Family Suidae

Phacochoerus africanus

Common Warthog *Phacochoerus africanus*
Male: Total length 1.3–1.8m; shoulder height 70cm; tail 45cm; mass 60–105kg.
Female: Total length 1.1–1.4m; shoulder height 60cm; tail 45cm; mass 45–70kg.
Identification pointers: Pig-like appearance; grey, sparsely haired body; wart-like lumps on face; thin tail with dark tufted tip, held erect when running; curved, upward-pointing tusks in adults.

Description: Often described as ugly and grotesque but not without appeal. Grey with sparse, dark, bristle-like hairs scattered over body, and mane of long erectile hair along back, which lies flat except when Warthog is under stress; mane may be yellowish-brown to black in colour. Tufts of pale whiskers lie along side of face. Snout is typically pig-like and prominent wart-like protuberances are present on face – two pairs in male, one less-conspicuous pair in female. Canine teeth of adults develop into long curved tusks; those of the boar may reach considerable lengths (record male 61cm) and make effective defensive weapons. Thin tail with its tuft of black hair is held erect when Warthog runs, unlike that of Bushpig.

Distribution: Northern and eastern areas of region. There is an expanding, introduced, population in the western sector of the Eastern Cape.

Habitat: Open country but also lightly wooded areas; savanna. Penetrates otherwise unsuitable country along watercourses.

Behaviour: Predominantly diurnal but sometimes nocturnal. Groups, or sounders, of Common Warthogs usually consist of sows and their young, or bachelor groups. Sexually active boars usually move freely and alone except when with a sow. Can dig their own burrows, but usually take over Aardvark or Porcupine holes. They frequently wallow in mud, especially during warmer weather.

Food: Mostly short grasses and grass roots. When grazing they usually kneel. Browse occasionally and rarely feed on animal matter.

Reproduction: Sow separates from sounder to give birth to litter of 2 or 3 (rarely up to 8, but most die) piglets in burrow, after a gestation period of about 170 days. Newborn piglets weigh 80–850g. Emerge from burrow about 2 weeks after birth. Seasonal breeders, with most births taking place early summer. Mammae: 1 pair abdominal, 1 pair inguinal.

Longevity: Captives to about 17 years (oldest captive 18 years 9 months); in the wild to about 17 years but most do not reach 12 years.

Common Warthogs require regular access to water for drinking and wallowing.

Common Warthogs have a prominent erectile dorsal crest and white cheek whiskers are often present.

The male Warthog has two pairs of warts on its face.

Common Warthog

45mm

right front

47mm

right back

Potamochoerus larvatus

Bushpig *Potamochoerus larvatus*

Total length 1.3–1.7m; shoulder height 55–88cm; tail 38cm; mass 60kg (46–115kg).

Identification pointers: Pig-like appearance; well-haired body; tufts of hair on ear tips; long head; tail held down when running – unlike the Warthog whose tail is held vertically upwards; facial hair much lighter in colour than rest of body.

Description: More typically pig-like than Common Warthog. Boar slightly larger than sow. Body is well covered with long bristle-like hair which, although variable, is usually reddish-brown to grey-brown. Mane of longer and paler hair extends from the back of neck to shoulders and facial hair is usually grey-white. Head is long and ears are pointed with tuft of longish hair at the tip. Older boars may develop a pair of warts on the muzzle, but not as large as those of Warthog. Thin tail has tassel of black hair at tip. Piglets dark brown with several longitudinal pale stripes along body. It is possible that the closely related Red River Hog (*P. porcus*) occurs in forested habitats in far northern Angola.

Distribution: Northern and eastern areas of the region south to Mossel Bay, South Africa. The population in southern South Africa is isolated, as is the case in other parts of its range as a result of habitat destruction.

Habitat: Forest, dense bush and riverine woodland, reed beds and stands of long grass where there is water. Can be a problem in farming areas.

Behaviour: Mainly nocturnal, but in areas where they are not disturbed, they may be seen during the day. Live in sounders of 4–10 individuals but larger groups have been recorded. A sounder consists of a dominant boar, a dominant sow, other sows and young. Solitary animals also occur, as well as bachelor groups. If wounded or cornered, Bushpigs can be dangerous. They are territorial, but their ways of marking territory are not well known. This may involve middens of droppings, urine and scent deposits from male facial glands. It has been suggested that secretions from these glands may also play a part in tree-bark tusking. In the latter, pieces of bark on the favoured trees are cut away by the tusks. In the Soutpansberg, Waterberry trees are frequently used for claw-scratching by Leopards and tusking by Bushpigs, often on the same trees.

Food: Bushpigs use their hard snouts to root for rhizomes, bulbs and tubers; areas where they have been active look like small ploughed plots. In some areas they do considerable damage to crops. They also browse. Animal matter may feature quite prominently in their diet and may include insects, other invertebrates, frogs and carrion; rarely sheep and goats. Bushpigs can detect the presence of carrion by scent from several kilometres distance. A cow carcass that had been lying for a week was visited by a sounder of Bushpigs from riverine thicket two kilometres away. The intervening vegetation comprised short grassland covering rocky hill slopes that were not normally frequented by Bushpig.

Reproduction: Most births occur in summer. The sow constructs a 'haystack' of grass, up to 3m in diameter and 1m in height, in bush cover. A litter consists of 2–4 piglets, up to 8, each weighing approximately 750g. The young are born in the centre of the stack. Apart from suckling, care of piglets is usually handled by the sounder boar. Mammae: 3 pairs abdominal.

Longevity: 12–15 years in the wild; one captive 21 years 7 months.

Bushpigs moving at night clearly showing the prominent mane that runs from the nape to just behind the shoulders.

Bushpig piglets are striped, whereas those of the Warthog are unstriped.

Bushpigs vary in colour, and some develop extremely hairy coats, with a mane of paler hair that extends from the back of the neck to the shoulders.

The Bushpig has a typical pig-like appearance.

Red River Hog

Bushpig

55mm

right
front

53mm

right
back

*Giraffa
camelopardalis*

■ present range
▨ historic range

Giraffe *Giraffa camelopardalis*

Male: total length 4.6–5.7m; height (top of head) 3.9–5.2m; height (shoulder) 2.5–3.5m; tail 95–150cm; mass 970–1,400kg.
Female: total length <5m; height (top of head) 3.7–4.7m; height (shoulder) 2–3m; tail 75–90cm; mass 700–950kg.
Identification pointers: Large size; long legs and neck; patchwork patterning. Cannot be mistaken for any other species.

Description: Giraffe apparently gets its name from the Arabic *xirapha*, which means 'one who walks swiftly'. Giraffe is the tallest animal in the world and with its long neck and legs is unmistakable. A lattice pattern consisting of large, irregularly shaded patches separated by networks of light-coloured bands covers the body. The colouring of the patches is variable, ranging from light fawn to almost black. Old bulls are often very dark. Knob-like horns are present on the top of the head and these will be well developed in adult bulls. Three races are sometimes recognized as occurring in southern Africa: the Angolan *(G. c. angolensis)* in northern Namibia and northern Botswana; the Southern *(G. c. giraffa)*, mainly restricted to South Africa and its northern fringes, and Thornicroft's *(G. c. thornicrofti)* of Zambia's Luangwa Valley.
Distribution: In southern Africa, the population that occurs in Mpumalanga and Limpopo provinces, South Africa, and adjacent areas of Mozambique and Zimbabwe is isolated. Giraffe also occur in western Zimbabwe and northern Namibia, extending from there into Angola and Zambia. Once occurring widely and continuously in savanna country south of the Sahara, they are now broken up into numerous isolated populations scattered throughout West and East Africa. Widely reintroduced in their original habitat, and introduced in the south to nature reserves and privately owned game farms, often well outside the traditional natural range; this includes those in the reserves of KwaZulu-Natal.
Habitat: Dry savanna woodland; in some areas, penetrating into the desert along wooded river courses. Particularly areas with trees such as *Vachellia* and *Senegalia* (formerly *Acacia*), *Commiphora* and *Terminalia*.

Note: Up to 70% of South Africa's Giraffe population, <5,500 animals, is located in Kruger National Park, with an estimated 3,000 in reserves and game farms in eastern Limpopo and Mpumalanga; KZN's population totals some 800, although Giraffes probably never occurred naturally in that province.

Behaviour: Diurnal and nocturnal, resting during the hot midday hours. They occupy large home ranges of 20–85km², but do not establish defended territories. Usually seen in herds of 4–30 individuals, although these groups are unstable and much wandering takes place. Bulls only associate with cows temporarily. Although Giraffes are generally believed to be silent, they do have a range of grunting and snorting calls.
Food: Giraffes are browsers, only rarely eating grass. Their long necks and legs give them access to a food supply beyond the reach of all other browsers. Although they feed from a fairly wide range of trees and bushes, they are selective in what they eat. Twigs are pulled into the mouth by the lips and the long, prehensile tongue, which may reach 45cm in length, and the leaves are shredded off into the mouth. Between 15 and 20 hours of each day may be spent feeding.
Reproduction: Calves weighing about 100kg (from 47kg) may be born at any time of year after a gestation period of about 450 days, the longest of any of the ungulates. The newly born calf can stand and walk within an hour of birth but remains isolated from the herd for up to 3 weeks. There is a very high mortality of calves in their first year, up to 70 per cent in some range areas. Mammae: 2 pairs inguinal.
Longevity: One individual recorded to live 26 years in the wild; one record of 36 years 2 months in captivity.

Giraffes are mainly browsers but they will also feed on grass, especially new growth.

Giraffe bulls are usually darker in colour than cows.
Inset: Giraffes have two short horns on the top of the head, ringed with black hairs at the tip.

The race Thornicroft's Giraffe occurs only in Zambia's Luangwa Valley.

Giraffe

180mm

right
front

170mm

right
back

Syncerus caffer
■ present range
▓ historic range

African Savanna Buffalo *Syncerus caffer*

Total length 2.9m; shoulder height 1.4m; tail 70cm; mass (M) 700kg, (F) 550kg.

Average horn length 100cm along curve from centre of boss to tip; record horn length (southern Africa) 124.8cm (Zimbabwe).

Identification pointers: Cattle-like appearance: large size; uniform dark brown or black colouring; heavily built; characteristically massive horns.

Description: These buffalo are massive, heavily built, cattle-like animals. Adult bulls are dark brown to black, cows are usually lighter and calves are reddish-brown. In northern Angola, Forest Buffalo *(S. c. nanus)* occur and they have red coats, especially cows, and more lightly structured horns. This race is smaller than African Savanna Buffalo. They have stocky, relatively short legs with large hooves, those on the forefoot being larger than those on the hind foot. The horns are heavy and massive, and the central horn base or 'boss' is particularly well developed in the bulls. The horns curve down and outwards, then upwards and inwards, narrowing towards the tips. When viewed from the front, the horns form a shallow 'W'. The horn boss is less pronounced in the cow and absent in younger animals. Ears are large and hang below the horns. The tail is cow-like with a tip of long brown or black hair.

Distribution: Once widely distributed in southern Africa, this buffalo is now restricted to the region's northern and eastern parts. The largest populations are in Kruger National Park (±30,000), Hwange and the Zambezi floodplain in Zimbabwe, and the Okavango complex in Botswana. Buffalo in the Hluhluwe/iMfolozi complex and other KwaZulu-Natal parks probably number fewer than 3,000 animals. Bovine TB is present in these populations, but the naturally occurring herds in Greater Addo National Park are classified disease-free and can be translocated to other reserves to form satellite populations. Despite wide distribution south of the Sahara, many buffalo populations have been fragmented by human expansion and the species now has a markedly discontinuous distribution. Populations in Angola have been decimated. It has, however, been reintroduced to several nature reserves and game-farms, such as the Great Fish River Conservation Area in the Eastern Cape, as well as Mountain Zebra, Karoo, Camdeboo and Mokala national parks, South Africa.

Habitat: The African Savanna Buffalo has a fairly wide habitat tolerance but requires areas with abundant grass, water and cover. It shows a preference for open woodland savanna and will utilize open grassland as long as it has access to cover.

Behaviour: They are gregarious, occurring in herds that may number several thousand. Smaller groups may break away from the herd only to rejoin it later. Bachelor groups may form and solitary bulls are common. Adult bulls within the mixed herd maintain a dominance hierarchy, the complexity of which is influenced by herd size. Cows establish a pecking order among themselves. Dominant bulls mate with receptive cows. Herds have clearly defined home ranges and herd areas rarely overlap. They come to water early morning and late afternoon and seek out shade during the day. They regularly wallow in mud, especially bulls. Mostly feed at night.

Food: Predominantly grazers but also occasionally browse, especially in dry season. Preference for grasses that grow in dense swards.

Reproduction: Seasonal breeders; the majority of calves are dropped in the wet and warm summer months. A single calf, weighing 30–40kg, is born after a gestation of about 340 days. Calves are born within the herd and are able to keep up within a few hours of birth. Mammae: 2 pairs inguinal.

Longevity: To 20 years in the wild; 26 years in captivity, one 29 years 6 months.

The African Savanna Buffalo is a herd animal but bulls may be solitary, or move in small groups away from the herds. **Inset:** A large Buffalo bull

The horns of the African Savanna Buffalo cow do not form the massive central boss seen in mature bulls.

The Forest Buffalo is smaller, richer in colour and has a different horn structure.

African Savanna Buffalo

120mm

right front

120mm

right back

311

*Taurotragus
(Tragelaphus) oryx*

■ present range
■ historic range

Common Eland *Taurotragus (Tragelaphus) oryx*

Male: total length 3–4.2m; shoulder height 1.7m; tail 60cm; mass 700kg (but up to 900kg).
Female: total length 2.2–3.5m; shoulder height 1.5m; tail 60cm; mass 450kg.
Average horn length (both sexes) 60cm; record horn length (Namibia) 118.4cm.
Identification pointers: Massive size; fawn-tawny with some grey on forequarters; both sexes with straight horns, each with a slight twist or spiral.

Description: The largest living antelope in the region, Common Eland has a cow-like appearance. Its general colour is usually fawn or tawny, turning blue-grey with age, particularly on the neck and shoulders. Adult bulls develop a patch of fairly long, dark, coarse hair on the forehead. A short, dark mane runs down the back of the neck. The tail is fairly long with a tuft of black hair at the tip. Older bulls typically develop a large dewlap on the throat. Both sexes have horns but those of the bull are thicker and the shallow spiral is marked by a prominent ridge. In the north of the region, Livingstone's Eland differs in having up to seven vertical, white stripes on each side.
Distribution: Once occurred widely in southern Africa but now restricted to the northern parts, except for a natural population in the Drakensberg and numerous localities where it has been reintroduced to farms and reserves. Occurs widely in Central and East Africa but is absent from the forested areas of equatorial Africa. The Eland population in Kruger National Park has been in decline since the 1980s and may number fewer than 500 today. There may be more than 2,000 Eland in the Kgalagadi Transfrontier Park, but these herds move freely in and out of the park on the Botswana side and so may be absent at times.
Habitat: Occupies a wide range of habitats from desert scrub to montane areas but shows a preference for open scrub-covered plains and woodland savanna.
Behaviour: Normally in herds of 25–60 individuals but temporary associations of over 1,000 are occasionally seen, usually during the rainy season. In some areas, Eland tend to be more or less sedentary, whereas in others, such as the Kalahari, they may move considerable distances in search of suitable sources of food. Although a hierarchy exists within herds, they appear not to defend territories. Eland are predominantly diurnal but also feed at night, particularly during summer months.
Food: Predominantly browsers, Common Eland do occasionally eat grass. They dig for roots and bulbs with their front hooves and also use their horns to knock down foliage. They are independent of water but will drink when it is available.
Reproduction: The dominant bulls mate with the receptive cows, and a single calf, weighing 22–36kg, is born after a gestation period of approximately 270 days. The calf remains hidden for the first 2 weeks after birth. Calves may be dropped in any month of the year but there is a peak in summer. They grow rapidly and can achieve a mass of 450kg by the end of their first year. Mammae: 2 pairs inguinal.
Longevity: One captive 23 years 6 months, several to 23 years, one unconfirmed captive 26 years; wild Eland are recorded as living for 14–17 years.
Note: Despite the massive size, Eland are excellent jumpers and can easily clear a 2m fence. When moving, they make a distinct clicking noise, which is believed to be caused by the two halves of each hoof striking together. This sound carries quite well and is sometimes the first indication of the species' presence. Eland feature frequently in San rock paintings. They have been successfully domesticated in Zimbabwe and Russia. Although the Zimbabwe programme, begun in 1954, has since collapsed, the Russian farming venture is still under way. Eland produce good quality meat and the milk has a very high fat content and is said to have great nutritional value.

Some of the largest herds of Common Eland are found in the Kalahari.

The race known as Livingstone's Eland occurs in the north of the region, and has vertical white stripes on the body.

Common Eland bulls and cows (here) both carry horns.

Common Eland

100mm
right front

85mm
right back

Tragelaphus
strepsiceros

Greater Kudu *Tragelaphus strepsiceros*

Current thinking splits this into two species – **Cape Kudu** (*T. strepsiceros*);
Zambezi Kudu (*T. zambesiensis*).
Total length 2.3–2.9m; shoulder height 1.2–1.55m; tail 43cm;
mass (M) 250kg, (F) 165–180kg.
Average horn length 120cm; record horn length (along the curve) 187.6cm.
Identification pointers: Large size; long legs; 6–10 vertical white stripes on
grey-brown sides; large rounded ears; bushy tail, blackish or brownish above,
white underneath; characteristic long, spiral horns of bull.

Horn Development

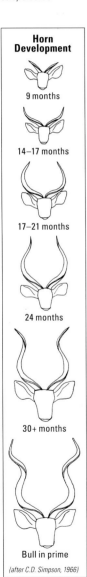

9 months

14–17 months

17–21 months

24 months

30+ months

Bull in prime

(after C.D. Simpson, 1966)

Description: This large and handsome antelope is grey-brown to rufous, with the
bulls being more grey than the cows and calves. The sides are clearly marked with
6–10 vertical white stripes. There is a distinct white band across the face, with white
spots on the cheeks. The bull has a prominent mane from the neck to beyond the
shoulders and a fringe of longer hair on the throat and lower neck. The blackish
or brown bushy tail is white underneath with a black tip. The ears are very large,
showing pink on the inside. Only the male has the long, spiral horns.
Distribution: Kudu occur principally in the northern and eastern parts of
southern Africa with apparently isolated populations in the south, where it has
spread westwards from the Eastern Cape into the northern Western Cape and
Northern Cape provinces over the past 20 years. Kudu can now be found in
the Nuweveld range near Beaufort West, the dry watercourses in the vicinity of
Williston, Carnarvon and Van Wyksvlei, with individuals being recorded as far
west as Nieuwoudtville on the western escarpment. Sightings are now regular
to the north of the Swartberg range which separates the Little and Great Karoo.
Outside of the region, Kudu occur widely in Central Africa south of the equatorial
forests, and through East Africa to Ethiopia, Sudan and Chad.
Habitat: The Greater Kudu is an antelope of wooded savanna. It may occur in
arid areas but only where there are stands of bush that provide cover and food.
It does not occur in open grassland or forest. It has, however, been able to
penetrate the Karoo and the Namib Desert along wooded watercourses. In many
areas it shows a preference for acacia woodland and rocky hill country.
Behaviour: Although it normally occurs in small herds, from 3–10 animals, larger
groups are occasionally seen. Outside the midwinter rutting period the adult bulls
are either solitary or join small bachelor herds. At the time of the rut an adult bull will
run with a group of cows and their young. Although usually active in early mornings
and late afternoons, in areas where they are disturbed or hunted they have taken to
nocturnal activity. They are well known for their jumping ability, having no difficulty in
clearing fences of up to 2m. Home range sizes are quite small, 100–3,200ha and are
a measure of food quality and abundance.
Food: Although predominantly a browser, it does occasionally graze. It eats a wider
variety of browse species than any other of our local antelopes. It is considered a
pest in some areas because it feeds on crops such as alfalfa, maize and vegetables.
Reproduction: Calves are born throughout the year but most births take place in
the summer months, the main rutting period being in midwinter. Like Sable and
Roan Antelopes, the Greater Kudu cow moves away from the herd to drop a single
calf, which weighs about 16kg. The gestation period is around 270 days. The calves
remain hidden for at least 2 months after birth, with the cows visiting them just once
a day to suckle. After this time, calves move with their mothers and join the nursery
herds. Mammae: 2 pairs inguinal.
Longevity: Average 7–8 years in the wild; 23 years in captivity, one confirmed at 22
years 3 months.

The Greater Kudu bull has, arguably, the most elegant of all antelope horns.

The Greater Kudu cow lacks the horns and long throat fringe of the bull.

Two Greater Kudu bulls showing the differing extent of white striping on the body.

Greater Kudu

78mm

right
front

61mm

right
back

Tragelaphus angasii

Nyala *Tragelaphus (Nyala) angasii*

Male: Total length 2.1m; shoulder height 1.15m; tail 43cm; mass 108kg.
Female: Total length 1.8m; shoulder height 97cm; tail 36cm; mass 62kg.
Average horn length 60cm; record horn length 83.5cm.
Identification pointers: Ram slate-grey to dark brown overall with long
mane along entire length of back, and long fringe hanging below underbelly
from throat to between hind legs; lower part of legs rufous or yellow-brown;
8–14 vertical white stripes on sides; tail quite bushy and white below; horns
spiralled but much shorter, lighter and less spiralled than those of Greater
Kudu (p.314). Ewe is smaller, has no horns and is yellow-brown to chestnut in
colour with up to 18 vertical white stripes on sides.

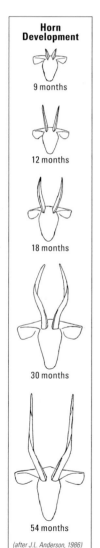

Horn Development

9 months

12 months

18 months

30 months

54 months

(after J.L. Anderson, 1986)

Description: Falls between Greater Kudu and Bushbuck in size. Like other
members of genus *Tragelaphus*, only the male Nyala has horns, but the sexes are
also markedly different in other aspects. Ram has fringe of long hair hanging
from underparts, from just behind chin to between hind legs, and a mane of hair
from back of head to rump. Mane normally lies flat but is raised during certain
behavioural interactions, such as on encountering another ram. Buttocks and
upperparts of hind legs are also lined with long hair. From 8–14 vertical white
stripes are present on the sides but these disappear or become less distinct in
older rams. Ground colour is slate-grey to dark brown. Lower parts of legs are
rufous to yellow-brown. There are 2 or 3 white cheek spots, and chin and upper
lip are also white. Shallow V-shaped white line runs between eyes. Ewe differs
from ram, being much smaller and lacking the long shaggy hair. In addition, ewes
and lambs have yellow-brown to chestnut ground colour and up to 18 vertical
white lines on sides of body. Ram's slightly spiralled horns curve outward after
the first turn. Horn tips are whitish-yellow.

Distribution: Occurs patchily in the north-eastern parts of southern Africa, with a
marginal occurrence north of the Zambezi in Mozambique and southern Malawi.
In South Africa there are two major centres of distribution: northern KwaZulu-
Natal and the lowveld of Mpumalanga and Limpopo provinces. Although some
populations have disappeared in recent years, others have expanded and increased
in numbers. Nyala have also been introduced to game farms well outside of their
traditional range, including into the Eastern Cape and Namibia and, in many cases,
thrive in these areas. Probably the best location to observe this antelope is uMkuzi
Game Reserve in KwaZulu-Natal.

Habitat: Restricted to dry savanna woodland and along watercourses. It may be
seen grazing in open areas adjacent to bush or tree cover.

Behaviour: Nyala rams are not territorial and seldom fight, but display by raising
the dorsal crest and 'slow-walking' in what is called the 'lateral presentation'. The
biggest ram wins and the competitor withdraws. However, when fighting does
take place it can be very intensive. Commonly seen in small groups, either ewes
and lambs, or all rams together. Solitary rams are often seen. Group composition
changes constantly, although ewe-and-lamb groups are the most stable. Larger
groups may be observed, but these are usually associated with a waterhole or a
localized abundance of food.

Food: Principally a browser, eating from wide variety of plants. Fresh grass taken
during rains. Like Bushbuck and Impala, Nyala will feed on fallen tree flowers and
fruits knocked down by foraging Baboons and Vervet Monkeys.

Reproduction: Single lamb, weighing 4.2–5.5kg, born at any time of year. Gestation
period 220 days. Remains hidden for first 2 weeks. Mammae: 2 pairs inguinal.

Longevity: Up to 14+ years in the wild; one captive 15 years 10 months.

Nyala ewe and fawn showing the distinct vertical white stripes.

Nyala ewes suckle their young for up to seven months.

The Nyala ram has a mane of long hair along the length of the back.

Nyala

57mm

right
front

53mm

right
back

Tragelaphus spekii

Sitatunga *Tragelaphus spekii*

Current thinking names it the **Zambezi Sitatunga** *(T. selousi)*.
Male: total length 1.72–1.95m; shoulder height 88–125cm; tail 22cm;
mass 115kg.
Female: total length 1.55–1.8m; shoulder height 75–90cm; tail 22cm;
mass 55kg.
Average horn length 60cm; record horn length 92.4cm.
Identification pointers: Semi-aquatic habitat requirements totally different
from those of Nyala (p.316); Sitatunga considerably larger than Bushbuck.
Hindquarters higher than front; fairly long, shaggy hair. Spoor unmistakable.

Description: Adult rams larger than ewes; shaggy-haired, drab, dark brown with no
body stripes – sometimes lighter marks on back. Ewes also dark brown or reddish-
brown but have black band down centre of back, four vertical stripes on side, white
lateral band and white spots on haunches. Both sexes have an incomplete white
band between eyes and white spots on cheeks. White patch above chest and another
below chin. Dark brown tail is white below; not very bushy. Hooves are extremely
widely splayed and up to 18cm long – an adaptation to marshy habitat. Only rams
have horns; quite long and similar in form to Nyala.
Distribution: In scattered, largely isolated, populations. Major populations in the
Okavango Delta and Linyanti in Botswana and Namibia, Kasanka and Kafue national
parks and Bangweulu in Zambia. Other populations are small and fragmented.
Habitat: Semi-aquatic and spends most of its time in dense reed beds with water
to a depth of one metre. Swims in deeper water to escape danger and cross to
feeding grounds.
Behaviour: Common grouping is adult ram with ewes and juveniles, but solitary
animals and groups of sub-adults are also seen. Active throughout day, but lies
up during hottest hours on trampled mats of reeds or other vegetation. Will also
feed at night. If alarmed, will swim to safety.
Food: Papyrus and other reeds; also grass and occasional browse.
Reproduction: Single calf born after 220-day gestation, usually in midwinter.
Mammae: 2 pairs inguinal.
Longevity: 16–22 years in captivity; in the wild, most live up to at least 11 years.

Tragelaphus
sylvaticus

Bushbuck (Imbabala) *Tragelaphus sylvaticus*

Male: total length 1.36–1.66m; shoulder height 80cm; tail 20cm; mass 45kg.
Female: total length 1.3–1.5m; shoulder height 70cm; tail 20cm; mass 30kg.
Average horn length 26cm; record horn length 54.3cm.
Identification pointers: Presence of vertical white stripes and spots on sides
of the body to a greater or lesser extent, more so in north; broad ears; short
bushy tail, dark above and white below; ram has short, almost straight horns
with slight spiral and ridge. Much smaller than Nyala (p.316).

Description: Small bright chestnut to dark brown antelope; those in north of
region more brightly coloured and clearly marked than those from south, but
considerable variation in colour and markings exists within populations. Patterns
of white lines and spots are present on the flanks to a greater or lesser extent, more
so in the north. Bushbuck may or may not have the broken white line between the
eyes, which is always present in Sitatunga, Nyala and Greater Kudu, but it has two
white patches on the throat. Crest of longish hair down back of ram is raised when

A young Sitatunga ram in Kasanka, Zambia

A Bushbuck ram of the Cape race *T. s. sylvaticus*

A Sitatunga ram of the southern race has very few white markings and is greyish-brown.

A Bushbuck ewe of the Limpopo race *T. s. roualeynei*

Sitatunga will readily swim to feeding-grounds and to escape predators.

Note the white patches on the throat and the overall bright colour of this Bushbuck ewe, race *T. s. ornatus*, from the Zambezi Valley.

Sitatunga

110mm
right front

80mm
right back

Bushbuck

44mm
right front

41mm
right back

it displays or threatens. Bushy tail white below and dark brown above. Only ram has horns, which project backwards in a single spiral with a prominent ridge along edge. Can be extremely sharp-pointed in young rams. Three subspecies generally recognized for region but currently designated as full species by some. Populations in far northern Angola may be Harnessed Bushbuck (Kewel) *(Tragelaphus scriptus).*
Distribution: Southern coastal belt and eastern and northern parts of region.
Habitat: Riverine woodland and bush associated with water, from coastal dune bush to montane forest, and from sea level to an altitude of 1,800m in South Africa.
Behaviour: Usually single but occasionally in pairs or small loosely knit groups of ewes and lambs. They may occur at high densities in prime habitat. Mainly nocturnal but also active during day in cooler or overcast weather. In region, home ranges 2.5–120ha. There are apparently differences between the behaviour patterns of west-central populations of *T. scriptus* and *T. sylvaticus* occurring in the region and extending into eastern Africa but these are little studied.
Food: Predominantly browsers but will take grass. May damage young trees in forestry plantations or agricultural crops.
Reproduction: Single young weighing 3.5–4.5kg born after gestation period of 180 days. Follows mother regularly after 4 months of remaining hidden. Mammae: 2 pairs inguinal.
Longevity: Up to 8–13 years in the wild; >12–16 years in captivity.

Hippotragus equinus

Roan Antelope *Hippotragus equinus*

Total length 2.26–2.89m; shoulder height 1.1–1.5m (average 1.4m); tail 54cm; mass 220–300kg (average 270kg).
Average horn length (bull) 75cm; record horn length (Zimbabwe) 99.06cm.
Identification pointers: Large size; greyish-brown colour with lighter underparts; black-and-white facial pattern; heavily ridged, swept-back, curving horns; long, narrow, tufted ears. See Sable Antelope (p.322).

Description: After Common Eland, Roan Antelope is the second-largest antelope species occurring in southern Africa. It has a somewhat horse-like appearance with a general colouring of greyish-brown, often with a reddish tinge ('roan' coloration). The underparts are lighter. The face is distinctly marked with black and white, giving it a slightly clown-like appearance and the long, narrow ears have prominent tassels of hair at the tip. The tail is long and tufted. A distinct, light-coloured, dark-tipped mane runs from between the ears to just beyond the shoulders. Both sexes carry the back-curved horns, but the cow's are lighter and shorter than the bull's.
Distribution: Restricted to the northern and north-eastern areas of southern Africa where it is considered to be rare. The total Roan population in South Africa is estimated to be about 1,500 animals, of which only a small number are in national parks. For example, they occur throughout Kruger National Park but by 2003 their numbers had dwindled to fewer than 50 individuals. Although widespread in Angola and Zambia, numbers are very low. Beyond the southern African region it occurs widely in Central Africa, western East Africa and through the savanna zone to West Africa. However, despite this wide distribution, it is considered to be rare and endangered throughout much of its range. Although numbers are slowly increasing in South Africa, there is concern that animals have been imported from West Africa and this could lead to genetic contamination of the local populations.

The Roan Antelope bull has large, back-curved horns that are heavily ringed along most of their length.

Roan Antelope have an erect, black-tipped, mane running from behind the ears to the shoulder region.

A young Roan Antelope clearly showing the distinctive facial markings

Roan Antelope

120mm

right
front

120mm

right
back

Habitat: Roan Antelope require open or lightly wooded grassland with medium to tall grass and access to water. They avoid areas with short grass.

Behaviour: Live in small herds (5–12) usually led by an adult bull. Larger herds (30–80) have been recorded. Nursery herds, consisting of cows and young animals, occupy fixed areas that are defended by dominant bulls from approaches by other bulls. The herd itself is usually led by a cow, which becomes dominant over the other cows and juveniles. The bull is responsible for breeding and keeping competitors away and the lead cow selects the feeding and resting areas. Two-year-old bulls are driven away from the herd by the herd bull and join together to form small bachelor herds. Adult bulls (5–6 years old) move off to live alone or to take over nursery herds. Most activity takes place during the day.

Food: Roan Antelope are principally grazers, selecting medium or long grasses. They rarely browse. Will seek out areas of new grass after fires.

Reproduction: Calves, weighing 15–18kg, may be dropped at any time of the year after a gestation period of about 280 days. Shortly before the birth the cow moves away from the herd and remains in bush cover until the calf is born. For the first few days the cow remains close to the calf, but then rejoins the herd, only visiting her calf in the early morning and late afternoon. When it is 2–6 weeks old the calf joins the herd. Although its facial markings are similar to those of the adults, its body colour is light to rich rufous-brown. Mammae: 2 pairs inguinal.

Longevity: 14–17 years in captivity.

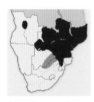

Hippotragus niger
■ present range
▨ historic range

Sable Antelope *Hippotragus niger*

Total length 2.3–2.56m; shoulder height 1.35m; tail 50cm; mass 180–270kg (bulls average 230kg).

Average horn length (bull) 102cm; record horn length (southern Africa) 140.65cm.

Identification pointers: Large size; contrasting black or dark brown upperparts with pure white underparts; long, transversely ridged, back-curved horns in both sexes. Different body colour from Roan Antelope (p.320), with a somewhat lighter build, longer horns and no tuft of hair at the tip of the ear.

Description: The adult bull Sable Antelope is shiny black with sharply contrasting white underparts and inner thighs. Cows and younger bulls are usually reddish brown above. The black-and-white facial markings are conspicuous. The face is mainly white, with a broad black blaze from the forehead to the nose and a black stripe from below the eye almost to the muzzle. There is an erect, fairly long mane running from the top of the neck to just beyond the shoulders. The ears are long and narrow but lack the tufted tips found in Roan Antelope. Both sexes carry horns but those of the bull are longer and more robust. The transversely ridged horns rise up from the skull and then sweep backwards in a pronounced curve.

Distribution: Restricted to the north-eastern parts of southern Africa but even here, distribution is patchy and not continuous. It occurs as far north as southern Kenya and marginally in south-eastern Angola. An isolated population occurs in northern Angola, but is considered to be a separate subspecies, the so-called Giant Sable *(H. n. variani)*. No recent counts have been made in Botswana or Zimbabwe, and within Namibia wild-ranging herds are restricted to the extreme north-east, although a small number of Sable Antelope have been introduced into Etosha National Park. Reasonable numbers still occur in Zambia, especially centred on Kafue and Luangwa. Sable populations in Kruger National Park have

Sable Antelope herd sizes range from 10–30 animals, but larger herds are known.

Sable Antelope bulls have strongly contrasting black-and-white coats.

The horns of the Sable Antelope cow are more slender than those of the bulls; body colouring is reddish to red-brown.

Sable Antelope

115mm

right front

104mm

right back

declined by 70 per cent in the past 15 years, and it has been predicted that they will continue to decline into extinction in that park. Most herds are intensively managed on private game farms, as Sables fetch high prices as breeding stock and the bulls are sought-after as hunting trophies. Unfortunately, some of the stock on South African game farms originates from Zambia, thus genetically contaminating the southernmost Sable populations.

Habitat: Sable are usually associated with dry, open woodland with medium to tall grass. They avoid dense woodland and short grassveld. Water is essential.

Behaviour: Sable Antelope live in herds usually numbering 10–30 individuals but occasionally larger groups come together. Territorial bulls establish themselves in territories overlapping those of nursery herds (cows and young animals). The nursery herds move within a fixed home range. During the rut the bull tries to keep the cows within his territory. As with Roan Antelope, a cow takes over leadership of a nursery herd. Young bulls grow up within bachelor herds, only seeking out their own territories in their fifth or sixth year. Most Sable Antelope activity takes place in the early morning and late afternoon.

Food: Sable Antelope are principally grazers but will take browse, particularly in the dry season. Regular access to drinking water is essential.

Reproduction: Sable Antelope is a seasonal breeder, dropping its calves January–March, although this varies according to area. A single reddish-brown calf, weighing 13–22kg, is born after a gestation period of about 270 days. The cow leaves the herd to give birth and the calf remains hidden for up to 2 months before joining the other animals. After each suckling, only once or twice a day, the calf moves to a new hiding-place and in this way reduces the chances of being found by a predator. Mammae: 2 pairs inguinal.

Longevity: One captive 22 years 3 months, several to 17 years.

Note: A pair of Sable Antelope horns collected in 1898 from Kruger National Park measured 140.65cm, exceeding the currrent official South African record of 127.6cm by more than 13cm. A Giant Sable *(H. n. variani)*, from northern Angola, holds the overall record horn length for the continent of 164.7cm.

Oryx gazella

Gemsbok (Southern Oryx) *Oryx gazella*

Total length 2.2–2.5m; shoulder height 1.2m; tail length 46cm; mass (M) 240kg, (F) 210kg.
Average horn length 85cm; record horn length (Kalahari) 125.7cm.
Identification pointers: Heavily built with short, thick neck; distinct black facial and body markings; long, black, horse-like tail; long, straight horns.

Description: Heavily built with a thick neck and distinct black-and-white markings on head, body and legs; long horse-like tail. Body colour greyish-fawn, separated from white underparts by black streak along flanks. Black patches on upper part of legs and along top of rump. Black stripe runs down front of neck. Calves fawn and lack black body markings. Both sexes carry long, almost straight, transversely ridged, rapier-like horns; those of bull are shorter and more robust.

Distribution: Arid south-west of the region, extending north into Angola. Reintroduced widely in the south throughout its historic range.

Habitat: Open, dry country but also open woodland, grassveld and dune country. Availability of water is not an essential habitat requirement.

Behaviour: Gregarious, occurring in herds of about 15, sometimes more, particularly during rains. They occur in mixed herds (consisting of bulls, cows and young of different ages) or nursery herds (cows and young); solitary bulls are

Gemsbok form herds averaging 15 individuals but many more animals may gather together after rains.

The long, rapier-like horns of the Gemsbok are carried by both sexes; those of the cow are longer but more slender than those of the bull.

Gemsbok (Southern Oryx)

110mm

right
front

80mm

right
back

often seen. A territorial bull will herd a mixed or nursery herd into his territory and only he will mate with receptive cows. Gemsbok are usually forced by their hostile environment to be nomadic, moving to fresh vegetation growth following rain.

Food: Although mainly grazers they also include browse, seed-pods and fruits such as tsamma melons in their diet.

Reproduction: Single calf, weighing about 15kg, dropped after a gestation of about 264 days, usually linked to seasonal rainfall. The calf hides and will move with the mother at night to a new resting-place. Calves usually 3–6 weeks old before joining the herd. Mammae: 2 pairs inguinal.

Longevity: One captive 18 years 1 month but up to 24 years claimed.

■ *Kobus ellipsiprymnus ellipsiprymnus*

■ *Kobus ellipsiprymnus defassa*

Waterbuck *Kobus ellipsiprymnus*

Total length 2.1–2.74m; shoulder height 1.3m; tail 35cm; mass 250–270kg (bulls heavier than cows).
Average horn length 75cm; record horn length (South Africa) 99.7cm.
Identification pointers: Large size; broad white ring around rump (Common Waterbuck, *K. e. ellipsiprymnus*); broad white rump patch (Defassa Waterbuck, *K. e. defassa*); coarse, shaggy grey-brown coat; long, ringed, forward-swept horns of the bull.

Description: Waterbuck are large, robust antelopes with coarse, long coats. The body colour is grey-brown with either grey or brown being dominant, scattered through with grey or white hairs. A broad white ring encircles the rump in the Common but in the Defassa this ring is replaced with a broad white rump patch, and a white band is present from throat to the base of the ears. The flanks are lighter in colour than the back and the hair around the mouth, nose and above the eyes is white. The ears are short, rounded, white on the inside with a black tip. The tail is quite long with a black tuft of hair at the tip. Only the bull has the long, heavily ringed horns that curve backwards and then forwards towards the tips.

Distribution: Waterbuck occur patchily in eastern and northern southern Africa and then northwards through East Africa to southern Somalia and across through West Africa. The Common is the only form occurring in South Africa, Botswana, Zimbabwe and Mozambique but both this and the Defassa occur in Zambia and only the Defassa in Angola. Historically, Waterbuck occurred in Angola, but their present status is unknown and we have not included the historic range on the map but it may still be present in the south-east close to the Zambian border and possibly elsewhere. Where the two forms have overlapping ranges they will interbreed.

Habitat: Always associated with water, preferring areas with reed beds or tall grass as well as woodland. They will utilize open grassland adjacent to cover.

Behaviour: Gregarious, occurring in herds of 5–10, sometimes up to 30. Larger herds usually seen during rainy season. Nursery herds may move through territories of several bulls. Bull attempts to establish territory during fifth or sixth year; when successful, holds it until dislodged by a competing bull. Bulls largely rely on elaborate displays but fights can be vicious. Younger bulls form bachelor herds. Often detected by the strong musky scent given off by their oily hair.

Food: Principally grass but also take browse.

Reproduction: A single calf, averaging 13.6kg, may be dropped at any time of the year but mostly in summer; the gestation period is about 280 days. After 3–4 weeks in hiding the calf follows the mother and joins the herd. Mammae: 2 pairs inguinal.

Longevity: In the wild, 4–5 years, rarely to 18 years; one captive lived for 30 years but usually much less.

Common Waterbuck bull and cows; the broad white ring encircling the rump is diagnostic, and only the bull has horns.

Young Waterbuck bulls test each other's strength.

The Waterbuck bull has heavily ringed, forward-curving horns.

The Defassa Waterbuck has a distinctive white patch on the rump.

Waterbuck

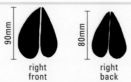

90mm
right
front

80mm
right
back

■ *Kobus leche leche*

■ *Kobus leche kafuensis*

▨ *Kobus leche smithemani*

Lechwe *Kobus leche*

All races of the Lechwe are endemic to the region and each is recognized as a full species in its own right by some authorities.

Male: total length 2m; shoulder height 1m; tail 34cm; mass 100kg.
Female: total length 1.9m; shoulder height 96cm; tail 34cm; mass 80kg.
Average horn length 70cm; record horn length 93.98cm.

Identification pointers: Medium size; rump higher than forequarters; ewe and young chestnut upperparts, white underparts, black markings on leading face of front legs; rams of different races range from similar to ewes to very dark; long, ridged, forward-pointing horns of the ram much longer than those of Puku. Semi-aquatic habitat sets Lechwe apart from other species. Different in appearance from Sitatunga (see p.318).

Description: Hindquarters are noticeably higher than the shoulders and the muzzle is quite short. The rams carry long, strongly laterally ridged, lyre-shaped horns. Three distinctive and non-overlapping subspecies (some place each as a full species in its own right) are recognized, within which the ewes and young are very similar to each other but adult rams are clearly separated by pelage coloration. All races and both sexes have black markings on the forward-facing surfaces of the legs, and the underparts are white; white facial patches are most prominent in the black race. The Red *(K. l. leche)* is overall bright chestnut-brown; the Kafue *(K. l. kafuensis)* ram has dark shoulder patches; the Black *(K. l. smithemani)* ram is blackish-brown over much of the body.

Distribution: In the region, Red Lechwe is restricted to the Okavango and Chobe areas of northern Botswana and the Caprivi Strip, Namibia, with small, isolated populations in western Zambia and adjacent areas of Angola. The Kafue Lechwe only occurs on the Kafue floodplains in south-central Zambia (Blue Lagoon and Lochinvar). Black Lechwe are centred on the floodplains of the Bangweulu Swamps in north-eastern Zambia. A possible newly recognized species occurs close to the Zambian border in DR Congo, Upemba Lechwe (*K. anselli* – proposed).

Habitat: Floodplains and seasonal swamps; rarely ventures more than 2–3km from permanent water.

Behaviour: Next to the Sitatunga, the Lechwe is the most water-loving antelope. It takes readily to water, both to feed and when threatened. It usually occurs in herds of up to 30 individuals, but occasionally many thousands may be seen together. Rams form small territories, rarely more than 150m across, within which they keep small groups of ewes for mating. Small groups of non-territorial rams congregate on the edges of the mating grounds. Ewe herds with their young move freely between ram territories. Lechwe are active during the early morning and late afternoon, lying up during the heat of the day and at night. Although quite slow on land, they can move rapidly in shallow water and swim readily.

Food: Mainly semi-aquatic grasses.

Reproduction: Although lambs may be seen at any time of year, there appear to be seasonal peaks, e.g. October–December in northern Botswana. A single lamb, weighing approximately 5kg, is born after a gestation period of about 225 days. Calves remain hidden for the first 2–3 weeks. Mammae: 2 pairs inguinal.

Longevity: One captive lived 15 years 1 month.

Ewes and young of all Lechwe races have reddish-brown coats with contrasting white underparts and black markings on the leading face of the front legs.

Red Lechwe ram

The Kafue Lechwe ram carries the most impressive horns.

The Black Lechwe ram has the darkest coat of all the Lechwe races.

Kafue Lechwe ewe

Lechwe

80mm
right
front

75mm
right
back

Kobus vardonii

Puku *Kobus vardonii*

Total length 1.5–1.7m; shoulder height 80cm; tail 28cm; mass (M) 74kg, (F) 62kg.
Average horn length 45cm; record horn length 56.2cm.
Identification pointers: Can be distinguished from Lechwe by the absence of black markings on the front of the forelegs and by the shorter horns of rams.

Description: The upperparts of this medium-sized antelope are golden-yellow with slightly paler sides. The underparts are off-white, as are the throat, the sides of the muzzle and around the eyes. The legs are uniform brown in colour, and the tail is golden-yellow. Only the ram has the relatively short, stout, lyre-shaped, well-ringed horns.
Distribution: In the region, occurs in several isolated populations with the bulk of the population located in the Luangwa Valley, Kasanka and Kafue in Zambia. A small population is centred on the Pookoo Flats in Chobe National Park, Botswana. Remnant herds probably survive in Angola.
Habitat: Open flatland adjacent to rivers and marshes but usually not on open floodplains favoured by Lechwe. Where they occur on dambos, they move out into the surrounding miombo woodlands during the rains.
Behaviour: Herds of Puku usually number from 5–30. Adult rams defend small territories for short periods, during which time they attempt to herd the ewes, which will, however, move across the territories of several rams. A distinctive, sharp, repeated whistle is given by territorial rams and as an alarm call.
Food: Predominantly grasses, with species selection in different seasons.
Reproduction: Young may be dropped at any time of the year but in the south of its range there is a birth peak during the dry winter months. The gestation period is approximately 240 days. The lamb (<6kg) hides for the early part of its life and, on joining the herd, usually moves with the other lambs as the mother/lamb bond is weak in comparison with other antelope species. Mammae: 2 pairs inguinal.
Longevity: One captive to 17 years.

Redunca fulvorufula

Mountain Reedbuck *Redunca fulvorufula*

Total length 1.3–1.5m; shoulder height 72cm; tail 20cm; mass 30kg.
Average horn length 14cm; record horn length 25.4cm.
Identification pointers: Grey-fawn upperparts; white underparts; bushy tail, grey above and white below; short, forward-curved horns of male. May be confused with Grey Rhebok (p.334) where they occur together, but the horns of the latter are straight and vertically set, and not forward-curved. Similar to Common Reedbuck but smaller, and has no dark brown line on front of the forelegs; different habitat.

Description: Upperparts grey-fawn and underparts white. Hair on the head and neck is usually more yellow-fawn. Bushy tail, grey-fawn above, white below, is held vertically when animal flees, prominently displaying white under-surface. Ears are long and narrow. Only male has short, stout, forward-curved and ringed horns.
Distribution: Patchy distribution in south-eastern parts of the region.
Habitat: The Mountain Reedbuck is restricted to mountainous and rocky areas. Preference for broken hill country with scattered bush, trees or grassy slopes but avoids steep rock-faces and boulder tangles. Water is essential.

The Puku ram has well-formed, lyre-shaped horns.

The Mountain Reedbuck ram has short, forward-pointing horns.

Puku ewes do not carry horns but are otherwise very similar to the rams.

The Puku lamb remains hidden for the first month of its life.

Unlike the Common Reedbuck, the Mountain Reedbuck has no black markings on the front face of the forelimbs.

Puku

67mm
right front

62mm
right back

Mountain Reedbuck

45mm
right front

45mm
right back

Behaviour: Territorial rams occupy their areas throughout the year but small groups of 2–6 ewes and young are unstable and move from herd to herd and over several ram territories. Bachelor groups may also be observed but these are unstable. This species is active both at night and during the day but lies up during the hottest hours.

Food: Grasses, with seasonal preferences.

Reproduction: Breeding takes place throughout the year with a birth-peak in the summer months. A single lamb with a mass of 3kg is born after a gestation period of approximately 242 days. The ewe gives birth to the lamb under cover and away from the group. The lamb remains hidden for 2–3 months before joining the other group members. Mammae: 2 pairs inguinal.

Longevity: Up to 12 years in the wild.

Redunca arundinum
■ present range
▨ historic range

Common (Southern) Reedbuck *Redunca arundinum*

Male: total length 1.6–1.8m; shoulder height 95cm; tail 25cm; mass 43–68kg.
Female: total length 1.4–1.7m; shoulder height 80cm; tail 25cm; mass 32–51kg.
Average horn length 30cm; record horn length 46.68cm.

Identification pointers: Forward-curved horns of the ram; white, bushy underside of tail is prominent when the animal is running away. Differs from Mountain Reedbuck in being larger, having brown or black lines on front surface of forelegs, and in ram having considerably longer horns. Habitat requirements of the two species are different and they are rarely found together.

Description: Medium-sized antelope with brown or greyish-fawn upperparts, although head and neck are slightly lighter. Underparts are white. The short, bushy tail is grey-fawn above and white below. There is a vertical, dark stripe on the forward-facing surface of forelegs. Ears are broad and rounded and white on the inside. Only the ram has horns and they are curved forward and transversely ridged from the base for two-thirds of their length. Base of horns narrowly ringed with pale grey growth tissue.

Distribution: Reedbuck has patchy distribution dictated by availability of suitable habitat, and is restricted to east and north of region. It has been eradicated in a number of areas, including extreme northern Namibia, although it still occurs in low numbers in parts of the Caprivi Strip. It is also now absent from the coastal plain of South Africa's Eastern Cape province; but some historic records indicate that it might once have extended into the Western Cape. The highest known densities reached in the region are in the Greater St. Lucia Wetland (iSimangaliso) in KwaZulu-Natal.

Habitat: The Common Reedbuck requires tall-grass areas and reed beds as well as permanent water. It avoids dense bush areas. They occur at altitudes ranging from near sea-level to about 2,000m in South Africa.

Behaviour: Usually in pairs or family groups but up to 20 individuals on occasion. A pair occupies a territory, which is defended by the ram. Both nocturnal and diurnal. Loud alarm whistle emitted through the nostrils when the animal is disturbed, or by rams advertising their territories.

Food: Reedbuck are predominantly grazers but do sometimes take browse.

Reproduction: Birth peak in summer. Gestation 220 days. A single lamb weighs 4.5kg, stays hidden for 2 months, and then accompanies the ewe;

The Common Reedbuck ram has forward-pointing and transversely ridged horns.

Common Reedbuck rams and ewes both have dark markings on the front faces of the forelimbs.

Common Reedbuck

65mm

right
front

65mm

right
back

both join the ram after 3–4 months. Mammae: 2 pairs inguinal.
Longevity: One captive 16 years 9 months; several in the wild to 10 years, but rarely more than 5 years.

Pelea capreolus
■ known current range
▨ limit of total range

Grey Rhebok *Pelea capreolus*

Total length 1.1–1.3m; shoulder height 75cm; tail 10cm; mass 20kg.
Average horn length 20cm; record horn length 30.16cm.
Identification pointers: Woolly grey coat; long, narrow ears; large black nose; straight, upright horns of ram. May be confused with Mountain Reedbuck (see p.330) where the two species occur together, but the latter's horns curve forwards at the tip.

Description: Gracefully built antelope with a grey, thick, woolly coat. The underparts are pure white. The short, bushy tail is grey above and white underneath and at the tip. Ears are long and narrow. Only the male has the vertical, almost straight horns. The large black nose has a somewhat swollen appearance.
Distribution: Almost entirely restricted to South Africa, Lesotho and Swaziland. This antelope has a patchy, discontinuous distribution and, despite its relatively large size, its range is not accurately known. There is a small population in the Huns Mountains *(Hunsberg)* in extreme south-western Namibia, close to the South African border. The largest population unit is located within the Drakensberg of KwaZulu-Natal. Relatively high numbers occur in the southern wheatlands of the Western Cape. It extends as far into the arid north-west as the Richtersveld and southwards into the Kamiesberg, but only in small numbers. There is a substantial population in the Karoo National Park and adjacent areas of the Nuweveld escarpment.
Habitat: Usually hill or mountain country, but also occurs in the wheatlands of the south-western Cape, particularly in the Bredasdorp and Swellendam districts.
Behaviour: Normally in small family parties consisting of a territorial adult ram, several ewes and their young. Active by day. Gives vent to a sharp snort at regular intervals when disturbed or alarmed. Runs with rocking-horse motion displaying white underside of tail as warning signal.
Food: Grasses and browse, the latter most important seasonally.
Reproduction: After a gestation period of 260 days, single lamb born in the wet season (September–January); remains hidden for several weeks. Mammae: 2 pairs inguinal.
Longevity: One captive lived to 12 years 4 months.

Connochaetes gnou

Black Wildebeest *Connochaetes gnou*

Male: total length 2.2–2.6m; shoulder height 1.2m; tail 46–61cm; mass 180kg.
Female: total length 1.9–2.3m; shoulder height 1.1m; tail 42–56cm; mass 100–140kg.
Average horn length 62cm; record double horn length (tip to tip) 74.62cm.
Identification pointers: Overall black appearance; long, white, horse-like tail; characteristic horn shape, extensive facial 'hairbrush'. Could be confused with Blue Wildebeest (p.338) but the ranges do not overlap, except where introduced. The white tail is characteristic of this species.

Grey Rhebok move in small family parties consisting of a ram, several ewes and their offspring of the season.

The Grey Rhebok ram has short, smooth, sharp-pointed horns. **Inset:** This buck's large black nose is obvious.

A pair of young Grey Rhebok in Swellendam district

Grey Rhebok

48mm

right
front

45mm

right
back

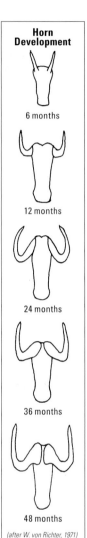

Horn Development

6 months

12 months

24 months

36 months

48 months

(after W. von Richter, 1971)

Description: More dark brown than black, but from a distance the Black Wildebeest does look black. Long, white, horse-like tail contrasts with body colour. Somewhat grotesque in appearance: shoulders are higher than rump and it has a large, broad-snouted head. Face covered in brush-like tuft of hairs which points outwards and there is long hair on throat and on chest between forelegs. Erect mane runs from top of neck to shoulders. Horns of cow are thinner and less robust than those of bull. They bend steeply downward, forward and upward; in mature bulls the horn base forms a 'boss' over top of head.

Distribution: Formerly distributed over a wide area of central South Africa, but brought to the brink of extinction towards the end of the 19th century. Numbers are now at least 22,000 in total, with perhaps 14,000 in South Africa. Widely introduced beyond former range. Some of the largest populations are located in Golden Gate Highlands National Park (>400) in the Free State and Mountain Zebra National Park (>300), near Cradock, in the Eastern Cape. There are more than 3,000 in various Free State provincial reserves, but by far the largest numbers (7,500) are kept on private land in that province. Of major concern is hybridization with Blue Wildebeest, and a number of populations are considered to be of dubious purity. A number of game farms run both species on the same property. Considerable numbers (±7,000) are kept in Namibia, far outside of their traditional range.

Habitat: Low karroid scrub and open grassland.

Behaviour: Bulls set up territories and, during rut will attempt to 'herd' cows within their areas. Herds, consisting of cows and their young, normally wander freely over bull territories. Bulls mark their territories with urine, droppings and scent secretions, reinforcing the effect by performing elaborate displays. Bachelor herds consist of bulls of all ages. Although, in the wild, wildebeest tend to flee from humans, in captivity they can be extremely dangerous. We have recorded several cases of people being attacked by captive animals, which can inflict serious wounds in these encounters. Most feeding takes place in the cooler daylight hours. When running, tend to zigzag, changing direction abruptly and swishing white tail from side to side.

Food: Principally grasses but browse on occasion. Browse becomes particularly important during the dry winter months. This varies from area to area, but probably ranges from 5–30 per cent of intake during this time. On some game farms, access to grasses is limited, and browse intake may be higher than usual. Drinking water essential.

Reproduction: The majority of calves are dropped during the midsummer months (December–January) but the peak period varies in different areas. A single calf, averaging 14kg, dropped after a gestation of about 250 days; can move with the herd shortly after birth. Mammae: 1 pair inguinal.

Longevity: May live for up to 14 years in the wild; one captive lived for 21 years 8 months.

Note: Also known as White-tailed Gnu, the latter part of the name coming from the characteristic nasal call 'ge-nu'.

The Black Wildebeest's horns have an overall dark appearance and a distinctive form; the bull's horns are heavier than those carried by the cow.

Note the white tail, facial 'hairbrush' and the erect, bi-coloured mane.

Black Wildebeest calf

Black Wildebeest

90mm
right
front

83mm
right
back

■ *Connochaetes taurinus taurinus*

■ *Connochaetes taurinus cooksoni*

■ *Connochaetes taurinus johnstoni*

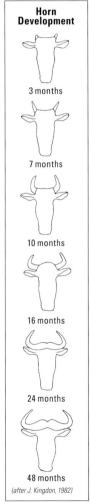

Horn Development

3 months

7 months

10 months

16 months

24 months

48 months

(after J. Kingdon, 1982)

Blue Wildebeest *Connochaetes taurinus*

Male: total length 2.4–3.3m; shoulder height 1.5m; tail 60cm (45–100cm); mass 250kg.
Female: total length 2.4–3.3m; shoulder height 1.3m; tail 60cm (45–100cm); mass 180kg.
Average horn length 60cm; record horn length 86.05cm (measured, like that of Black Wildebeest, from tip to tip along both horns).

Identification pointers: Forequarters higher and heavier than hindquarters; dark grey with some brown in younger animals and cows, with darker, vertical stripes on neck and chest; broad snout; superficially buffalo-like horns, but much lighter than African Buffalo (p.310). Distinguished by black tail (as opposed to white tail of Black Wildebeest, p.334).

Description: This wildebeest has lightly built hindquarters and is more robust at the shoulders. The head is large with a broad snout. Adult animals are dark grey tinged with brown, and in certain light conditions a silvery sheen is discernible. A number of vertical, darker stripes are present from the neck to just behind the rib-cage; it is frequently referred to as the Brindled (brown-streaked) Gnu for this reason. There is a mane of long black hair down the back of the neck and a beard of black hair on the throat. The front of the face is almost black, although an area of brown hair may be present at the horn base, particularly in younger animals. The race known as Cookson's Wildebeest *(C. t. cooksoni)* forms an isolated population in Zambia's Luangwa Valley and differs in usually having a more brown cast to the coat. In far northern Mozambique, centred on Niassa National Park, the wildebeest are designated as Johnston's or Nyassa *(C. t. johnstoni)* and are distinguished by a white chevron across the muzzle. Johnston's is sometimes considered to be a separate species. The calf is rufous fawn with a darker face and a dark vertebral stripe. Both sexes have horns, although those of the cow are less robust. The horn bases form a boss over the top of the head and the horns themselves grow outwards, turn sharply up and then inwards. The tail is black and horse-like.

Distribution: Largely restricted to the northern and central areas of southern Africa but it has been reintroduced and introduced widely to reserves and farms further south. Now found throughout its historical range. It extends from northern Namibia into southern Angola and western Zambia, with an isolated population in the Luangwa Valley (Cookson's). There is a break in distribution, with separate populations occurring in Tanzania and Kenya. In recent years, there has been a massive decline in numbers in Mozambique, as well as serious reductions in numbers in Botswana. In the former country, this can be ascribed to hunting levels and in the latter, to the network of veterinary fences that criss-cross the country, preventing access to traditional migration routes.

Habitat: Preference for open savanna woodland and open grassland. Access to drinking water is essential.

Behaviour: Although Blue Wildebeest occur in herds of up to 30 individuals, much larger concentrations may be observed, numbering many thousands. These are formed during migrations to new feeding-grounds but the smaller herd units maintain their identity. Such mass movements still take place in Botswana but the erection of veterinary cordon fences in that country has disturbed a number of the traditional routes. Territorial bulls defend a zone around their cows, even when on the move. A bull may have between two and 150 cows with their young within his territorial control. Cows may move through the territories of a number of bulls and mate with more than one. Outside the mating season, the cow herds move freely and are not herded by territorial bulls. Bachelor herds

Blue Wildebeest have to drink on a regular basis. Herd size averages 30 individuals but larger numbers commonly gather.

The Blue Wildebeest *(C. t. taurinus)* has by far the greatest range in the region. **Inset:** In young Blue Wildebeest calves the head is darker than the rest of body.

Cookson's Wildebeest occurs only in Zambia's Luangwa Valley. **Inset:** Johnston's Wildebeest has a distinct white chevron on the muzzle.

Blue Wildebeest

100mm

right
front

100mm

right
back

are usually found around the edge of the main concentration. Blue Wildebeest are active by day but seek out shade during the hottest hours.

Food: Essentially grazers, showing a preference for short green grass when available.

Reproduction: The mating season is usually March–June, with most calves dropped from mid-November to end-December, although this varies in different areas and may be influenced by factors such as drought or early rains. A single calf, weighing about 22kg, is born after a gestation period of approximately 250 days. The calf is able to run with the mother a few minutes after birth. Mammae: 1 pair inguinal.

Longevity: Up to 14 years in the wild, with one estimate to 18 years; captives have lived 21–24 years.

Alcelaphus caama

Red Hartebeest *Alcelaphus (buselaphus) caama*

Total length 2.3m; shoulder height 1.25m; tail 47cm; mass (M) 150kg, (F) 120kg.

Average horn length 52cm; record horn length 74.93cm.

Identification pointers: Much higher at shoulder than at rump; golden-brown colour with black leg markings; long face with black blaze; unusual horn shape. Similar to Lichtenstein's Hartebeest (see p.342) but distributions do not overlap (see maps), and to Tsessebe (p.346), but their horns are differently shaped.

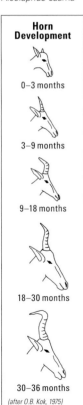

Horn Development

0–3 months

3–9 months

9–18 months

18–30 months

30–36 months

(after O.B. Kok, 1975)

Description: High-shouldered, awkward-looking antelope with long, pointed head. Body colour fawn to golden-brown, but darker from shoulders down centre of back to rump, particularly in bulls. Rump and upper thighs paler than rest of body. Black blaze down front of face and black markings on all four legs. Tail is pale at base, with black hair over remainder. Horns in both sexes; those of bull are heavier but both are set close together at the base, curving forwards and out and then twisting in and back.

Distribution: Now restricted to arid western parts of region, but formerly found as far south as Cape Town. Reintroduced widely throughout its historical range.

Habitat: Open savanna country and open woodland. Drinking water not essential.

Behaviour: Normally in herds numbering from about 20 to several hundred, occasionally thousands; larger groups usually forming at onset of summer rains. In arid areas, travels great distances in search of fresh grass. Adult bulls are territorial. Harem herds consisting of cows, young animals and a territorial bull occupy the best grazing, with bachelor herds having to make do with what is left. Mostly active by day.

Food: Mainly grasses but also browse, depending on season and conditions.

Reproduction: Single calf, weighing 12–14kg, born away from herd, after gestation period of 240 days, usually in early summer (October–December). It remains hidden until it is strong enough to keep up with the other animals. Mammae: 1 pair inguinal.

Longevity: Some 10–12 years in the wild, one report to 20 years but exceptional.

Red Hartebeest are essentially herd animals but solitary bulls are quite common.

A Red Hartebeest bull showing the distinctive black markings. **Inset:** The cow's horns are more slender than those of the bull.

The horns of the Red Hartebeest bull are heavier than those of the cow. **Inset:** Young calves have no dark markings.

Red Hartebeest

100mm

right
front

96mm

right
back

341

Alcelaphus lichtensteinii

Lichtenstein's Hartebeest *Alcelaphus lichtensteinii*

Total length 2.01–2.5m; shoulder height 1.25m; tail 48cm; mass
(M) 160–204kg, (F) 160–180kg.
Average horn length 52cm; record horn length 61.92cm.
Identification pointers: Higher at shoulders than rump; yellow-tawny body
colouring; characteristic Z-shaped horn. Compare with Tsessebe (p.346)
where range overlaps.

Description: A clumsy-looking antelope with its shoulders higher than its
hindquarters. Yellow-fawn body with slightly darker 'saddle' from shoulders to
rump. Flanks and underparts are lighter with an off-white area on rump. Dark
stripe runs down front of forelegs. Tail base is white but remainder of tail is covered
in longish black hair. Both sexes have horns flattened at base, strongly ringed,
except at the tips, with a Z-shaped curvature similar to those of Red Hartebeest.
Distribution: Occurs in Mozambique and south-eastern Zimbabwe, with largest
populations in Zambia. Introduced to Kruger National Park from Malawi.
Habitat: Savanna woodland where it abuts on vleis or floodplains. Access to
surface water is essential.
Behaviour: Small herds of up to 10 individuals; occasionally larger groups.
A territorial bull stays with a number of cows and calves within a fixed area.
Bachelor herds subsist in less favourable habitat. Mainly active by day but
partly nocturnal.
Food: Grasses, but occasionally browse from a range of tree species.
Reproduction: Single calf weighing about 15kg is born after a gestation period
of 240 days, usually in June–September. Can follow mother soon after birth but
usually lies up between feeds; makes no attempt to hide. Mammae: 1 pair inguinal.
Longevity: Not known but probably similar to Red Hartebeest.

■ *Damaliscus pygargus dorcas*

■ *Damaliscus pygargus phillipsi*

Bontebok *Damaliscus pygargus dorcas*

Total length 1.7–2m; shoulder height 90cm; tail 30–45cm;
mass (M) 62kg.

Blesbok *Damaliscus pygargus phillipsi*

Total length 1.7–2m; shoulder height 95cm; tail 30–45cm;
mass (M) 70kg.
Average horn length (both subspecies) 38cm; record horn length 52.39cm
(Blesbok), 43cm (Bontebok).

Identification pointers: Bontebok has a rich, dark brown body colour with
pure white buttocks, open white blaze from muzzle to between horns; **Blesbok**
has a reddish-brown colour with pale brown buttock patch, white blaze on
muzzle broken by brown between the eyes. No other hartebeest-like antelope
has white on the face.

Description: The Bontebok and Blesbok are separate and distinct subspecies of
D. pygargus, although recent thinking has raised each to full species status. The
differences between the two are outlined in the table on p.344. Both subspecies
are higher at the shoulder than at the rump and have long, pointed heads with
both sexes carrying simple lyre-shaped horns. They are thus similar in general
appearance to the other hartebeests and the Tsessebe. The ewe's horns are more
slender than those of the ram.

Lichtenstein's Hartebeest occupies savanna woodland and reaches its highest numbers in the northern miombo belt.

Bontebok are more richly coloured than Blesbok.

Blesbok usually have a much wider distributional range than Bontebok.

Lichtenstein's Hartebeest

100mm

right
front

96mm

right
back

Bontebok showing continuous facial blaze

Blesbok showing broken facial blaze

	Bontebok	Blesbok
Body colour	Rich, dark brown with purple gloss, particularly rams; darker on sides and upper limbs	Reddish-brown; no gloss
Face	White blaze usually unbroken but narrows between eyes (this character not 100%)	White blaze usually broken by brown band between eyes (this character not 100%)
Buttocks	Always white	Usually pale but rarely white
Limbs	Lower part usually white	Rarely as white as in Bontebok
Horns	Usually black on upper ringed surface	Usually straw-coloured on upper ringed surface

Distribution: **Bontebok** historically restricted to the Bredasdorp and Mossel Bay areas of Western Cape. After near-extinction, now safe on several reserves and private farms. Largest single population occurs in De Hoop Nature Reserve near Bredasdorp. **Blesbok** occur throughout the central grasslands of the Free State, and in the Eastern Cape, as well as marginally in KwaZulu-Natal. Both have been moved extensively outside their traditional range. (Largely uncontrolled transportation of the two subspecies into areas outside their traditional ranges has resulted in hybridization, where herds have been deliberately or accidentally mixed. This has resulted in an unknown number of populations being labelled as suspect as far as subspecies/species purity is concerned.)

Habitat: **Bontebok:** coastal plain within Cape fynbos vegetation zone; require short grass, water and some cover. **Blesbok:** open grassland with water.

Behaviour: Both **Bontebok** and **Blesbok** are diurnal, but are less active during hotter midday hours. Both characteristically stand head-down in groups facing the sun. Territorial **Bontebok** rams hold their areas throughout the year and ewe/lamb groups numbering some 6–10 wander at will through adjoining territories. Ewe groups are herded during January–March rut. Bachelor herds usually establish home ranges away from those held by territorial rams. **Blesbok** ewes move in harem herds numbering from 2–25, each herd attended by a territorial ram. Unlike **Bontebok**, where herd structure remains largely unchanged throughout the year, **Blesbok** do not occupy the same home range continuously, but come together in large mixed herds during the dry winter months.

Food: Grasses but will browse occasionally.

Reproduction: Most **Bontebok** lambs born September–October with a few being dropped as late as February. Most **Blesbok** lambs born November–January with a peak in December. Gestation period is approximately 240 days and the lamb has a mass of 6–7kg at birth. It is pale fawn to creamy in colour and can run with the mother within 20–30 minutes of birth. Mammae: 1 pair inguinal.

Longevity: One **Bontebok** lived to 15 years 7 months in captivity; **Blesbok** to 21 years 8 months. Given the lack of major predators in the locations where these buck occur, these ages may well be reached in the wild.

Young Bontebok and Blesbok lambs lack the distinctive markings of adults.

Adult Blesbok are overall reddish-brown, lacking the gloss of the Bontebok.

Most Bontebok have an unbroken white facial blaze and black horn faces.

Blesbok usually have a broken facial blaze and straw-coloured horn faces.

Bontebok & Blesbok

62mm

right front

63mm

right back

Damaliscus lunatus

Tsessebe *Damaliscus lunatus*

Total length 1.9–2.3m; shoulder height 1.2m; tail 45cm; mass (M) 140kg, (F) 126kg.
Average horn length 34cm; record horn length 46.99cm.
Identification pointers: Higher at shoulder than rump; characteristic horn shape; head dark in contrast to reddish-brown upperparts. See Red Hartebeest and Lichtenstein's Hartebeest (pp.340, 342) where distributions overlap.

Description: Rather hartebeest-like in general appearance, with long face and sloping back. Upperparts dark reddish-brown with distinct purplish sheen. Head, lower shoulder and upper parts of legs darker in colour than rest of body. Lower parts of legs are brownish-yellow, with pale fawn tail base and inner thighs. Black tassel on end half of tail. Bulls darker than cows. Both sexes have horns; lyrate and ringed except at the tip.
Distribution: Occurs patchily in north and north-eastern areas of the region. Herds numbering in the thousands sometimes gather on the floodplain woodlands fringing the Bangweulu Swamp in north-eastern Zambia. This isolated Tsessebe population is recognized as a full species by some authorities based on pelage colour and some skull differences (Bangweulu Tsessebe, *D. superstes*) but the authors consider this to be unlikely.
Habitat: Open savanna woodland with adjacent grassland and surface water.
Behaviour: Small herds of 5 or 6 individuals but sometimes number up to 30 or more, especially near water or favourable grazing. Larger numbers gather on the Bangweulu floodplains. A territorial bull maintains a defended area, within which the cows and young animals live permanently. Groups of young males form fluid bachelor herds that circulate around perimeter of established territories, usually with access to less-favourable grazing. Territory-holding bulls mark their territory with heaps of droppings and facial-gland secretions.
Food: Grasses, especially medium-length to long species.
Reproduction: Single young, with a mass of 10–12kg, born after a gestation of 240 days, usually October–December. Calves run with the herd shortly after birth. Mammae: 1 pair inguinal.
Longevity: One estimate of 15 years in the wild; one captive lived 9 years 4 months.

■ *Aepyceros melampus melampus*

■ *Aepyceros melampus petersi*

Impala *Aepyceros melampus*

Total length 1.6–1.72m; shoulder height 90cm; tail 28cm; mass (M) 45–80kg (50kg), (F) 34–52kg (40kg).
Average horn length 50cm; record horn length 80.97cm. Black-faced Impala record horn length 67.9cm.
Identification pointers: Long, graceful, lyrate horns of the ram; black tuft of hair above the hoof on the rear surface of hind leg; thin black line down centre of white tail and vertical black line on each buttock.

Description: Impala is a medium-sized, lightly built antelope. Upperparts are reddish-fawn becoming paler on sides; chest, belly, throat and chin are white. Tail is white with central black line on upper surface, and each buttock has vertical black blaze. The tuft of black hair on lower rear edge of hind leg is a character unique to Impala. The ears are black-tipped. Only rams carry the long, graceful, lyrate horns. Black-faced Impala (*A. melampus petersi*) of northern Namibia differs at subspecies level from the eastern populations of

The Tsessebe stands much higher at the shoulders than at the rump.

Impala fawns gather in 'crèches', particularly when resting.

Only the Impala ram carries the long, graceful, lyrate horns. **Inset:** This is the only antelope with black buttock stripes.

The Tsessebe has a distinctive horn shape and dark facial blaze. **Inset:** Young Tsessebe lack the dark markings of the adult.

Impala ewes and lambs closely resemble each other.

Tsessebe

90mm — right front
90mm — right back

Impala

90mm
right front

90mm
right back

47 mm — right front
46 mm — right back

347

Note: In the 1960s, the Black-faced Impala was facing extinction in its limited Namibian and Angolan range. Some 180 were captured and released in the south-west of Etosha National Park. They have since spread throughout the park and number almost 3,000 individuals. Common Impala were introduced onto surrounding game farms and hybridization has unfortunately taken place between the two subspecies/ species.

Impala *(A. melampus melampus)*; the black blaze down the front of the face of *petersi* is distinctive. The two subspecies have been raised to full species level by some taxonomists.

Distribution: Widespread in north-eastern areas of the region and northwards to Kenya. In South Africa, Impala have been widely introduced into areas far outside their natural range, including parts of the semi-arid Karoo, where they do particularly well. The greatest numbers in South Africa occur in Limpopo, Mpumalanga and KwaZulu-Natal. An isolated subspecies, Black-faced Impala (see 'Description' on p.346), is found in north-western Namibia and extends into Angola.

Habitat: Open or light savanna woodland; avoids open grassland unless there is scattered bush cover. Absent from mountains. Surface water must be available.

Behaviour: Rams are extremely vocal during the mating season and give vent to growls, roars and snorts. They are only territorial during the rut, January–May, spending the rest of the time in bachelor herds. The home range of a breeding herd, consisting of ewes and young animals, may overlap with the territories of several territorial rams. Rams separate harem herds of 15–20 ewes (with their young) for mating. This disrupts the composition of the herds but they reunite at the conclusion of the rut. Bachelor herds tend to occupy areas away from the breeding herds. Impala are active mainly during the cooler daylight hours but there is some nocturnal activity.

Food: Short grasses and browse; proportions vary with area and season.

Reproduction: Single lamb, weighing approximately 5kg, is born in early summer after gestation of 196 days. Mammae: 2 pairs inguinal.

Longevity: Up to 12 years in the wild; one captive lived to 17 years 9 months; some captive individuals have reached 25 years.

Antidorcas marsupialis

Springbok *Antidorcas marsupialis*

Total length 1.12–1.27m; shoulder height 75cm; tail 25cm; mass (M) 32–46kg, (F) 26–38kg.
Average horn length (ram) 35cm; record horn length (ram) 49.22cm.
Identification pointers: Dark brown band separating upper- from underparts; white head with brown stripe through eye to corner of mouth; short lyrate horns in both sexes; broad white crest on back visible when pronking.

Description: Hindquarters of this distinctive antelope appear to be slightly higher than shoulders. Dark red-brown band along flanks separates fawn-brown upperparts from white underparts. Head is white with a brown stripe running through eye to corner of upper lip. A large white patch on rump is bordered by brown stripe. A long-haired, white dorsal crest extends from the midpoint of the back to the rump; this is normally seen only when the crest is erected, for example, during 'pronking'. The pronk, or stotting, is a jump performed with stiff legs accompanied by arching of the back. Tail is white with tuft of black hairs at tip. Both sexes have heavily ringed, lyre-shaped horns but ram's are thicker and longer. Three races, the Karoo *(A. m. marsupialis)*, Angolan *(A. m. angolensis)* and Kalahari *(A. m. hofmeyeri)*, recognized, the last somewhat larger. Some authorities believe each of these subspecies should be raised to full species level. Game farmers and conservation authorities have, however, mixed these subspecies populations extensively throughout the range of Springbok on game farms and reserves.

Distribution: More arid western areas of the region and into south-western Angola. Now one of South Africa's most important game-farming species.

The Black-faced Impala differs from the Common Impala by having a dark facial blaze and a bushier tail.

Black-faced Impala ewe showing the distinctive dark facial blaze

Springbok, here a ram, have a dark stripe separating the brown upperparts from the white underparts.
Inset: A black Springbok

The Springbok ewe's horns are more slender than those of the ram.

Springbok

55mm
right
front

54mm
right
back

Habitat: Open, arid plains and avoids dense cover. Surface water not essential.
Behaviour: Normally in small herds but when moving to new feeding-grounds may congregate in herds of many thousands in some areas. Small herds may be mixed or consist of rams only; solitary rams are frequently encountered. Springbok rams are territorial and when in rut will herd ewe groups; they do not, however, remain in their territories throughout the year. Territory-holding rams have elaborate displays to intimidate potential rivals. Springbok are active during the cooler daylight hours but also partly at night.
Food: Grass and browse; will dig for roots and bulbs.
Reproduction: A single lamb weighing about 3.8kg is born after a gestation period of about 168 days, usually during rains. Joins herd after 2 days. Mammae: usually 1 pair inguinal.
Longevity: Up to 19 years in captivity; probably 7–10 years in the wild.
Note: Springbok are farmed for their venison and skins. Aberrant Springbok with white, black or copper coats appear from time to time, and are often selectively bred as they fetch high prices at sales of game animals and from trophy hunters.

Madoqua damarensis

Damara Dik-dik *Madoqua damarensis*

Total length 64–76cm; shoulder height 38cm; tail 5cm; mass 5kg.
Average horn length 8cm; record horn length 10.48cm (Namibia).
Identification pointers: Small size; elongated nose; crest of erectile long hair on forehead. No similar species occur within southern African distribution range.

Description: Very small; characterized by having elongated, very mobile nose. Upperparts yellowish-grey with grizzled appearance; neck paler than shoulders and flanks. Underparts white to off-white. Tuft of long hair on forehead is erected when the dik-dik is alarmed or displaying. Rams have short, spike-like horns that slope back at angle of facial profile.
Distribution: Northern and north-western Namibia and into south-western Angola.
Habitat: Damara Dik-dik show a strong preference for fairly dense, dry woodland. They penetrate deep into the Namib Desert along riverine woodland. Bush-covered hillsides and adjacent scrub are also occupied.
Behaviour: Usually single, in pairs or in small family parties. Pairs establish communal dung middens within home range; territorial. Nocturnal and diurnal. Both ram and ewe defend the territory, with ram chasing away other rams and ewes seeing off other ewes. Use same pathways between resting and feeding sites in territory. Also dig for roots with front hooves. In Namibia's Etosha, average territory size is 3.5ha.
Food: Although they are chiefly browsers they do take some grass during the rainy season. They will utilize leaves, pods and flowers knocked down by larger species, such as Elephant and Greater Kudu.
Reproduction: After a gestation period of approximately 170 days, a single fawn with a mass of 620–760g is dropped during the summer months. Mammae: 2 pairs inguinal.
Longevity: Probably <5 years in the wild but possibly up to 10 years; 15–16 years in captivity, one captive lived 16 years 6 months.

The Damara Dik-dik ram has short, spiked and strongly ringed horns.

The Damara Dik-dik ewe lacks horns.

Note the long snout, white eye-ring and short, ringed horns.

Damara Dik-dik

21mm

right
front

23mm

right
back

Nesotragus moschatus

Suni *Nesotragus moschatus*

Total length 68–75cm; shoulder height 35cm; tail 12cm; mass 5.1–6.8kg (male slightly heavier than female).
Average horn length 8cm; record horn length 13.34cm.
Identification pointers: Very small size; constantly flicking white-tipped tail; pink-lined, translucent appearance of ears. Much smaller than Sharpe's Grysbok (p.360); while white flecks on the upperparts distinguish Suni from similar-sized Blue Duiker (p.362).

Description: Tiny, elegant antelope with rich rufous-brown upperparts flecked with white hairs, and white underparts. Two slightly curved white bars on throat. Above each hoof is a narrow dark band. Tail fairly long and is dark brown above with a white tip and is regularly flicked from side to side. Pink-lined ears give the appearance of being almost translucent. Only the ram has horns and these are quite thick, prominently transversely ridged and slope backwards in line with facial profile. Prominent gland in front of each eye of the ram.
Distribution: Widespread in Mozambique, but occurs only marginally in northern KwaZulu-Natal, and south-east and north-east Zimbabwe. Because of the marginal nature of this antelope's range, there are only three substantial populations in South Africa: Thembe Elephant Reserve (>3,000); Phinda Resource Reserve (500) and False Bay Park (350), all in KwaZulu-Natal. There is probably a total of about 5,000 Suni in South Africa. Numbers elsewhere are not known.
Habitat: Dry thickets and riverine woodland with dense underbrush.
Behaviour: Usually occur in pairs or small groups consisting of one adult ram and up to four ewes. Ram is territorial, marking areas with glandular secretions and dung middens. Home ranges of rams in KwaZulu-Natal cover from 0.5ha to just over 1ha, whereas those of ewes range from just under 1ha to 4.6ha. Some nocturnal activity but are also active during early mornings and late afternoons. When disturbed they take off in a rapid zigzag resembling that of a startled hare. They follow regular pathways, which leaves them vulnerable to snaring. Group members use the same dung-heaps, which are scattered through the territories.
Food: Principally browse, but take a wide range of plant food.
Reproduction: Single fawn (750g) is born at any time of the year; gestation about 180 days. Remains hidden for several weeks, only emerging to suckle. Mammae: 2 pairs inguinal.
Longevity: One captive to 13 years 6 months, 9 years for several captives.

Oreotragus oreotragus

Klipspringer *Oreotragus oreotragus*

Total length 80–100cm; shoulder height 50–60cm; tail 8cm; mass (M) 10kg, (F) 13kg.
Average horn length 8cm; record horn length (South Africa) 16.19cm.
Identification pointers: Stocky appearance; short muzzle; walking on hoof tips; associated with rocky areas where it displays great agility.

Description: A small, stocky antelope with coarse, spiny hair. Heavily built appearance is caused by hair standing on end instead of lying flat as in other antelope. General colour yellow-brown to grey-yellow, with an overall grizzled appearance. Underparts, chin and lips are white. Ears are rounded, broad and bordered with black. Only the ram has horns; these are short, widely separated

Only the Suni ram carries the short, straight and heavily ringed horns.
Inset: The ewe does not have horns.

The Suni has pink-lined inner ears.

A pair of Klipspringer in the Waterberg of northern South Africa.

Among Klipspringers in the region, only rams carry horns.

Klipspringer ram in the lower Orange River broken veld

The Klipspringer is the only antelope that walks on its hoof tips.

The Klipspringer has a short muzzle.

Suni

23mm

right front

22mm

right back

Klipspringer

20mm

right front

21mm

right back

353

at the base, vertically placed and ringed only near base. Characteristically walks on the tips of hooves, the only antelope to do so. Four, possibly more, subspecies recognized for the region, based on coat coloration variables but some believe them to warrant full species status. They are Zambian Klipspringer *(O. o. centralis)*; Cape Klipspringer *(O. o. oreotragus)*; Transvaal Klipspringer *(O. o. transvaalensis)* and Angolan Klipspringer *(O. o. tyleri)*.

Distribution: Wide but patchy distribution in rocky habitats.

Habitat: Rocky habitat only, from coastal and other mountain chains, crossing open plains between isolated rock outcrops. From near sea level to high altitudes, rain regimes from 100mm to >1,500mm.

Behaviour: Occur in pairs or small family groups. Adult ram is territorial, marking twigs with secretions from preorbital gland. Ewe also marks in this way but less frequently than ram. Extremely agile in moving across rocky terrain and up steep rock-covered slopes. Frequently stop to look back when running from a disturbance and both sexes give loud nasal alarm whistles. Use communal dung-heaps, which are usually situated on flat areas. Active in morning and in later afternoon but throughout day when cool. Recorded home ranges cover 8–49ha.

Food: Predominantly browse, but grass taken occasionally.

Reproduction: Klipspringer probably give birth at any time of the year but some records indicate many births in the region are linked to summer rains. A single lamb, weighing about 1kg, is born after a gestation period of 210 days (214–225 days). The lamb remains hidden for 1–3 months after birth. Mammae: 2 pairs inguinal.

Longevity: One captive lived 17 years 10 months, several to 15 years; estimate for wild 6–8 years.

Note: Popular opinion has it that the Klipspringer's coarse, bristly, hollow hair has a cushioning function when the animal falls. However, it is more likely that it serves as a heat regulator. Klipspringer hair was once prized for stuffing saddles.

Raphicerus campestris

Steenbok *Raphicerus campestris*

Total length 75–90cm; shoulder height 50cm; tail 5cm; mass 11kg (9–13kg). Average horn length 9cm; record horn length 19.05cm.

Identification pointers: Small size; large ears; clearly demarcated reddish-fawn upperparts and white underparts; very short tail; only ram has short, vertical horns. Could be confused with Oribi, but the latter is larger, has smaller ears, longer neck, a black tail tuft and the Oribi ram's horns are ridged for part of their length. Also see Cape and Sharpe's Grysbok (both pp.358, 360).

Description: Small, elegant, large-eyed antelope, normally rufous-fawn above but varies from pale fawn to reddish-brown. Underparts including insides of legs are pure white, and there is a white patch on throat and above eyes. Very short rufous-fawn tail. Only the ram carries short, sharp-pointed, smooth-surfaced, vertical horns. Although five subspecies recorded for the region, their validity is suspect as there is much variation within any one population.

Distribution: Widespread in region; separate population in East Africa. The East African range is much smaller than that of the southern African populations, being restricted to southern Kenya and the adjacent area of Tanzania. It is believed that the original separation of the species was a consequence of the dry climatic conditions that prevailed during the Pleistocene, and linked north and south, being replaced by a higher-rainfall regime that created the wooded belt across southern Central Africa. This dense woodland, known as miombo, was unsuitable for Steenbok, which retreated from this area, or died out.

The Steenbok ram carries straight, sharp-pointed, smooth-surfaced, vertical horns.

The Steenbok ewes lack horns.

Note the large ears, short horns and the short black blaze on the lower muzzle.

The Steenbok's eyes are large with white rings.

Steenbok

39mm

right
front

40mm

right
back

Habitat: Open country, with some cover. In arid areas inhabit dry river-beds. Does not require access to drinking water. Can reach high densities in optimal habitat. Authors counted 16 individuals in one stretch of 10km in Great Karoo.

Behaviour: Occur singly or in pairs. Territorial and both sexes strongly defensive of jointly held territories. Unlike other small antelope, Steenbok defecate and urinate in shallow scrapes dug by front hooves, then covered. These latrines appear to be mainly located around the perimeter of territories, and serve a marking role. Steenbok have glands between the hooves, on the throat and in front of each eye; it is presumed the secretions from these glands also play a role in marking territories. Steenbok lie up in cover during the heat of day, feeding in the early morning and late afternoon; they are also active at night, particularly in areas where they suffer disturbance.

Food: Mixed feeders taking grasses, browse, seed-pods and fruit; dig for roots and bulbs with the front hooves, but browse is the most important food source.

Reproduction: Single lamb, approximately 900g, born after gestation of 170 days at any time of the year, but usually summer. Remains hidden up to 3 months but usually less. Mammae: 2 pairs inguinal.

Longevity: 10–12 years in captivity, although only one official record of 8 years 2 months.

Ourebia ourebi

Oribi *Ourebia ourebi*

Total length 1.1m; shoulder height 60cm; tail 6–15cm; mass 14–20kg (ram averages 2kg lighter than ewe).

Average horn length 10cm; record horn length 19.05cm.

Identification pointers: Steenbok-like but larger; rufous yellow-orange above, white below; short, black-tipped tail; long neck. The ram has erect, partly ridged horns, unlike the smooth horns of the Steenbok ram.

Description: Largest of the 'small' antelope. Upperparts rufous yellow-orange and underparts white. White hair extends onto front of chest. Relatively long neck, medium-sized ears and short tail with distinguishing black tip. Has pale throat patch and off-white areas on either side of nostrils and above eyes. Hair on back and underparts may have a curly appearance, particularly during winter. Only the ram has horns and these are short, erect and partly ringed towards the base. Three subspecies recognized but differences minimal *(O. o. hastata; O. o. ourebi; O. o. rutila).*

Distribution: Widely separated areas in eastern and northern parts of the region. Widespread in sub-Saharan Africa. Populations greatly reduced and fragmented, especially in South Africa and Zimbabwe.

Habitat: Open short grassland with taller grass patches for cover.

Behaviour: Occur in pairs or small parties consisting of one ram and up to four ewes. The ram is vigorously territorial and frequently marks grass stalks with secretion from preorbital gland. Communal dung-heaps serve a territorial marking function. When disturbed Oribi give a sharp whistle or sneeze and run off rapidly with occasional stiff-legged jumps displaying black-tipped tail. Inquisitive, however, and will turn to look back at source of disturbance after running a short distance. Also lies down in taller grass if disturbed, with head erect; in this position they are difficult to detect.

Food: Principally grazers but occasionally browse, with a marked preference for short grass, moving if grass becomes too long. Will seek out freshly burned grassland for new growth. Independent of drinking water.

Oribi ewe has a short, black tail and a fairly long, wavy dorsal coat.

In the Oribi, only the ram carries the erect, partly ridged horns.

The white hair of the underparts extends onto the front of the Oribi's chest.

Oribi

40mm

right front

42mm

right back

Reproduction: Births have been recorded throughout the year but the majority of lambs are dropped during the wet summer months (October–December). A single lamb is born after a gestation period of about 210 days. The lamb remains hidden for as long as 3–4 months before joining the group. Mammae: 2 pairs inguinal.
Longevity: One captive 15 years 10 months, others to 14 years.
Note: Oribi are endangered in South Africa. The largest populations (totalling some 3,000 individuals) occur in the Drakensberg fringes and KwaZulu-Natal Midlands. Small populations in Eastern Cape number perhaps 500 antelope. Threats include destruction of, or changing, habitat, poor veld-burning practices, illegal hunting with dogs (so called 'taxi-hunting') and increased predation by Black-backed Jackal and Caracal, as well as domestic and feral dogs.

Raphicerus melanotis

Cape (Southern) Grysbok *Raphicerus melanotis*

Total length 72–81cm; shoulder height 54cm; tail 5.5cm; mass 10kg.
Average horn length 8cm; record horn length 13.34cm.
Identification pointers: Similar to Sharpe's Grysbok (see p.360) but distribution ranges do not overlap (see maps). Brown underparts and rufous-brown upperparts flecked with white distinguish it from Steenbok (p.354).

Description: A small, squat antelope characterized by rufous-brown upperparts abundantly flecked with white hairs. Flanks and neck have fewer white hairs and underparts are lighter brown than upperparts. Tail very short and grey-brown ears are proportionately large with white hairs on inside. Only the ram has short, smooth, slightly back-angled horns. Pair of 'false hooves' above the fetlock.
Distribution: Restricted to a narrow belt along south-western and southern coastal belt and the adjacent interior.
Habitat: An inhabitant of relatively thick scrub-bush, it is almost entirely restricted to the Cape fynbos (heathland) vegetation. It is found in a variety of situations, from scrub-covered sand-dunes to wooded gorges on mountain slopes. In the areas where it enters the extreme southern Karoo, it can be found along rivers and on scrub-covered hillsides. It is frequently found along the fringes of agricultural land where belts of natural vegetation remain.
Behaviour: Mainly nocturnal but active in early morning and late afternoon if not disturbed, or on overcast and cool days. Usually single except when mating or when ewes are tending lambs. Males territorial and frequently mark twigs with secretions from preorbital glands; range size dictated by season. Male territories are particularly small and their ranges do not overlap but those of females do. Droppings are deposited in substantial middens and may be used by several individuals.
Food: It is mainly a browser but will take fresh grass. In the south-western Cape vineyards it is considered to be a nuisance as it eats the young grapes and terminal buds. Also feeds in rooibos tea plantations along the western escarpment.
Reproduction: Although lambs may be dropped at any time of the year, most are born September–December. A single lamb is born after a gestation period of approximately 180 days. Mammae: 2 pairs inguinal.
Longevity: One captive 7 years, potential for longer.

Only the Cape Grysbok ram carries the short, smooth, sharp-pointed horns.

The Cape Grysbok ewe does not have horns.

The Cape Grysbok has a rufous-brown coat abundantly flecked with white hairs.

Cape Grysbok

34mm

right
front

35mm

right
back

Raphicerus sharpei

Sharpe's Grysbok *Raphicerus sharpei*

Total length 65–80cm; shoulder height 50cm; tail 6cm; mass 7.5kg (7–9kg). Average horn length 6cm; record length 10.48cm (6.35cm for region).

Identification pointers: Similar to Cape Grysbok but distribution ranges do not overlap (see maps). The white freckling and buff underparts distinguish it from the Steenbok (p.354). Although larger and distinct in other ways, it could possibly be confused with Suni (p.352) where ranges overlap.

Description: Small, stoutly built antelope with reddish-brown upperparts liberally flecked with white hairs. Incidence of white hairs diminishes down sides and legs. Underparts are buff-white, and area around mouth and eyes is off-white. Only the ram has the short, sharp, slightly back-angled horns. 'False hooves' are normally absent (see Cape Grysbok, p.358). Two species sometimes recognized, Limpopo Grysbok *(R. colonicus)* and Sharpe's Grysbok *(R. sharpei)*.

Distribution: Restricted to the north-eastern parts of southern Africa, into Malawi, Zambia, Tanzania and southern Congo.

Habitat: Sharpe's Grysbok requires good vegetation cover, preferring low thicket with adjacent open patches of grass. It is also found on vegetated rocky hills and in the scrub at their base.

Behaviour: Almost entirely nocturnal but can be seen in the cool early morning and late afternoon. Although usually seen singly, it is possible that a pair may live in loose association within a home range. Rams are probably territorial as they mark twigs with secretions from the preorbital gland and both sexes deposit droppings at midden sites scattered through the range. Because of its largely nocturnal activity and secretive nature, very little is known about this small antelope.

Food: Mostly browse but also grass. It will take fruits, berries and pods. Especially during the dry season will dig for roots and bulbs with the front hooves.

Reproduction: Lambs, weighing <900g, may be dropped at any time of the year but more are probably born during the wet summer months than in any other season. A single lamb is born after a gestation period of approximately 200 days. Mammae: 2 pairs inguinal.

Longevity: Probably to at least 10 years.

Cephalophus
natalensis

Natal Red Duiker *Cephalophus natalensis*

Total length 80–110cm; shoulder height 45cm; tail 9–15cm; mass 10–16kg. Average horn length 6cm; record horn length 10.48cm (East Africa).

Identification pointers: Uniform rich reddish-brown coat; small size; black-and-white tipped tail; prominent crest on top of head. Lacks the white flecking of either Sharpe's Grysbok or Suni (p.352). Walks with a 'hunchback' gait.

Description: A small, thickset antelope with relatively short legs. The general colour is rich reddish-brown, with underparts being slightly paler, and chin and throat paler than rest of the body. Although short, the tail is the same colour as the body at the base, with a well-developed tuft of mixed black-and-white hairs. A long crest is present on top of the head, sometimes obscuring the short horns. Both sexes have horns, which slope backwards at the same angle as the face.

Distribution: Occurs along the eastern coastal plain with an isolated population in the Soutpansberg range of northern South Africa. It occurs as far north as southern Sudan and Somalia, although northern population often ascribed to Harvey's Red Duiker. Harvey's Red Duiker is now believed to occur in northern Malawi and

Sharpe's Grysbok is very similar to the Cape Grysbok but their ranges do not overlap.

The Sharpe's Grysbok ewe does not carry horns.

The Natal Red Duiker has a uniform rich reddish-brown coat and a short, black-and-white-tipped tail.

Sharpe's Grysbok

25mm — right front

25mm — right back

Natal Red Duiker

30mm — right front

31mm — right back

361

Cephalophus
harveyi

adjacent Zambia, centred on the Nyika Plateau. It differs only slightly from Natal Red Duiker. Largest estimated population in iSimangaliso Wetland Park along narrow coastal strip of northern KwaZulu-Natal, some 1,000 individuals.
Habitat: Forest and dense woodland with permanent water.
Behaviour: Because of the dense habitat that it favours, and its secretive nature, little is known about this duiker's behaviour. It is usually solitary but it seems probable that a pair may live in loose association within the same home range. The dung pellets are deposited in specific areas and there are often many small piles of currant-sized pellets at these sites. Mainly active in daylight.
Food: They are browsers, taking leaves, shoots, fruits and berries. Also feeds below trees where monkeys and baboons forage.
Reproduction: Fawns are probably dropped at any time of the year but peak in the summer months. Single fawn (<1kg) after gestation of about 210 days. Mammae: 2 pairs inguinal.
Longevity: Unconfirmed captive to 15 years, others to 12 years; estimates of 8-9 years in the wild.

Philantomba
monticola

Blue Duiker *Philantomba (Cephalophus) monticola*

Total length 62–84cm; shoulder height 30–35cm; tail 7–12cm; mass 4kg (3.5–6kg).
Average horn length 3cm; record horn length 7.3cm (East Africa).
Identification pointers: Smallest southern African antelope; grey to brown coloration with blue-grey sheen. Short horns in both sexes. Skulking nature.

Description: The smallest antelope occurring in southern Africa. The upperparts vary from slate-grey to dark brown with a grey-blue sheen and the underparts are white or off-white. Legs light brown to grey-brown. A constantly wagging tail is characteristic of this duiker. The tail is quite long, bushy and black, bordered with white. Short, strongly ringed horns are present in both sexes but these are often hidden by the crest of hair on top of the head. Five species sometimes recognized from the region, others place them as subspecies, all are readily recognizable as Blue Duiker. They are Angolan Blue Duiker *(P. m. anchietae)*; Zimbabwe Blue Duiker *(P. m. bicolor)*; Zambian Blue Duiker *(P. m. defriesi)*; Malawi Blue Duiker *(P. m. hecki)*; Cape Blue Duiker *(P. m. monticola)*.
Distribution: The population in Mozambique and adjoining eastern Zimbabwe is isolated, as are the scattered populations in the narrow belt along the coast from George in the south to KwaZulu-Natal, South Africa. It occurs widely in Angola, Zambia and Malawi and patchily in East Africa.
Habitat: Blue Duiker are confined to forests and dense stands of bush. They utilize open glades when feeding. Water is an essential habitat requirement.
Behaviour: It usually occurs singly, or in pairs during courtship. Mated pairs occupy small, permanent territories with a common range averaging less than 1ha. Territory marked with secretions from preorbital gland, tree-horning and piles of droppings in concentrated areas but not true middens. It is very timid and is rarely seen, its dung-pellet heaps usually being the only indication of its presence. The level of disturbance probably influences times of activity but it is known to feed both at night and during the day. It uses regular pathways to feeding and drinking sites, which makes it vulnerable to snaring.
Food: The Blue Duiker is a browser, and includes fruits and berries in its diet. As is common to other duiker species, some animal food is included in the diet, especially insects.

The Blue Duiker is the smallest of the forest duikers, with pelage colouring varying from slate-grey to dark brown.

The very short horns are present in both sexes.

The Blue Duiker has a large preorbital gland that is used for scent marking.

Blue Duiker

24mm

right
front

22mm

right
back

Reproduction: The young are born throughout the year with a possible peak in the summer months. A single lamb weighing an average 726g (some figures 400g) is born after a gestation period of up to 207 days; some published accounts as little as 120 days but unlikely. Mammae: 2 pairs inguinal.
Longevity: Estimates of 7–10 years in the wild, but no certain records.

Cephalophus dorsalis

Bay Duiker *Cephalophus dorsalis*
Total length 78–110cm; shoulder height 40–55cm; tail 8–15cm; mass 19–25kg.
Horn length 5.5–10.5cm.
Identification pointers: Brown-yellow to brown-red; distinct dark dorsal stripe from nose to tail base; dark on legs; medium-sized.

Description: Bright brownish-yellow to brownish-red coat with a distinct dark dorsal stripe extending from nose to base of tail. Dark markings on legs (in some individuals all of legs darker in colour), extending onto shoulders and rump. Forehead crest is poorly developed and may be almost absent.
Distribution: Northern third of Angola.
Habitat: Lowland and dense secondary forest.
Behaviour: Little known, except they are solitary or live in mated pairs and are apparently territorial. Said to be mainly nocturnal but this may be more a measure of disturbance levels. Use the same pathways that radiate from resting locations.
Food: Wide range, including fruits and possibly some animal food.
Reproduction: Probably aseasonal, with a single lamb, weighing approximately 1.6kg, born after an estimated gestation period of about 238 days. Mammae: 2 pairs inguinal.
Longevity: Captives said to live for up to 18 years.

Cephalophus nigrifrons

Black-fronted Duiker *Cephalophus nigrifrons*
Total length 95–120cm; shoulder height 45–55cm; tail 10–15cm; mass 13–16kg.
Horn length 4–12cm.
Identification pointers: Reddish to dark brown overall; distinct very dark to black facial blaze, crest.

Description: Overall body colour a deep chestnut, or dark red-brown, with lower leg colouring darker to black. The main distinguishing character is the broad black blaze running from nose to forehead, usually incorporating the crest and often extending a short distance down the back of the neck. The tail is black with a white tip.
Distribution: Far northern Angola.
Habitat: Lowland and gallery forests.
Behaviour: Little known but probably solitary or in pairs living within a defended territory.
Food: Wide range of plant food but probably takes some animal food.
Reproduction: Nothing known but probably a single lamb dropped at any time of year.
Longevity: No records.

The Bay Duiker occupies areas of lowland and dense secondary forest in northern Angola.

The Black-fronted Duiker takes its name from the broad, black facial blaze.

Bay Duiker

Although the form of the tracks is known, the measurements are not.

right front

right back

Black-fronted Duiker

25mm

regs voor

27mm

regs agter

Cephalophus
silvicultor

Yellow-backed Duiker *Cephalophus silvicultor*

Total length 1.26–1.6m; shoulder height 65–85cm; tail 11–18cm;
mass 45–80kg.
Average horn length 8.3cm; record 21.2cm.
Identification pointers: Very large; dark black-brown glossy coat, distinct
yellow patch on rump.

Description: Largest of all the duikers and easy to identify. Overall dark brown
to blackish coat with distinctive yellow rump patch, which is broadest above the
tail and tapers along the spine ending in a point behind the shoulders. The rump
patch hairs are raised when animal alarmed but may also serve some behavioural
function. Hair around muzzle may be silvery white and the head crest may be
dark or dull chestnut.
Distribution: In the region, occurs patchily across northern Angola
and Zambia.
Habitat: Virtually all forest types, as well as savanna and miombo woodland.
Behaviour: Known to be diurnal and nocturnal but this may be a measure of
local disturbance. They lie up in fixed locations, scattered through a territory,
from which pathways radiate to feeding areas. Pairs live in a defended territory
but the male and female have only a very loose association. The territory is
marked with glandular secretions and with dung middens.
Food: A range of plant parts, including leaves and fruits, as well as fungi and
possibly some animal food.
Reproduction: Births possibly at any time but there may be some seasonality in
parts of its range. A single lamb (rarely twins), weighing 2.3–6.1kg, dropped after
an estimated 210–280-day gestation, lies hidden for the first few days after birth.
Mammae: 2 pairs inguinal.
Longevity: Few records but probably 10–12 years; 18–23 years in captivity.

Sylvicapra grimmia

Common Duiker *Sylvicapra grimmia*

Total length 90–135cm; shoulder height 50cm; tail 10–22cm; mass (M) 18kg,
(F) 21kg.
Average horn length 11cm; record horn length (South Africa) 18.1cm.
Identification pointers: Crest of long hair usually present on top of head;
uniform grey-brownish (generally darker animals in the south getting lighter to
the north) colouring of upperparts and paler underparts; usually black blaze
(vertical stripe) on face; fairly short tail – black above and white below. Ears
are long and somewhat narrow.

Description: Uniform grey-brown to reddish-yellow upperparts, with paler
(sometimes white) underparts. Black blaze of variable length on face. Short tail,
black above and white below. Front surfaces of slender forelegs are dark brown
or black. On top of head there is usually a pointed crest of long hair. Ram has
well-ringed, sharp-pointed horns that are in line with the slope of the face. Some
females, especially on South Africa's western coastal plain, also carry slender,
deformed horns. As many as six subspecies have been described from the region
based on coat colour variations but it is unlikely that all, if any, are valid.
Distribution: Found throughout the region except for the Namib Desert.
Habitat: Wide range of habitats but prefers scrub and bush-covered country.

The Yellow-backed Duiker has a triangular patch of whitish-yellow erectile hair on the back.

The Yellow-backed Duiker is the largest duiker species in the region.

The crest of long hair, which is present on both sexes, is clearly visible on this female Common Duiker from the southern coastal plain of South Africa. **Inset:** Only the male usually carries horns.

Yellow-backed Duiker

Although the form of the tracks is known, the measurements are not.

right front

right back

Common Duiker

40mm

right front

42mm

right back

Behaviour: Usually single but sometimes pairs. Ram holds and marks a territory within which there is usually one, occasionally two, ewes. Ram drives away other rams, ewe drives away intruding females. Active in early morning and late afternoon but also at night. Lies low when disturbed but on too-close approach takes off at a fast zigzag run. Home ranges extend from 6–27ha. Although they can reach high densities in optimum habitat, they always keep a distance from each other, although they may feed within a few metres. On one night drive in South Africa's Eastern Cape, the authors counted 38 Common Duiker along a 6km stretch of farm track running through Fish River Valley bushveld. Similar densities have been seen at two other locations, once in southern Kalahari scrub, and the other in Cape heathland on South Africa's western escarpment. Nine individuals were observed feeding on fallen pears at an abandoned farmstead, intermingling with no aggressive interactions.

Food: Wide variety of browse species; also agricultural crops; some animal food. Will actively hunt small vertebrates.

Reproduction: Single 1.6kg lamb may be born in any month after an average 190 days (range 189–216 days). Mammae: 2 pairs inguinal.

Longevity: In the wild, 6–8 years; captives from 11–26.5 years.

DEER Family Cervidae

Note: There is no distribution map available for this species.

European Fallow Deer *Cervus (Dama) dama* (Introduced)
Shoulder height 90cm; mass (buck) 95kg.
Identification pointers: Distinctive white spotting; males carry branched palmate antlers for much of the year. Restricted to enclosed farms, but numerous escapes.

Description: Variable in colour and patterning, with the summer coat being rich yellowish-fawn above, spotted boldly in white. White stripe along each flank. Underside of tail and surrounding areas conspicuously white. Underparts and inner leg areas are pale. Winter coat duller and hair longer. Males carry palmate antlers shed during midsummer months to make way for new set.

Distribution: Introduced from Europe to private farms in South Africa but there have been numerous escapes, especially on the Great Karoo plateau and in the Eastern Cape.

Habitat: Open woodland to scrub or grassland.

Behaviour: Adult buck establish territories during the rut and form harem herds. Sexes are separate outside rut.

Food: Principally browse but also grass.

Reproduction: Usually single fawn (rarely twins), weighing about 4.5kg, born in summer after a ±230-day gestation. Mammae: 2 pairs inguinal.

Longevity: Several records of up to 20 years in captivity.

European Fallow Deer buck develop branched palmate antlers that are shed each year.

Fallow deer doe in white-spotted summer coat

Fallow deer doe in duller winter coat

European Fallow Deer

62mm

right
front

60mm

right
back

MARINE MAMMALS

SEALS Order Carnivora

FUR SEALS Family Otariidae

Only three species of fur seal have been recorded from southern African waters, one as a permanent resident and the others as rare vagrants. The Antarctic Fur Seal *(Arctocephalus gazella)* is recorded from the Southern Ocean islands that fall under South African jurisdiction (namely the Prince Edward Islands) and one individual recently recorded from South Africa. Fur seals have small but obvious ear pinnae.

Arctocephalus pusillus

■ occasional

+ principal breeding-ground

Cape Fur Seal *Arctocephalus pusillus*
Also known as Brown, or Afro-Australian, Fur Seal; same species occurs in southern Australian waters.
Male: length 2.2m; mass 247–360kg (190kg).
Female: length 1.5–1.8m; mass 40–80kg (75kg).
Identification pointers: Large size; only seal likely to be encountered in southern African waters, along west coast and as far east along south coast as East London. Males lack crest on top of head found in Sub-Antarctic Fur Seal.

Description: Males much larger than females (up to 300kg or more in summer), with powerfully developed necks. When moving on land, hind limbs are brought forward to support some body mass and forelimbs bend out and slightly backwards. Dark brown to golden brown but bulls tend to be darker. Coarse outer hair of bulls may be greyish-black with a tinge of brown. Females tend to be more brownish-grey. Newborn pups have black velvety coat. Have obvious ears.
Distribution: Offshore islands and along parts of the mainland of the western and southern coastline to Port Elizabeth but rarely as far as East London. Stragglers along the Angolan coast but rarely beach.
Behaviour: Within southern African waters there are estimated to be almost 2 million fur seals in some 25 breeding colonies, or rookeries. The largest colony, of some 500,000 animals, is located on South Africa's west coast at Kleinzee, with that at Cape Cross, Namibia, being the second largest. In mid-October mature bulls move to the breeding sites to establish territories and these are actively defended against rival bulls. Territory-holding bulls are sometimes called 'beach masters'. The cows arrive several weeks later to give birth. A territorial bull establishes a harem of several cows. Mating takes place about 5–6 days after the cow has given birth. The territories and harems break up before the end of December. Can dive to at least 200m and stay under for as long as 7.5 minutes. When resting on sea surface will often float on back with flippers out of the water.
Food: Shoaling fish such as pilchards; other fish, squid and some crustaceans. Opportunistically take seabirds, such as Cape Gannets, both on land and at sea.
Reproduction: Pups weighing 4.5–6.5kg dropped after a gestation of about 360 days. Mammae: 2 inguinal teats, with mammae forming sheet under the blubber layer.
Longevity: Wild fur seals to at least 18–21 years.

Cape, or Brown, Fur Seal cows are considerably smaller than mature bulls.

During the breeding season mature bulls hold, defend and mate with harems of cows until they disperse in December.

The seal has short, pointed, external ears.

Cape Fur Seal

*Arctocephalus
tropicalis*
(occasional)

Sub-Antarctic Fur Seal *Arctocephalus tropicalis*

Male: total length 1.8–2m; mass 88–165kg.
Female: total length 1.4m; mass 25–55kg.
Identification pointers: Yellow-brown face, and chest lighter than rest of
body, contrasting with brown upperparts. Males have short crest and cape of
long hair on top of head – a feature not found in Cape Fur Seal.

Description: Similar in form to Cape Fur Seal but differs in colouring. Upperparts
are variable grey-brown to brown, with the head, shoulders and flippers being
darker and the face and chest being yellow-brown or creamy brown. Mature bulls
have a short, tufted crest on top of head, raised when animal excited, and cape of
longish hair on the head and shoulders. Newborn pups black to very dark brown.
Distribution: They occur in sub-Antarctic waters and haul out on small oceanic
islands such as Gough and the Prince Edward islands. Some 200,000 are
located on Gough Island, roughly two-thirds of the total population. Vagrants
occasionally haul out on the coastline of South Africa and Namibia.
Behaviour: Behaviour is similar to that of Cape Fur Seal. Recorded maximum dive
208m, staying under for 6.5 minutes.
Food: Squid and fish seem to be of equal importance, but crustaceans (krill) are
occasionally taken.
Reproduction: This species does not breed within southern African waters. Most
pups are born in mid-December. Mammae: 2 inguinal teats, with mammae
forming sheet under the blubber layer.
Longevity: Up to 25 years in the wild.

---

*Arctocephalus
gazella*

Antarctic Fur Seal *Arctocephalus gazella*

Male: total length up to 2m; mass 110–230kg.
Female: total length 1.4m; mass 22–51kg.
Identification pointers: Bull considerably larger than cow, and very
dark brown, grizzled grey on crown; cow paler and grey-brown with
paler underparts.

Description: Bull uniform dark to very dark brown, with grey grizzling on
crown and onto neck, fairly heavy but short mane on forequarters. Cow
much smaller and overall lighter coloured than bull, with light grey to light
grey-brown underparts and face. Flippers very dark, also dark ring around
eye. Very long (up to 50cm) facial whiskers that are light in colour. When wet,
animal appears black.
Distribution: 95 per cent of population breeds on South Georgia Island, from
61°S to Antarctic Convergence. Vagrants occasionally to southern Australia,
Argentina and one South African record.
Behaviour: Recorded dives up to 181m and as long as 10 minutes. During
breeding season 'beach masters' hold harems of up to 20 cows.
Food: Crustaceans (krill), fish, squid and penguins.
Reproduction: Does not breed in South African waters. Births and matings
November–December. Mammae: 2 inguinal teats, with mammae forming sheet
under the blubber layer.
Longevity: No defined records but probably up to 25 years in the wild.

Sub-Antarctic Fur Seals breed on islands in the southern Atlantic, but occasionally come ashore along the region's coastline.

Antarctic Fur Seals are known to haul out on the Prince Edward Islands in the Southern Ocean.

Sub-Antarctic Fur Seal

Antarctic Fur Seal

Three species of true seal have been recorded along the coastline of southern Africa, but all as rare vagrants. Leopard Seal (p.376) has only been recorded twice on the southern African mainland. Weddell Seal *(Leptonychotes weddellii)* has never been recorded on the southern African mainland but there is a record from the South African-administered Marion Island, in the South Atlantic Ocean. As there are records from Uruguay and Australia, it is possible that the Weddell Seal could, in time, be recorded on the South African coastline. True seals have no external ear pinnae.

Mirounga leonina
- landings
- occasional occurrence

Southern Elephant Seal *Mirounga leonina*

Male: total length 4.5–6.5m; mass 3,700kg.
Female: total length 2.5–4m; mass 350–800kg.
Identification pointers: Massive size, particularly in the case of bulls; bulls also have a swollen, prominent snout.

Description: This is the largest of all living seals. The massive bulls have a short, prominent, bulbous proboscis, which projects from just below the eye and hangs over the mouth. This organ can be inflated during threat displays. Fur colour is usually greyish-brown to brown but in mature males, and before the moult, the fur takes on a yellowish-brown colour. Old bulls are usually heavily scarred on the head and shoulders from territorial fighting.

Distribution: This seal has a circumpolar distribution, largely restricted to a belt of sub-Antarctic waters extending to the southern tip of South America. Vagrants occasionally beach on the southern African coastline. More than 50 records, including as far north as Angola. Total population >600,000 animals.

Behaviour: The Elephant Seal moults on land, remaining there throughout the duration of the moult. Much of the winter spent at sea.In spring adult bulls haul out on island beaches for mating. Mature bulls arrive first to establish the territories in which they will keep their harems of up to 100 (average 30) cows. Bulls with territories are known as 'beach masters'.

Food: Southern Elephant Seals feed mostly on squid and fish but some crustaceans are also taken. When hunting, they can dive to depths of >1,400m and remain submerged for more than an hour (one record gives two hours), but usually dives more shallow and for shorter duration.

Reproduction: The pregnant cows haul out shortly after the bulls and the pups conceived the year before are born within about one week of their arrival. Newborn pups average about 1.3m in length and weigh 36–50kg. The females come on heat 2–3 weeks after the pups are born and are mated by their harem bull. Mammae: 2 inguinal teats, with mammae forming sheet under the blubber layer.

Longevity: 15–25 years in the wild.

Southern Elephant Seal bull: note the short, prominent proboscis from which the common name is derived.

The Southern Elephant Seal bull may weigh up to 10 times more than the female.

Southern Elephant Seal

375

Lobodon carcinophaga (occasional)

Crabeater Seal *Lobodon carcinophaga*

Total length 2–2.7m; mass 180–410kg.
Identification pointers: Sleek, long body; usually silvery-grey but no prominent markings; distinctly serrated edge to each cheek-tooth. Vagrants in southern African waters, with less than 20 records.

Description: This slender and agile seal has a general body colour of silvery grey-fawn with paler underparts. Numerous brown markings are scattered on the shoulders and sides of younger animals. The flippers are darker than the rest of the body. The fur becomes creamy-white towards the moult and older animals become paler with age. Females slightly larger than males. The cheek-teeth have up to six cusps each and have a distinctive saw-like profile. When the jaws are closed the teeth interlock neatly and are used to sieve out the small crustaceans upon which this seal feeds.

Distribution: Crabeater Seal is by far the most abundant seal in the world and is confined to the pack-ice zone around Antarctica. Hauls out rarely on the southern African coast.

Behaviour: It is estimated there are 30–50 million (one estimate 10–15 million; another as many as 75 million) Crabeater Seals in Antarctica. Despite their abundance, the harsh environment in which they live makes them extremely difficult to study and therefore little is known about them. In contrast to fur seals and elephant seals, during the breeding season Crabeater Seals associate in family pairs, comprising mother and newborn pup, with an attendant bull waiting nearby for the female to come into oestrus after the birth. Outside of the breeding season, Crabeater Seals form large or small groups of both sexes. Recorded diving to 530m but most to between 20–30m and lasting up to 5 minutes.

Food: Despite their name, Crabeater Seals do not eat crabs but feed almost exclusively on krill, a small crustacean that abounds in Antarctic waters. Their technique is to swim into a krill shoal with open mouth and then close their jaws, forcing the water out between closely fitting teeth and swallowing the krill that remains in the mouth. Feed mostly at night. Some squid and fish also eaten.

Reproduction: Single pup, weighing some 36kg and 1.3m long, born September–November on ice-floes in the pack-ice zone. Mammae: 2 inguinal teats with mammae forming sheet under the blubber layer.

Longevity: Average 20 years but some individuals known to have reached 40 years.

Hydrurga leptonyx
● landings
■ occasional occurrence

Leopard Seal *Hydrurga leptonyx*

Male: total length 2.8–3.3m; mass 300kg.
Female: total length 3.8m; mass 450–500kg.
Identification pointers: Sleek; silvery-grey above, white below; numerous dark spots especially on throat, shoulders and sides; only two records from the coast of southern Africa.

Description: These are slender, agile seals, with silvery-grey fur on the upperparts and (usually) white fur on the underparts. There is a liberal scattering of darker grey to black spots, particularly on the sides, throat and shoulders. The head is long and slender and it has a large 'gape'.

Crabeater Seal is mainly found in the pack-ice zone around Antarctica, rarely hauling out in southern African waters.

Penguins comprise a major part of the Leopard Seal's diet.

Crabeater Seal

Leopard Seal

377

Distribution: Predominantly a species of the Antarctic pack-ice, but in winter and spring it moves towards the sub-Antarctic islands and may enter Argentinian, South African and Australian waters. Very rare vagrant to South African shores.

Behaviour: Leopard Seal is a solitary species, which spends summer and autumn around the pack-ice and which tends to disperse towards the small mid-oceanic islands of the sub-Antarctic in winter and spring. Population estimates from 100,000–450,000 animals, almost impossible to count accurately.

Food: Leopard Seal takes a wide variety of food items, predominantly penguins, but also fish, squid and krill, and the young (possibly also adults) of other seals.

Reproduction: Little is known about its reproduction. After gestation period of about 335 days, single pup, weighing some 30kg and about 1.1m long, born on the pack-ice September–January (most November–December). Mammae: 2 inguinal teats with mammae forming sheet under blubber layer.

Longevity: One in the wild 26 years.

Leptonychotes weddellii

Weddell Seal *Leptonychotes weddellii*
Male: total length 2.5–3m; mass 360–600kg.
Female: total length 2.6–3.3m; mass 400–600kg.
Identification pointers: Not as streamlined as Crabeater Seal; relatively small head; dark brown-grey to almost black above; white streaks and splashes on sides and back; underparts mainly white.

Description: Stoutly built, with rather small head. Upperparts are dark, and sides and back are flecked and splashed with pale grey to white. Underparts are predominantly white to pale greyish blotched but generally darker in male. Flippers small when compared with other southern seals. Female slightly larger than male.

Distribution: Difficult to assess, but probably numbers at least 500,000 individuals. This seal is largely restricted to the inshore rim of Antarctica. It is the most southerly occurring of the seals. One live specimen found on Marion Island, a South African possession. Records from Uruguay, Chile, New Zealand and Australia indicate that, in time, it might beach on the South African mainland.

Behaviour: In winter, most time is spent in the water under the ice. Breathing holes are kept open by regular sawing with the teeth. Most dives in the 50–500m range but recorded to 750m, lasting 15–20 minutes. Very docile and said to be easy to approach.

Food: Mainly fish but some squid, crustaceans and penguins.

Reproduction: Pregnant cows concentrate from August, dropping single pups, about 1.35m long and weighing 25kg, in September–October. Mammae: 2 inguinal teats with mammae forming sheet under blubber layer.

Longevity: About 25–30 years.

Leopard Seals live amongst the pack-ice of Antarctica, moving towards the sub-Antarctic islands in winter and spring.

Weddell Seal occurs mainly in Antarctica.

Weddell Seal

WHALES & DOLPHINS Order Whippomorpha Suborder Cetacea
Baleen or Whalebone Whales Infraorder Mysticeti

Ten species of baleen whale have been recorded off the coastline of southern Africa.

RORQUALS (PLEATED WHALES) Family Balaenopteridae

Long, slender, streamlined whales with flattened heads, pointed flippers and a small, back-curved dorsal fin set far back along body. Rorquals are characterized by a large number of grooves, or pleats, running longitudinally from throat and chest to upper abdomen.

Balaenoptera acutorostrata

Common (Northern) Minke Whale *Balaenoptera acutorostrata*
Total length 6.8–7.8m; mass 6–8t.

Antarctic (Southern) Minke Whale *Balaenoptera bonaerensis*
Total length 7–10m; mass 6–10t.

Identification pointers: Smallest of the rorquals; white patch on upper flipper surface. Antarctic Minke usually lacks white flipper patch. Flippers of Humpback Whale (p.386) are much longer and usually more white. Indistinct blow.

Balaenoptera bonaerensis

Description: These, the smallest of the rorquals, have 1–3 ridges running along top of head. Upperparts are dark blue-grey to almost black, with lighter-coloured whitish underparts. Flippers sometimes have a bright white patch on upper surface, extending onto body, and very occasionally are wholly white. Tail-flukes are rarely raised above the water. With 52–60 throat grooves. The slightly smaller 'Dwarf' Minke Whale is now recognized as a distinct sub-species of Common (Northern) Minke Whale. Antarctic (Southern) Minke Whale usually lacks the white flipper patches. In the two species, cows shorter than bulls. (Very closely related to Antarctic (Southern) Minke Whale *(Balaenoptera bonaerensis)*, may in fact be same species. Some authorities believe it is a species on its own account.).
Distribution: southern hemisphere. Infrequently off southern African coast and rarely comes to shore; usually off continental shelf. Antarctic Minke tends to stay well offshore and does not extend as far north into tropical waters but there are records of individuals migrating to the Arctic. The regularity of such movements is unknown.
Behaviour: Singly or in pairs but larger groups, up to eight, at feeding-grounds. Dives may last up to 20 minutes and swimming speed may reach 38km/h.
Food: Krill and to a lesser extent small fish and squid.
Reproduction: Approximately 2–2.8m calf born after 10-month gestation period. The few records indicate a breeding peak during the summer months. There are records of the two species interbreeding. Mammae: 1 pair mammary slits.
Longevity: 30–60 years.

The Common (Northern) Minke Whale, the smallest of the rorquals, has a white patch on the upper flipper surface.

Common Minke Whale

Antarctic Minke Whale

Balaenoptera edeni
■ population concentrations
▨ occasional occurrence
? extent not known

Balaenoptera borealis

Bryde's Whale *Balaenoptera edeni*

Total length 10–15.6m; (female on average about 1m longer than male) mass 12–20t (to 24t) .

Sei Whale *Balaenoptera borealis*

Total length 15–21m; mass 15–30t.

Identification pointers: Medium to large size; **Bryde's Whale** has three ridges on top of head; only one in **Sei Whale**. Two forms of **Bryde's Whale** have been recognized in South African waters, a smaller, resident form and a larger form that is migratory and stays in deeper water beyond the continental shelf. (Globally, **Bryde's Whale** may yet be found to be a complex of species.)

Description: **Sei Whale** is a slender blue-black whale with white band from chin to abdomen, broadening dorsally. Throat grooves stretch back to flippers. **Bryde's Whale** similar but light grey underparts. The main distinguishing character is that there are three ridges on the head of **Bryde's Whale** from around the blowholes to the tip of the snout, and only one (the median ridge common to most baleen whales) on the head of the **Sei Whale**. These whales submerge gently and their flukes and flippers do not show when they dive down from the surface. **Bryde's Whale** usually has around 45 throat grooves; **Sei Whale** has 60–65 throat grooves. Both **Sei** and **Bryde's Whales** have a fairly prominent dorsal fin set well down on the back, but that of the former slightly longer, and those of both sickle-shaped. **Bryde's Whale** believed to consist of a complex of at least three species but these would be virtually impossible to separate in the field.

Distribution: **Sei Whale** worldwide but **Bryde's** largely restricted to tropics and adjacent waters. Some **Bryde's** resident off southern African coast. **Sei Whale** is a deep-water species and rarely observed from land. **Sei Whale** in southern hemisphere possibly numbers some 40,000, with perhaps some 90,000 **Bryde's Whales** worldwide.

Behaviour: Both species are usually encountered in small pods of about 5 or 6 individuals but both may form groups numbering more than 100, but solitary individuals and groups of 2 or 3 not uncommon. **Bryde's Whale** is often seen close inshore.

Food: Both species feed on planktonic crustaceans and small fish, with **Bryde's Whale** off the west coast, for example, taking shoaling fish such as pilchards.

Reproduction: **Sei Whale** calves, measuring about 4.5m and weighing some 650kg , born in June–July after a gestation of 11–13 months; **Bryde's Whale** calves are about 50cm shorter at birth. **Bryde's Whale** may be a seasonal breeder, but the inshore form is aseasonal. Mammae: 1 pair mammary slits.

Longevity: Up to 74 years in **Sei Whale**; not known for **Bryde's** but probably similar.

Bryde's Whale

Above: Bryde's Whale has three ridges on the top of the head, extending from around the blowholes to the tip of the snout.
Left: The Sei Whale has 60–65 throat grooves.

Sei Whale

383

Fin Whale *Balaenoptera physalus*

Total length 17–27m (female to 5m longer than male); mass 30–81t.
Identification pointers: Large size; dark upperparts and light to white underparts with the right lower jaw being white, the left black. Rear end raised before diving but flukes not raised above water. Fin appears after the blow.

Balaenoptera physalus

Description: Second-largest living mammal. Unique colour pattern. Upperparts are dark grey and underparts lighter or white, but right lower jaw, right front baleen plates and undersides of flippers and flukes are white; left half of lower jaw is black and left-side baleen plates are bluish-grey. The asymmetrical colour pattern of the lower jaw gives it a somewhat twisted or lop-sided appearance. There are 50–60 throat grooves. Southern form genetically isolated from northern form and sometimes referred to as *B. p. quoyi*.
Distribution: Worldwide. Not usually seen offshore, favouring deep waters. One estimate indicates a worldwide population of >100,000 animals.
Behaviour: Occurs in groups of 3–7 (6–10), but very rarely up to 100, with larger numbers at principal feeding-grounds. Most dives in the range 100–230m and lasting 3–15 minutes.
Food: Krill, fish and squid.
Reproduction: One calf, measuring 6–7m and weighing 1–1.9t, born after gestation of up to 12 months in warmer waters during winter. Mammae: 1 pair of mammary slits.
Longevity: Up to 90 years; some believed to have lived over 100 years.

Blue Whale *Balaenoptera musculus*

Total length 20–33.6m; mass 80–150t (to 190t) (female slightly larger than male).
Identification pointers: Massive size; blue-grey colour with lighter mottling. When diving, performs a smooth, even roll with no humping; the tail-flukes emerge shallowly and briefly. Fin only shows in dive.

Balaenoptera musculus

Description: Largest mammal on Earth. The taxonomy of this giant whale is in a state of flux and in southern African waters may involve at least two forms, the Pygmy *(B. m. brevicauda)* at a mere 22m, and the Southern Blue *(B. m. intermedia)*. Upperparts blue-grey mottled with light grey spots; underparts of body and under-surface of flippers much lighter in colour. There are 88–94 throat grooves. Dorsal fin small and set very far back; not exposed while blowing but may be seen when whale dives. Flukes show briefly just above surface when diving. Blow may reach a height of 12m.
Distribution: Worldwide in virtually all parts of principal oceans and seas, from Arctic to Antarctic. Perhaps no more than 6,000 animals in the southern hemisphere.
Behaviour: Usually occurs singly or in groups of three or four, but up to 50 have been seen together on feeding-grounds. southern hemisphere populations migrate to Antarctic waters in summer to feed on krill, returning

Fin Whale

Left: Fin Whale has dark grey upperparts and white underparts.
Below: Blue Whale, the largest mammal in the world, can measure over 30m – nearly one-third the length of a football field.

Blue Whale

to warmer waters in the winter to breed. Most dives last 5–20 minutes and are as deep as 200m, but known to drop to 500m below the surface.
Food: Various species of krill, especially *Euphausia superba*, taken at depths of less than 100m. Can eat up to 10t of krill per day.
Reproduction: A single calf, up to 7m and weighing 2.5–4t, born during early winter after a gestation of 11 months. Mammae: 1 pair of mammary slits.
Longevity: Up to 90–110 years.

Humpback Whale *Megaptera novaeangliae*

Total length 11–18m; mass 24–40t (male slightly shorter than female).
Identification pointers: Very long flippers, white below, and variable black or white or both above; body dark above, light to white below including flukes. Dorsal fin shows when blowing; when diving, flukes raised high above water. Often shows flippers and jumps (breaches) clear of water.

*Megaptera
novaeangliae*
■ migration routes
■ occasional
    occurrence

Humpback Whale
tail-fluke

Humpback Whale
flipper

Description: Humpback easily distinguishable from other rorquals because of less streamlined appearance, small dorsal fin situated further forward than in other members of this group, knobbly head and extremely long flippers which may measure up to one-third of body length. Leading edges of flippers are serrated and may be partly or entirely white. Upperparts of Humpback are dark grey to black and underparts are usually dark although throat grooves are white. With 30 or fewer throat grooves – considerably fewer than in other baleen whales. Animals in southern African waters probably *M. n. lalandii*.
Distribution: Worldwide. Occurs off the southern African coast in midwinter and in spring on their way to and from the breeding-grounds. May cover to 16,000km on these movements. Roughly perhaps 17,000 in the southern hemisphere but not known how many migrate past southern Africa.
Behaviour: In the southern hemisphere they migrate from their Antarctic feeding-grounds to over winter and breed in tropical waters, passing up and down the west and east coasts. Breeding-grounds off Angola in the Atlantic and in Mozambique Channel to Kenya in Indian Ocean. They remain in warmer waters for a short period before moving southwards again. Breaching, tail-fluke and flipper slapping common. Groups of 12–15, sometimes more, at feeding-grounds but usually cow/calf. Dives to 150m and average 3–15 minutes.
Food: Mainly krill/plankton feeders, but they also take small shoaling fish. Individuals may feed alone or cooperatively. Frequently emit circular 'curtain' of bubbles then rush through to gulp prey thus trapped.
Reproduction: Calves are born in tropical waters during winter (July–August) after a gestation period of almost 1 year. At birth, the calf measures about 4.5m and weighs 1–2t; during the first 10 months of life, it doubles in length. Mammae: 1 pair of abdominal slits.
Longevity: Records to 50 years but some estimates to 77 years.
Note: Grey Whale *(Eschrichtius robustus)*. An extraordinary multiple sighting of this Northern Pacific Ocean whale off Walvis Bay, Namibia, in 2013 was positively confirmed. This large whale (reaching 15m in length and 15–35t) has never previously been recorded off the southern African coastline or in the southern hemisphere for that matter. It is not known whether this species has been overlooked in the past, whether it was a once-off visit, or a pattern that may develop. It occurred in the North Atlantic until some 200 years BP. They are unique in the world of large mysticetes whales in that they give birth to their young in warm, shallow waters on the Pacific coast of Mexico, and they are bottom-feeders.

The Humpback Whale has characteristic long flippers, with a serrated leading edge. **Inset:** Grey Whale (*Eschrichtius robustus*)

Humpback Whales often jump clear of the water, an action known as breaching.

Humpback Whale

Right Whales, of which one species occurs in southern African waters, were so called because they are slow-moving and were easily caught by early whalers; when killed they floated, allowing the whalers to tow the carcasses to land, hence they were the 'right' whales to hunt. They are characterized by their large heads with arched jaw-line and smooth ungrooved throat.

Eubalaena australis
■ main
   concentration
■ occasional
   occurrence

Southern Right Whale
tail-fluke

Southern Right
Whale flipper

Southern Right Whale *Eubalaena australis*

Total length 11–17m; mass 20–30t.
Identification pointers: Large size; no dorsal fin; lumpy white growths on head; broad-tipped flippers; very large flukes; overall dark colour with occasional white patches on underparts; no throat grooves. Blows when much of back exposed, and when diving the flukes are clear of water. Flippers often seen. V-shaped blow. Frequently seen close inshore in South Africa.

Description: This is a relatively easy whale to identify. There is no dorsal fin, there are no grooves or pleats on the throat, the flukes are large and pointed at the tips and the head is very large with a deeply arched jaw-line. The head and back are more or less on the same level. The flippers are broad-tipped. A distinguishing character is the presence of numerous white callosities on the head; the largest (the 'bonnet') is situated at the front of the snout. The overall body colour is dark grey-black with occasional white markings on the underparts.

Distribution: Extreme southern Pacific, Atlantic and Indian oceans. Breeds off southern Argentina, South Africa and southern Australia. This is the easiest large whale to observe close inshore in South African waters (May–December). Some of the best viewing sites are Hermanus (Walker Bay), the inshore trough at De Hoop Nature Reserve near Bredasdorp, Mossel Bay (especially from Reebok and Tergniet) and Plettenberg Bay, particularly off Robberg Peninsula. It is now known that some (several hundred) Southern Right Whales move up the West Coast, especially off St. Helena Bay, and remain here into the summer and even autumn; there is an abundance of plankton in this area. Total population for Southern Ocean about 7,000 individuals.

Behaviour: A typical pod of Southern Right Whales usually consists of fewer than six individuals and is normally a family unit of 2 or 3, rarely to 12 animals. A regularly monitored and steadily increasing population is frequently seen in sheltered bays off the southern and western coast of South Africa. Southern Right Whales move north into southern African coastal waters from about May–October, spending the summer and autumn months in their Antarctic feeding-grounds. They glide and roll on the surface, when the flippers and flukes are clearly visible, and not infrequently jump or 'breach' clear of the water – a sight once seen, never to be forgotten. Dive usually 10–20 minutes, but stay under for more than 50 minutes, to depths of 184m recorded.

Food: Plankton.

Reproduction: Calves (1t), some 4.5–6m long, are born in southern African waters from about June to September with an August peak in sheltered bays. Mature bulls have the largest testes in the animal kingdom, the pair weigh about 1t. Mammae: 1 pair of mammary slits.

Longevity: Very few records but one cow known to have reached 70 years.

The Southern Right Whale is the most frequently seen large whale in South African waters between May and October.

Baleen of a Southern Right Whale

The distinguishing white callosities on the head are clearly visible.

Southern Right Whale

PYGMY RIGHT WHALE Family Cetotheriidae

Caperea marginata

Pygmy Right Whale *Caperea marginata*
Total length 6–6.5m; mass 2.8–3.5t.
Identification pointers: Small size and similar appearance to Southern Right Whale but note possession of dorsal fin and absence of white head callosities. No throat grooves. When it rises to breathe, usually only the head breaks the surface and then it sinks quietly back without exposing the back.

Description: The smallest of all the baleen whales, with an arch to the lower jaw like that of the Southern Right Whale; the head, however, is comparatively small. Unlike Southern Right Whale, Pygmy Right Whale possesses a dorsal fin, but as the flukes of this species are never raised above water; the fin is rarely seen. The overall colour is dark grey-blue, with a paler band around the neck, and grey-white underparts. Two lighter coloured chevrons across the back in vicinity of flippers. There are no callosities on the head, unlike Southern Right Whale.
Distribution: Circumpolar distribution south of the tropics. Rarely seen off the southern African coast.
Behaviour: Usually seen in pairs or small groups of up to 10 individuals, although some records indicate that rarely larger numbers may come together. It frequently associates with other whale as well as dolphin species.
Food: Plankton (including copepods and amphipods) skimmed off the surface.
Reproduction: Calves are 1.6–2.2m in length. Mammae: 1 pair of mammary slits.
Longevity: No records.
Note: This, the smallest of the baleen whales, has recently been found not to be a right whale but a member of the cetotheres, a family of baleen whales believed to have been long extinct, and is now referred to as a 'living fossil'. Previously the sole species in the family Neobalaenidae. It is believed to be more closely related to the Grey Whale and the rorquals than it is to the right whales.

Toothed whales & dolphins Infraorder Odontoceti

Thirty-five species of toothed whales and dolphins have been recorded off the coasts of southern Africa.

BEAKED WHALES Family Ziphiidae

Ten (possibly 11) species of beaked whales have been recorded from southern African waters but most are known from very few specimens and sightings. This is the second-largest cetacean family, with 21 species worldwide. A number of species have not been identified at sea and are best known from strandings. For convenience, the 10 species have been divided into two groups (pp.392, 394).

Pygmy Right Whale is the smallest of the baleen whales.

Pygmy Right Whale

Berardius arnuxii
■ occasional
   occurrence
x strandings

Hyperoodon planifrons

Ziphius cavirostris
■ occasional
   occurrence
x strandings

Arnoux's Beaked Whale *Berardius arnuxii*
Total length 7.8–9.8m; mass 7–10t.

Southern Bottlenose Whale *Hyperoodon planifrons*
Total length 6–7.5m; mass 7–8t.

Cuvier's Beaked (Goose-beaked) Whale *Ziphius cavirostris*
Total length 4.7–7m; mass 2–3.4t.

Identification pointers: Cuvier's Beaked Whale with white to pale beak, head and on back to variable extent; head only slightly swollen. **Southern Bottlenose Whale** with very swollen head or 'melon'. Nothing distinctive about **Arnoux's Beaked Whale**, but if a stranded specimen should be encountered, note that it is our only beaked whale with two pairs of teeth in the lower jaw and our only beaked whale in which the female has visible teeth.

Description: Arnoux's Beaked Whale is a medium-sized, dark grey or black whale with paler underparts. The beak and forehead 'melon' are prominent. Both sexes have two pairs of teeth close to the tip of the lower jaw, which protrudes beyond the tip of the upper jaw. The front teeth are about 8cm long; the back ones are shorter. This species is known from four records in southern African waters, one a specimen stranded near Port Elizabeth.

Southern Bottlenose Whale is smaller than Arnoux's, with a stubby beak; its bulging dome-like forehead rises vertically above the beak and is rounded onto the back. Dorsal fin is fairly prominent, situated well back and slightly curved at the tip. The colour of the upperparts is bluish-grey, often with light brownish tinge, and the throat and belly are off-white or grey. Melon, beak and face may be paler to dirty white. Males have only one pair of teeth in the lower jaw; in the females the teeth do not erupt through the gums.

Cuvier's Beaked Whale has a stubby beak and the domed head or 'melon' is poorly developed. This species may be separated from other species by the fact that the snout, head and sometimes partially the back are white to paler, while the rest of the body is usually grey to black but often with browner tinge. The male has a single pair of teeth, each about 7cm long, at the tip of the lower jaw; the female's teeth do not erupt through the gums.

Distribution: Only Cuvier's Beaked Whale has a worldwide distribution in temperate and tropical seas, although it is absent from Arctic and Antarctic waters. Southern Bottlenose Whale and Arnoux's Beaked Whale are only found in the southern hemisphere, south of the Tropic of Capricorn.

Behaviour: Cuvier's Beaked Whale is an animal of deep waters and is usually seen alone or in small groups of 3–12 but larger groups have been observed. Dives recorded for this species may last to 40 minutes. Also a deep-water whale, Arnoux's Beaked Whale is usually solitary although 6–10 (to 80) individuals may on occasion be seen together. Most dives last from 12–25 minutes but sometimes exceed one hour. Southern Bottlenose Whale in small tight-knit groups.

Food: Arnoux's Beaked Whale and Southern Bottlenose Whale feed predominantly on squid and cuttlefish but some fish also taken; Cuvier's Beaked Whale also takes fish, crabs and starfish.

Reproduction: Calves of the Southern Bottlenose Whale (newborn 2.7–3.6m) and Cuvier's Beaked Whale (newborn to 2.7m, 250–300kg) are apparently born in the early summer months, although births all-year round seem possible. Arnoux's newborn 4–5m. Mammae: 1 pair of mammary slits.

Longevity: Cuvier's estimated from 36–62 years; Arnoux's estimated to 84 years (male), 54 years (female); Southern Bottlenose at least 37 years.

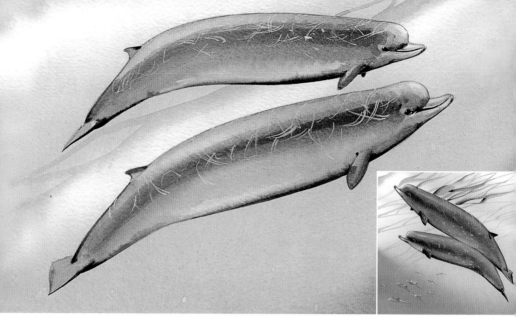

The Southern Bottlenose Whale has a bulging, dome-like forehead, or 'melon' and a prominent beak.
Inset: Arnoux's Beaked Whale has a prominent forehead 'melon'.

Arnoux's Beaked Whale

Southern Bottlenose Whale

Blainville's Beaked Whale

Hector's Beaked Whale

Strap-toothed Beaked Whale

Cuvier's Beaked Whale has a stubby beak and a poorly developed domed head, or 'melon'; the dorsal fin is small.

Arnoux's Beaked Whale

Southern Bottlenose Whale

Cuvier's Beaked Whale

393

Mesoplodon densirostris

Mesoplodon grayi

Mesoplodon hectori
■ occasional
  occurrence
x strandings

Mesoplodon layardii
■ main
  concentration
■ occasional
  occurrence

Mesoplodon mirus
■ occasional
  occurrence
x strandings

Blainville's Beaked Whale *Mesoplodon densirostris*
Total length 4.5–6m; mass 700kg–>1t.

Gray's Beaked Whale *Mesoplodon grayi*
Total length to 4.5–5.7m; mass 1–1.5t.

Hector's Beaked Whale *Mesoplodon hectori*
Total length 3.9–4.4m; mass 1–2t.

Strap-toothed (Layard's) Beaked Whale *Mesoplodon layardii*
Total length 5–6.2m; mass 1.5–3.4t.

True's Beaked Whale *Mesoplodon mirus*
Total length 4.8–5.5m; mass <1–1.5t.

Shepherd's Beaked Whale *Tasmacetus shepherdi*
Total length 6–7m; mass 2.3–3.5t.

Longman's Beaked Whale (Tropical Bottlenose Whale)
Indopacetus pacificus
Total length 6m; mass none known.

Identification pointers: See descriptions for specific pointers.

Description: All southern African species in the genus *Mesoplodon*, as well as Shepherd's and Longman's, are very difficult to identify in the field. This is compounded by there being considerable variation in body colour within any one species. Only an examination of the male's teeth can ensure positive identification; like most beaked whales, female *Mesoplodon* whales lack visible teeth. The species most likely to be seen in southern African waters is **Blainville's Beaked Whale**; the male of this species can be identified by a massive upward extension of each side of the lower jaw. One tooth is situated about midway along each jaw, at the apex of the extended portion but, although each tooth is about 10cm long, only a small portion is visible above the jaw. Upperparts medium- to dark brown to black with white underparts. Longish beak and indistinct melon.

Gray's Beaked Whale is usually dark grey above and whitish or light grey below; its head is almost flat on top and is not markedly swollen and has a prominent and pale beak.

Hector's Beaked Whale is only sketchily known from six or seven skulls and a few specimens found worldwide. Head small with only slight melon and shortish beak; upperparts and sides dark grey to brown-grey with lighter underparts and pale collar between head and flippers. Very rarely seen.

Strap-toothed Beaked Whale is blackish above but there is a grey area from the distinct (but not large) 'melon' to a point halfway along the back to dorsal fin. The underparts are also blue-black but the front half of the beak, the throat, and a patch around the genital area are white. White patch on throat and top of head joined behind eye. The male is clearly identified by the two 6cm-broad, curved, tusk-like teeth, one to each lower jaw, which protrude from the jaw and curve over the top of the beak; these teeth apparently prevent the mouth from opening more than a few centimetres.

True's Beaked Whale has a smallish but clearly bulbous 'melon' and its single pair of small teeth is situated at the tip of the lower jaw. It has a distinctive colour pattern, being blackish overall but white on the lower jaw, around the genital

Blainville's Beaked Whale can be identified by the upward-curving jaw. **Inset:** Gray's Beaked Whale is dark grey, with a flat head.

Hector's Beaked Whale is seldom encountered; it appears to inhabit colder waters.

Strap-toothed Beaked Whale has a grey area across the back and some of the frontal underparts.

Blainville's Beaked Whale

Gray's Beaked Whale

Hector's Beaked Whale

Strap-toothed Beaked Whale

Tasmacetus shepherdi

Indopacetus pacificus
■ occasional occurrence
x strandings

area and on the posterior section of both upperparts (including the dorsal fin) and underparts (including underside of the tail-flukes). The edges of the jaw and throat are speckled with black on a light grey background.

Longman's Beaked Whale only known from very few strandings and sightings at sea. Long beak and large melon on head, with darker upperparts and pale underparts, as well as light to white head; dorsal fin relatively large. Beak and melon often exposed on surface when swimming.

Shepherd's Beaked Whale has a pronounced melon, dolphin-like beak, brownish-black upperparts with off-white underparts, broad off-white belt between dorsal fin and flukes, as well as pale patch above flipper and melon.

Distribution: Gray's and Strap-toothed Beaked Whales are confined to the seas of the southern hemisphere mainly south of the Tropic of Capricorn. Although little is known of **Hector's Beaked Whale**, it appears to have a circumpolar distribution in the colder waters of the southern hemisphere but not closely entering Antarctic waters. **True's** and **Blainville's Beaked Whales** both occur in the northern and southern hemispheres; Blainville's appears to prefer tropical waters while **True's Beaked Whale** is found in both subtropical and temperate waters but apparently patchily. **Shepherd's** in temperate waters in the south below the tropic but not extending into Antarctic waters. **Longman's** only known from east coast of the region but present in warmer waters across southern Indian and Pacific oceans.

Behaviour: Although available information is scanty, **True's Beaked Whale** is thought to occur in pairs or as a cow with calf but possibly more; **Blainville's Beaked Whale** is normally seen in groups of 3–6 but also solitary and up to 12 in a pod; can dive to at least 1,000m. All species are usually associated with deeper waters. **Shepherd's** solitary or in small groups. **Longman's** in pods of 15–20 animals but sightings of up to 100. **True's** seen in pods of 1–6; lands on side when breaching. **Gray's** is solitary or in pods of up to six individuals, but mass strandings involving more animals have taken place. The beaked whales are unique in the cetacean world in that they have a wax ester type blubber.

Food: Squid appears to be the principal food of some species but fish is included in the diet of at least **Blainville's Beaked Whale**. Some beaked whales, certainly **Strap-toothed**, also eat crustaceans, including krill. Apparently most food is taken close to the sea floor. They are suction-feeders, aided by funnel-like grooves in the throat.

Reproduction: Very little known. Newborns of **Shepherd's Beaked Whale** are 3m in total length; **Gray's Beaked Whale** 2–2.4m; **Strap-toothed Beaked Whale** 2.2–2.5m; **Blainville's Beaked Whale** 1.9–2.6m, mass 60kg. Calving of **Longman's** believed to take place September–December in South African waters. Mammae: 1 pair of mammary slits.

Longevity: Most age estimates range from 27–39 years for all species but based on very few records. Records for **Baird's Beaked Whale**, which does not occur in our region although many believe it to be the same species as **Arnoux's Beaked Whale**, is 54–84 years.

Note: Andrew's Beaked Whale *(Mesoplodon bowdoini)* may occur in southern African waters but is apparently known only from strandings in Australia and New Zealand at this stage. Very similar to **Blainville's Beaked Whale** (3.4–4.9m, to 1.5t), although adult male has white-tipped beak, strongly arched lower jaw and heavy scarring.

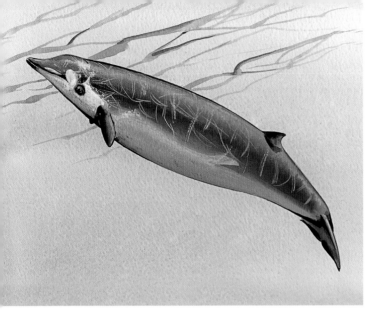

Left: True's Beaked Whale has a small forehead 'melon'.
Below: Shepherd's Beaked Whale

Longman's Beaked Whale

True's Beaked Whale

Shepherd's Beaked Whale

Longman's Beaked Whale

All three members of these two families have been recorded from southern African waters. Characterized by having square heads and by the possession of teeth on the lower, but not the upper jaw. They derive their name from the large spermaceti organ situated in a depression in the upper part of the front of the skull. Spermaceti wax is believed to assist in regulating the whales' buoyancy in deep diving and may also focus sound used in echolocation.

Family Kogiidae

Kogia breviceps

Kogia sima

Pygmy Sperm Whale *Kogia breviceps*
Total length 3.5m; mass 350–450kg.

Dwarf Sperm Whale *Kogia sima*
Total length 2.7m; mass 135–272kg.

Identification pointers: Difficult to tell apart but head shape and body size should separate them from any other species. 'False gill' marking of **Pygmy** and **Dwarf Sperm Whales** is characteristic, as is the mid-back placement of the larger dorsal fin of the **Dwarf Sperm Whale**.

Description: Species similar in appearance but differ considerably in size. Snout area swollen and projects beyond lower jaw, a feature that gives these two small whales a somewhat shark-like appearance. Dorsal fin of **Dwarf Sperm Whale** is large and situated halfway down the back, whereas that of the **Pygmy Sperm Whale** is smaller and situated further down the back. Both dark grey above and white to pinkish-white or light grey below. White 'false gill' marking is often present on head of both species but can be less distinct in **Dwarf**.
Distribution: Both species have an extensive distribution within the tropics, but extend into the temperate seas of both northern and southern hemispheres. **Dwarf** is more coastal and inshore than **Pygmy**.
Behaviour: Both species may be seen singly or in small groups to seven, the **Dwarf Sperm Whale** in schools of up to 10 individuals but also solitary.
Food: Principally squid, fish and crabs; squid and octopus particularly important in diet of **Pygmy**. **Dwarf** feeds in shallower waters than **Pygmy**.
Reproduction: Little is known. The gestation period may be 9–11 months; newborn of **Pygmy** is about 1.2m in length, **Dwarf** around 1m long. Most births off South Africa recorded December–March. In **Pygmy Sperm Whale** the calf is birthed head first, which is unusual for cetaceans. Mammae: 1 pair of mammary slits.
Longevity: Pygmy Sperm Whale estimated to live to 22 years.

Family Physeteridae

Physeter catodon

Sperm Whale *Physeter (macrocephalus) catodon*
Total length 8–18m; mass (M) 43–56t, (F) 13–20t.
Identification pointers: Cannot be mistaken for any other species. Large size; high, blunt snout; dorsal hump instead of fin; forward blow.

Description: Unmistakable profile with enormous square head, blunt snout and relatively small and narrow, undershot jaw. Head occupies nearly one-third of total length and contains vast spermaceti organ. No true dorsal fin but there is a distinct dorsal hump about two-thirds of way along back; behind this in

The Pygmy Sperm Whale's snout gives it the appearance of a shark. Note the white 'false gill' marking on the head.

The dorsal fin of the Dwarf Sperm Whale is situated halfway down the back.

Pygmy Sperm
Whale

Dwarf Sperm
Whale

Sperm Whale

Sperm Whale tail-fluke

male is usually a line of 4 or 5 smaller humps. Flippers short and stubby; tail-flukes broad and powerful. Males larger than females. Body skin has a series of longitudinal corrugations. Upperparts are dark grey-blue to black; underparts are paler. Skin around lips is usually white, with occasional white patches on the body. Blowhole is at tip of front of head and angled forward, giving a characteristic blow at an angle of approximately 45°. Sperm Whales occasionally breach or leap from the water.

Distribution: Worldwide, with preference for deep waters.

Behaviour: Sperm Whales descend to great depths to feed and stay down for lengthy periods. Accurate sonar tracking has shown that they can certainly reach at least 1,200m (probably up to 3,000m); long dives, of 1–1.5 hours, are on record. Most dives are to around 400m and last 35 minutes. Adult bulls hold harems, forming groups of 20–30 individuals. Nursery pods of 10–50 spread over several square kilometres outside breeding season. The species is not currently under threat of extinction: one estimate puts southern hemisphere stocks of Sperm Whales at some 350,000, but no certainty on this although populations have increased in recent decades.

Food: Mostly large squid, but also fish and crustaceans. It has been estimated that the total population of Sperm Whales consume 90 million tonnes of food annually.

Reproduction: After a gestation period of about 15 months, a calf, measuring about 4m and weighing >800kg, is born; in the region births are November–June, with a peak in February and March. Mammae: 1 pair of mammary slits.

Longevity: 60–70 years.

WHALE DOLPHINS, PILOT WHALES, KILLER & FALSE KILLER WHALES Family Delphinidae

Lissodelphis peronii
■ offshore population
■ occasional occurrence

This is a diverse group of small whales and dolphins, of which 23 species have been recorded in southern African waters. They can be divided into four main groups on the basis of their general appearance, namely:
1. No dorsal fin; beak present (one species)
2. Blunt or rounded head; beak absent; dorsal fin present (seven species)
3. Beak present, but very short; dorsal fin present (three species)
4. Long beak; dorsal fin present (12 species).

1. NO DORSAL FIN; BEAK PRESENT

Southern Right Whale Dolphin *Lissodelphis peronii*
Total length 1.8–3m; mass 60–116kg (male bigger than female).
Identification pointers: Small size; only dolphin with no dorsal fin; black above and white below; white beak, forehead, flippers and underside of tail-flukes.

Description: This small dolphin is unique in that it has no dorsal fin, and the back curves smoothly from the tip of the nose to the tail. It is further characterized by having a black dorsal surface and white underparts, with a clear dividing line between these colours along the side. The white coloration is continuous from the underside of the tail-flukes along the belly and flanks onto the flippers, throat and beak; it extends over the whole beak onto the forehead.

Distribution: From Tropic of Capricorn southwards to about 50°S. Extends higher up Namibian coast by following cold north-pushing current.

The Sperm Whale has a characteristic large square head and blunt snout, and longitudinal corrugations along the body.

The Southern Right Whale Dolphin has no dorsal fin.

Southern Right Whale Dolphin

Behaviour: This is usually a deep-sea species but it occasionally comes close inshore. Normally school size varies from about 20–200 but over 1,000 have been observed together. Commonly travels with other dolphin species. Poorly known.
Food: Fish and squid, octopus, as well as krill.
Reproduction: Poorly known but newborns are 80cm to 1m in length.
Longevity: No records.

2. BLUNT OR ROUNDED HEAD; BEAK ABSENT; DORSAL FIN PRESENT

Orcinus orca

Killer Whale dorsal fin; male

Killer Whale dorsal fin; female

Killer Whale *Orcinus orca*
Male: total length 7–9.8m; mass 3.8–5.5t.
Female: total length 4.5–8.5m; mass average 3t.
Identification pointers: Large size; prominent dorsal fin; distinctive black-and-white markings; characteristic white oval patch behind eye; rounded head.

Description: This species is unmistakable with its large size, heavy build, blunt or rounded head, large paddle-like flippers, bold black-and-white coloration and very tall dorsal fin. The fin of the male may be up to 2m in height and is erect and sometimes forward-pointing, while the female fin is smaller, and more shark-like in form. They are jet-black above, and white below from the chin to the vicinity of the anus and sometimes beyond. A short 'arm' of white extends from the ventral area onto the side in an angle towards but not reaching the tail. There is a characteristic oval white spot just above, and stretching a short way back from the eye. A greyish patch or saddle is usually present on the back behind the fin. By far the largest of all dolphins. Taxonomy in flux – based on genetic and behavioural differences, more than one species may be involved.
Distribution: Worldwide, but most common in colder waters.
Behaviour: Usually encountered in pods of 3–30 individuals in the region, but herds up to 200 individuals are known; they hunt in packs, hence the name 'wolves of the sea'. Pods consist of mixed sex and ages, with oldest female usually dominant. They have very complex social lives and are considered to be highly intelligent. Often very active on surface, spy hopping, flipper and fluke slapping, as well as breaching. Maximum diving depth recorded 260m, lasting up to 17 minutes.
Food: Wide variety of vertebrate food, including fish, birds, seals, dolphins and even large whales. Not all pods take the full range of foods but some specialize. Little known in region. Only cetacean to prey regularly on warm-blooded species.
Reproduction: After gestation of 12 months, young born measuring 2.1–2.7m and weighing 160–200kg. Mammae: 1 pair of mammary slits.
Longevity: Male 50–60 years (mean 29 years); female: 80–90 years (mean 50 years).

A female Killer Whale, or Orca, is identifiable by the characteristic dorsal fin.

The Killer Whale has very distinctive black-and-white coloration and a large dorsal fin.

Killer Whale

Pseudorca crassidens
- ■ principal range
- ■ occasional occurrence
- x strandings

False Killer Whale *Pseudorca crassidens*

Male: total length 3.7–6.1m; mass 2t.
Female: total length 3.5–5m; mass 1.2t.

Identification pointers: Dark and slender; dark grey to black with no distinctive markings or white scars from interspecific fighting (see Risso's Dolphin, p.408); prominent, centrally situated dorsal fin; flippers pointed, narrow with 'elbow'. At a distance it could be mistaken for Killer Whale (p.402), Pilot Whale (p.406), Pygmy Killer Whale (p.404) or Melon-headed Whale (p.408) – but all of these have distinctive white or pale markings. For further differences see individual species accounts. The False Killer Whale is the largest species likely to be seen sporting in the bow-waves of ships.

Description: This is a long and slender species with a slightly rounded head; the upper jaw projects slightly over the mouth. The flippers are pointed and narrow with a distinct bend or 'elbow'. Dorsal fin is situated at about mid-back and is prominent, narrow and strongly curved; it is never as strongly developed as in the Killer Whale. Overall colour is dark grey to black with a narrow grey blaze ventrally. The common name is presumably derived from the fact that these whales have a wide gape and well-developed teeth.

Distribution: False Killer Whales are found worldwide in all tropical and temperate seas, usually in deep water.

Behaviour: Usually travel in small family pods but several such pods may come together to form larger groups of 10–50 but 300–800 known, with the latter involving a mass stranding. This species appears to be prone to stranding; the first recorded stranding in southern Africa was of 108 individuals on the beach at Kommetjie, near Cape Town, in 1928. Among other strandings, 58 died at St. Helena Bay, north of Cape Town, in 1936, and 65 stranded and died on the same 1,500m stretch of beach in 1981. Often swims with mouth open; recorded diving to 500m.

Food: Squid and large pelagic fish. Occasionally hunt dolphins and larger whales.

Reproduction: After gestation of about 11–16 months, young born, measuring 1.5–1.9m and weighing about 80kg. Said to produce young at any time of year, but may have a peak. Mammae: 1 pair of mammary slits.

Longevity: Record to 63 years.

Feresa attenuata
- ■ principal range
- ■ occasional occurrence
- x strandings

Pygmy Killer Whale *Feresa attenuata*

Total length 2.1–2.6m; mass 110–170kg.

Identification pointers: Much smaller than either Killer or False Killer Whale; rounded head with white lips and chin patch; could be confused with Melon-headed Whale (p.408) but the latter species' head is curved into a 'parrot beak' and the white of its lips does not extend onto chin.

Description: Pygmy Killer Whale has a slender tapered body, with a compressed, narrow and rounded head. Dorsal fin is long, pointed, with the tip curved towards the tail. The flippers are relatively short and rounded at the tip. Much of the body is black, although the sides may have a greyish tinge, and a pale grey anchor-shaped blaze is situated between the flippers. There is a large white anal patch and this may stretch back almost to the tail. They have white lips and a white patch at the tip of the chin as an extension of the white on the lips.

Distribution: Found in warmer deep waters worldwide.

Left: The False Killer Whale is a long, slender species with a slightly rounded head and a prominent dorsal fin situated at mid-back.

The Pygmy Killer Whale has a slender, tapered body and a long, thin dorsal fin that is curved towards the tail.

False Killer Whale

Pygmy Killer Whale

Behaviour: Hunts in groups of about 15–25 (occasionally 50–100) individuals. It rarely moves close inshore and is essentially a species of the open sea.
Food: Fish and squid, and it has been suggested that it may also hunt dolphins.
Reproduction: Poorly known. Young, measuring about 80cm, believed to be born in summer months. Mammae: 1 pair of mammary slits.
Longevity: No records.

Globicephala
macrorhynchus
■ principal range
▨ occasional
occurrence

Short-finned Pilot Whale   *Globicephala macrorhynchus*
Total length 3.6–7.2m; mass 1–4t.

Long-finned Pilot Whale   *Globicephala melas*
Male: total length 4–7.6m; mass to 3t.
Female: total length 3.8–6.5m; mass 2–2.5t.

Identification pointers: Prominent fin, slightly forward of mid-body; rounded head with prominent 'melon'; dark or black dorsal surface and sides, with a grey patch behind dorsal fin of **Long-finned Pilot Whale**. White anchor-shaped blaze along belly of **Long-finned**; dark grey anchor-shaped blaze in **Short-finned Pilot Whale**. Distinguished from False Killer Whale by that species' more tapered head, narrow, more pointed fin and all-black back. False Killer Whale frequently sports in bow- and stern-waves of boats but this is extremely rare in the case of the pilot whales. **Short-finned Pilot Whale** is most likely to be seen off the east coast of the region and **Long-finned Pilot Whale** off the west coast.

Globicephala melas
■ principal range
▨ occasional
occurrence

Description: Difficult to tell apart. They are long, thin and rather cylindrical with blunt, rounded and bulbous heads; this 'melon' is usually better developed in old males. Head of **Short-finned** more prominent and rounded than that of **Long-finned**. Flipper form is characteristic: in **Long-finned**, the flippers are long (18–27 per cent of body length) and pointed, with a distinct bend or 'elbow'; in the **Short-finned** they are 15–18 per cent of body length and lack the 'elbow'. Prominent and back-curved dorsal fin of both is set slightly forward of body midpoint. Upperparts of both dark grey or black but there is distinct pale grey patch situated behind dorsal fin in **Long-finned**. White anchor-shaped blaze runs from throat to belly in **Long-finned**; **Short-finned** dark grey anchor-shaped blaze is only on belly, from between flippers to anal region. Longish eye-stripe may be present.
Distribution: Short-finned Pilot Whale occurs worldwide in warmer waters. Long-finned has two populations, one south of the Tropic of Capricorn and the other in the North Atlantic.
Behaviour: Both species come together in large schools, but group size may vary from fewer than 10 to several hundred individuals; several thousand **Long-finned Pilot Whales** have been observed together. Both species usually in pods of 15–50. When on the move, **Short-finned** travel in single file. Often float on the surface. **Short-finned** dives to 900m and can stay down for 27 minutes. Pods are highly stable and are considered to be matrilineal societies.
Food: Predominantly squid and some octopus, but also fish. Apparently most hunting done at night.
Reproduction: Gestation about 16 months in both species. **Short-finned** calves are 1.4–1.9m, weighing about 60kg; **Long-finned** calves are 1.75–2m and 75–80kg. Mammae: 1 pair of mammary slits.
Longevity: Short-finned to 63 years; Long-finned to at least 60 years; generally more than 46 years.

The Short-finned Pilot Whale has a grey patch behind the dorsal fin, and a prominent, rounded head.

The Long-finned Pilot Whale has a distinct 'elbow bend' on the flippers, and a white blaze on the belly.

Short-finned
Pilot Whale

Long-finned
Pilot Whale

Peponocephala electra
■ principal range
▨ occasional occurrence
? presence not recorded
x strandings

Melon-headed Whale *Peponocephala electra*

Total length 2.1–2.8m; mass to 210kg.

Identification pointers: Fairly slender with prominent centrally situated fin; overall dark upper sides and flanks without markings; rounded head; white lips but no white chin patch, as found in the fairly similar Pygmy Killer Whale (p.404). Presumably very rare in southern African waters.

Description: A fairly long and slender whale, which superficially resembles Long-finned Pilot Whale; despite the implication of its common name, however, the swelling on the head is not as pronounced as that of the pilot whales, the head more closely resembling that of False Killer Whale. The front of the head has a 'parrot-beak' appearance. The fin is prominent, about 25cm high, and strongly curved and set more or less in mid-back. Body is dark grey to black (but with dark patch along centre of back, extending down flanks on either side of dorsal fin), with a white or pale grey ventral anchor-shaped patch between the flippers and throat and a lighter coloured patch around the anal and genital area. The lips are white but there is no white chin patch as in Pygmy Killer Whale.
Distribution: Worldwide in warm waters. Only one stranding reported for South Africa; probably only rarely enters the country's waters.
Behaviour: Very little is known, but schools from around 20 to several hundred individuals have been recorded – usually 100–500 and very rarely to 2,000 – mainly in deep waters. A victim of mass strandings.
Food: Fish, squid and some crustaceans.
Reproduction: In the southern hemisphere, calves are born August–December after a gestation period of about 12 months. Newborns about 1m long; weighs some 15kg. Mammae: 1 pair of mammary slits.
Longevity: Up to 47 years recorded.

Grampus griseus
■ principal range
▨ occasional occurrence

Risso's Dolphin *Grampus griseus*

Total length 2.6–4m; mass 300–500kg.

Identification pointers: Usually overall grey with darker appendages; skin covered with numerous fine white scratch-marks – thus differs from False Killer Whale (p.404), which never has these scratches, and from the pilot whales, which rarely carry obvious scratch-marks. Prominent crease running from blowhole to upper lip. Teeth only on lower jaw; this is the only member of the dolphin family Delphinidae without teeth on the upper jaw.

Description: Similar in appearance to the pilot whales. It is robustly built in front of a tall, thin, back-pointing fin situated in mid-back, but behind the fin the body tapers and narrows rapidly towards the tail. There is no beak and the head bulges slightly. This species can be easily identified at close range as it is the only species with a deep crease down the centre of the head, from the blowhole to the upper lip. The flippers are fairly long (but shorter than in the pilot whales) and pointed and the flukes are broad and deeply notched. This dolphin is dark grey above and pale grey below, with dark grey flippers, dorsal fin and tail-flukes. With increasing age, the body may become paler, to almost white on the belly, face and anterior portion of the back. Fin, flukes and flippers retain their dark colour with age; however, there is considerable variation in overall colour. The body is usually criss-crossed with numerous fine white lines produced by teeth of fellow members of this species during fights; perhaps also by squids.

The Melon-headed Whale is fairly slender, with a centrally situated fin, an overall dark cololur, and white lips.

Risso's Dolphin has a deep crease down the centre of the head, from the blowhole to the upper lip. The grey skin is usually covered in scratches, either from fighting or from encounters with squid, a favoured prey.

Melon-headed Whale

Risso's Dolphin

Distribution: This species is found worldwide but avoids very cold waters.
Behaviour: Between three and 30 individuals make up the normal school but larger groups (several hundred temporary) have been observed and solitary individuals and pairs sometimes seen. Found mainly in deep waters along and beyond the continental shelf. Dives to at least 300m and these may last 30 minutes.
Food: Squid, cuttlefish, octopus as well as krill hunted mainly at night.
Reproduction: Calves are apparently born during the summer after a gestation period of about 13–14 months. They have a length at birth of about 1.5m and weigh 20kg. Mammae: 1 pair of mammary slits.
Longevity: At least 30 years.

---

3. BEAK PRESENT, BUT VERY SHORT; DORSAL FIN PRESENT

Three species occurring in southern African waters have short but clearly visible beaks: they are Haviside's Dolphin, Dusky Dolphin and Fraser's Dolphin.

Cephalorhynchus heavisidii
■ principal range
▨ occasional occurrence

Haviside's Dolphin *Cephalorhynchus heavisidii*
Total length 1.2–1.75m; mass 40–75kg.
Identification pointers: Small size; distinctive black-and-white markings; flattened, broad head; stocky body. Only likely to be seen off the west coast of southern Africa. Should not be confused with any other species.

Description: Haviside's Dolphin is easily distinguishable from the other two dolphins with short beaks because of its small size and stocky appearance. In addition it has black upperparts, which contrast with white areas on the lower throat, chest and abdomen, with white extending from the throat towards the eye, and from above the flipper towards the eye. Another broad white band extends from the abdomen in a shallow sweep across the flank back towards the tail to a round-ended point just beyond the back line of the fin. The fin is broad-based and triangular. The head is broad and flat, without a real beak, although from a distance the flattened head could appear to have such an extension.
Distribution: Apparently restricted to cold waters of Benguela Current off southern Africa's west coast, although recent records to Plettenberg Bay on south coast.
Behaviour: Little known, but it is said to form small schools only, usually very close inshore, usually not in water deeper than 100m. Normal group size is up to 10 but up to 30 observed. Commonly interact with boats and frequently breach, with some spectacular leaps.
Food: Squid, octopus and bottom-dwelling fish, with some crustaceans.
Reproduction: Calves are born October–January. Birth length is 80–85cm and weight 9–10kg. Mammae: 1 pair of abdominal slits.
Longevity: Minimum 20 years.

Haviside's Dolphin is small and stocky, with black upperparts. A white band extends from the abdomen towards the tail.

Haviside's Dolphin is the smallest in the region and executes spectacular leaps out of the water.

Haviside's Dolphin

Lagenodelphis hosei

Lagenorhynchus obscurus

Fraser's Dolphin *Lagenodelphis hosei*
Total length 2.1–2.7m; mass 160–210kg.

Dusky Dolphin *Lagenorhynchus obscurus*
Total length 1.5–2.2m; mass 70–90kg.

Identification pointers: Fraser's Dolphin: dark above, white below, separated by two stripes, a lighter upper stripe broadening over upper hindquarters and a darker lower stripe from corner of mouth and through eye to anus.
Dusky Dolphin: dark above, whitish below and grey along flanks with two dark blazes from black upperparts extending into the grey in broad backward- and downward-pointing sweeps. Fin has pale concave edge behind. Both species have short beaks. Both species rare in southern African waters.

Description: Both species have definite, very short beaks. Typical dolphin appearance but flippers and fin of Fraser's are shorter than those of Dusky Dolphin. Fraser's Dolphin is dark grey-blue above (from head to three-quarters along back beyond the fin), pinkish-white below, with two parallel stripes along body length creating a boundary between dark upper- and light underparts. Upper stripe, pale grey to cream, runs from above and in front of eye along the side to below the fin where it widens over the upperparts behind the fin as a light grey area extending to the tail. More prominent lower stripe, black or dark grey, runs from the beak through the eye along the flank to the anus. Throat, chin and rest of the underparts are white. Edge and tip of lower jaw are usually black. Dusky Dolphin has dark grey to black upperparts, flippers and flukes, the fin having a light grey to white margin to its trailing edge. Underparts are white and between upper- and underparts is a broad band of light grey along the flanks. Intruding into the grey of the flanks are two backward-pointing blazes of blackish coloration extending downwards from blackish upperparts. No other species should be confused with Dusky Dolphin.
Distribution: Dusky Dolphin has a circumpolar but very patchy distribution south of the Tropic of Capricorn. Fraser's Dolphin is apparently restricted to tropical and subtropical waters on both sides of the equator. Race of Dusky off South African west coast is nominate form *(L. o. obscurus)*.
Behaviour: Both species usually observed in small groups but Fraser's has been recorded in schools of up to 500, even thousands, and Dusky as many as 300, but these large groups are probably temporary. Dusky Dolphin is more coastal than Fraser's Dolphin, often accompanying ships and riding the bow-waves. Normal group size of Dusky 6–20 but occasionally thousands in some parts of range. Dives to at least 150m made by Dusky and 600m by Fraser's.
Food: Both species feed on squid and fish, as well as some crustaceans.
Reproduction: Fraser's Dolphin newborn are about 1m long; mass about 20kg. The calves of Dusky Dolphin are apparently unusually small and are born after a gestation period of about 11–13 months. The newborn are 55–91cm long; mass about 3–10kg. Mammae: 1 pair of mammary slits.
Longevity: No records.

Fraser's Dolphin is dark grey-blue above and pinkish-white below with two parallel stripes running the length of the body.

The Dusky Dolphin has dark grey to black upperparts, flippers and flukes and white underparts, separated by a band of light grey along the flanks.

Fraser's Dolphin

Dusky Dolphin

4. LONG-BEAK; DORSAL FIN PRESENT

Sousa chinensis

Sousa teuszii

Indian Humpback Dolphin *Sousa plumbea*
Total length 1.8–3m; mass 250–285kg.
Identification pointers: Long prominent hump supporting dorsal fin.

Description: Easily distinguished from other long-beaked dolphins by long thickened ridge along the middle of the back, supporting a pointed dorsal fin. Dark grey to black upperparts fade gradually to off-white underparts, extending from lower jaw to vicinity of genital opening.
Distribution: Largely restricted to coastal areas of Indian Ocean and as far as eastern India. Unlikely to be seen west of the Gouritz River in the region. It was generally held that the species in southern African Indian Ocean waters was *S. plumbea* but it is now accepted that it falls within *S. chinensis,* which occurs from South Africa, India, south-east Asia into the western Pacific. No overall estimates of numbers but about 450 individuals in South Africa's Algoa Bay.
Behaviour: School size 1–30 (average 7) but much movement in and out of schools; shallow coastal waters, including bays, mangrove swamps and areas of extensive sandbanks. Usually only makes short dives of 1–5 minutes.
Food: Fish, mostly from reefs near rocky coastlines, squid, octopus and crustaceans.
Reproduction: After gestation of 11–12 months, calves born weighing some 14kg and 1m long; births any time of year, with peak in spring/summer. Mammae: 1 pair of mammary slits.
Longevity: At least to 40 years.
Note: The Atlantic Humpback Dolphin *(S. teuszii)* is very similar to the Indian Humpback Dolphin both in appearance and behaviour and occurs along at least part of the northern Angolan coastline – see map. Range may be more limited than shown.

Stenella attenuata
■ principal range
x strandings

Pantropical Spotted Dolphin *Stenella attenuata*
Total length 1.6–2.6m; mass 90–120kg.
Identification pointers: Long, dark beak with white lips; dark grey body spotted with white.

Description: Prominent, curved dorsal fin, long flippers and marked ventral keel towards end of tail-stock. Dark slate-grey above, paler to pinkish below; fin, flippers and flukes are dark. Blackish circle around eye connected to blackish line around beak base, extending further as dark band from jaw to flipper. Beak black with pink or white lips. Some may have white tip to beak. Numerous white spots on body, particularly on sides and underparts posterior to genital aperture. Young animals have few or no spots.
Distribution: Worldwide in tropics; in the region only likely to be seen off east coast from KwaZulu-Natal northwards and from Angolan coast. Mainly oceanic and along continental shelf.
Behaviour: Large schools (100+) and may come together in thousands but most commonly 10–20 members. May be in nursery, bachelor or mixed-sex schools. Mainly a surface-feeder. Commonly bow-rides.
Food: Squid, fish and crustaceans.
Reproduction: After 11-month gestation period, calf born measuring 80–90cm long. Mammae: 1 pair of mammary slits.
Longevity: To 46 years.

The Indian Humpback Dolphin has a prominent ridge, or hump, below a small dorsal fin.

Pantropical Spotted Dolphin has a darkish circle around the eye, and numerous white spots on the body.

Indian Humpback
Dolphin

Pantropical Spotted
Dolphin

Stenella
coeruleoalba
- **principal range**
x strandings

Striped Dolphin *Stenella coeruleoalba*
Total length 1.8–2.7m; mass 90–156kg.
Identification pointers: Distinctive light and dark longitudinal striping. Stripes appear to commence around eye and diverge from each other posteriorly.

Description: Upperparts usually dark greyish-blue, with or without a brownish tinge; on death darkens to deep blue. White underparts. Black stripe from eye along side to anus and another dark stripe from eye to flipper. V-shaped lighter band runs above main side stripe, its shorter upper arm running towards fin and longer lower arm extending towards tail.
Distribution: Worldwide from southern continental tips northwards to northern hemisphere. Most likely to be encountered off the southern and eastern coastal areas of southern Africa although generally in deeper waters and not considered to be a coastal dolphin.
Behaviour: Large schools of 20–50 (over 100 individuals) moving in tight-knit groups. Although said to be surface-feeders, they are known to dive as deep as 700m.
Food: Squid and shoaling fish; some reports also mention crustaceans.
Reproduction: Cows calve at 3-year intervals. Calf measuring 90–100cm and weighing around 20kg born after a gestation of around 12 months. Mammae: 1 pair of mammary slits.
Longevity: 58 years recorded.

Stenella frontalis

Atlantic Spotted Dolphin *Stenella frontalis*
Total length 1.6–2.3m; mass 100–143kg.
Identification pointers: Rather resembles bottlenose dolphins but usually well covered in light-coloured spots; frequently breaches; attracted to fast-moving boats. More robust than Pantropical Spotted Dolphin.

Description: 'Chunky' dolphin with similar form to bottlenose dolphins. Colour ranges from light to dark grey, with males usually darker than females. Most individuals have variable amount of light spotting over the body – some are heavily spotted with younger animals sometimes uniform, without spots. Schools always have some heavily spotted individuals.
Distribution: In the region, off the Angolan coast but extent not known. Otherwise wide range in Atlantic tropical belt.
Behaviour: Most pods number less than 50 individuals but inshore pods are smaller. Commonly breach and make relatively short dives (2–6 minutes) to depths of 40–60m.
Food: Fish, squid and other invertebrates.
Reproduction: Poorly known, but young said to have length of 90–110cm at birth.
Longevity: No records.
Note: Another dolphin species that probably occurs off the Angolan coast but has not been confirmed is Clymene Dolphin *S. clymene*. Could easily be confused with other dolphins along that country's coastline.

Striped Dolphin has distinctive light and dark stripes, with a black stripe running along the side from the eye to the anus.

In the region, the Atlantic Spotted Dolphin is known only off the Angolan coast.

The Clymene Dolphin has not been confirmed off the Angolan coast but it is very likely to occur there.

Striped Dolphin

Atlantic Spotted Dolphin

Stenella longirostris
■ principal range
x strandings

Long-snouted (Spinner) Dolphin *Stenella longirostris*

Total length 1.75–2.4m; mass 75kg.

Identification pointers: Habit of 'spinning' while jumping out of water.

Description: Very long rostrum or beak, and long, pointed flippers. Upperparts dark grey-brown with pale grey to white underparts, spotted with small darker areas. Difficult to identify on appearance but its striking behaviour is diagnostic: individuals from its large schools periodically hurl themselves into air, twisting and spinning their bodies along longitudinal axis – thus the name Spinner Dolphin. Dorsal fin triangular, flippers and flukes pointed.

Distribution: Worldwide in tropical waters. Very few records off southern Africa.

Behaviour: Schools of 30 to several hundred, with sometimes thousands congregating. Deep-water feeder, hunting mainly at night. Have been noted diving to 600m.

Food: Predominantly fish but some squid taken.

Reproduction: After a gestation of 10–11 months, calf born measuring 70–85cm long, weighing little more than 10kg. Calving interval just over 2 years. Mammae: 1 pair of mammary slits.

Longevity: No records.

Tursiops aduncus

Indian Ocean Bottlenose Dolphin *Tursiops aduncus*

Total length 2.6m; mass 230kg.

Identification pointers: Dark grey and plain coloured, with no distinctive identifying features. Smaller than the next species.

Description: Robust with tall, curved fin and medium-length beak that is wide and rounded at the tip. Lower jaw projects slightly beyond upper jaw. Usually dark grey back with paler grey sides and ventral area. Thin pale line usually runs from eye to flipper. A fairly high percentage of animals may have distinct, or less so, spotting on undersides and lower flanks. Some taxonomists believe this dolphin is more closely related to the *Stenella* dolphin species than to the Atlantic (Common) Bottlenose Dolphin.

Distribution: Coastal waters of Indian Ocean, extending to China and Australia. This is a common inshore dolphin seen along the region's south and east coasts.

Behaviour: Can live in large schools of several hundred (even to 1,000) but 5–15 usual. Inshore and deep sea. Mingles with other inshore dolphin species.

Food: Mostly fish, but also squid, often taken on reefs and seabed.

Reproduction: After a 12-month gestation period, calf born measuring 84–110cm long, weighing 9–21kg. Mammae: 1 pair of mammary slits.

Longevity: Probably more than 40 years, although some populations shorter lived.

The Long-snouted Dolphin
has a very long beak.

Bottlenose dolphins are dark grey and plain coloured and it is hard to distinguish one species from the other.

Long-snouted Dolphin

Indian Ocean
Bottlenose Dolphin

Common (Atlantic Ocean) Bottlenose Dolphin
Tursiops truncatus
Total length 1.9–4.1m; mass 150–650kg.
Identification pointers: Dark grey and plain coloured, with no distinctive identifying features.

Tursiops truncatus
■ two separate populations, one inshore and the other in deep water, which apparently rarely intermingle
▨ occasional occurrence

Description: As for Indian Ocean Bottlenosed Dolphin (p.418). Rarely spotting on undersides and, if so, usually indistinct. Larger animals tend to be deep-sea dwellers, with smaller animals inshore. It is possible that several species are involved and not just inshore and deep-sea forms.
Distribution: Widespread; found in North Sea and Mediterranean Sea, as well as the North and South Atlantic, Pacific and Indian oceans; only absent from Arctic and Antarctic waters.
Behaviour: Large schools, numbering up to several hundred (usual 15–25+). Occur both inshore and in deeper seas. Recorded diving to more than 500m but usually less, although deep-sea dwellers tend to have the deepest and longest dives.
Food: Fish and squid. Schools will work together, herding fish to facilitate capture and occasionally driving them into the shallows.
Reproduction: After a 12-month gestation period, calf born measuring 84–140cm long, weighing 15–30kg. Calving interval possibly 2 years. Mammae: 1 pair of inguinal slits.
Longevity: Up to 52 years.
Note: Some scientists believe the Indian Ocean and Atlantic Ocean Bottlenosed dolphins are the same species.

Short-beaked Common Dolphin *Delphinus delphis*
Long-beaked Common Dolphin *Delphinus capensis*
Total length 1.6–2.3m; mass 150kg.
Short-beaked Common Dolphin is a deep-water species; the **Long-beaked Common Dolphin** is now recognized as the inshore species.
Identification pointers: Clear 'figure-of-eight' pattern along flanks.

Delphinus delphis
■ main deep water range
▨ occasional incursions between the continental shelf and the mainland

Description: Sleek and streamlined; pointed flippers and a prominent back-curved fin. Rostrum or beak is long. Dark grey to brown-black above and pale grey below. Characterized by having elongated 'figure-of-eight' or 'hour-glass' pattern on each side, from eye to tail-flukes. Colouring of 'hour-glass' variable but section from eye to mid-body is commonly brown-grey (occasionally tinged yellow), while hind section usually pale grey. Thin black line from corner of mouth to flipper. **Long-beaked Common Dolphin** similar in appearance to **Short-beaked**.
Distribution: Worldwide in tropical and warm temperate waters, both in deep water and inshore. Apparently in the region, **Short-beaked** is most frequently seen off south and east coasts, rarely inshore. **Long-beaked** common inshore. According to some biologists, **Short-beaked** does not occur in southern African waters. There is still no clarity on this but it is possible that all inshore sightings in the region are **Long-beaked**. It is virtually impossible to separate the two in the field. **Long-beaked** numbers perhaps 20,000 off South Africa's east coast.

Delphinus capensis
■ principal range
? range limit unknown

The common dolphins are fast, graceful swimmers.

The common dolphins are known for making regular leaps out of the water.

Common Bottlenose
Dolphin

Short-beaked
Common Dolphin
Long-beaked
Common Dolphin

Behaviour: Short-beaked is usually in schools of about 20 but can be up to several hundred or even thousands. **Long-beaked** in schools of 10–30 but schools come together to form aggregations of up to 500. Feeds in deeper waters. Most Short-beaked dives down to 90m, lasting around 3 minutes; **Long–beaked** recorded to 280m but average dive around 2 minutes.
Food: Squid; cuttlefish; small schooling fish and some crustaceans, such as krill.
Reproduction: Newborn calves around 85cm long, born after 10–11-month gestation. Most births in spring and autumn. Mammae: 1 pair of mammary slits.
Longevity: Up to 35 years.

Steno bredanensis
■ occasional
    occurrence
x strandings

Rough-toothed Dolphin *Steno bredanensis*
Total length 2.1–2.65m; mass 90–160kg.
Identification pointers: Dark purplish-grey above; white under-jaw, throat and belly; flanks blotched with pinkish-white.

Description: Centrally placed sickle-shaped fin. Flippers distinctly large. Dark grey above with white throat and belly as far as genital area. Dark flanks blotched with pinkish-white. Off-white to pinkish beak tip. The conical head and long snout are characteristic.
Distribution: Only three records from southern Africa. Found worldwide in the deep waters of tropical, subtropical and warm temperate seas.
Behaviour: In groups of 10–20, rarely as many as 300. Has been timed to dive for up to 15 minutes, and to depth of 70m. In other parts of its range it is known to mix with other species of dolphin and whale.
Food: Fish, including some large species, and cephalopods; sometimes hunt cooperatively.
Reproduction: Little is known. Newborns measure about 1m in length. Mammae: 1 pair of mammary slits.
Longevity: Up to 32–36 years.

DUGONG & MANATEES Order Sirenia
DUGONG Family Dugongidae

Dugong dugon
■ common
■ rare

Dugong *Dugong dugon*
Total length 2.5–3m (rarely to 4m); mass 250–420kg.
Identification pointers: Cigar-shaped body with flippers and tail-flukes. Completely aquatic; found only in shallow waters.

Description: Entirely aquatic, never on land. Forelimbs are paddle-like flippers; no hind limbs. Large, fleshy, boneless tail flattened horizontally and shallowly forked. Skin greyish-brown with sparsely scattered bristles; upperparts slightly darker than underparts. Front of mouth and lower lip covered with short, thick bristles. These are the only truly herbivorous marine mammals. They have a distant taxonomic relationship with elephants, hyraxes and Aardvark, and all are referred to as sub-ungulates. The only character they share with other marine mammals is that they are aquatic. There are three other close relatives in the order, the Amazonian Manatee, West Indian Manatee and West African Manatee (see next species).

Rough-toothed Dolphin has a centrally placed sickle-shaped dorsal fin and dark flanks blotched with pinkish-white.

The Dugong, an entirely aquatic mammal, inhabits shallow coastal waters and lagoons, where it feeds on sea grass.

Rough-toothed Dolphin

Dugong

423

Distribution: In the region restricted to sheltered areas along Mozambique coast but stragglers occasionally seen in northern KwaZulu-Natal. It occurs from the south-west Pacific, including New Caledonia, Micronesia, Philippines, Taiwan, New Guinea, Australia and westwards along the coastlines of countries fringing the Indian Ocean. Some of the highest populations are to be found off the tropical coastline of Australia (total some 85,000 in that country). Shark Bay, on that country's west coast, is estimated to be home to as many as 10,000 Dugong. Elsewhere, it is hunted heavily for its palatable meat and many populations are in decline, or have disappeared completely. Other reasons for declines include silting over of sea grass beds that form the bulk of its food, disturbance at feeding-grounds and pollution.

Habitat: Shallow, sheltered waters close to the coastline.

Behaviour: Although usually seen singly, in pairs or in family parties up to six, groups of up to 30 have been recorded in southern Africa. They are slow swimmers (2 knots) but can achieve speeds of up to 5 knots to escape danger; able to remain submerged for over 5 minutes although the average dive lasts for just 1–4 minutes.

Food: Several species of sea grass in sheltered shallow bays and lagoons. They can consume up to 15 per cent of their body mass during each feeding day.

Reproduction: Single young (rarely twins) born mainly November–January. Gestation period apparently 12–14 months and newborns weigh 20–35kg, with total length of 1–1.5m. The mother suckles the young for up to 18 months, and the calf drinks the milk underwater. Mammae: 1 pair pectoral.

Longevity: Up to 73 years.

MANATEES family trichechidae

*Trichechus
senegalensis*

West African Manatee *Trichechus senegalensis*
Total length 2.5–3.3m (to 4m); mass 400–500kg.
Identification pointers: Large, seal-like 'cigar-shaped' body; broad, rounded tail-fluke; short, paddle-shaped flippers (forelimbs); large, blunt snout.

Description: Long, cigar-shaped body with a large, flattened and rounded tail, short, paddle-shaped forelimbs and relatively small head with a squared-off, blunt snout. Body hairless and grey to greyish-brown overall with marginally lighter underparts.

Distribution: West African coast to northern Angola. Has been recorded in the Loge, Dande, Bengo and Cuanza rivers, among others, in Angola.

Habitat: Shallow inland waters, estuaries, mangroves and may penetrate deep, and be resident in, river systems.

Behaviour: Virtually nothing known but probably similar to the Amazonian Manatee. Solitary or in small groups. There is apparently some seasonal movement up and down river systems.

Food: Aquatic grasses and other plants.

Reproduction: Most mating takes place during the wet season, when several males may compete for access to a receptive female. After a gestation of about 360 days, young born weighing 30kg on average, and about 1.5m long. Mammae: 1 pair pectoral.

Longevity: Few records but up to 60 years.

This image of the very similar West Indian Manatee *(T. manatus)* shows the long, cigar-shaped body and large, rounded tail. There are few good images of the West African Manatee.

The head of the West African Manatee is relatively small and the snout is squared.

West African Manatee

SKULLS

On occasion, all there is to view of an animal is its skeletal remains, of which the most recognizable part is the skull, and this can be identified to a particular species. In some cases, even a cursory examination will show whether a skull belonged to a male or female. This section will aid identification and enhance knowledge with regard to the dentition and skull form of the species. The measurements shown are averages for total length.

Golden moles

Giant Golden Mole
Chrysospalax trevelyani
42mm   p.36

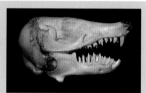

Cape Golden Mole
Chrysochloris asiatica
25mm   p.36

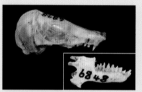

Sclater's Golden Mole
Chlorotalpa sclateri
29mm   p.36

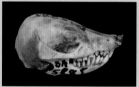

Yellow Golden Mole
Calcochloris obtusirostris
21mm   p.36

Four-toed Sengi
Petrodromus tetradactylus
56mm   p.42

Round-eared Sengi
Macroscelides proboscideus
30mm   p.42

Eastern Rock Sengi
Elephantulus myurus
38mm   p.44

Southern African Hedgehog
Atelerix frontalis
47mm   p.48

Greater Red Musk Shrew
Crocidura flavescens
26mm   p.54

Greater Dwarf Shrew
Suncus lixus
20mm   p.56

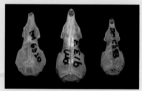

Myosorex (left), ***Crocidura***
(middle), ***Suncus*** (right)
comparison   p.50

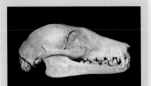

Straw-coloured Fruit-bat
Eidolon helvum
55mm   p.58

Wahlberg's Epauletted Fruit-bat
Epomophorus wahlbergi
42mm   p.64

Egyptian Fruit-bat
Rousettus aegyptiacus
40mm   p.60

Mauritian Tomb Bat
Taphozous mauritianus
20mm   p.70

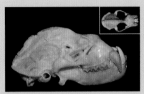

Giant Leaf-nosed Bat
Hipposideros gigas
32mm   p.72

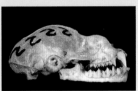

Sundevall's Leaf-nosed Bat
Hipposideros caffer
28mm   p.72

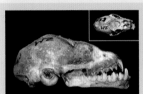

Egyptian Slit-faced Bat
Nycteris thebaica
20mm   p.76

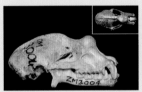

Hildebrandt's Horseshoe Bat
Rhinolophus hildebrandtii
28mm   p.80

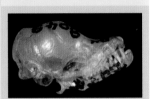

Lesser Long-fingered Bat
Miniopterus fraterculus
14mm   p.86

Temminck's Myotis
Myotis tricolor
20mm   p.88

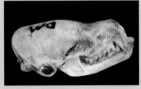

Dusk Pipistrelle
Pipistrellus hesperidus
12mm   p.94

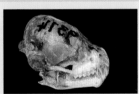

Variegated Butterfly Bat
Glauconycteris variegata
13mm   p.98

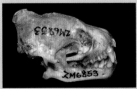

Giant Yellow House Bat
Scotophilus nigrita
24mm   p.104

Large-eared Giant Mastiff Bat
Otomops martiensseni
26mm   p.108

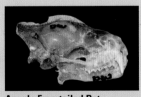

Angola Free-tailed Bat
Mops condylura
22mm   p.110

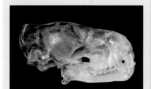

Ansorge's Free-tailed Bat
Chaerephon ansorgei
16mm   p.108

Yellow Baboon (female)
Papio cynocephalus
177mm   p.112

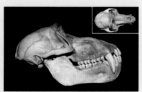

Yellow Baboon (male)
Papio cynocephalus
240mm   p.112

Vervet Monkey
Chlorocebus pygerythrus
100mm   p.116

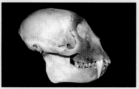

Sykes's Monkey
Cercopithecus albogularis
108mm   p.120

Thick-tailed Galago
Otolemur crassicaudatus
72mm   p.126

Southern Lesser Galago
Galago moholi
40mm   p.128

Ground Pangolin
Smutsia (Manis) temminckii
82mm   p.132

Cape Hare
Lepus capensis
88mm   p.134

Scrub Hare
Lepus saxatilis
95mm   p.134

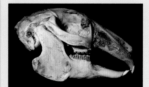

Smith's Red Rock Rabbit
Pronolagus rupestris
84mm   p.138

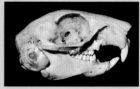

**Southern African Ground
Squirrel** *Xerus inauris*
60mm   p.144

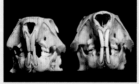

Damara (left) & **Southern
African Ground Squirrel** (right)
teeth   p.144

Tree Squirrel
Paraxerus cepapi
44mm   p.150

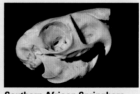

Southern African Springhare
Pedetes capensis
90mm   p.160

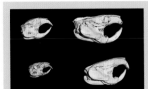

Rodent Moles (Mole-rats)
Family Bathyergidae
p.162

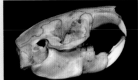

Namaqua Dune Mole-rat
Bathyergus janetta
49mm   p.162

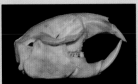

Cape Mole-rat
Georychus capensis
43mm   p.164

Common Mole-rat
Cryptomys hottentotus
33mm   p.162

Cape Porcupine
Hystrix africaeaustralis
150mm   p.166

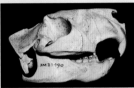

Greater Cane-rat
Thryonomys swinderianus
85mm   p.168

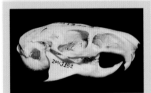

Dassie Rat (Noki)
Petromus typicus
34mm   p.170

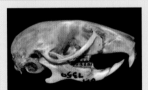

White-tailed Mouse
Mystromys albicaudatus
33mm   p.172

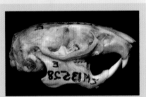

Pouched Mouse
Saccostomus campestris
32mm   p.174

Gambian Giant Pouched Rat
Cricetomys gambianus
70mm   p.174

Cape Short-tailed Gerbil
Desmodillus auricularis
36mm   p.182

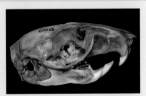

Bushveld Gerbil
Gerbilliscus leucogaster
39mm   p.184

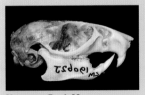

Namaqua Rock Mouse
Micaelamys namaquensis
32mm   p.188

African Marsh Rat
Dasymys incomtus
35mm   p.192

Single-striped Grass Mouse
Lemniscomys rosalia
33mm   p.194

Acacia Rat
Thallomys paedulcus
32mm   p.202

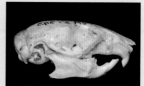

Woodland Thicket Rat
Grammomys dolichurus
31mm   p.204

Verreaux's White-footed Mouse
Myomyscus verreauxii
30mm   p.208

Southern African Vlei Rat
Otomys irroratus
38mm   p.216

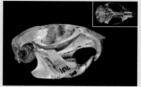

Laminate Vlei Rat
Otomys laminatus
39mm   p.216

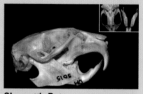

Sloggett's Rat
Myotomys sloggetti
41mm   p.216

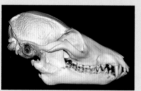

Bat-eared Fox
Otocyon megalotis
118mm   p.222

Cape Fox
Vulpes chama
115mm   p.222

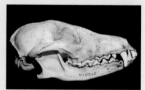

Black-backed Jackal
Canis mesomelas
170mm   p.224

Side-striped Jackal
Canis adustus
170mm   p.226

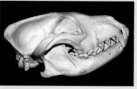

African Wild Dog
Lycaon pictus
210mm   p.228

Cape Clawless Otter
Aonyx capensis
134mm   p.230

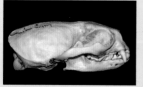

Spotted-necked Otter
Hydrictis maculicollis
101mm   p.232

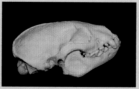

Honey Badger
Mellivora capensis
146mm   p.232

African Striped Weasel
Poecilogale albinucha
48mm   p.234

Striped Polecat
Ictonyx striatus
62mm   p.236

Banded Mongoose
Mungos mungo
70mm   p.236

Meller's Mongoose
Rhynchogale melleri
90mm   p.240

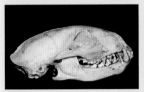

Bushy-tailed Mongoose
Bdeogale crassicauda
96mm   p.240

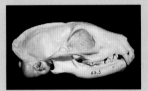

Selous's Mongoose
Paracynictis selousi
90mm   p.242

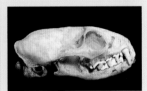

Small Grey Mongoose
Galerella pulverulenta
68mm   p.242

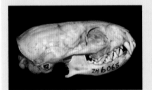

Slender Mongoose
Galerella sanguinea
63mm   p.244

Large Grey Mongoose
Herpestes ichneumon
98mm   p.246

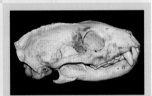

Water (Marsh) Mongoose
Atilax paludinosus
110mm   p.248

Dwarf Mongoose
Helogale parvula
48mm   p.250

White-tailed Mongoose
Ichneumia albicauda
108mm   p.252

Yellow Mongoose
Cynictis penicillata
60mm   p.252

Suricate (Meerkat)
Suricata suricatta
62mm   p.254

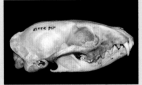

Small-spotted Genet
Genetta genetta
93mm   p.256

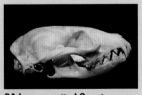

SA Large-spotted Genet
Genetta tigrina
92mm   p.256

African Civet
Civettictis civetta
150mm   p.260

African Palm Civet
Nandinia binotata
90mm   p.260

Spotted Hyaena
Crocuta crocuta
280mm   p.262

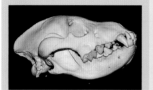

Brown Hyaena
Hyaena brunnea
263mm   p.264

Aardwolf
Proteles cristatus
135mm   p.266

African Wild Cat
Felis silvestris cafra
95mm   p.268

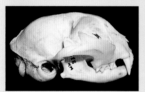

Small Spotted Cat
Felis nigripes
84mm   p.270

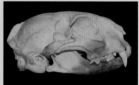

Serval
Leptailurus serval
124mm   p.272

Caracal
Caracal caracal
135mm   p.272

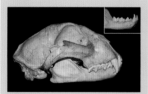

Cheetah
Acinonyx jubatus
170mm   p.276

Lion (male)
Panthera leo
420mm   p.278

Leopard
Panthera pardus
210mm   p.280

Aardvark
Orycteropus afer
198mm   p.282

African Elephant
Loxodonta africana
1.136m   p.284

Rock Dassie (Hyrax)
Procavia capensis
90mm   p.288

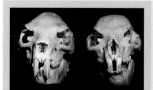

Rock Dassie male (left) and
female *Procavia capensis*
p.288

Hartmann's Mountain Zebra
Equus zebra hartmannae
560mm   p.294

Plains Zebra
Equus quagga
530mm   p.296

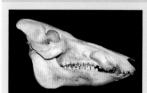

Bushpig
Potamochoerus larvatus
372mm   p.306

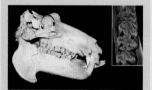

Hippopotamus
Hippopotamus amphibius
642mm   p.302

Giraffe
Giraffa camelopardalis
540mm   p.308

Grey Rhebok (ram)
Pelea capreolus
284mm   p.334

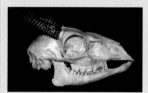

Suni (ram)
Nesotragus moschatus
118mm   p.352

Damara Dik-dik (ram)
Madoqua damarensis
118mm   p.350

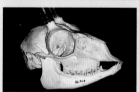

Klipspringer (ram)
Oreotragus oreotragus
155mm   p.352

Klipspringer (ewe)
Oreotragus oreotragus
145mm   p.352

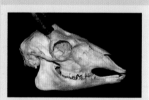

Oribi (ram)
Ourebia ourebi
149mm   p.356

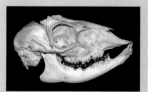

Cape Grysbok (ram)
Raphicerus melanotis
140mm   p.358

Cape Grysbok (ewe)
Raphicerus melanotis
142–149mm   p.358

Steenbok (ram)
Raphicerus campestris
140mm   p.354

Blue Duiker (female)
Philantomba monticola
122mm   p.362

Natal Red Duiker
Cephalophus natalensis
155mm   p.360

Common Duiker (ram)
Sylvicapra grimmia
170mm   p.366

Cape Fur Seal (male)
Arctocephalus pusillus
270mm   p.370

Cape Fur Seal (female)
Arctocephalus pusillus
190mm   p.370

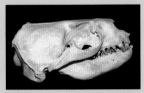

Sub-Antarctic Fur Seal
Arctocephalus tropicalis
217mm   p.372

Southern Elephant Seal (male)
Mirounga leonina
440mm   p.374

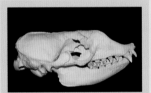

Crabeater Seal
Lobodon carcinophaga
290mm   p.376

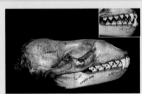

Leopard Seal
Hydrurga leptonyx
320mm   p.376

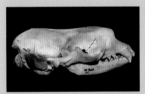

Weddell Seal
Leptonychotes weddellii
275mm   p.378

Blue Whale
Balaenoptera musculus
about 6m   p.384

Southern Right Whale
Eubalaena australis
4.2–5.4m   p.388

Strap-toothed (Layard's) Beaked Whale *Mesoplodon layardii*
1.1m   p.394

Pygmy Sperm Whale
Kogia breviceps
430mm   p.398

Dwarf Sperm Whale
Kogia sima
270mm   p.398

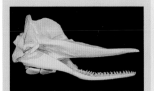

Sperm Whale
Physeter catodon
3–5m   p.398

Killer Whale
Orcinus orca
860mm   p.402

False Killer Whale
Pseudorca crassidens
600mm   p.404

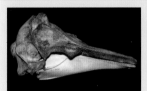

Melon-headed Whale
Peponocephala electra
460mm   p.408

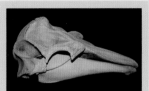

Risso's Dolphin
Grampus griseus
550mm   p.408

Haviside's Dolphin
Cephalorhynchus heavisidii
340mm   p.410

Dusky Dolphin
Lagenorhynchus obscurus
400mm   p.412

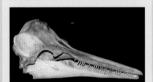

Indian Humpback Dolphin
Sousa chinensis
540mm   p.414

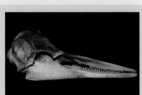

Pantropical Spotted Dolphin
Stenella attenuata
445mm   p.414

Striped Dolphin
Stenella coeruleoalba
440mm   p.416

Long-snouted (Spinner) Dolphin
Stenella longirostris
400mm   p.418

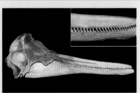

Short-beaked Common Dolphin
Delphinus delphis
500mm   p.420

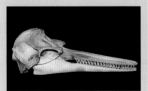

Rough-toothed Dolphin
Steno bredanensis
510mm   p.422

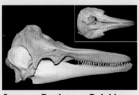

Common Bottlenose Dolphin
Tursiops truncatus
550mm   p.420

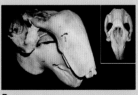

Dugong
Dugong dugon
350mm   p.422

GLOSSARY

Alpha male/female The dominant male or female within a social group; often the only breeders.
Anterior Of or near the head; also at or near the front.
Aquatic Living in or near water.
Arboreal Adapted for life in trees.
Baleen Comb-like structures in mouths of baleen whales, used for filtering plankton from the water.
Bifurcated Forked or divided into two branches.
Biome An ecological region, usually extensive, characterized by a dominant type of plant life.
Biotic zone A geographical area that, in terms of its ecological character and the nature of its life forms, is recognized as a coherent ecosystem distinguishable from its adjacent areas.
Canine The tooth that lies between the incisors and premolars, usually cone-shaped and pointed and used as part of the killing apparatus in many carnivores.
Cheek-teeth Molar and premolar teeth lying behind the canines or incisors. Also called carnassials.
Crepuscular Active during the twilight hours of dawn and dusk.
Diurnal Active during the daylight hours.
Dorsal The back- or upper-surface.
Drey A domed nest of leaves and twigs constructed by some species of tree squirrels.
Ecosystem Unit of the environment within which living and non-living elements interact.
Ecotone The zone between two major ecological communities.
Endangered Refers to a species that is facing a very high risk of extinction.
Endemic Native to a particular country, region or restricted area.
Exotic Not native to a country or region but introduced from other countries or areas. Also 'alien'.
Feral Having reverted to a wild state.
Flehmen Grimace in which an animal's lips are pulled back, the teeth are exposed and the nose wrinkled, usually associated with males sniffing urine from an oestrus female.
Foraging Searching for or seeking out food.
Fossorial Burrowing animals, adapted to spend most, or part, of their life underground or in burrows.
Genus A taxonomic group containing one or more species.
Gestation The period between conception and birth in which offspring are carried in the uterus.
Gregarious Living together in groups, herds or colonies.
Guano Accumulations of droppings, usually of bird and bat colonies.

Herbivore Animal that feeds principally on plants. Large mammalian herbivores may be classed as 'grazers' (subsisting largely on grasses) or 'browsers' (subsisting largely on woody or herbaceous plants).
Home range The area covered by an animal in the course of its day-to-day activities.
Incisors Sharp-edged front teeth, usually in both the upper and lower jaws.
Inguinal In the vicinity of the groin; between hind limbs.
Insectivore A mammal that subsists largely on insects.
Interfemoral membrane The thin membrane situated between the hind legs of bats.
Introduced (also alien, exotic) Species brought by man from areas where it occurs naturally to areas where it has not previously occurred. Some introductions are accidental, others deliberate.
Krill Small shrimp-like marine crustaceans.
Lateral At the side or sides.
Longevity Length of time an animal lives; lifetime; age.
Mammae The milk-secreting organs of female mammals.
Midden (latrine) Place where droppings (scats) are regularly deposited.
Molar Tooth adapted for grinding food, situated at the back of the jaws.
Moult The process in which old hair is shed to make way for new hair.
Nocturnal Active during hours of darkness.
Nuchal patch A contrasting patch of hair in the nape (between and behind the ears).
Oestrus (heat) Period during which female animals are sexually receptive to males.
Omnivore An animal that feeds on both plant and animal food.
Order A taxonomic group that contains one or more families of species.
Pectoral On the chest or thorax.
Pelage Hair covering or coat.
Plankton Mainly microscopic organisms, both plant and animal, that drift or float in the surface layers of the sea or fresh water.
Pod A group of whales with some kind of social structure.
Post-partum oestrus Renewed ovulation and mating within hours or days of giving birth.
Predator An animal that preys on other live animals for its food.
Preorbital gland A gland in front of the eye socket.
Rare A loose term for a species that is uncommon or whose numbers have recently decreased, but which is not endangered; not a recognized conservation category.

Riparian In close association with rivers and river-bank habitats.

Rooting behaviour Digging at roots with feet and snout.

Ruminant Mammal with a specialized digestive system typified by behaviour of chewing the cud; an adaptation to digesting the cellulose walls of plant cells.

Rut Period of sexual excitement (in male animals) associated with the mating season.

Scats Faeces or droppings.

Scavenger Animal that feeds on dead or decaying organic matter.

Scrotum The pouch that contains the testes in most mammals.

South African Red Data Book A publication listing and describing the conservation status of species of a particular taxon (for example, mammals, birds or plants) that are vulnerable or endangered.

Species A group of interbreeding individuals of common ancestry, reproductively isolated from all other groups.

Subterranean Living underground.

Taxonomy The classification of organisms into logical groups.

Terrestrial Living on land.

Territory A restricted area inhabited by an animal, usually for breeding purposes, and actively defended against other individuals of the same species.

Tragus (pl. tragi) Small cartilaginous process situated in the external ear-opening of most species of bat.

Ungulate Mammal that has its feet modified as hooves (of various types).

Vibrissae (s. vibrissa) Prominent coarse hairs or whiskers, usually on the face.

Vulnerable Referring to a species that faces a high risk of extermination in the medium-term future.

Withers Area behind the neck and between the shoulders of an animal.

SUGGESTED FURTHER READING

Dorst, J. & Dandelot, P. 1983. *A Field Guide to the Larger Mammals of Africa*. Macmillan, Johannesburg.

Haltenorth, T. & Diller, H. 1984. *A Field Guide to the Mammals of Africa including Madagascar*. Collins Publishers, London.

Hunter, L. 2011. *Carnivores of the World*. Princeton University Press, Oxford.

Kingdon, J.S. *et al.*(Eds) 2013. *Mammals of Africa*. 6 vols. Bloomsbury Publishers, London.

Monadjem, A. *et al*. 2010. *Bats of Southern and Central Africa – a Biogeographic and Taxonomic Synthesis*. Wits University Press, Johannesburg.

Skinner, J.D. & Chimimba, C.T. 2005. *The Mammals of the Southern African Subregion*. Cambridge University Press, Cambridge.

Stuart, C. & Stuart, M. 2009. *Pocket Guide Mammals of East Africa*. Random House Struik, Cape Town.

Stuart, C. & Stuart, M. 2011. *Pocket Guide Mammals of Southern Africa*. Random House Struik, Cape Town.

Stuart, C. & Stuart, M. 2013. *A Field Guide to the Tracks and Signs of Southern, Central and East African Wildlife*. Struik Nature, Cape Town.

Stuart, C. & Stuart, M. 2014. *Southern, Central and East African Mammals: a Photographic Guide*. Struik Nature, Cape Town.

Stuart, C. & Stuart, T. 2007. *Field Guide to the Larger Mammals of Africa*. Struik Publishers, Cape Town.

PHOTOGRAPHIC CREDITS

All photographs in this book have been taken by the authors, with the exception of those listed below. Copyright rests with individual photographers.

Doug Allen/naturepl.com: 377 (bottom)

P.K. Anderson: 423 (bottom)

Antwerp Zoo: 127 (middle right)

Laila Bahaa-el-din: 85 (bottom right inset), 231 (middle right), 263 (top)

Laila Bahaa-el-din/Panthera: 261 (bottom right), 275 (top right, middle, bottom left and inset), 285 (top main), 365 (top, bottom), 367 (top left)

Daryl and Sharna Balfour/Wildphotos: 243 (top)

Guy Balme/Panthera/Ezemvelo KwaZulu-Natal: 241 (middle right), 253 (middle left)

Rebecca Banasiak: 199 (middle, bottom)

Phil Berry: 329 (middle right, bottom left)

Tony Bruton: 173 (bottom)

Duncan Buchart: 283 (middle left)

John Carlyon: 73 (top right), 217 (bottom right), 227 (bottom main and inset), 239 (middle right), 247 (top), 253 (top main), 259 (top), 273 (top left), 361 (bottom), 373 (bottom), 375 (top, bottom), 377 (top), 379 (bottom)

Danita Dellmont/Gallo Images: 411 (bottom)

Nigel Dennis/Images of Africa: 255 (top), 335 (top), 357 (bottom right)

N. Dippenaar: 51 (top left)

Andrew Duthie: 141 (middle left)

Th. Engel: 241 (bottom right)

Chris and Monique Fallows: 421 (bottom)

Ken Findlay: 387 (bottom), 389 (bottom left)

Pat J. Frere: 293 (bottom right)

Roger Fussell/Big Sky Lodges: 245 (top left)

Nick Gordon/Ardea: 125 (bottom right)

Mike Griffin: 39 (top), 101 (top), 165 (top right), 185 (top left and right)

Todd Kaplan/Wildlife Campus: 161 (bottom left)

Karoo Images: 141 (bottom left and right)

Pam Laycock: 75 (top)

Bryan Lenz: 123 (bottom right)

Ian Manning: 319 (middle left, bottom left)

W. Massyn: 113 (top left)

David R. Mills/Panthera: 127 (top), 135 (top, bottom left)

Ara Monadjem: 61 (bottom right), 63 (bottom right and left), 67 (top right, bottom right), 69, 73 (bottom right), 75 (bottom), 77 (bottom right, top right), 83 (bottom left), 85 (top right, bottom left inset), 87 (top right), 95 (bottom left), 103 (bottom), 111 (bottom left)

Nature Picture Library: 379 (top)

Brent Naudé: 203 (bottom main)

Rory Nefdt: 87 (bottom left)

U. de V. Pienaar: 241 (top)

Galen Rathbun (California Academy of Sciences): 43 (top right), 45 (top main, top right inset, middle left)

I.L. Rautenbach: 77 (top left), 87 (bottom right), 91 (bottom left), 97 (bottom left), 105 (top), 109 (top right, bottom left)

Joan Ryder/ABPL: 265 (bottom main)

E. Seamark and T. Kearney: 81 (top right), 95 (top main and inset)

E. Seamark: 71 (bottom right inset), 73 (middle left, bottom left inset), 81 (middle right, bottom left and inset, bottom right), 83 (bottom right and inset), 85 (top left and middle), 87 (middle right), 89 (top right, bottom main), 91 (top main and inset, middle right, bottom right), 93 (top right, bottom left and right), 95 (bottom right), 97 (middle right, bottom right and inset), 99, 103 (top), 105 (bottom left and right), 107 (top right, middle right), 109 (top left), 111 (middle right), 113 (middle left and right, bottom left)

Alex Sliwa: 271 (bottom left and right)

Bill Stanley/FMNH, Chicago: 85 (bottom main), 155 (bottom), 165 (bottom right), 177 (bottom main), 197 (bottom left), 211 (top right), 213 (top, middle left, bottom right)

Lorna Stanton/ABPL: 131 (top right)

Kyle Stuart: 123 (bottom left)

Warwick Tarboton: 149 (bottom)

Peter Taylor: 79 (bottom left), 111 (bottom right)

Tobo Aquarium/Tokyo: 425 (bottom)

Merlin Tuttle (BCI): 61 (bottom left), 65 (bottom main)

Harry van Rompaey: 131 (bottom right), 133 (top left)

John Visser: 55 (middle left), 101 (bottom), 373 (top)

Jane Waterman: 145 (bottom)

Alan Weaving: 223 (top main), 265 (top main), 267 (top right), 277 (top), 281 (bottom right), 283 (top left), 361 (top left)

Lajuma Wilderness: 131 (top left), 261 (bottom left), 307 (top, bottom left)

Mark Williams/Ashanti African Tours, Ghana: 143 (left)

INDEX

English names are in **demi-bold**, scientific names in *italic*, Afrikaans names in roman and German names in grey.